ONE DAY IN HISTORY

The Days That Changed the World

JULY 4, 1776

ONE DAY IN HISTORY

The Days That Changed the World

JULY 4, 1776

Rodney P. Carlisle, Ph.D., General Editor

Collins

An Imprint of HarperCollinsPublishers

Special Thanks to:

Dik Daso from the National Air and Space Museum, Smithsonian Institution

FIRST EDITION

Library of Congress Cataloging-in-Publication Data

One day in history: July 4, 1776 / Rodney P. Carlisle, general editor. — 1st ed.
   p. cm.
   Includes bibliographical references and index.
   ISBN-13: 978-0-06-112032-9
   ISBN-10: 0-06-112032-4
   1. United States — History — Revolution, 1775-1783 — Encyclopedias. 2. Fourth of July — Encyclopedias. I. Carlisle, Rodney P. II. Title.

E208.O54 2006
973.303—dc22   2006049087

06 07 08 09 10 TPNJ 9 8 7 6 5 4 3 2 1

Photo Credits

National Archives and Records Administration: Pages 3, 5, 9, 18, 20, 23, 29, 41 bottom, 44 right, 47, 48, 57, 77, 86, 91, 96, 104, 105 left and right bottom, 112, 119, 128, 131, 143, 149, 154, 157, 161, 163, 165 top, 169, 176, 179, 193, 200, 202, 206, 213, 215, 217, 219, 221, 223, 236, 238, 257; Loretta Carlisle Photography: Pages 10, 17, 22, 24, 35, 40, 44 left, 50 far left to far right, 54, 62, 70, 73, 75, 100, 105 top left and right (courtesy Benninghoff Foundation), 108, 110, 115, 124, 136, 147, 171, 173 (courtesy Benninghoff Foundation), 174, 182, 185, 189, 227 top (courtesy Benninghoff Foundation), 227 bottom, 228, 230 bottom, 232, 235 top and bottom, 238 top and center; Thomas Jefferson Foundation/Robert C. Lautman: Page 116; Corbis: Pages 86, 98, 150; Library of Congress: Pages ii-iii, iv-v, xvi, 31, 41 top, 43, 58, 61, 65, 69, 78, 81, 85, 135, 144, 165 bottom, 187 top and bottom, 196, 210, 230 top, 240, 244 top left and right, 246; National Park Service: Page 26; Getty Images: Pages 102, 141; © iStock International: Page 101; ©Jupiterimages Corporation: Page 122; OAR/National Undersea Research Program (NURP): Page 205. www.virtualology.com; Pages 138, 201.

Golson Books, Ltd.

President and Editor	J. Geoffrey Golson
General Editor	Rodney P. Carlisle
Design Director	Kevin Hanek
Designer	Mary Jo Scibetta
Compositor and Editor	Linda C. Angér
Copyeditor	Martha Whitt
Proofreader	Felicity Tucker, Barbara Paris
Indexer	JS Editorial, LLC

CONTENTS

Articles are presented in alphabetical order. Cross-references to other articles are in SMALL CAPS *within the text.*

PREFACE

BY GORDON S. WOOD

JULY 4, 1776, is the most important day in American history, and because of the emergence of the United States as the most powerful nation the world has ever known, it is surely one of the most important days in world history as well. July 4, 1776, is important because that was the day the Continental Congress formally adopted the Declaration of Independence, which announced that the American colonies had severed their ties to the empire of Great Britain. Independence itself had been approved on July 2, and the actual signing of the Declaration took place more than a month later. Yet Americans, as they created their nation, had created an iconic date that would resonate through history.

July 4, 1776, became the country's birthday, for the Declaration approved on that day legally created the United States of America. The Declaration told a "candid world" that "these united Colonies are, and of Right ought to be Free and Independent States . . . Absolved from all Allegiance to the British Crown." But the Declaration went further than just announcing that the American people were assuming "among the Powers of the earth, the separate and equal station to which the Laws of Nature and Nature's God entitle them." It went on to state that all governments everywhere were supposed to derive "their just powers from the consent of the people," and when any one of these governments became destructive of the people's rights and liberties, the people had the right to alter or abolish that government and institute a new one.

These words have served as inspiration for peoples everywhere. Colonial rebellions against imperial regimes throughout the world have looked to the Declaration to justify their cause. In declaring Vietnam independent from France in 1945 Ho Chi Minh cited the American Declaration of Independence. Members of Solidarity in Poland and dissidents in Czechoslovakia invoked its words to oppose Soviet domination in the 1980s. And the Chinese students who occupied Tiananmen Square in 1989 used its language. The Declaration of Independence has become one of the most influential documents in world history.

But for Americans the Declaration has taken on a special significance. It infused into the culture most of what the American people came to believe and value. The noblest ideals and highest aspirations of Americans—their belief in liberty, equality, and individual rights, including the right of every person to pursue happiness—came out of the Declaration of Independence. Consequently, it is not surprising that every reform movement in American history—from the abolitionists of the 1830s, to the feminists at Seneca Falls in 1848, to the civil rights advocates of the 1960s—invoked the words and ideals of the Declaration. It was Abraham Lincoln who made the most of the Declaration, particularly its assertions of human equality and inalienable rights. Thomas Jefferson, the principal drafter of the Declaration, said Lincoln, "had the coolness, forecast, and capacity to introduce into a merely revolutionary document, an abstract truth, applicable to all men and all times, and so to embalm it there, that today, and in all coming days, it shall be a rebuke and stumbling block to the very harbingers of re-appearing tyranny and oppression." A century later on the steps of the Lincoln Memorial Martin Luther King, Jr., took inspiration from this abstract truth embodied in the Declaration.

For Americans the words of the Declaration have become central to their sense of nationhood. Because the United States is composed of so many immigrants and so many different races and ethnicities, it could never assume its identity as a matter of course. The nation has had to be invented. At the end of the Declaration the members of the Continental Congress could only "mutually pledge to each other our Lives, our Fortunes, and our sacred Honor." There was nothing else but themselves that they could dedicate themselves to—no patria, no fatherland, no nation as yet. In comparison with the 230-year-old United States, many states in the world today are new, some of them created within the fairly recent past. Yet many of these states, new as they may be, are undergirded by peoples who had a preexisting sense of their ethnicity, their blood-connections, their nationality. In the case of the United States the process was reversed: Americans were a state before they were a nation, and much of American history has been an effort to define that nationality. In fact, even today America may not be a nation in any traditional meaning of the term. Americans have had to rely on ideas and ideals in order to hold themselves together and think of themselves as a single people. And the Declaration has embodied these ideas and ideals more fully than any other single document in American history. No wonder the Declaration has been transformed into America's most sacred text. And no wonder that July 4, 1776, the day that gave birth to the Declaration, is the most important day in American history.

INTRODUCTION

As the delegates filed into the State House on Thursday, some rankled at the fact that the windows remained closed. It was going to be another hot July day in Philadelphia, and some fresh air would be a help. Even with the redolent odor of horse manure and the more distant hints from the fish market, some outside air would be welcome. But the decision had been made to keep the windows closed so word of the deliberations would not be overheard by passers-by on Chestnut Street.

Furthermore, tempers were flaring. Despite entreaties from others, the New York delegation continued to balk. They had no instructions from the state and could vote against the resolution. Furthermore, it looked as if the two delegates from Delaware were deadlocked. Unless Caesar Rodney got in to town in time for the vote, July 4, 1776, promised to be just another day of delay and political wrangling.

Finally, Rodney arrived, his horse in a lather and with mud on his breeches and coat. The New York delegates did not vote against the resolution, but chose to abstain. Then there was a discussion of who should sign the document, and only John Hancock, president of the Continental Congress and Charles Thompson, secretary, put their names on the document. Copies were sent by couriers to the states and commanders in the field.

On Monday, July 8, the declaration was publicly proclaimed from the balcony of the State House, known thereafter as Independence Hall. Only later, in August 1776, some of the delegates to the Congress signed the Declaration, and through November others signed, for a total of 56 signatures, including one member who had not been present for the original vote. Thereafter, July 4 celebrations always had a bit of irony because they did not honor the date of the crucial vote. The day marked an agreement on a final version of a document approved two days earlier and signed several weeks and months later. However, John Adams had it almost right when he wrote to Abigail on July 3: "The Second Day of July 1776, will be the most memorable Epocha, in the History of America—I am apt to believe that it will be celebrated, by succeeding Generations, as the great anniversary Festival."

In another sense, however, July 4 is important because it represents the date when the final decision was taken by 13 English colonies on the continent of North America to declare themselves free and independent states united in their purpose to form a new nation. The approval of that decision on July 4 represented the culmination of a debate that had started in early June. North Carolina and Virginia had taken the lead, with conventions in those states authorizing their delegates to vote for independence. After Congress appointed a committee to draft the declaration, that committee assigned the actual writing of the Declaration to Thomas Jefferson. Over a period of about three weeks in June 1776, Jefferson prepared the draft, drawing on his understanding of the Enlightenment philosophy of natural rights, and spelling out a long list of despotic abuses by the English monarch, George III.

Jefferson remembered, "I turned to neither book nor pamphlet while writing the Declaration." Instead, he relied on his understanding of John Locke's *Second*

Treatise of Government and the principle of the social compact that had become part of his thinking.

The words and logic of the Declaration approved on July 4 and the larger events that surrounded that decision shaped the destiny of the world, creating a new nation that would build on the principles enunciated then. The doctrine proclaimed in the Declaration could be seen as very revolutionary. The Declaration stated that when a government abused the natural rights of its subjects or citizens, those people had a natural right and a duty to establish a new government that would protect those rights. That concept would shape the destiny not only of the 13 colonies, but would be emulated and echoed over the next two centuries and more, in nations in Latin America and the Caribbean and then around the world. The vast empires built by Britain, France, Spain, and other European countries all dissolved under the doctrine proclaimed in July 1776.

Questions about the Declaration haunted Americans for decades. Jefferson wrote and the delegates approved this sentence: "We hold these truths to be self evident, that all men are created equal, that they are endowed by their Creator with certain unalienable Rights, that among these are Life, Liberty, and the Pursuit of Happiness." Did Jefferson and his contemporaries mean to include African Americans in this statement? Jefferson, at least, apparently did not think so, as he remained a slaveholder the rest of his life. The delegates approved the language: "We, therefore, the Representatives of the United States of America solemnly publish and declare . . . that as Free and Independent States, they have full Power to levy War, conclude Peace, contract Alliances...." Did the writers mean to say that each of the colonies was a free and independent state, sovereign in its own right? Eighty-five years later Jefferson Davis would claim that they meant that, while Abraham Lincoln believed that sovereignty resided with the United States as a nation, not with the states.

Clearly, however, a new kind of nation had emerged. Edmund Burke remarked: "A great revolution has happened—a revolution made, not by chopping and changing of power in any of the existing states, but by the appearance of a *new state*, of a *new species*, in *a new part of the globe*. It has made as great a change in all relations...as the appearance of a new planet would...."

In the 21st century, the nature of the society and the events that led up to this crucial date in history seem distant and strange, with some hauntingly recognizable characteristics. How this startling and world-changing document came to be written, what events had led up to its preparation, and the consequences of the actions of the delegates in Philadelphia in that hot summer of 1776 are worthy of close attention.

Partly because many modern American institutions and elements of the way of life derive from that period, much of it seems familiar. Even some of the very same homes of the delegates to Congress and other leaders of the period are occupied today, while others are preserved for tourists. The delegates gathered at City Tavern, which continues to serve food and beverages, three blocks from Independence Hall. Beer in mugs and whiskey in glasses were downed then as now, while recipes from the era remain in use for certain soups, puddings, and stews. Delegates attended Christ Church on Second and Church Street, five blocks from Independence Hall, and the building is open for visits and worship today. Thousands of visitors look into the hall where the vote was taken on the Declaration, while others view the reconstructed Graff House at Seventh and Market where Jefferson drafted the document, or tour nearby Valley Forge where George Washington encamped with his army through the winter of 1777–78.

Despite the seeming familiarity of the settings, however, much of life was very different in that era. In several of the colonies, women who owned property could vote, but for the most part, women and men without property were excluded from participation in the political affairs of the day. Throughout the colonies, most African Americans and many Native Americans were held in slavery, and opposition to slavery among whites tended to be found only among some Quakers.

Mills, forges, foundries, ropewalks, and shipbuilding yards represented a thriving industrial base that would grow in later years. In the age before steam engines, electric motors, and internal-combustion power, heavy power was available from waterwheels, windmills, and animal power. Unlike steam engines and gas engines that require expensive fuel, waterwheels ground on as long as gravity drained a stream through a mill race to the wheel, and windmills, too, were powered by a free force of nature. Craftsmen specialized in making carriages and wheels, barrels, leather goods, silverware, and iron and steel tools. Much of the clothing, hats, and textiles were imported to the colonies, although during the Revolution, Americans turned increasingly to homespun thread and hand-loomed fabric produced locally.

Travel between cities was mostly by water, with tenuous carriage routes over dirt roads marked by fords, ferries, bridges, and tavern stops. Today throughout the states that were the original 13 colonies, towns bear the names of particular 18th century ways of life. Valley Forge, Chadd's Ford, Harper's Ferry, and hundreds of others carry the legacy of the era into the present.

If the roads, towns, houses, and ports of the era seem at once familiar and strange, the same can be said of the leaders and their ideas. One of the enduring debates in American history cen-ters around the issue of just how revolutionary the American Revolution was. After all, the Declaration of Independence voted on July 4 did not propose many new ideas. Rather, it simply accepted existing views of the relationship between government and governed, and listed the excesses and violations of that relationship that could be laid at the feet of George III. When historians look at men like John Adams, John Hancock, Thomas Jefferson, and George Washington, some see them as conservatives attempting to preserve a system while others depict them as radicals setting out to overthrow a government.

Gaining a flavor of the era and its lifestyle is a challenge, as is knowing the leaders and their ideas. Biographies can help yield an understanding of the merchants, craftsmen, planters, military officers, and journalists who emerged as the founding fathers. Analysis of their writings can give some access to their thought. But to understand what it was like to live in the colonies in the 1770s, we have to look at the physical remains, the objects that serve as documents of day-to day-life.

The artifacts, tools, weapons, and structures that people lived with give a feel for the fabric of home, work, family, and society. Some of it may be alien to the modern eye, but thinking about such traces of the past can yield insights into how hard it was to cook a meal, take a bath, or find a comfortable bed in 1776. Surprisingly, much of the equipage of the 18th century is little changed in the 21st century, from tools like rakes and hammers, through household utensils, mugs, plates, and dishes, to everyday items like buttons, boothooks, bottles, wheelbarrows, and windows. At once alien and familiar, the era of the 1770s is both immediate and distant.

While July 4 is rightly thought of as a date that shaped the history of nations, laden with political meaning that would alter the world, understanding the life and times of 1776 requires a view far beyond the meeting in Independence Hall and the rooms above city traffic in the Graff House where Jefferson drafted the list of grievances against King George. Documents and proclamations take on a life of their own, but they come out of a rich context of people, life, culture, and events.

This book gathers 100 articles that focus on the day and the document, but that also reach out in concentric circles to Philadelphia in 1776, to Pennsylvania and the other colonies, to some of the notable signers, and to the life and times of the ordinary people of the period. In tracing the causes and consequences of that day, the entries in this book move back in time to the source of the grievances that led up to the Declaration, and to the war that was fought to secure national independence. Through this collection of information and illustration, we hope to make this one day in history more immediate, the era less distant, and the Declaration itself less obscure.

—**RODNEY P. CARLISLE**
GENERAL EDITOR

READER'S GUIDE TO ARTICLES

This list is provided to assist readers in finding related articles by topic.

DECLARING INDEPENDENCE

Committees of Correspondence
Continental Congress, First and
    Second
Declaration House (Jacob Graff
    House)
Declaration of Independence
Declaration of Independence,
    August 2, Embossed
Declaration of Independence, Drafts
    and Copies
Declaration of Independence, Signers
Drafting Committee
Dunlap's Broadsides
Independence Hall
Jefferson, Thomas
July 2 Vote
July 4 Celebrations
July 8 Proclamations
National Archives
Self-Evident Truths
Speeches on July 4 Commemorations
Syllogism
Unanimity

HISTORY & CULTURE

African Americans
Bicentennial
Boston in the Revolution
Charleston in the Revolution
Colonies, Loyal
Colonies or States
Commerce and Trade
Culture, 1776

Daily Life, 1776
Disease and Medicine, 1776
Farm Life, 1776
Flags of the Revolution
France, Reaction in
Frontier in the American Revolution
Great Britain, Reaction in
Independence Hall
Loyalists
Memoirs of the Revolution
Native Americans
Navigation Acts
Philadelphia
Plantation Life and Slavery, 1776
Recreation and Leisure, 1776
Religion, 1776
Revolution, Theory of
Seafaring, 1776
Sons of Liberty
Taverns and Residences, 1776
Travel, 1776
Whigs, English
Women in the Revolution

PEOPLE

Adams, Abigail
Adams, John
Adams, Samuel
Arnold, Benedict
Braxton, Carter
Burgoyne, John
Carroll of Carrollton, Charles
Chase, Samuel
Clark, George Rogers
Franklin, Benjamin
George III
Gerry, Elbridge
Hamilton, Alexander
Hancock, John
Henry, Patrick
Howe, Richard

Jefferson, Thomas
Jones, John Paul
Kosciusko, Thaddeus
Lafayette, Marquis de
Lee, Richard Henry
Livingston, Philip
Marion, Francis
Morris, Robert
Rochambeau, Comte de
Rodney, Caesar
Rush, Benjamin
Rutledge, Edward
Sherman, Roger
Stockton, Richard
Washington, George

WAR OF INDEPENDENCE

American Revolution, Causes of
American Revolution, Events of
    April 1775–July 1776
American Revolution, Events of
    August 1776–September 1783
American Revolution, Results of
Connecticut in the Revolution
Delaware in the Revolution
Georgia in the Revolution
Loyalists
Maryland in the Revolution
Massachusetts in the Revolution
New Hampshire and Vermont in the
    Revolution
New Jersey in the Revolution
New York in the Revolution
North Carolina in the Revolution
Pennsylvania in the Revolution
Rhode Island in the Revolution
Soldiers, American
Soldiers, British
South Carolina in the Revolution
Virginia in the Revolution

JULY 4, 1776:
TIMELINE

The sun rose at 4:37 A.M. and set at 7:32 P.M. on July 4, 1776. On what became known as Independence Day, members of the Second Continental Congress officially voted to become the United States of America. On that date, Thomas Jefferson left his suite of rooms at the Graff House at around 6 A.M. to attend committee meetings. This was not unusual. Generally, sessions of Congress began at 10 A.M. each day and continued into the evening hours whenever matters were pressing.

During less urgent times, sessions ended at three or four o'clock in the afternoon, when the delegates broke for dinner. On those evenings that Congress did not continue its sessions, members used the time for committee meetings. Because the issue of independence was of utmost importance, regular sessions had been scheduled to begin an hour earlier in the day.

At 9 A.M. on July 4, Congress took up an emergency measure dealing with the purchase of flints from New York for use in Pennsylvania; then agreed to request that Pennsylvania and Delaware dispatch troops to be used in the defense of Philadelphia. Afterward, Congress resolved itself into a body of the whole. The Declaration of Independence was read as amended; and with Benjamin Harrison presiding, the debate on the Declaration continued. The debate dealt with toning the Declaration down to refrain from alienating the British population. In the early evening hours, members of the Second Continental Congress completed all changes to the Declaration of Independence, and John Hancock returned to his chair. After reading the Declaration aloud one final time, the delegates approved the document, with each colony having one vote. The secretary called the roll from north to south, beginning with New Hampshire and ending with Georgia. The former British colonies were now American states. John Adams, the foremost advocate for independence, announced to his colleagues, "It's done." After completing other minor business, Congress adjourned.

Congressional secretary, Charles Thompson, recorded in the *Journal* for July 4, 1776, that the whole Congress had approved the motion for independence. He enclosed a broadside of the Declaration, which had been signed, "by order and in behalf of the congress," John Hancock, President." Thompson had attested Hancock's signature, which he had intentionally made three times its normal size. Hancock joked that the British might raise the price on his head from the current £500 when they saw his signature on the treasonous document. No other signatures were added to the Declaration on July 4. Congress voted to distribute the document among the colonies to be read in public places and to all members of the military.

The bell upstairs in the Philadelphia State House had been designated as the signal to announce independence to the crowds waiting below. After the bell rang out, a celebration started that lasted throughout the night. Even those Philadelphians who wished to sleep would have found it difficult because cannons were discharged, drums rolled, people shouted and cheered, and all the church bells chimed in to announce the birth of the United States of America. Messengers jumped on their horses and spread the news to surrounding areas. Philadelphians gathered again on July 8 when the first official reading of the Declaration of Independence took place at the Liberty Bell.

On July 19, Congress voted to have an engrossed copy of the Declaration prepared. This document became the official Declaration of Independence, and it was this document that the 56 signers signed on August 2, 1776. That version of the Declaration of Independence was released to the public on January 18, 1777.

A footnote to the signing of the Declaration of Independence on July 4, 1776, occurred on the 50th anniversary of the nation's independence. On July 4, 1826, former presidents Thomas Jefferson and John Adams died within hours of each other as the United States celebrated its birthday.

—ELIZABETH PURDY

THE REBELS OF '76.
THE GREAT
OR, THE FIRST ANNOUNCEMENT OF
DECLARATION.

EXPLANATION.—It is sunset on the 4th of July, 1776. The members of the old Conti-nental Congress, having signed the Declaration, are seen in the act of leaving the Hall of Independence. HANCOCK, distinguished by his dark dress, stands on the steps in front of the hall-door, announcing to a friend that the Declaration has just been signed. FRANKLIN is seen at his right, JEFFERSON leans against the right pillar of the door. ADAMS is con-versing with Jefferson—between their heads is seen the face of LIVINGSTON, and against the left pillar stands ROGER SHERMAN. These form the group on the steps. We then com-mence on the left of the picture, and counting every figure, discover the following persons: 1, a citizen; 2, WILSON, a signer; 3, a citizen; 4, a tory; 5, a signer; 6, a lady; 7, her father; 8, the Indian who bore the Declaration to the camp of Washington; 9, Thomas Paine, talking with No. 10, BENJAMIN RUSH, and 11, ROBERT MORRIS, both signers. Behind them the heads of citizens are seen, and to the right, a crowd of patriots, Quakers, tories, &c. eagerly disputing the nature and merits of the Declaration.

Entered according to act of Congress, in the year 1869, by P. Adams, in the Clerk's Office of the District Court of the U. S. for the Eastern District of Pennsylvania.

A

Adams, Abigail (1744–1818)

A letter from Abigail Adams to her husband, JOHN ADAMS, dated Sunday, July 14, 1776, read, in part:

By yesterdays post I received two Letters dated 3 and 4 of July and tho your Letters never fail to give me pleasure, be the subject what it will, yet it was greatly heightned by the prospect of the future happiness and glory of our Country; nor am I a little Gratified when I reflect that a person so nearly connected with me has had the Honour of being a principal actor, in laying a foundation for its future Greatness. May the foundation of our new constitution, be justice, Truth and Righteousness. Like the wise Mans house may it be founded upon those Rocks and then neither storms or temptests will overthrow it.

I cannot but feel sorry that some of the most Manly Sentiments in the Declaration are Expunged from the printed coppy. Perhaps wise reasons induced it.

The correspondence between John and Abigail Adams not only helps illuminate the events of July 4, 1776, in PHILADELPHIA, but also provides light on the home front, from Abigail's point of view. In the above letter, she is surely referring to the final changes made to the Declaration prior to proclamation.

Born Abigail Smith on November 11, 1744, at Weymouth, Massachusetts, the future first lady was grounded on both sides of her lineage by generations of community leaders within the colonies. Abigail Adams was schooled at home due to her fragile health. The lack of a formalized education did not hinder Adams's intellectual development and fostered her love of reading. Her voracious appetite for literature bolstered her sharp wit and gave her the foundation for her above-average intelligence.

In 1764 at the age of 19, she married a young Harvard law graduate, John Adams, who felt that he had found his mental, emotional, and intellectual equal. The union produced two sons and three daughters. The family lived between their small farm at Braintree and in Boston as John Adams's legal practice began to grow. When John became a circuit court judge and was required to spend inordinate amounts of time traveling, Abigail proved herself a capable mistress at Braintree, managing the affairs of the family as well as the farm. Their legendary letters spell out their longing for each other while apart, as well as their personal opinions on the political events of the day.

Abigail was fiercely patriotic and urged her husband to "... remember the ladies ..." as a prominent member of the fledgling government. Abigail was one of the first American suffragists who lobbied for women's rights long before the right to vote was granted in 1920. She wrote frequently to her husband as confidant and advisor in all matters, personal and political. Those letters added another dimension to their strong bond, and a chronology of the issues faced by the newly forming nation.

Abigail remained in the colonies in 1778, as John became the first diplomat to France and then England. By 1783 she had joined him in Europe; all six family members arrived safely, although the cow they had shipped did not. Abigail and her children explored western Europe with her husband until his appointment as vice president of the United States in 1789. She was present for only about 18 months of her husband's presidency, first in Philadelphia, then in Washington, D.C., where she and John were the first to live in the White House.

After John lost his bid for reelection, the couple returned to their home in Quincy, Massachusetts, bitter at the loss to their former friend, THOMAS JEFFERSON. Abigail's interest in politics did not retire along with her husband, and she continued to remain keenly attentive to the political happenings of the day. Abigail passed away on October 28, 1818, of typhoid fever at her home in Quincy. Her son, John Quincy Adams, would become president six years later.

Further Reading: Charles W. Akers, *Abigail Adams, An American Woman* (Longman, 2005); Edith B. Gelles, *Portia: The World of Abigail Adams* (Indiana University Press, 1992); Cokie Roberts, *Founding Mothers: The Women Who Raised Our Nation* (HarperCollins, 2005); "Adams Family Papers," Massachusetts Historical Society, www.masshist.org/digitaladams/ aea/cfm/doc.cfm?id=L17931219ja (cited March 2006); Frank Shuffleton, ed., *The Letters of John and Abigail Adams* (Penguin, 2003).

—CARLISE E. WOMACK

Adams, John (1735–1826)

By some accounts, the Second Continental Congress (see CONTINENTAL CONGRESS, FIRST AND SECOND) ratified the Declaration of Independence at about 2 P.M. on the afternoon of July 4. Submitted by John Adams, along with BENJAMIN FRANKLIN and the document's primary author, THOMAS JEFFERSON, this DRAFTING COMMITTEE had spent the morning of the 4th in discussion and editing of the document to secure a unanimous vote.

Adams would become the first vice president of the newly formed United States and the second president. He began his life in Braintree, Massachusetts (which would later become Quincy, named after the maternal lineage of his wife, ABIGAIL ADAMS), and received a common school education. The future president received a scholarship to Harvard and graduated by age 20 with a law degree in 1755.

He and Abigail made their first home on the small farm where Adams had been raised and spent their time between Braintree and Boston, as his practice began to grow and expand. As his practice and notoriety grew, Adams became an integral part of the colonial government and the underlying struggle to free the colonies from Great Britain. He was involved with freeing the colonies from the beginning, yet, demonstrating his adherence to principle, he also served as lead defense lawyer when soldiers in Boston were arrested for the Boston Massacre.

Adams served in the Massachusetts legislature from 1768 to 1774 and was selected to represent his colony at the First Continental Congress in 1774, which would lay the framework for the fledgling government. He was a signer of the Declaration of Independence and assisted Thomas Jefferson with the drafting of the Constitution.

He later served as the diplomat to France, the Netherlands, and Great Britain, returning to become the first vice president under GEORGE WASHINGTON. Adams found little he enjoyed about the office. In one of his famed letters to Abigail he wrote, "My Country has in its Wisdom contrived for me the most insignificant Office that ever the Invention of Man contrived or his Imagination conceived."

Adams was elected as the nation's second president in 1796. The Adams administration was

Last Words

AS JOHN Adams lay dying on July 4, 1826, he spoke two phrases that have survived the test of time. "Independence Forever!" was his tribute to the celebration of independence from Great Britain. But his softly spoken final words were of his close friend and political rival: "Thomas Jefferson survives." Adams was unaware that just hours before, Jefferson, too, had died.

UPPER RIGHT *Photo of a portrait of Abigail Adams painted by John S. Copley. Abigail was an early proponent of women's rights.* LOWER RIGHT *Photo of a portrait of John Adams painted by C. W. Peale.*

constantly involved in foreign affairs, especially with Great Britain and France. Adams assisted in negotiating a peace treaty between the hostile nations, but his troubles with France were not over. American trade vessels were all but helpless against French marauders, and Adams petitioned Congress for funding for a provisional army to quell the threat.

Congress also passed the Alien and Sedition Acts, which Adams accepted as measures of national security in an emergency situation, after diplomats returned from France with stories of corruption and the threat by the French to refuse to negotiate trade agreements unless a sizable bribe was offered. Adams was deeply angered and, in what would later be known as the XYZ Affair, managed to bring together the nation again with an upwelling of national pride. Under his administration the purpose of the acts was to scare any foreign dissidents as well as attempt to hamper vicious editorials written by Republican editors, attacking Adams.

Shortly before the presidential election of 1800, Adams arrived in the new capital city of Washington, D.C., to a country estate referred to as the Executive Mansion, which was to be the executive seat of the American government. On his second night in the new presidential home, he wrote in another letter to his wife, "Before I end my letter, I pray Heaven to bestow the best of Blessings on this House and all that shall hereafter inhabit it. May none but honest and wise Men ever rule under this roof."

His tenure in the White House was short. Though Adams was widely popular, the Federalists were deeply divided and the Republican Party was strong and unified. In the presidential election of 1800, he was defeated by a narrow margin, by his old friend Thomas Jefferson.

In 1825, his son John Quincy Adams became the fifth president of the United States. Adams died on July 4, 1826, and was laid to rest in the United First Parish Church cemetery.

Further Reading: John Adams, *The Adams Papers*, Lyman H. Butterfield et al., eds. (Harvard University Press, 1961); John Ferling, *John Adams: A Life* (University of Tennessee Press, 1992); James Grant, *John Adams: Party of One* (Farrar, Straus, and Giroux, 2005); David McCullough, *John Adams* (Simon and Schuster, 2001); "Adams Quotations," www.masshist.org/digitaladams/aea/cfm/doc.cfm?id=L17931219ja (cited July 2006).

—CARLISE E. WOMACK

Adams, Samuel (1722–1803)

Samuel Adams has been called the "firebrand of the Revolution" and was in many ways the inventor of agitprop (agitation propaganda), long before the Bolsheviks gave it that name in their own revolution against Russia's tzar.

Adams was a complex figure, for whom failure was as familiar a companion as success. Born in Boston, he was one of 12 children of a prosperous landowner and brewer. Though educated at Harvard, he never held down a steady job, perhaps because his naturally rebellious personality chafed against submitting to a boss. He studied law for a while, but when it did not work out, he bounced from one job to another. He worked at his father's brewery, at a colonial financial institution, then started and lost his own business.

After his father died, he ran the family brewery into the ground. He spent some time as the city tax collector, but fell so far in arrears on his collection that he was in danger of losing the run-down family home that was his last possession. The only occupation at which he had any success was politics. Adams emerged as the leader of the opposition against the conservative aristocracy and used

Sam Adams: Tory Propaganda

SOME HISTORIANS suggest Samuel Adams's reputation as the great fire-brand of the Revolution may have been as much the work of his enemies as of his supporters. There is evidence that Tories attempted to blacken his reputation by portraying him as a dangerous radical and traitor. His record of statements and actions as a political official, however, show a strong preference for established authority and limiting the franchise and political office to the wealthy. Adams was a revolutionary in his 18th-century culture in that he rejected monarchy. AT LEFT a painting of Samuel Adams by John S. Copley.

his skill as a writer to fan public discontent against important tax legislation, including the Sugar Act and the Stamp Act. He was one of the organizers of the SONS OF LIBERTY, and his stridency disturbed even such patriots as JOHN HANCOCK and his second cousin JOHN ADAMS.

The Tea Act of 1773 was critical in Adams's drive to spark a rebellion. He was a key player in inciting the Boston Tea Party, and may well have participated in the rebellion. He narrowly escaped capture after the Battle of Lexington, and before he set off to the Second Continental Congress (see CONTINENTAL CONGRESS, FIRST AND SECOND), he organized the committee that issued the Suffolk Resolves, a document declaring Massachusetts to be in rebellion against the British Crown (see MASSACHUSETTS IN THE REVOLUTION).

In spite of his fiery reputation as an agitator in Boston, he played a low-key role in PHILADELPHIA. Adams knew his radicalism would be startling to the delegates from other colonies, particularly those who were still undecided about independence. After the independence vote, he continued to serve in Congress until 1781. He participated in Massachusetts's constitutional convention, after which he confined his political activities to his home state.

He served in the state senate, ultimately presiding over that legislative body. Because of his opposition to strengthening the national government, he refused to participate in the Constitutional Convention and subsequently was one of the more notably unenthusiastic delegates in the state's ratifying convention.

The last act of his political career was to be elected lieutenant governor of Massachusetts in 1789. After the death of Hancock, he was briefly interim governor before being elected to the governorship in his own right. He died in 1803 and was buried at the Old Granary Burying Ground.

Further Reading: John K. Alexander, *Samuel Adams: America's Revolutionary Politician* (Rowman & Littlefield, 2002); Ralph V. Harlow, *Samuel Adams: Promoter of the American Revolution* (Reprinte Services, 2001); Ray Raphael, *Founding Myths: Stories That Hide Our Patriotic Past* (The New Press, 2004); John Tebel, *Turning the World Upside Down: Inside the American Revolution* (Orion, 1993).

—**LEIGH KIMMEL**

African Americans

By March 5, 1770, relations between the British soldiers and American colonials were strained. There had been brawls and fights, including one instance where the locals beat and drove out of town three soldiers, who returned later with reinforcements. On the 5th, a group of soldiers walked out of their barracks to face a small crowd of boys, including Irish, blacks, and others. After trading insults, they began to fight. The colonials, under the leadership of Crispus Attucks, chased the soldiers back into their barracks.

While this was going on, an apprentice with a bloody head claimed that he had been bludgeoned by a sentry. Attucks led the crowd to the sentry, who called for reinforcements. When seven reinforcements arrived, the crowd dared them to fire. Struck by a stick on the side of his head, one soldier fired—directly into Attucks. In all, five people died in the Boston Massacre (see BOSTON IN THE REVOLUTION).

Slaves such as Attucks were a complication for the patriots of the 1770s. At the time of the Revolution, about 20 percent of the colonial population was African American, and over 90 percent were slaves. Every colony had legal slavery. Still, most blacks were in the south, where the plantation economy had taken hold (see PLANTATION LIFE AND SLAVERY, 1776). The plantations, in a preindustrial era, required large numbers of seasonal laborers. Most plantation owners held themselves as absolute masters of all they owned, including their slaves. Slaves had neither rights, privacy, nor recourse. They could only resist by work slowdown, sabotage, or on occasion, mutiny. Arming them was not an attractive option.

SLAVE UNREST IN THE EARLY 1770S

In July 1772, African Americans learned that James Somersett, an American slave, ran away to England, and won his freedom because slavery was illegal in England. Although the Somersett ruling applied only to England, by January 1773 American slaves were petitioning Boston's General Court for their freedom. Virginians' fears of slave revolt increased when, in 1774, a conspiracy by slaves to desert to English troops was unmasked. At that point, James Madison told William Bradford that he suspected the British would foment a slave revolt.

In March 1775, Virginia governor Lord Dunmore armed his slaves. In April, Dunmore sent the Royal Marines to take the Williamsburg Magazine and its gunpowder. He backed off in the face of Virginian violence and paid restitution, but threatened to free the slaves and see Williamsburg in ashes. By June 1775 Dunmore was taking sanctuary in a British man-of-war ship off Yorktown. About 100 blacks joined the fleet in the fall of 1775.

When Dunmore bested a troop of Virginia militia in November 1775, he proclaimed that all male indentures and slaves belonging to the rebels were welcome to join his forces. By December 1, he had roughly 300 runaways in "Dunmore's Ethiopian Regiment." These soldiers wore "Liberty to Slaves," on their chests. About half of Dunmore's force at the Battle of Great Bridge on December 9 were freed slaves.

By the summer of 1776 Dunmore had over 800 black troops. Fever and disease killed over half, and Dunmore left 300 to fend for themselves when he left Virginia on August 7.

THE AMERICAN SIDE

In September 1776 Congress ordered the raising of 88 infantry battalions. Southern pressure had initially forced black militiamen out of the Continental Army, but the states needed bodies, so Congress authorized the states in January 1777 to take whatever measures they needed to meet their quotas. Virginia, with a quota of 10,200, considered a draft of the militias after the call for volunteers fell short.

Wanting to keep its armed militia close to home for self-protection and to control the slaves, Virginia sent free blacks first. New Jersey authorized the use of slaves as substitutes in May 1777. New Hampshire and Connecticut subsequently allowed recruitment of slaves to meet their Continental quotas.

By the winter of 1777–78, the Continental Army was down to 18,000 troops due to disease and desertion. Washington needed troops. His general order of January 12, 1777, called on recruiters to enlist freemen only but said nothing about skin color. Virginia tightened up its recruiting standard, requiring proof of free status prior to enlistment.

African Americans were at Valley Forge in 1777–78. Washington approved the 1st Rhode Island Regiment, composed of black slaves, in January 1778. Black soldiers drilled with whites by February 1778 when Baron von Steuben was forming a ragtag group into a European-style army. At Monmouth in June, about 700 blacks fought alongside white troops. By August the Continental Army reported 755 black members.

After blacks proved their worth in the colonial success at Monmouth, Sir Henry Clinton, new com-

James Armistead

THE MARQUIS DE LAFAYETTE's success in tracking British General Charles Cornwallis in Virginia was due in large part to James Armistead. Born around 1760 in New Kent County, Armistead had approached Lafayette in Williamsburg in early 1781. Armistead's master had offered him as a servant, but Lafayette used him as a spy in British headquarters. Armistead was able to tell Lafayette that Cornwallis was fortifying Yorktown, so there, in September, Lafayette began the final siege of the war. Armistead left Yorktown before the siege, and in October 1784 Lafayette wrote that Armistead had provided essential service. Armistead took Lafayette's document to the legislature, which considered his case and finally freed him in 1787.

mander of British forces, moved the war to the south and promised any African American who crossed his lines the opportunity to choose his own occupation. He attracted tens of thousands of slaves.

After the provisional treaty of November 1782, the British prepared to evacuate. When the Americans demanded their slaves back, the British commander, Sir Guy Carleton, refused. The British commandant of New York City, General Samuel Birch, created *The Book of Negroes,* a list of the thousands of claimants to the British promise of protection and freedom. Three to four thousand black LOYAL-ISTS sailed from New York for Nova Scotia, Jamaica, and Britain.

An estimated 100,000 blacks escaped, died, or were killed during the war. The Continental Armies had 5,000 blacks, and many hundreds of blacks were in the navy. When the French combined forces with the Americans at White Plains in June 1781, Baron Closen of the French Royal Deux-Ponts estimated that about 1,200 to 1,500 of the 6,000 Continentals were black.

ABOLITIONIST MOVEMENT

Black participation in the war encouraged the abolitionist movement. Quakers, the Society of Friends, had been the first to denounce slavery. The Quaker influence led to the creation of the London Committee to Abolish the Slave Trade in 1783.

Another influence was the Enlightenment, which challenged the structure of society, rejected class for equality, and defined natural rights as the property of all human beings. Many felt guilty at the hypocrisy of demanding life, liberty, and the pursuit of happiness for some, while denying all three to a sizeable population.

By 1799 most of the northern states had abolished slavery. When the Reverend Absalom Jones and 70 freemen of color of PHILADELPHIA petitioned Congressman Robert Waln for protection against slavery, the slave trade, and the fugitive slave trade, they cited the absence in the Constitution and Bill of Rights of any restriction on the rights of slaves or people of color to its guaranteed liberties. When Waln submitted the petition, a furious debate ensued before the House voted to refer it to committee, where it died, as did the revolutionary fervor and the hope for black rights arising from the Revolutionary War.

Further Reading: Robert N. Buckley, *Slaves in Red Coats: The British West India Regiments, 1795–1815* (Yale University Press, 1979); Bernard C. Nalty, *Strength for the Fight: A History of Black Americans in the Military* (The Free Press, 1986); Robert A. Selig, "The Revolution's Black Soldiers," www.americanrevolution.org/blk.html (cited December 2005); WGBH, "The Revolutionary War: Africans in America," www.pbs.org/wgbh/aia/part2/2narr4.html (cited December 2005).

—JOHN H. BARNHILL, PH.D.

American Revolution, Causes of

The intellectual underpinnings of the American Revolution were in English common law, the Enlightenment philosophy, and English political tradition. These three elements produced an American sense of entitlement to specific rights due to all humankind. Violation of these "unalienable" rights led to the Revolution.

PHILOSOPHICAL ROOTS

The colonists grew up with English common law, in which cases were judged individually with allowance for circumstances not previously foreseen. The exceptional circumstance that the revolutionaries identified concerned obedience to the English king. Thus, the Declaration of Independence enunciated the right of the people to overthrow any form of government inimical to their well-being. Common law promoted the continual reconsideration of tradition and custom.

Rather than taking everything on faith, 18th-century Enlightenment thinkers began reexamining and challenging values and took social ideas into new directions. Inherent in this philosophy was a challenge to authority. Enlightenment philosopher John Locke wrote that all people had rights to "life, liberty, and the pursuit of property," which the government had to protect. The king of England had denied the colonists those natural rights, so he had lost authority over them.

IMPACT OF THE FRENCH AND INDIAN WARS

British victory in the French and Indian Wars of 1754–63 brought the French holdings in Canada and the Spanish possession of Florida into the empire. Britain took for granted that its colonies would share the burden of repaying the war debt.

The colonies were not all that certain. Until the wars, British had imposed duties to regulate trade, as prescribed by standard mercantilist policy. At the same time, the British policy of salutary neglect had meant lax law enforcement. During the French and Indian Wars, the colonial assemblies acted with increasing independence. When coupled with the debt, colonial behavior led the British to take a postwar second look at their colonial policy. The colonies regarded taxation and other reassertions of British control as interference with internal matters. Because only the people of Britain, not the people of the empire, voted for Parliament, the colonies claimed Parliament had jurisdiction over external affairs but not internal ones. It could legislate for the empire but tax only Britain itself.

PAUL REVERE'S ETCHING OF THE BOSTON MASSACRE AT LEFT *On March 5, 1770, a British sentry was taunted and harassed by American patriots outside Boston's Customs House on King Street. Church bells rang, which usually signaled a fire, and the crowd thickened, surrounding British army captain Thomas Preston and seven or eight soldiers who had arrived on the scene to preserve order. Whether from fear or malice remains a historical mystery, but the soldiers did open fire, killing five and wounding several more. The incident is remembered today as the Boston Massacre. (See* Boston in the Revolution.*)*

British policy changes came quickly. The Currency Act of 1764 banned colonial legislatures' use of paper money for payment of debts. The Sugar Act of 1764 was a revenue measure that reduced the tariffs set by the Molasses Act but was enforced diligently on sugar, molasses, and rum. The Quartering Act of 1765 required the colonies to house and supply British troops. This was too much change for the colonies after enjoying half a century of salutary neglect.

THE STAMP ACT

When, in 1765, British Prime Minister George Grenville's government levied a direct tax requiring colonials to use revenue stamps for all legal documents as well as deeds, newspapers, dice, playing cards, and pamphlets, the colonists strongly opposed. No taxation without representation was the colonial demand.

The Stamp Act led to immediate opposition. After its passage in March, PATRICK HENRY of Virginia asked the House of Burgesses to condemn the measure. Nine of the colonies met in October in New York City, where delegates petitioned for repeal. Many British merchants agreed because they did not want to risk losing millions of pounds of debts should the colonists refuse to pay.

Other colonists did more than talk. On October 31, the day before the Stamp Act was to take effect, 200 New York merchants agreed that they would import no more British goods. This was the First Nonimportation Movement.

Local nonimportation agreements were established in several cities throughout the colonies, and artisan groups used force to prevent distribution of the stamps and to force local stamp collectors to resign. Wherever the colonials challenged British authority, the British backed off, either due

Colonial Economy and Nonimportation

PRIOR TO the French and Indian Wars, the colonists had exported enough to pay for what they imported from Great Britain. The wars brought prosperity to many colonists, and they began buying farm equipment and household goods. Quickly, the colonists were buying 20 percent of all British exports, and becoming deep in debt. The wartime boom gave way to postwar recession, with bankruptcy for some and hard times for all. The last thing the colonists needed in 1767 was higher taxes.

When coupled with the moralistic objection by New England Puritans and American women to extravagances such as fancy carpets, carriages, and elegant apparel and furnishings, the economic argument was sufficient to bring about the boycotts.

ABOVE *After the French and Indian Wars, prosperous colonists began buying equipment and household goods, such as this colonial-era writing chair.*

to lack of power or lack of will. Pressured by British merchants, the new British prime minister, Charles Wentworth, Marquess of Rockingham, repealed the Stamp Act in 1766.

THE TOWNSHEND ACTS

The Townshend Acts of 1767 taxed glass, paint, paper, lead, and tea, to support British troops in America and to pay the salaries of British officials.

BENJAMIN FRANKLIN in 1769 called on the ministry to repeal the laws, renounce the right to tax, and return to salutary neglect. Lord Frederick North conceded to an extent, repealing most of the Townshend acts. The British troops remained, and Parliament kept the tax on tea to show its supremacy.

FAILED ATTEMPTS AT COMPROMISE

The Massachusetts assembly proposed two separate governments—British and American—under the single king. Parliament was unlikely to accept renunciation of its sovereignty, and confrontations in the colonies made the matter mostly moot. The British ministers hoped that time and patience would solve the crisis. Parliament wanted stronger action.

North hoped to split the more moderate colonies from radical Massachusetts. Although THOMAS JEFFERSON denounced Parliament when the colonies met at the First Continental Congress (see CONTINENTAL CONGRESS, FIRST AND SECOND) in Philadelphia in September and October 1774, Joseph Galloway of Pennsylvania proposed an American parliament with legislative and taxing powers that would be able to veto by a crown-appointed governor general. Galloway's plan was narrowly defeated. The radicals issued the Declaration of Rights and Grievances, declaring British reform unconstitutional, dangerous, and damaging to freedom. Congress established the Third Nonimportation Movement and a Continental Association to enforce the boycott and whip up local patriotic feeling.

The British refused to budge. In 1775 General Thomas Gage, governor and military commander of Massachusetts, received orders to close the illegal Massachusetts assembly, arrest its leaders, and capture the arms the radical militias had been stockpiling outside Boston. On April 19, Gage sent troops to Concord. At Lexington shots were fired, and at Concord the Americans ambushed the British, who retreated with 270 casualties. American casualties were under 100. Parliament blockaded the colonies and prohibited trade with them in December. Thomas Paine published *Common Sense* in January 1776, and skirmishes began. Finally, Congress established the Continental Army and declared independence with a July 4, 1776, restatement of the causes of the Revolution.

Further Reading: Carl Degler, *Out of Our Past* (HarperCollins, 1984); Eric Foner, *The Story of American Freedom* (W.W. Norton, 1999); Ray Raphael, *A People's History of the American Revolution* (The New Press, 2001); Simon Schama, *Rough Crossings: Britain, the Slaves, and the American Revolution* (Ecco Press, 2006).

—JOHN H. BARNHILL, PH.D.

American Revolution, Events of April 1775–July 1776

The British Parliament had declared the colonies in a state of rebellion on February 9th, 1775—well before there was a Declaration of Independence or any Continental Army.

Just before the days of Paul Revere's ride and the first fighting at Lexington and Concord, the British Parliament passed the New England Restraining Act. With the Boston Massacre and the Boston Tea Party (see BOSTON IN THE REVOLUTION), and the seizure of arms at Fort William and Mary in New Castle, New Hampshire, New England was a particular source of political irritation and matter of lost revenue for the English.

William Pitt, the venerable Earl of Chatham, proposed that, if the 13 colonies would formally recognize Parliamentary supremacy, then the Continental Congress would not only be recognized, but afforded the authority to raise revenues in its sphere of authority. Such an act might have forestalled armed rebellion.

Instead, King GEORGE III signed the New England Restraining Act: Effective July 1, 1775, New England trade was to be limited to Britain and the British West Indies.

1775

By mid-April SAMUEL ADAMS, JOHN HANCOCK, and many other patriots had sought refuge in the countryside outlying Boston, fearing they would be arrested by the British army. Paul Revere correctly surmised that the British might land in force and march to Concord to seize a cache of arms and munitions. On April 18, Revere, William Dawes, and Dr. Samuel Prescott alarmed the countryside and mustered the Minutemen.

The battles of Lexington and Concord began the following day, and the Second Continental Congress (see CONTINENTAL CONGRESS, FIRST AND SECOND) convened in PHILADELPHIA on May 10. On the same day, Ethan Allen seized Fort Ticonderoga, assisted by Connecticut militia under BENEDICT ARNOLD.

GEORGE WASHINGTON was named commander in chief of the Continental Army on June 15, and two days later British marines and soldiers stormed American positions on the high ground north of Boston in the battle of Bunker Hill.

On July 5, John Dickenson sent the Olive Branch Petition to King George III, who refused to read it. The next day, Thomas Jefferson and John Dickinson authored the *Declaration of Causes of Taking Up Arms*, a statement by the Congress asserting that war was not a desire, but that oppression required a readiness to resist. George III declared the American colonies in rebellion on August 23, the second such declaration emanating from England.

In November, the Americans established the U.S. Marine Corps, the Continental Navy, and the Committee of Secret Correspondence—the first American intelligence system. On December 22, Parliament passed the American Prohibitory Act, forbidding all trade with the colonies and authorizing the seizure of American ships and cargo.

1776

New Hampshire ratified the first state constitution independent of the British Crown on January 5, adopting the state motto "Live Free or Die."

The Continental Navy and Marines seized Nassau in the Bahamas on March 3, in the first amphibious assault in American history, and took Dorchester Heights on March 4. With this capture, the Continental Army held a critical tactical advantage over the British.

On March 17, in one of the few political and military strategic decisions by the British that made sense during the entire war, the British withdrew from Boston.

In June, RICHARD HENRY LEE introduced the formal resolution that culminated in the Declaration of

Common Sense

THOMAS PAINE'S *Common Sense*, published on January 15, 1776, inspired the revolutionary movement in the 13 colonies. Quotations include:

We have it in our power to begin the world anew... America shall make a stand, not for herself alone, but for the world.

Tyranny, like hell, is not easily conquered.

A long habit of not thinking a thing wrong, gives it a superficial appearance of being right.

Government even in its best state is but a necessary evil.

For all men being originally equals, no one by birth could have a right to set up his own family in perpetual preference to all others for ever.

Of more worth is one honest man to society and in the sight of God, than all the crowned ruffians that every lived.

As to religion, I hold it to be the indispensable duty of all government, to protect all conscientious professors thereof, and I know of no other business which government hath to do therewith.

Independence, and the British moved 30 ships and 30,000 troops into New York. Congress approved the independence resolution on July 2.

For the first time in the history of the world, a royal sovereign was renounced by his subjects when the Declaration of Independence was approved on July 4. (See also AMERICAN REVOLUTION, EVENTS OF AUGUST 1776–SEPTEMBER 1783.)

Further Reading: David Hackett Fischer, *Paul Revere's Ride* (Oxford University Press, 1994); Pauline Maier, *American Scripture: Making the Declaration of Independence* (Alfred A. Knopf, 1997); Pauline Maier, *From Resistance to Revolution* (W.W. Norton, 1991); Charles Royster, *A Revolutionary People at War* (University of North Carolina Press, 1996); Stanley Weintraub, *Iron Tears: America's Battle for Freedom, Britain's Quagmire* (Simon and Schuster, 2005).

—RAY BROWN

American Revolution, Events of August 1776– September 1783

When the official copy of the Declaration of Independence was signed on August 2, 1776, 56 representatives from the 13 colonies affixed their signatures. The United States now faced the daunting task of driving British soldiers from America and convincing the king that he no longer had any authority over the new country.

REVOLUTION

With independence as a goal, the colonies turned their attention to war. Both the British and Americans held New York's ports as significant. After the Battle of Long Island on August 27, General GEORGE WASHINGTON reluctantly left the British to occupy New York City. By November 15, Congress had approved the Articles of Confederation, a document that created a loose league of friendship among the 13 sovereign states.

After the British captured Fort Washington on November 16, Washington headed to New Jersey. Four days later American troops retreated to

Pennsylvania after the capture of Fort Lee. Washington retrieved his reputation on Christmas night in 1776 with his daring passage over the frozen Delaware River and his surprise attack on the British in the Battle of Trenton. Washington was forced to retreat from General Charles Cornwallis on January 2, 1777, but staged a victory the following day at the Battle of Trenton. On July 23, Howe arrived in PHILADELPHIA, and the Battle of Brandywine Creek ensued on September 11. By September 26, the British had gained control of Philadelphia. Unwilling to concede the city, Washington's troops converged on the British at Germantown on October 4. Howe repelled the attack, and Washington's forces again withdrew. Nevertheless, the British suffered a major defeat on October 17, in the Battle of Saratoga.

During the winter of 1777–78, Washington's troops endured a harsh winter with diminishing supplies at Valley Forge. Washington was heartened by news that on February 6, 1778, America and France had signed an alliance. Eleven days later France declared war on Britain. Anxious to see its enemy defeated, France had been sending weapons as well as money to the colonies. While foreign aid was essential, it was not enough to make up for Congress's shortage of revenue.

On June 17, after facing Washington's troops at the Battle of Monmouth, the British again retreated to New York. Two months later, a joint Franco-American attempt to recover Rhode Island failed. The British had captured Savannah, Georgia, in December 1777, effectively ensuring British control of America's newest and southernmost colony, so the major focus was on Virginia and the Carolinas. On March 3, 1779, American forces were defeated at Briar Creek, and were repelled in an attempt to recapture Augusta, Georgia. Spirits rose briefly when

Equal Power

AWARE THAT it was necessary to form a national government in addition to 13 sovereign state governments, the Continental Congress (see CONTINENTAL CONGRESS, FIRST AND SECOND) appointed a committee comprised of members from each state to determine how the United States would operate as a confederation of 13 states with equal power. The result was the Articles of Confederation, which Congress approved on November 15, 1776. Because of state sovereignty, the Articles required the approval of all 13 states to be ratified. The Articles, finally ratified on March 1, 1781, were flawed from the beginning because of the many compromises made to protect state interests. The major weakness in the Articles was the lack of power at the national level. Congress had no power to levy taxes, regulate commerce, or pass and enforce national laws. Ultimately these weaknesses led to the Philadelphia Convention of 1787 that produced the U.S. Constitution.

Spain declared war on Britain. Despite this good news, Americans were soon reeling from the fiasco in which a Franco-American plan to recapture Savannah failed after weeks of effort.

The autumn of 1779 presented America with a stunning sea victory when Captain JOHN PAUL

JONES, the "Father of the American Navy," attacked Britain's HMS *Serapis* and HMS *Countess of Scarborough.* Other members of Jones's squadron sank the USS *Bonhomme Richard.* During the battle in which over half of his crew was lost, Jones uttered the words for which he became known, "I have not yet begun to fight."

On May 12, 1780, the British captured Charleston, South Carolina. The Battle of Camden on August 16 was one of the bloodiest of the entire war. The treason of former American war hero BENEDICT ARNOLD dealt a crushing blow to the colonists, who were subsequently heartened by the news that American forces had defeated a large Tory unit in the Battle of King's Mountain.

Americans were also delighted with the news that the Netherlands had declared war on Great Britain, and greatly encouraged by an American victory at the Battle of Cowpens. With victory in sight, the last state had ratified the Articles of Confederation on March 1, 1781.

VICTORY

While the South Carolina campaign was taking place, General Nathanael Greene initiated his legendary cat-and-mouse strategy, outmaneuvering the British and forcing them to chase him. On March 15, Greene's force of 4,400 faced a British onslaught of 1,900 men. Cornwallis ordered his men to shoot indiscriminately into the ranks, and both British and American soldiers fell as Greene was forced to retreat. After the battle, Cornwallis set out on his ill-fated march northward through Virginia. On April 29, Virginians celebrated the arrival of the MARQUIS DE LAFAYETTE.

On August 8, Cornwallis marched into Yorktown with no way of knowing that it would be his downfall. On August 13, French Admiral François-Joseph-Paul de Grasse left New York and steered his fleet toward Virginia, arriving on August 30. Nine days before his arrival, Washington had also begun his journey to Virginia. From September 5 to September 9, the Battle of the Capes raged. When it was over, the French fleet controlled the Chesapeake.

After the Battle of Eutaw Springs on September 8, the Franco-American forces consolidated their plans to surround Cornwallis. Between September 14 and September 26, both Washington and Rochambeau arrived in Williamsburg with reinforcements, and Cornwallis was forced to surrender to Washington on October 19, 1781. Although the war was not officially over, the tables had completely turned.

On April 15, 1783, Congress ratified the Preliminary Articles of Peace, followed by the signing of the Treaty of Paris on September 3, 1783. On November 15, the British finally left New York City.

Overall, some 250,000 men fought for the patriot cause. Although the British army and navy had been victorious in battle after battle, and the Americans appeared to be constantly retreating, they had fought for a cause in which they believed. The French later applied that same conviction to overthrowing its monarchy in the French Revolution (1789–95).

Further Reading: Ian Barnes, *The Historical Atlas of the American Revolution* (Routledge, 2000); Robert D. Bass, *Swamp Fox: The Life and Campaign of General Francis Marion* (Sandlapper, 1976); Edward G. Lengel, *General George Washington: A Military Life* (Random House, 2005); Cathy D. Matson and Peter S. Onuf, *A Union of Interests: Political and Economic Thought in Revolutionary America* (University of Kansas Press, 1990); Gary B. Nash, *The Unknown American Revolution: The Unruly Birth of Democracy and the Struggle to Create America* (Viking, 2005); Elswyth Thane, *The Fighting Quaker: Nathanael Greene* (Hawthorn, 1972); Harry M. Ward, *The American Revolution: Nationhood Achieved* (St. Martin's, 1995).

—ELIZABETH PURDY, PH.D.

American Revolution, Results of

Important internal consquences emanated from the American emancipation. Suffrage was extended to males in regions that were previously underrepresented in the legislatures, such as the scarcely inhabited western regions of the states.

The representatives in the senates, first chambers, or upper houses of the states were no longer appointed by the king or the governor but elected by the people, as were a number of offices previously assigned by the king or governor.

Before the Revolution, holding an office meant serving the king. After July 4, 1776, it meant serving the people. The popular participation in the general democratization brought along a political system that was closer to the common man than anything before. Political processes and proceedings were no longer an elitist leisure-time activity, but of general interest, discussed in popular newspapers.

Increasing political mobilization, broadening of political share, overcoming localisms, nation-building, and the revolution of communication and media usage were integral parts of the rapidly changed social structure within the states. Many citizens previously barred from direct political participation, or not active in politics, started to run for offices. Minorities, like the Germans who comprised one-fourth of PHILADELPHIA's population, enjoyed for the first time the effects of participatory politics.

The Revolution transformed the American mind and soul, and self-perception. In 1760 only 17 newspapers existed in North America. After the establishment of the new federal constitution in 1790, 92 newspapers existed in the United States. This broadening of state-citizen interaction culminated in the sanctioning by the Constitution of the configuration in which the legislative, executive, and judicial branches were all elected by direct or indirect popular vote. A close look at the turnout in the elections on a state level shows that despite the founding myths of the unanimous nation (see UNANIMITY), the identification with the state was much higher than the identification with the United States of America.

The political theorists of the Enlightenment advocated in favor of the common people's right to overthrow governments if their ruling was unjust. The American Revolution took the ideas of the Enlightenment a step further in establishing a government from the people and for the people.

The most telling effects were in France. The American Revolution significantly added to the uprising in France, proving that there could be a successful overthrow of power, the establishment of a new state, and the erection of a new political order.

For the British Empire and its elite, the Revolution meant loss of prestige, and a large part of their transatlantic possessions. Britain lost its 13 colonies, and had to leave Minorca and Florida to the Spanish, Santa Lucia and Tobago to the French, and Ceylon to the Dutch. Furthermore, the American Revolution demonstrated the inability of the British to win a battle on land without the help of allies, if the opponent was not already weakened in fights at sea.

The Revolution created the mental and institutional preconditions for economic growth and political self-assertion, as well as the base for a modern nation-state that served as a role model for the formation of the nation-states in Europe in the 19th century.

From the very beginning of the United States, the question of states' rights triggered off a heated debate. The first American constitution, the Articles of Confederation, left most of the rights with the states. The Articles were in existence for only 10 years before they were overruled by the federal constitution of 1790 that gave more power to the federal administration.

Further Reading: Jeremy Black, *Revolutions in the Western World, 1775–1825* (Ashgate, 2005); Richard D. Brown, *Major Problems in the Era of the American Revolution, 1760–91* (Houghton Mifflin, 2000); Francis D. Cogliano, *Revolutionary America, 1763–1815* (Routledge, 1999); Stanley Elkins and Eric McKitrick, *The Age of Federalism: The Early American Republic, 1788–1800* (Oxford University Press, 1993); Gordon S. Wood, *The Radicalism of the American Revolution* (Alfred A. Knopf, 1992).

—ALEXANDER EMMERICH

Arnold, Benedict (1741–1801)

Benedict Arnold was one of the greatest enigmas of the Revolutionary War. As the "Hero of Saratoga," he laid claim to substantial military fame. Conversely, as the embittered hero, he could never get along with others, and betrayed the country he had vowed to serve.

Arnold was born in Norwich, Connecticut, the grandson of a Rhode Island governor. At the age of 14, his mother apprenticed him as an apothecary. Twice, young Arnold ran away to fight in the French and Indian Wars, deserting on both occasions. After his apprenticeship, Arnold opened his own apothecary/bookstore in New Hampshire and became a successful businessman and trader.

When tensions in the American colonies increased in response to British taxes, Arnold was named captain of the local militia. Arnold marched his small force to Massachusetts upon hearing of the hostilities at Lexington and Concord. After being commissioned as a colonel in the Continental Army, Arnold's forces joined Ethan Allen's forces in the May 10, 1775, surprise attack on Fort Ticonderoga. A week later, Arnold led an attack on the British garrison at St. John's, Canada.

Because of these successes, Arnold was chosen to lead the American campaign to capture Quebec.

HOUSEHOLD ITEMS *typical of colonial homes included a butter churn,* **AT LEFT,** *used to agitate milk to bring the fat globules together into butter; butter paddles,* **AT RIGHT,** *used to smooth out the consistency of the butter; and copper hot water 'bottles,'* **BELOW,** *heated on the hearth.*

After a two-month trip over the rugged terrain of Maine and the Canadian wilderness in which he lost one-fourth of his men, Arnold arrived outside Quebec with 700 men on November 9, 1775. There he was joined by General Richard Montgomery. During the unsuccessful Siege of Quebec, Arnold was seriously wounded and Montgomery was killed. Quebec remained part of the British Empire and continued to provide the British military with a major supply base.

As a new brigadier general, Arnold determined to prevent the British from retaking Fort Ticonderoga in the autumn of 1776. He put together a fleet of 15 boats and a force of 800 men and sailed for Valcour Bay. When the battle came, Arnold lost the entire fleet and a third of his forces. Nevertheless, he had successfully delayed the British, who decided to set up winter headquarters before staging an attack against Fort Ticonderoga the following summer. Arnold continued to skirmish with the British and was promoted to major general. His ultimate chance for glory came during the Battle of Saratoga against General Horatio Gates in the fall of 1777, earning him the nickname "hero of Saratoga."

Congress appointed Arnold the military commander of PHILADELPHIA in June 1778. A widower with three sons, Arnold met and married Philadelphian Peggy Shippen, a member of a prominent loyalist family. Peggy introduced him to wealthy contacts who offered him incentives for betraying his country. Believing that he would never be appreciated by Americans, Arnold sold out for £20,000, a commission in the British military, and the promise of land and annuities. In 1926, new information pinpointed the beginning of Arnold's treachery as the summer of 1779. Afterward, he continued to provide the British with minute details about the movements of the American military.

In August 1780, Arnold was named commander of West Point and made plans to turn the base over to the British. However, on September 23, Arnold's contact, Major John André, was arrested. Officials discovered the plot, and André was hanged as a spy. Arnold escaped. Modern historians believe that Peggy Shippen was heavily involved in the plot to betray America and that her hysterics upon being informed of her husband's treason were simply a ploy to give him time to escape to the British. Arnold was also involved in the Virginia campaign of 1781 that ultimately led to the surrender of General Charles Cornwallis and the end of the war.

Further Reading: Thomas Desjardin, *Through a Howling Wilderness: Benedict Arnold's March to Quebec* (St. Martin's, 2006); Willard Sterne Randall, *Benedict Arnold: Patriot and Traitor* (William Morrow, 1990); Barry K. Wilson, *Benedict Arnold: A Traitor in Our Midst* (McGill-Queen's University Press, 2001).

—ELIZABETH PURDY, PH.D.

B

Bicentennial

The Bicentennial of the American Revolution was an official celebration in the United States that ran from 1974 to 1977, commemorated by a series of loosely connected events throughout the country.

The focal event was the 200th anniversary of the signing of the DECLARATION OF INDEPENDENCE on July 4, 1976. The largest celebrations were held in Washington, D.C., PHILADELPHIA, and New York City. President Gerald R. Ford spoke at Independence Hall in Philadelphia in the morning and at the U.S. Capitol in Washington, D.C., in the afternoon. The New York City celebration included a water parade of tall ships from around the world, and lighting of the top of the Empire State Building in red, white, and blue.

The four souvenir sheets of special postage stamps issued from the U.S. Postal Service on July 4, 1976, are among the most valuable philatelic issue of the past 70 years. The U.S. Mint issued quarters, half dollars, and dollar coins in 1975 and 1976 with special designs on the reverse and the date "1776–1976."

President Ford sought an expansion of the national parks system as a national bicentennial project. Some states issued special license plates. Cities and towns engaged in commemorative public projects, particularly rehabilitating parks or public spaces. New York City engaged in the renewal of Union Square. Warwick, Rhode Island, built an art museum. The University of Florida renovated its auditorium.

AT LEFT *Benedict Arnold, in an engraving by H.B. Hall, 1879. Arnold gained great fame in the Continental Army, eventually earning the status of major general. He was called "The Hero of Saratoga" for his part in the 1777 Battle of Saratoga against British General Horatio Gates. In the summer of 1779, Arnold sold out to the British for the sum of £20,000, a commission in the British military, and the promise of land and annuities. His name has since become synonymous with betrayal and treachery.*

There was a program of Bicentennial sister cities. This involved the pairing of cities and towns with the same name in different states. These cities sent delegations and exhibits to visit the sister city.

Many local historical societies published history books tied to the anniversary, and private firms issued books and memorabilia. Only a small number of these items were licensed to carry the official Bicentennial logo. One particularly ambitious project was the American Freedom Train, a traveling exhibit of American memorabilia housed in 26 railroad cars that visited all 48 contiguous states between April 1975 and December 1976.

The CBS television network produced a unique series called *Bicentennial Minutes* that aired daily in prime time from July 4, 1974, through December 31, 1976. A celebrity read a brief narrative describing the events that happened 200 years ago that day, often accompanied by artworks of the events. The final episode in this series was hosted by President Ford.

—TONY HILL

Boston in the Revolution

B oston was the powder keg of the American Revolution. It was here the Sons of Liberty was formed, here the first battles were fought, and

ABOVE LEFT *An engraving of Paul Revere's famous ride to warn the colonials of the British march on Concord. Revere was one of three riders sounding the alarm that day.* **ABOVE RIGHT** *An engraving titled "The Bostonians in Distress," published in London in 1774, shows caged Bostonians hanging from the Liberty Tree while British ships and troops gather in the background.*

here where General GEORGE WASHINGTON first assumed command of the Continental Army. Boston was home to the Minutemen, Paul Revere, and JOHN HANCOCK.

There had always been uneasiness between Boston and the Crown. The first white inhabitants of Massachusetts came not as the king's agents, but as religious pilgrims seeking liberty. Those who followed were seeking to begin a legacy of freedom, not to continue one of homage to royalty.

Prior to the American Revolution, New England had flexed military muscle during the French and Indian Wars, fighting against the Abenakis and the French armies who ventured south. That they had fought alongside the British army left the belief that they had earned respect as Englishmen, not lesser colonial subjects. When they found the respect wanting, they were not hesitant to again take up arms.

Taxation and regulation in the colonies had been in "salutary neglect" for many years. That condition would change when, in March 1765, the British Parliament imposed the Stamp Act, essentially a tax on the purchase of paper. This caused great discontent in the 13 colonies, particularly in Boston, where shopkeepers and artisans formed the Sons of Liberty in August 1765. These inspired citizens, or hooligans to some, harassed agents of the Crown and burned them in effigy.

In March 1770, a British sentry outside Boston's Customs House was being taunted, harassed, and probably threatened. Someone began ringing church bells, which usually meant a fire. British army captain Thomas Preston and seven or eight soldiers arrived on scene to preserve order. The situation worsened as the British soldiers were surrounded by a crowd. Whether from fear or malice remains a historical mystery, but the soldiers did open fire, killing five and wounding several more, and the incident is remembered today as the Boston Massacre.

The British planned to assist the East India Company at the expense of Boston. On December 13, 1773, some 50 members of the Sons of Liberty, some disguised as Mohawks, stormed three ships in Boston Harbor and threw the contents of 342 chests of Darjeeling tea, worth 9,659 pounds sterling, into the harbor water.

Parliament was outraged. The port of Boston was closed and four British regiments were sent to Boston. Massachusetts's agent in London, Benjamin Franklin, was excoriated before the Privy Council. While he was being berated, Franklin was heard to mutter, "I shall make your king a little man for this."

In May 1774, Hutchinson was replaced by British army general Thomas Gage, a brave and capable soldier, but an affront to the citizens of Massachusetts. Instructed by the Crown to establish order, Gage marched with 700 troops in April 1775 to seize a colonial arsenal in Concord, instigating Paul Revere's ride and the Battles of Concord and Lexington. The Minutemen and militia were then fully mobilized and proceeded to Boston in the thousands.

In July, General George Washington assumed command of the Continental Army in Cambridge, just across the Charles River from Boston. The siege of Boston went on for many months. When the British did evacuate, it was only to land a large army in New York and battle toward PHILADELPHIA. (See also MASSACHUSETTS IN THE REVOLUTION.)

Further Reading: Esther Forbes, *Paul Revere and the World He Lived In* (Houghton Mifflin, 1999); A.J. Langguth, *Patriots: The Men Who Started the American Revolution* (Diane Publishing, 2004); Arthur B. Tourtellot, *Lexington and Concord* (W.W. Norton, 2000).

—RAY BROWN

Braxton, Carter (1736–97)

Carter Braxton was appointed to the First Continental Congress (see CONTINENTAL CONGRESS, FIRST AND SECOND) in 1775. Contemporaries said that the Virginians were "so alarmed with the Idea of Independence that they have sent Mr. Braxton on purpose to turn the vote of that colony, if any question on that subject should come before Congress."

Braxton was well positioned to take an authoritative role in Virginian politics. As a young man, he spent nearly two years in England forming ties within the British court. On his return to America, he married Elizabeth Corbin, the daughter of Colonel Richard Corbin, the receiver-general of customs for the king in Virginia.

While serving in the House of Burgesses during the turbulent 1760s, Braxton continually took Virginia's side in the dispute over taxation and representation with Great Britain. His name, along with those of GEORGE WASHINGTON, THOMAS JEFFERSON, and PATRICK HENRY, was signed to the May 18, 1769, agreement protesting the Townshend Acts.

Braxton took his seat in Congress on February 23, 1776. Four months later, he was alarmed by the introduction of a resolution for independence presented by RICHARD HENRY LEE. In a personal letter to his friend Landon Carter, dated April 14, 1776, Braxton wrote that independence "is in truth a delusive bait which men inconsiderately catch at, without knowing the hook to which it is affixed."

On August 2, 1776, Braxton affixed his signature to the official copy of the DECLARATION OF INDEPENDENCE along with other members of congress. Because of his previous hopes for a peaceful resolution with Britain, it is safe to assume that he was one of the delegates whom JOHN ADAMS described as having "signed with regret." Nine days after the historic signing, Braxton's term as a delegate ended and he returned to his Virginia estate.

Braxton loaned large amounts of money to the struggling new government for which he was never repaid. During the war, he sought to increase his fortune by outfitting numerous merchant ships to carry American goods to other countries. One by one, his ships were captured by the British fleet and he sank further into debt. Forced to give up his country estate and move to Richmond in 1786, Braxton again found purpose by serving as representative for Henrico County to the Virginia Legislature from 1786 until his death in 1797.

Further Reading: Alonzo Thomas Dill, *Carter Braxton, Virginia Signer: A Conservative in Revolt* (University Press of America, 1983); Joseph J. Ellis, *Founding Brothers: The Revolutionary Generation* (Alfred A. Knopf, 2002).

—VICTORIA EASTES

ABOVE *A British Revolutionary War cannon and cannonball. An inscription, carved into the base after the cannon was recovered, reads, "Cannon from British Flagship* Agusta, *destroyed at battle of Redbank, NJ, Oct. 23, 1777."*

Burgoyne, John (1722–82)

In February 1775, British General John Burgoyne was appointed as an advisor to Thomas Gage on military matters in America, which he tried to decline because it was not an independent command. Burgoyne made himself odious in Boston by writing a prologue to the play *Zarah* that mocked Puritans and using Old South Meeting House as a cavalry-training center. Having accomplished little, he returned to London in November 1775 to complain about his position in America to Lord George Germain, newly made secretary at war.

Born in 1722, Burgoyne was rumored to be the bastard offspring of Robert Benson, Lord Bingley, who provided money for his education and officer's commission. Burgoyne parlayed a school friendship with the son of the powerful Earl of Derby into both a prestigious commission and an elopement with Lady Charlotte Stanley, the earl's daughter. Burgoyne missed serving in the 1745 Jacobite rebellion as well as the War of the Austrian Succession and sold his commission to pay gambling debts in 1749. Intervention from his in-laws restored him to the army in 1756, and by 1758 he was a lieutenant colonel of the Coldstream Guards.

During the 1760s, Burgoyne served as a Member of Parliament, where he voted against repeal of the Stamp Act and for the Declaratory Act and gave a speech in which America was portrayed as a spoiled and indulged child. In March 1768, he won a hotly contested election in Lancashire after authorities interpreted a 1661 charter to include all adult males in the area as voters, although he was handed a substantial fine for inciting a riot during the voting.

Burgoyne's subsequent October 1776 pursuit of the rebels stalled at the Battle of Valcour Island, and Carleton refused him permission to attack Fort Ti-

ABOVE *Engraving of a formal portrait of John Burgoyne.*

conderoga. After one more huffy return to London, Burgoyne was the linchpin of the 1777 strategy to attack down the Hudson Valley and cut off New England. Unfortunately, changes in plan left Burgoyne alone marching from Quebec, and although his early successes at Crown Point, Fort George, and Ticonderoga were rapturously received in London, he blundered into the battles of Bennington and Saratoga, where he surrendered to General Horatio Gates.

Burgoyne returned to London and his Parliament seat, where, in 1781, he admitted in a speech that American independence was inevitable. Burgoyne joined the faction supportive of the French Revolution before dying in London on August 4, 1782.

Further Reading: Richard M. Ketchum, *Saratoga: Turning Point of America's Revolutionary War* (Henry Holt, 1999); Max Mintz, *The Generals of Saratoga: John Burgoyne and Horatio Gates* (Yale University Press, 1990).

—MARGARET SANKEY

C

Carroll of Carrollton, Charles (1737–1832)

Charles Carroll of Carrollton was born in Annapolis, Maryland, into one of the wealthiest families in America and became the last surviving signer of the Declaration of Independence. Carroll was Catholic, a rarity among the founding fathers. He was sent abroad to be educated by French Jesuits. After attending the College of St. Omer and the College of Louis le Grand in France, he studied law in London. In 1765 Carroll returned to Maryland after a 17-year absence.

Although he was an early supporter of the colonists' cause against Great Britain, Carroll did not become active until he wrote a series of articles in the *Maryland Gazette* in 1773. Responding to a defender of Maryland's government and Parliament's policies, Carroll, writing as "First Citizen," argued that Great Britain had no right to tax the colonists without proper representation. The articles established him as one of the leaders of that colony's opposition.

In May 1774 Carroll was appointed to the Annapolis committee of correspondence (see COMMITTEES OF CORRESPONDENCE). The next year he was a delegate to the revolutionary Convention of Maryland. In 1776 Congress appointed him, along with BENJAMIN FRANKLIN and SAMUEL CHASE, as continental commissioners to Canada to try to persuade the Canadians to give up their allegiance to Great Britain. Following this mission, he was elected as a delegate to the Continental

Congress on July 4, 1776. Although not present for the actual vote on the DECLARATION OF INDEPENDENCE, Carroll did sign the document as a member of Maryland's delegation on August 2, 1776.

Carroll was an active member of the Board of War during his time in Congress. He finished his term in 1778 and was elected a member of the Maryland state senate. He was again elected to the Continental Congress (see CONTINENTAL CONGRESS, FIRST AND SECOND) in 1780, but declined to serve. In 1789 he was elected to the U.S. Senate and he remained a Senator until 1792, when a new state law forced him to resign his seat to remain a Maryland state senator. Carroll retired from public life in 1801. He died in Baltimore on November 14, 1832.

Further Reading: Thomas Hanley, *Charles Carroll of Carrollton: The Making of a Revolutionary Gentleman* (Loyola University Press, 1982); Ronald Hoffman, Sally D. Mason, and Eleanor S. Darcy, eds., *Dear Papa, Dear Charley: The Peregrinations of a Revolutionary Aristocrat, as Told by Charles Carroll of Carrollton and His Father, Charles Carroll of Annapolis* (University of North Carolina Press, 2001).

—JOSHUA P. SCHIER

Charleston in the Revolution

The modern city of Charleston, lying at the tip of the seven-mile peninsula connecting the Ashley, Cooper, and Wando Rivers, was named after Charles II, ruler of Britain from 1649 to 1660. As tensions with the mother country grew in 1775, it became obvious that Charles Town, as it was originally known, would need protection from a probable invasion of British soldiers.

City officials began fortifying Fort Johnson on James Island and building Fort Sullivan on Sullivan Island. The new fort was only half completed when the British fleet arrived on November 11, 1775. Fort Sullivan was placed under the command of Colonel William Moultrie in January 1776, and it was subsequently renamed in his honor.

ABOVE *General Nathanael Greene (1742–1786) of the Continental Army. He succeeded Horatio Gates as commander in the South in 1780, taking part in battles at Cowpens and Charleston. Painting by Charles Wilson Peale, from life 1783.*

On June 28, 1776, the second battle for Charleston began. The British suffered over 200 casualties, while only 12 Americans were killed and 25 wounded. As a result of their ignominious defeat, the British temporarily abandoned the South and turned their attention northwards. Ignoring a partial British blockade, South Carolina was able to obtain supplies and even formed a small navy to harass the British and engage in privateering.

On May 11, 1779, a force commanded by General Augustine Prevost advanced on Charles Town with an estimated 8,000 men. The South Carolina militia, which consisted of 4,000 troops, was reinforced by 4,000 members of the Continental Army under General Benjamin Lincoln. When Sir Henry Clinton returned to Charles Town with a fleet and 13,500 men on February 11, 1780, it became clear that South Carolina was no longer capable of repelling the third attack.

By April 15, Charles Town was surrounded. On May 12, the City of Charles Town surrendered. It was a major defeat for the patriot cause. Savannah was already under British control; thus, the American supply line was cut.

Even though Charles Town was now in the hands of the British, the war continued along the frontier under partisans Thomas Sumter, FRANCIS MARION, and Andrew Pickens. Subsequently, American forces began to win the war, and the British left Charles Town on December 14, 1782, as Continental forces under General Anthony Wayne arrived to retake the city. (See also SOUTH CAROLINA IN THE REVOLUTION.)

Further Reading: Walter J. Fraser, Jr., *Charleston! Charleston! The History of a Southern City* (University of South Carolina Press, 1989); Benton Rain Patterson, *Washington and Cornwallis: The Battle for America, 1775–83* (Taylor Trade Publishing, 2004).

—ELIZABETH PURDY, PH.D.

Chase, Samuel (1741–1811)

As a representative from Maryland, Samuel Chase voted for independence on July 4, 1776. Chase was born on April 17, 1741, in Somerset County, Maryland, and at the age of 18, went to Annapolis to study law under John Hall.

Chase's entry into politics in 1761 coincided with the beginning of the American colonies' hostilities with Great Britain. In 1764 he was elected to the Maryland General Assembly, and he served there until 1784. He took an active role in the opposition to Britain and its policies, helping to organize the SONS OF LIBERTY in Maryland.

In 1774 Chase was elected a delegate to the Continental Congress (see CONTINENTAL CONGRESS, FIRST AND SECOND). Proving himself in Congress, Chase was chosen by that body to travel to Canada with BENJAMIN FRANKLIN and CHARLES CARROLL OF CARROLLTON to obtain the Canadians' support against Great Britain. On August 2 he signed the DECLARATION OF INDEPENDENCE.

Following the war, Chase focused his political activity in Maryland. In 1786 he moved to Baltimore and became a judge in that city's criminal court in 1788. A member of Maryland's ratifying convention for the Constitution, he did not support it and voted against it. Despite this initial opposition, by the mid-1790s Chase was an ardent Federalist.

In 1791 Chase became judge of the general court of Maryland. In 1796 President GEORGE WASHINGTON appointed him an associate justice of the U.S. Supreme Court. While a member of the judiciary Chase continued to be an active Federalist, and he campaigned against THOMAS JEFFERSON in 1800. After the election, Chase continued his assault against Jefferson and his party. As a result, in 1804 the Jeffersonian majority in the House of

Representatives impeached Chase on charges of misconduct stemming from several trials he had conducted. Chase was acquitted of all charges and resumed his seat on the Supreme Court. He died in Washington, D.C., on June 19, 1811.

Further Reading: Biographical Directory of the United States Congress, Chase, Samuel, http://bioguide.congress.gov/scripts/biodisplay .pl?index=C000334 (cited December 2005); James Haw, *Stormy Patriot: The Life of Samuel Chase* (Maryland Historical Society, 1980); William H. Rehnquist, *Grand Inquests: The Historic Impeachments of Justice Samuel Chase and President Andrew Johnson* (William Morrow, 1992).

—JOSHUA SCHIER

The Impeachment of Samuel Chase

THE EIGHT articles of impeachment that were brought against Samuel Chase stemmed from his behavior during the treason trial of John Fries and the sedition trials of Thomas Cooper and James T. Callender. A charge Chase made to a Maryland grand jury in 1803 brought matters to a head.

In that charge, he lamented the loss of the judiciary's independence and stated that recent political events would lead to "mobocracy." Jefferson saw this charge as a blatant attack at him and wrote to Maryland Representative Joseph H. Nicholson, encouraging that something be done about Chase. Nicholson and the other Jeffersonian leaders in the House quickly assembled articles of impeachment and voted against Chase.

From the beginning, it was obvious that the case against Chase was weak. Of the eight charges brought against Chase, only three received a majority of votes. The Chase acquittal meant that the members of the judiciary were safe from the improper use of impeachment as a weapon and helped to establish the judicial branch's independence.

Clark, George Rogers (1752–1818)

A tall, imposing frontiersman and natural leader, George Rogers Clark was one of the most important figures in what was the American West during the Revolutionary era. His victories over the British in the Northwest Territory helped ensure that the region would remain in American hands once the Revolutionary War ended in 1783.

The second son in a family of 10 children, Clark was born on a farm two miles from Charlottesville, Virginia. At the age of 11, he was sent to a private school that included among its students future president James Madison. Clark eventually became a surveyor. In 1772 he made his first trip into what would become the state of Kentucky, where a few scattered settlements were developing in direct violation of a 1763 British edict that forbade colonial settlement west of the Appalachian Mountains.

Clark organized militia in the region to defend against Native American raids and with the outbreak of the American Revolution became a key figure on the frontier. Once the war began he went to Virginia and successfully lobbied Governor PATRICK HENRY and the legislature for war supplies and additional men. Clark then launched an offensive

Memorials and Namesakes

THERE ARE a number of memorials to Clark scattered through Kentucky, Ohio, Indiana, and Tennessee. Clark County, Kentucky, and Clark County, Ohio, were named for him, as were Clarksville, Indiana, and Clarksville, Tennessee. There are major memorials recognizing Clark's achievements in Louisville, Kentucky, Springfield, Ohio, and at what is believed to be the site of Fort Sackville. His brother William led the famous Lewis and Clark expedition for **THOMAS JEFFERSON.**

ABOVE LEFT *Clark's attack on Fort Sackville.* **ABOVE RIGHT** *Clark's march against Vincennes across the Wabash River; photos of paintings by Ezra Winter.*

against the British in the Northwest Territory that gained him great fame.

In 1778 Clark led a small force of just over 150 troops down the Ohio River, and more than 100 miles overland, to capture British installations at Kaskaskia and Cahokia along the Mississippi River near St. Louis. On May 27, 1778, he founded a settlement that eventually became the city of Louisville, Kentucky.

The British sent a force under the command of Henry Hamilton to stop Clark. Hamilton delayed his attack, choosing instead to go into winter quarters at Fort Sackville near Vincennes, Indiana. Clark marched his men into the area, surrounded the fort and demanded that the British surrender. Believing he was significantly outnumbered, Hamilton surrendered Fort Sackville on February 25, 1779. Clark's activities in the Northwest Territory helped secure the area for the Americans and neutralize the British threat along the frontier.

Clark had financed many of his campaigns himself and never received adequate compensation from the United States. Plagued by financial problems and pursued for years by creditors, Clark finally retired in 1803 to a two-room cabin overlooking the Ohio River at Clarksville, Indiana, which was named for him. At Clark's funeral on February 13, 1818, Kentucky jurist John Rowan said of the fallen hero, "The father of the western country is no more."

Further Reading: Michael Burgan, Arthur Meier Schlesinger, eds., *George Rogers Clark* (Chelsea House, 2001); Lowell Hayes Harrison, *George Rogers Clark and the War in the West* (University Press of Kentucky, 2001); George Rogers Clark, *Colonel George Rogers Clark's Sketch of His Campaign in the Illinois, 1778–1779* (Applewood Books, 2002).

—BEN WYNNE, PH.D.

Colonies, Loyal

When the American Revolution began in 1775, British colonies included a section of over 20 colonies stretching from the northernmost reaches of Canada to the Caribbean islands. Although Americans remember the "13 colonies" that participated in the rebellion, the rest remained loyal.

The British West Indies were of great economic importance to the mother country because they provided more revenue to the Crown than either America or Canada. Nevertheless, both America and Canada included large areas that were ripe for development and exploitation of resources.

Despite differences with the mother country, Canada, Nova Scotia, and the Caribbean remained loyal to Britain, providing support and supplies during the American Revolution.

CANADA

Britain's battle with France during the Seven Years' War led to a prolonged struggle for control of Canada. In September 1760, the French ceded Canada to Britain. Britain allowed the Canadians to retain their own religion and culture, simply requiring that they accept that they were subjects of the king of England and no longer owed allegiance to France. A trading partnership between Canada and Britain developed in which Canada provided timber needed to build British factories and mills.

Quebec assumed major importance for both the Americans and the British. After the province rejected an invitation to join the colonies in rebellion, plans were made to invade Quebec. Many Americans thought if Britain were defeated in Quebec, the whole of Canada would join the American rebellion.

In the spring of 1775, BENEDICT ARNOLD accompanied Ethan Allen and his Green Mountain Boys in boldly capturing Fort Ticonderoga in New York. Hoping to build on this victory, Arnold set out the following fall with plans to capture Quebec. Because Congress had decided to turn the siege into a major campaign, the British were given ample time to prepare defenses. After two months of traversing through wilderness, Arnold's troops were near starvation. Smallpox was rampant, and Arnold lost one-fourth of his forces during the journey.

With only 700 men, Arnold arrived outside Quebec on November 9, 1775, where he joined forces with his superior officer, General Richard Montgomery, a former British officer. The British decided to evacuate Montreal, which was considered indefensible, and left Nova Scotia open to attack in favor of reinforcing Quebec. If Arnold had attacked Nova Scotia rather than Quebec, he would have returned to America a hero. He chose, however, to continue in his ill-fated quest for glory at Quebec.

The siege began on December 31, 1775, with Arnold attacking on the west and Montgomery coming in from the river. Quebec had experienced a blinding snow storm the previous day. Snow and ice covered the ground, and a deserter had provided the British with detailed plans of the attack. The Americans suffered a devastating defeat. Montgomery was killed and Arnold seriously wounded. In the spring, when British ships arrived to reinforce Quebec, Americans were convinced that further attempts to take Quebec would be useless.

NOVA SCOTIA

Britain had gained control of Nova Scotia, Newfoundland, and Hudson's Bay at the end of the Seven Years' War. With the French still in control of parts of Canada, Nova Scotia looked to the British military for protection. The colonial governor hired private vessels and established regular communication

Loyalist Exile

WHEN THE American Revolution began in 1775, some LOY-ALISTS moved to nearby Nova Scotia to wait for the British to bring the colonists to their senses. However, after the Battle of Saratoga on October 17, 1777, ended with an American victory and the surrender of General JOHN BURGOYNE's army, many American loyalists realized that the Revolutionary War might not end in a British victory. As a result, new groups of loyalists began fleeing to Nova Scotia. For other loyalists, the American victory at Yorktown, Virginia, in October 1781 provided a basis for reassessing loyalties. Large numbers of loyalists chose to live in harmony with their neighbors and retain their property. Consequently, scores of loyalists deserted the British army and returned to their homes to await the official end of the war.

On February 23, 1782, Sir Guy Carleton took over the command of the British forces in North America and was charged with overseeing the British withdrawal of Savannah, Charleston, and New York and with providing transport home for thousands of British and Hessian soldiers (see HESSIANS). By default, he became responsible for overseeing the resettlement of American loyalists in Canada and Nova Scotia. By the end of the war, some 29,000 American loyalists had resettled in Nova Scotia, doubling the province's population. Among those loyalists settling in Nova Scotia, including New Brunswick, were 3,500 black loyalists who had gained their freedom by fighting on the British side during the Revolution.

ABOVE *A view of Louisbourg during the siege of 1758, showing the headlands above the lighthouse with ships in the harbor. Drawn on the spot by Captain Lince of the 35th Regiment.*

Despite the fact that many Nova Scotians had previously emigrated from New England, loyalists were not universally welcomed. Many loyalists complained that Britain had not adequately rewarded them for their service to the Crown. Those loyalists who remained became a strong element in Nova Scotia's continued loyalty to Britain. After Britain ceased providing free provisions and granted portable pensions, many loyalists returned to America. A large contingent of African American loyalists sailed from Nova Scotia to found Freetown, Sierra Leone, in West Africa in 1791. In addition to the thousands of loyalists who migrated to Nova Scotia, scores of others moved to Quebec, Montreal, and Halifax. As a result, Canadian cities became overcrowded, and tensions mounted. Loyalists clamored for a new colony, and New Brunswick was established with its own government in 1784.

routes between Nova Scotia and the surrounding outposts. In spite of these efforts, France continued to make its presence known. In 1755, Boston and Halifax banded together to run the French out of the area. The following year, a resounding victory added Louisbourg, Halifax, and Montreal to the British holdings in Canada.

In 1759, the governor of Nova Scotia invited New Englanders to relocate to the province. The following year, the bond between northern America and her neighbor was further strengthened when Britain completely defeated France and paved the way for the rest of Canada and Acadia to become British possessions. Ties continued to strengthen between Nova Scotia and America, and when the Revolution broke out in 1775, many Americans believed that the strong New England influence in Nova Scotia would move the province to join the rebellion. Some scholars contend that if Americans had not tried to push Nova Scotians into rebellion by invading the province, Nova Scotia would have become part of the United States.

The first attempt to capture Nova Scotia began two months after the fighting at Lexington and Concord when rebel Jonathan Eddy of Cumberland County arrived with a small force. Eddy was easily routed. When the British decided to evacuate Boston in March 1776 for Halifax, they reinforced Nova Scotia and made it less vulnerable to attack. When the tide turned in favor of America, the French signed an alliance with the new country to fight her old enemy. Nova Scotians began living in constant fear of invasion.

In June 1777, the invaders arrived in a fleet of whaling boats. However, the British rescued their colony. The following year, Captain JOHN PAUL JONES began waging war on British strongholds, burning and commandeering ships and taking prisoners. Jones subsequently turned to more productive ventures, and Nova Scotia remained in British hands. Although BENJAMIN FRANKLIN attempted to gain Canada and Nova Scotia during peace negotiations with Britain, he was unsuccessful.

CARIBBEAN COLONIES

In 1775, British Caribbean colonies included Jamaica, Barbados, the Leeward and Windward Islands, and the Bahamas. Like the Americans, residents of the Caribbean islands claimed British citizenship along with the rights that had been granted in the English Bill of Rights of 1689. Some scholars believe that Barbados was the first nation to send up an outcry against "taxation without representation."

Despite some dissatisfaction, the islands chose to continue their relationship with Britain rather than breaking away. A major factor in this decision was that many island residents had little interaction with North America except as a trading partner, and the children of wealthy families were educated in England. In the America colonies, emerging nationalism was turning loyalties toward America and away from the mother country.

Unlike America, the British West Indies had little to complain about economically. Because of low production costs, their chief exports of sugar and rum were competitive in British markets. In addition to sugar, cotton and tobacco provided export revenue, as did Brazil wood and logwood. Jamaica was a major exporter of cocoa and indigo, and the Leeward Islands had a thriving livestock industry. The Caribbean islands were heavily dependent on British protection from France, Spain, and the island's slave population. Despite continued loyalty among Caribbean islands, riots did occur on St. Kitts and Nevis and other Leeward Islands after the Stamp Act was passed in 1766. Antigua also experienced protests

A Conservative Revolution

THE AMERICAN Revolution has been called a conservative revolution, which seems to be a contradiction in terms. However, there is a large body of literature that supports the fact that the colonists seceded from Britain not because they wanted to overturn the existing social and political order, but because they were being denied the rights guaranteed to English citizens. The rationale for the secession was in great part based on the theories of English philosopher John Locke, who believed in the natural rights that were given to all humans by their Creator. It is significant that the government created by the states when the Constitution was written in 1787 was based in large part on the English system of government that had been instituted after the Glorious Revolution (1688) and the recognition of the English Bill of Rights. The most notable difference in the American and English political systems, of course, was the absence of the monarchy in America.

against British taxes, and pro-American feeling was high in certain areas. Jamaica and Barbados accepted the Stamp Act without controversy.

The Caribbean continued to be a major supply depot for both sides because the French and Spanish maintained control of sections of the West Indies. After the Franco-American alliance was signed in 1778, the British were willing to direct major resources to protecting the Caribbean from encroachment and to gain possession of French islands in the area.

As a result of the Battle of the Saints and negotiations during the peace treaty of 1783, Britain recovered its Caribbean possessions. Even though trade between the United States and Britain resumed after the war, the Navigation Acts continued to prohibit American trade with British possessions in the West Indies.

Further Reading: Selwyn H. H. Carrington, *The British West Indies during the American Revolution* (Foris, 1988); Robert L. Dallison, *Hope Restored: The American Revolution and the Founding of New Brunswick* (New Brunswick Military Heritage Project, 2003); Julian Gwyn, *Frigates and Foremasts: The North American Squadron in Nova Scotia Waters, 1745–1815* (UBC Press, 2003).

—ELIZABETH PURDY, PH.D.

Colonies or States

Of the 13 colonies, Massachusetts and Virginia had the smallest number of LOYALISTS. States with large groups of British supporters included New York, New Jersey, Pennsylvania, Georgia, and the Carolinas. Loyalty to Britain was most likely to be found in the largest cities and along the coast where trade relations played a significant role in the formation of political positions.

On May 15, 1776, the Virginia Convention passed what became known as the Virginia Resolution, which declared that the colonies should be free of British tyranny, setting forth their grievances against Britain. On June 28, Richard Henry Lee introduced this resolution at the Second Continental Congress (see CONTINENTAL CONGRESS, FIRST AND SECOND) in PHILADELPHIA. Initially, Massachusetts had instructed its congressional delegates to work toward reconciliation with Great Britain. However, as hopes of reconciliation faded, the Massachusetts legislature gave its delegation full authority to vote for independence, and JOHN ADAMS became the moving force in Congress for secession. Adams pressed Thomas Jefferson of Virginia into writing the DECLARATION OF INDEPENDENCE, which the Massachusetts delegation unanimously supported on July 4, 1776.

Within a week of the Virginia Resolution, Connecticut had declared its independence from Britain and given permission for its delegation to support Lee's plan. The New Hampshire delegation was free to follow its own dictates by voting for independence when the mood of Congress swung in that direction.

Rhode Island passed its own resolution of independence a month before the Virginia Resolution was introduced in Congress. When the vote on the Virginia Resolution ended in a tie, Rhode Island cast the deciding vote for the resolution.

When the initial vote on independence was taken, New Jersey was not represented. On July 4, however, new delegates arrived who had been instructed to vote for independence.

As the newest colony, Georgia's ties with Britain were still strong. However, as the outrages committed by King GEORGE III continued, Georgians were determined to protect their own interests. When Button Gwinnett and George Walton joined Dr. Lyman Hall in Philadelphia on May 20, 1776, they carried instructions from the Georgia legislature that allowed them to vote in the interests of Georgia and of the colonies as a whole.

Maryland was convinced that only independence would free the colony from exorbitant taxes and allow Maryland to conduct its own affairs. Due to the urgings of Samuel Chase, Maryland gave its delegation full authority to vote for independence. On July 3, Maryland's legislature established the Free State of Maryland.

Delawareans were heavily influenced by Philadelphia and ordered its delegates to work toward reconciliation with Britain. However, Caesar Rodney and Thomas McKean convinced the legislature to vote for independence, and Delaware subsequently declared its own independence.

When Jefferson and the DRAFTING COMMITTEE presented their draft of the Declaration of Independence to Congress, the document included a statement accusing the king of violating the rights of life and liberty of innocent people by exporting them to other hemispheres, where they were enslaved. Jefferson felt strongly that a declaration of equality was hypocritical as long as slavery existed in the United States. South Carolina refused to sign, and convinced North Carolina and Georgia to support the objections.

Knowing that the Declaration would not be unanimously approved without southern support, Jefferson removed the offending statement. This shift left only Pennsylvania voting against independence.

On June 8, the Pennsylvania legislature rescinded its restrictions on the delegation and allowed the delegates to concur with the majority opinion.

The large loyalist base and the close economic and trade ties with Britain had made New York reluctant to forego loyalty to the Crown. However, New York chose to protect its interests by siding with its sister colonies.

On July 9, New York declared itself independent and sent new instructions to its congressional delegation. The official signing that took place on August 2 included signatures of 56 delegates from all 13 colonies.

Further Reading: Alf J. Mapp, Jr., *The Virginia Experiment: The Old Dominion's Role in the Making of America, 1607–1781* (Hamilton, 1987); Joseph S. Tiedemann, *Reluctant Revolutionaries: New York City and the Road to Independence, 1763–76* (Cornell University Press, 1997).

—ELIZABETH PURDY, PH.D.

Commerce and Trade

On July 4, 1776, the United States was, for the most part, an agricultural nation. Commerce and trade were limited to a few large towns and cities on the coast or close by in river ports that contained only a fraction of America's population. America's merchant class was small—making up only about 10 percent of the colonial population.

In cities like PHILADELPHIA, New York, Boston, Providence, and Newport, merchants and shippers controlled most of the wealth and guided its economy. Wealthy merchants were often the political leaders of their communities. In Massachusetts, merchants formed half of the membership of the lower house of the state legislature and completely dominated the upper house. Merchants' dissatisfaction with increasing British interference with colonial commerce and trade in the 1770s made northern cities and port towns hotbeds of revolutionary fervor. Leading figures in the shipping and manufacturing industries sought to win allies to their cause with a host of arguments against particular measures. Their complaints eventually

ABOVE *The window display of a recreated 18th century apothecary, the precursor to the modern pharmacy.*
AT RIGHT *A present-day replica of an 18th century printing shop. Two ink balls hang on the wall to the left of the hand-operated press.*

became the list of grievances in the Declaration of Independence.

Sailors, as well as craftsmen and laborers involved in the colonial shipbuilding industry, realizing that disruptions in commerce would also affect them, found themselves drawn to the politics of revolution. Early showdowns between British soldiers and officials and angry colonists often involved sailors, dockworkers, and men employed in the shipping industry.

SHIPBUILDING

By July 4, 1776, Massachusetts had come to dominate the colonial shipbuilding trade, producing roughly three times as many ships as the other colonies.

The neighboring colony of Rhode Island also produced large numbers of ships designed for various maritime activities, including the transportation of slaves. Philadelphia was also a major shipbuilding center. Ironically, before the outbreak of the Revolution, shipyards in these cities had also produced about one-third of British merchant ships.

Shipbuilding played a major role in the colonial economy, producing not only vessels, but also creating work for numerous laborers. While sawyers cut the needed wood, shipwrights designed the vessel and began its assembly. As the pieces of the ship came together, skilled craftsmen called joiners carefully fitted the ship's planks together. Carpenters might be employed to finish the ship's interior, especially the captain's cabin. Caulkers then sealed any remaining gaps with tarred pieces of hemp grown by local farmers. Once the masts were installed, blacksmiths produced iron bands and chains to hold the masts and spars in place.

In nearby sail lofts, sail makers cut pieces of canvas and stitched the lengths together to form a sail. Ropes and lines for rigging the ship were produced

Journeymen and Apprentices

COLONIAL ARTISANS often depended on journeymen and apprentices to provide labor for their craft shops. Children were often apprenticed by their families at a young age to learn a skilled trade. The master contracted to teach the apprentice, for an agreed-upon fee, the "mysteries" of his craft. Apprentices often lived with their masters and were subject to their discipline. The average apprenticeship lasted seven years, although some trades, such as ship carpentry, lasted longer.

Most girls were apprenticed to local women to learn the "domestic arts." Following the period of trade apprenticeship, young men found work as journeymen, hiring themselves out to master craftsmen, and usually paid a daily or monthly wage. In addition to wages, employers often provided their workers with food and alcohol. The goal of every journeyman was to save enough money to open his own business and become a master himself. In the American colonies, journeymen were often paid double what they would have received in England, and did not have to toil long before they were able to open their own shops.

in ropewalks. Glassworkers made portholes. Painters finished the ship in bright colors or simply coated the boards with turpentine. In port towns from which ships regularly set to sea, coopers manufactured barrels to hold both the ship's provisions and goods. Coopers, in turn, called upon stave cutters and blacksmiths to produce the wooden staves and iron bands that they needed to make barrels. Taverns and inns provided food, drink, and lodging to sailors and men who worked in the shipyards.

RUM DISTILLING

The American colonists' drink of choice was rum. In one day, a common laborer could earn enough money to supply himself with enough rum to last an entire week.

Besides delighting colonial palates, rum also played an important role in colonial trade and manufacture. Before the Revolution, rum distilling was the leading industry in the northern colonies. In the decades immediately preceding the Revolution, Boston, Providence, Newport, New York, and Philadelphia were major centers of rum production. By the beginning of the Revolution, Boston and Newport boasted 30 distilleries apiece. Manhattan had 17 distilleries, followed closely by Philadelphia with 14. Rum distilleries employed many people and brought huge profits to their owners.

Rum, which could be easily stored and transported, could withstand extreme heat and humidity, and did not deteriorate with age, was perfectly suited to serve as a trade good. Although nearly 90 percent of the rum produced in the northern colonies was consumed by Americans, northern merchants often used the remainder to purchase slaves. The slaves could then be exchanged in the Caribbean for molasses and sugar—from which more rum could be produced. Rum was thus a key to the lucrative triangular trade that ran from New England to Africa, Africa to the Caribbean, and the Caribbean to New England.

The British closing of the port of Boston and the higher price of Caribbean molasses and sugar, the result of British legislation, had made rum fairly expensive and often hard to come by. After July 4, 1776, British blockades made it nearly impossible to secure the molasses needed for rum production. Unable to provide soldiers with their customary daily rum ration, the Continental Army doled out whiskey instead. By the end of the war, whiskey had become the distilled liquor of choice in the new United States.

GLASSMAKING

At the time of the American Revolution, all glass was blown by hand. Sand, potash, and lime were heated and fused at extremely high temperatures, then cooled. Hollow wares, such as drinking glasses, were produced by blowing into a mass of molten glass at the end of a hollow tube. The glass bubble was then rolled on a solid surface. The process of blowing and rolling was repeated until a container of the desired size and shape was produced. Window glass was produced by spinning molten glass into a flat disk and cutting it into panes.

Because making glass was such a difficult and lengthy process, glass was fairly expensive. When people built or moved into a new house, they often removed the window panes from their old dwelling and took them with them. European glassmakers had traditionally formed a largely closed society, and immigrant artisans were reluctant to pass on their knowledge to American craftsmen. Making glass was also an uncomfortable process; because of the intense heat of the furnace, glassworks could not operate during the warmer months of the year.

IRON PRODUCTION

By 1776, the American colonies were producing approximately 14 percent of the world's iron.

The iron produced in the colonies was largely pig iron or bar iron—the raw, unfinished iron that issued forth from the iron furnace. The pig iron, which was quite brittle, could be heated in a large forge and hammered into wrought-iron bars for sale to artisans who would use it to produce horseshoes, wheel rims, pots, pans, tools, and farm implements.

The American iron industry blossomed with the coming of the Revolution, and following July 4, 1776, American ironworks not only produced iron but also used it to cast cannon, shot, and shells for the Continental Army. Although many ironworks were located in the middle colonies of Pennsylvania and New Jersey, the difficulty of moving cannon and munitions overland meant that local ironworks supplied the needs of the army as the theater of war shifted. Thus, at the beginning of the Revolution, New England foundries produced cannon and shot for the patriot cause. Unfortunately, a lack of men skilled in the production of close-tolerance artillery pieces and the poor working conditions in furnaces and foundries limited the number of weapons that could be manufactured for the army.

THE GUNPOWDER INDUSTRY

Prior to the Revolution, the British government had restricted the production of gunpowder in the colonies and had allowed only a few mills to operate. After July 4, 1776, the gunpowder mills of Virginia produced as much gunpowder as possible. Nevertheless, the Continental Army often lacked sufficient supplies of the valuable material with which to fight the British army during the Revolutionary War.

Further Reading: Carl Bridenbaugh, *Cities in Revolt: Urban Life in America, 1743–1776* (Alfred A. Knopf, 1995); Michael Burgan with Timothy J. Shannon, *Voices from Colonial America: New York 1609–1776* (National Geographic Society, 2006); Niall Ferguson, *Colossus: The Price of America's Empire* (Penguin Group, 2004); Mark Edward Lender and James Kirby Martin, *Drinking in America: A History* (The Free Press, 1982); David McCullough, *1776* (Simon & Schuster, 2005); W. J. Rorabaugh, *The Alcoholic Republic: An American Tradition* (Oxford University Press, 1979); Peter Stockman, ed., *Early Nineteenth-Century Crafts and Trades* (Dover Publications, 1992); Edwin Tunis, *Colonial Craftsmen and the Beginnings of American Industry* (World Publishing, 1972).

—ANN KORDAS, PH.D.

The Raleigh Tavern Meeting

ON MARCH 4, 1773, a group of Virginia Burgesses convened in the Raleigh Tavern in Williamsburg. Among the group were THOMAS JEFFERSON, PATRICK HENRY, RICHARD HENRY LEE, Francis Lightfoot Lee, and Dabney Carr. Those in attendance intended to call on the House of Burgesses to propose an intercolonial standing committee of correspondence. Jefferson was asked to present the matter, but he demurred, so on Friday, March 12, 1773, Dabney Carr spoke before a committee of the whole. Carr asked for a standing committee to obtain knowledge of parliamentary behavior or acts of interest to the colonies, and to inquire of Britain about the propriety of sending colonists overseas to stand trial. All resolutions passed, and Virginia had created the only committee of correspondence that reached outside Virginia. With this action, Virginia had given the first hint that a united America was possible.

Committees of Correspondence

The American colonies chose the committee of correspondence as a means of communication. The first formal committee, established in 1764 in Boston, was intended to generate opposition to the Currency Act and changes in the customs service. New York established a committee the next year to generate united opposition to the Stamp Act's new taxes. Massachusetts responded to New York by calling for the Stamp Act Congress of the fall of 1765.

The Stamp Act Congress attracted representatives from nine of the colonies, but no permanent organization resulted. SAMUEL ADAMS and Joseph Warren of Massachusetts formed a committee in 1772 to protest the decision to remove control over gubernatorial and judicial salaries from the colonial legislatures. In the months to come, over 100 Massachusetts towns and villages formed committees, and eventually every colony had them. Over half of Massachusetts's 260 towns formed committees and sent replies to Boston.

Virginia proposed in 1773 that the committees of all colonies become permanent. Those committees planned the First Continental Congress of September 1774. The Second Continental Congress established its own committee to deal with foreign countries and spread the American interpretation of events (see CONTINENTAL CONGRESS, FIRST AND SECOND).

Correspondents, often legislators and members of the SONS OF LIBERTY, had the obligation of ensuring that the right information got to the right people and places at the right time. Coordination was slow, and only after the Boston Port Bill was coordinated action against Great Britain a reality.

The committees were important in the years leading to the Revolution because they helped to spread a common colonial view of British behavior. They united the opposition, established joint plans, and laid the basis for the later formal union of the colonies.

Further Reading: Eric Burns, *Infamous Scribblers: The Founding Fathers and the Rowdy Beginnings of American Journalism* (Public Affairs, 2006); John E. Ferling, *A Leap in the Dark: The Struggle to Create the American Republic* (Oxford University Press, 2004); Gordon S. Wood, *American Revolution: A History* (Random House, 2003).

—JOHN H. BARNHILL, PH.D.

Connecticut in the Revolution

Known as the "Arsenal of the Nation," Connecticut served as the major supplier for the Continental Army. Connecticut had been founded in 1614 by Dutch settlers, but after Puritan settlers arrived, the area developed distinctly English characteristics. Colonial Connecticut acted much like an extended family. Among themselves, the people were known to be quarrelsome and quick to litigate. However, they were ready to pull together when it was necessary. Religion was a major issue in Connecticut, where most Puritans believed the Church of England was unholy and considered it their mission to introduce God to its unenlightened members.

Politically, Connecticut was in a different position than the royal colonies. The colony elected its own governor who worked with the legislature to govern the colony. Elections for the lower house of

Roger Sherman (1721–93)

ROGER SHERMAN of Connecticut was the only individual involved in the signing of all major documents that established the United States. A self-educated lawyer, surveyor, and mathematician of Puritan stock, Sherman served in both the First and Second Continental Congresses. Sherman signed the Declaration in August 1776, the Articles of Confederation in November, 1776, and the Peace of Paris in 1783. Overall, Sherman served in the Continental Congress from 1774 until 1789 when a new government was established.

In 1787, Sherman introduced the Connecticut Plan, designed to protect the interests of the smaller states from being overwhelmed by those with the largest populations. He subsequently signed the U.S. Constitution. Thomas Jefferson said Roger Sherman was a man who had never said a foolish thing in his life.

Roger Sherman and the other signers used quill pens and inkwells such as those shown AT LEFT to sign the Declaration, the Articles of Confederation, and the Peace of Paris.

the assembly were held frequently, and those males eligible to vote were avid participants in the political process. Only Rhode Island had more freedom from British control than Connecticut. The colony's economy was not dependent on Britain because it had no particular products to trade with the mother country.

After Parliament passed the Stamp Act, Connecticuters responded by soundly defeating conservatives in the election of 1766, giving liberal Whigs (see WHIGS, ENGLISH) control of the governorship and both houses of the legislature. The shift away from old loyalties had evolved gradually in Connecticut, but when it occurred, Connecticuters turned into loyal patriots.

In 1764 in response to the Sugar Act, Governor Fitch and the legislature wrote a pamphlet, "Reasons Why the British Colonies in America Should Not Be Taxed," which was published in newspapers and read all over Connecticut. The pamphlet was also sent to the king, who subsequently used it to justify his harsh treatment of Connecticut.

By the time a group of British soldiers fired into a Boston crowd on March 5, 1770, revolutionary fervor had already taken over Connecticut (see BOSTON IN THE REVOLUTION). In May 1775, the Connecticut legislature drew up their own list of grievances against Britain and laid claim to the rights that were being denied Connecticuters as English citizens. When the Olive Branch Petition of July 5, 1775, failed to bring about the necessary changes, Connecticut decided to send delegates to the national legislature.

Word of the confrontations with the British at Lexington and Concord reached Connecticut on April 20, 1775, and was closely followed by a report that the Americans had captured Fort Ticonderoga. Connecticut responded by sending 3,600 militia and Sons of Liberty to Massachusetts. Connecticut also held a state convention and signed a nonimportation agreement that ended all trade with Britain.

When the Second Continental Congress convened in Philadelphia in May 1776, the delegates voiced their approval of the Virginia Resolution. When the embossed copy of the Declaration was signed in Philadelphia on August 2, Connecticut's signers included Roger Sherman, Samuel Huntington, William Williams, and Oliver Wolcott.

Out of the 15,000 men involved in the Siege of Boston, 3,000 of them came from Connecticut, where 46 of the colony's 72 towns had responded to the call for reinforcements. The legislature doubled the colony's supply of powder, balls, and flints. By 1774, membership in the Connecticut militia had risen to 26,260 men. Overall, Connecticut's contributions to the Continental Army included four regiments of traditional cavalry and three legions that were a combination of mounted and foot soldiers. Together, Connecticut forces made up one-sixth of the Continental Army.

In addition to the state's contribution of forces, Connecticut's supplies were integral to winning the Revolutionary War. Because of Connecticut's role as a supply line for the Continental Army, the state experienced a number of raids on supply depots. For example, an April 1777 raid in Danbury led by General William Tryon resulted in the destruction of 1,800 bushels of corn and 1,000 tents. A raid at Fairfax in July 1779 resulted in economic losses of over £14,000 and the destruction of more than 200 buildings.

Further Reading: Patricia Harris and David Lyon, *Connecticut: The Spirit of America* (Harry N. Abrams, 2000); David M. Roth and Freeman Meyer, *From Revolution to Constitution: Connecticut 1763 to 1818* (Pequot Press, 1975); Peter D.F. Thomas, *Tea Party to Independence: The Third Phase of the American Revolution, 1773–76* (Clarendon Press, 1991).

—ELIZABETH PURDY, PH.D.

Continental Congress, First and Second

The First and Second Continental Congresses were the legislatures of the newly declared United States until 1781. The Second Continental Congress was later displaced by the Congress of the United States.

ABOVE *The Second Continental Congress convenes to vote for independence in a paintng by John Trumbull.*
BELOW *Federal Hall in New York City, the meeting place of the First Continental Congress.*

The most important product of the First Continental Congress was the composition of the Articles of Association against the Intolerable Acts as well as the Quebec Act. The Articles were dated October 20, 1774, and provided the structural framework to form a union among the colonies to boycott British goods and to cease exports to Britain if the Intolerable Acts were not repealed by the British.

However the First Continental Congress was not ready to really question the British authority to rule the colonies. On September 28, 1774, the members of the Continental Congress voted loyalist Joseph Galloway's plan of a union with six to five votes. Galloway's proposal recommended that every colony itself should deal with its internal affairs, and there should be an elected council for external affairs consisting of all of the North American colonies. They would respect the decisions of the English Parliament and would bind their rulings to them. The king should appoint a president general as executive power for the colonies.

The majority of the Congress wanted more autonomy from the British than Galloway's proposal had suggested. On October 14, they agreed that the English Parliament could be left in charge of the regulations of trade, but the colonies should be in charge of levying and collecting taxes. On October 26, 1774, the First Continental Congress was dissolved after it was decided that the delegates would reassemble the following year if the situation had not improved significantly. The boycott was successfully implemented, but its long-term effects were cut off by the outbreak of open fighting in 1775.

THE SECOND CONTINENTAL CONGRESS

On May 10, 1775, the Second Continental Congress assembled for the first time. None of the declared demands from the First Continental Congress was fulfilled by the British. The Congress resolved that Great Britain had declared war against them on March 26 of the same year.

The delegates of the Second Continental Congress created the Continental Army on July 8, 1775, and appointed General GEORGE WASHINGTON commander in chief of the troops. On July 8, 1775, the Second Continental Congress forwarded the Olive Branch Petition to the Crown in a last attempt to reach reconciliation, but GEORGE III refused to receive it.

On April 6, 1776, the Congress reopened American ports for every foreign ship except for the British, in defiance of the Navigation Acts. This economical declaration of independence happened before political independence was declared.

On July 6, 1775, the Congress passed "The Declaration of the Causes and Necessity of Taking Up Arms," the direct forerunner of the DECLARATION OF INDEPENDENCE. The declaration of armed resistance embodied the natural freedom of men and declared colonial rule to be discriminating.

On Friday, June 27, 1776, Jefferson handed in his proposal for the Declaration of Independence to the president of the Congress. The final version was passed on July 4, 1776, in unison but without the vote of the State of New York.

On November 17, 1777, the Congress passed the Articles of Confederation, the first written constitution for the United States of America. Finally, on March 1, 1781, the Articles of Confederation were ratified. The Second Continental Congress adjourned, and then the same delegates met the next day as the first legislature for the United States of America. Seven months later, October 19, 1781, the United States was victorious at the Battle of Yorktown, which ended military operations in the colonies.

Further Reading: Francis D. Cogliano, *Revolutionary America, 1763–1815* (Routlege, 1999); H. James Henderson, *Party Politics in the Continental Congress* (Rowman and Littlefield, 2002); John Reardon, *Peyton Randolph, 1721–75: One Who Presided* (Carolina University Press, 1981).

—ALEXANDER EMMERICH

Culture, 1776

American colonists established a flourishing culture that was a mixture of elite and popular trends, heavily influenced by British culture yet uniquely American. All of the traditional "high culture" of Europe was present in the colonies, existing side by side with the interests of the farmers, sailors, and artisans who scorned British pretension and regarded American culture as superior to the elite culture of the mother country.

In the minds of many Americans, European gentility, which included an interest in high forms of culture, was a cover for corruption, vanity, greed, and moral laxity. JOHN ADAMS, for example, was suspicious of the political sympathies of the genteel and sophisticated and considered simplicity and crudeness to be the mark of a true patriot.

MUSIC

European art forms that made the transition to American soil were often altered to suit the interests, tastes, and desires of American colonists. This was especially true in the early years, and nowhere

Broadsides and Proclamations

BROADSIDES WERE documents printed on one side of a page only. When they were printed on both sides, they became known as broadsheets. Broadsides often contained news, reports of recent incidents, and unpublished songs. Broadsides were nailed to walls so that people might read the news or learn the lyrics and melodies of the songs. Some broadsides were copied down and preserved in private diaries.

The American anthem "Yankee Doodle" first appeared as a broadside entitled "The Yankey's Return from Camp" in 1775. In the years preceding the Revolution, colonists composed hundreds of satirical "liberty songs" that mocked British troops and often referred to Mother England as a "whore."

ABOVE LEFT *A rare broadside of the Declaration of Independence printed and distributed by order of the Continental Congress, 1776.*
ABOVE RIGHT *A broadside announcing a 1779 lottery to raise funds in support of the Revolutionary War.*

ABOVE LEFT *18th century American gardens reflected the highly stylized topiary arts practiced in Europe. Gardens generally included raised beds, carefully shaped trees and shrubs, and maze-like walkways.* **ABOVE RIGHT** *A cartoon engraving by Paul Revere showing "The Able Doctor," with a feminine personification of America swallowing and spitting out the bitter draught of British tea. In the background, ships commandeer Boston Harbor. The cartoon was created for the* **Royal American Magazine** *in 1774.*

more so than in music. The first music to become popular in the colonies was religious. The first organ appeared in New England in 1708. It was rejected by the Puritans as being too "Catholic," and given to the Anglican Church in Boston. By July 4, 1776, many of the Puritan residents of Providence, Rhode Island, were having difficulty becoming accustomed to the organ that had been installed in their church a few years earlier. These musical "rebels" were the first Puritan congregation to allow an organ to be installed inside their meeting-house—now called the Congregational Church of Providence.

By July 4, 1776, even staid New Englanders had come to love and embrace various forms of music. Itinerant musicians and traveling singing teachers held "singing schools" in communities throughout the colonies. Their main goal was to teach people to read music. These young people might then be able to teach their friends and fellow congregants to follow musical notation and to sing on key.

In some communities, public concerts were a regular feature, and the end of a singing school term was usually marked by a recital. The wealthy, in contrast, often formed clubs that presented concerts, the tickets to which were usually "by subscription only." Public concerts, on the other hand, were often free of charge.

For those who preferred to enjoy music at home, a wide variety of sheet music and musical instruments was available, and Boston was the sheet music capital of the colonies. People such as artisans and farmers often owned spinets, harpsichords, violins, horns, lutes, and guitars. Singing and fiddling were popular at harvest time.

Unpublished ballads, which recounted tales from everyday life and were often composed when the incident involved took place, were extremely popular. Among these unpublished songs were satirical verses, many sung at rowdy gatherings. The favorite among these songs was a "ribald" number entitled "Our Polly Is a Sad Slut." By the time of the Revolution, many of these songs had taken on a political tone and were printed on broadsides that were later published in newspapers or nailed to walls.

THEATER

Theater was not widely performed in any of the colonies in the 18th century. Stage plays were considered socially disruptive, sometimes contained sexual scenes, and were often intended to arouse dissent against the government or cause conflict with established religion.

Although strictly barred from New England, theater did take root in other parts of the American colonies. In 1752, William Hamlin, a professional actor, came to the colonies accompanied by his English theatrical troop, the American Company. Their staging of *The Merchant of Venice* in Virginia caused a great sensation, and the American Company began to travel throughout the colonies performing Shakespeare, Greek tragedies, and some contemporary comedies. However, when the American Company attempted to bring its repertoire to Newport, Rhode Island, and then to Providence, voters banned the performance of any forms of theater. Massachusetts followed suit. Both Massachusetts and Connecticut, however, allowed private plays staged by the students of Harvard and Yale to continue. Theater was never really accepted in New England until after the Revolution.

PRINT CULTURE

While musical culture was fraught with contradictions, print culture was less so. Many American colonists were avid readers. Protestantism, the religion espoused by the largest number of American settlers of European descent, had always stressed basic literacy so that Christians could read and understand the Bible for themselves. To meet these ends, Massachusetts towns quickly established a system of grammar schools, which were attended by children of similar ages and levels of reading ability. As a result, New England had the highest level of literacy in the colonies. In the southern colonies, public education was not considered a major priority, and private tutors were scarce and expensive. The southern colonies thus had far higher levels of illiteracy. Newspapers and pamphlets were read aloud at taverns. Even at work, it was quite common for one person to be assigned to read newspapers, books, and sermons while the others worked. Families often read together in the evenings.

For the most part, newspapers were more popular than books and were more widely read. Newspapers were fairly inexpensive, and newspaper purchasers might pass them on to others when they had finished reading them. Because news traveled slowly in 1776, newspapers contained large amounts of poetry and political essays from local contributors. Newspapers that voiced sentiments that were unpopular with the majority of the paper's readers might be shut down. On occasion, their presses were destroyed.

With a few exceptions, nearly all of the books the colonists read and purchased came from England. Although there were a substantial number of printers in the American colonies, most devoted their time to publishing newspapers and government documents.

Bibles were the most common books owned, and nearly every household had one. Books on more "practical" matters such as animal husbandry, agriculture, surveying, and home medical care were widely available, as were almanacs, which guided colonial farmers in their yearly round of planting, harvesting, and slaughtering. Basic law books and legal dictionaries were also available to assist the ever-litigious American colonists in their perennial disputes over land and inheritance. Books on mathematics and botany to further the ongoing education of the self-taught were featured in many bookshops. In addition, books on politics were popular—especially books by such writers as Locke, Hobbes, Montesquieu, and Milton.

Southern gentlemen often stocked their shelves with plays by Shakespeare, Addison, and Sheridan. The colonial elite collected and read the Greek and Roman classics and works of British history. It was also on the shelves of these men that one could find more esoteric works of science, law, and medicine.

The period also witnessed the publication of a large number of books designed to transform humble Americans and their simple wives and daughters into items of elegance and fashion. Ironically, at the same time that Americans were seeking to differentiate themselves from their English overlords, many of them were also obsessed with learning how to walk and bow and what to do with such odd implements as teacups and punch bowls.

CULTURE OF THE STREET

While the socially and economically elite and their families attended concerts and plays, practiced the harpsichord, and debated the evils and virtues of reading novels, other Americans—the small artisans, the journeymen and apprentices, the tavern keepers, and the unskilled laborers of the streets—had invented a culture of their own, focused on the street.

Public celebrations were common in colonial America. Harvard Commencement Day, Militia Day, and Election Day drew great crowds and were often accompanied by celebrations in the streets. All of these occasions might also serve as an opportunity for the public consumption of alcohol.

VISUAL ARTS

While street demonstrations were undoubtedly the most ungenteel of all American cultural forms, both the sophisticated and the unwashed could find something to admire in the visual arts. Wealthy colonists engaged in art collecting, often traveling to Europe for the purpose.

One of the favorite topics for American painters was portraiture. At first, many painters depicted their subjects as European notables, smiling and wearing magnificent clothing in the midst of beautiful gardens or other natural surroundings.

Many other American painters, like John Singleton Copley, painted their subjects in a more naturalistic fashion, depicting them in natural poses, performing ordinary activities in ordinary settings. Other American artists turned to painting distinctly American scenes and personages. Philadelphia artist Charles Wilson Peale painted famous Philadelphian David Rittenhouse, and Rhode Island artist Gilbert Stuart painted GEORGE WASHINGTON.

Those Americans who could not own portraits of their family members or of famous Americans bought prints and engravings to decorate the walls of their homes. Reproductions of portraits of such American worthies as William Penn and SAMUEL ADAMS were sold. Prints depicting American cities, buildings, gardens, harbors, and colleges also sold well. (See also DAILY LIFE, 1776; RECREATION AND LEISURE, 1776.)

Further Reading: Richard L. Bushman, *The Refinement of America: Persons, Houses, Cities* (Alfred A. Knopf, 1992); Bruce C. Daniels, *Puritans at Play: Leisure and Recreation in Colonial New England* (St. Martin's Griffin, 1995); Mason I. Lawrence, Jr. and Georgia B. Bumgardener, eds., *Massachusetts Broadsides of the American Revolution* (University of Massachusetts Press, 1976); Simon P. Newman, *Parades and Politics of the Streets: Festive Culture in the Early American Republic* (University of Pennsylvania Press, 1997); David W. Stowe, *How Sweet the Sound: Music in the Spiritual Lives of Americans* (Harvard University Press, 2004).

—ANN KORDAS, PH.D.

Pamphleteering

AMONG THE literate in the colonies, pamphlets were great favorites. Often formed of broadsheets folded in four, pamphlets contained short accounts of political happenings or political arguments.

Pamphlets often contained reprints of newspaper articles or essays that had not been published by their authors. Pamphlets often undertook to inform people of their liberties and the ways in which they were being deprived of them "by ministerial and regal practices." Other pamphlets made light of Britain's supposed might and military power; Thomas Paine, for example, in his famous pamphlet "Common Sense" (1776), ridiculed the idea that a relatively tiny English nation should consider it within its right and its power to attempt to dominate the vast continental expanse that was the United States.

Some pamphlets, such as "Letters from a Farmer in Pennsylvania to the Inhabitants of the British Colonies" (1767–68), written by John Dickenson, one of the foremost writers of the Revolution, took deliberate aim at the hated Townshend Acts. Some writers recounted British atrocities in order to arouse America's fighting spirit; others related tales of the misery of England's poor and the ways in which the Crown was depriving them of their traditional rights—shades, perhaps, of things to come for Americans who preferred to ignore such graphic hints as to the fate of America.

BROADSIDES AND PAMPHLETS *were frequently used to detail military information such as the 1776 muster records* AT LEFT, *to publish amusing and often political verse such as the 1778 "Battle of the Kegs,"* BOTTOM LEFT, *and to promote adherence to religious and social mores of the time, such as "The Great Evil of the Sin of Drunkenness," circa 1760,* BOTTOM RIGHT. *While numerous copies of 18th century broadsides have been preserved, few pamphlets remain.*

IN CONGRESS, JULY 4, 1776.

THE UNANIMOUS

DECLARATION

OF THE

THIRTEEN UNITED STATES OF AMERICA.

WHEN, in the Course of human Events, it becomes neceſſary for one People to diſſolve the Political Bands which have connected them with another, and to aſſume, among the Powers of the Earth, the ſeparate and equal Station to which the Laws of Nature and of Nature's GOD entitle them, a decent Reſpect to the Opinions of Mankind requires that they ſhould declare the Cauſes which impel them to the Separation.

We hold theſe Truths to be ſelf-evident, that all Men are created equal, that they are endowed, by their CREATOR, with certain unalienable Rights, that among theſe are Life, Liberty, and the Purſuit of Happineſs.—That to ſecure theſe Rights, Governments are inſtituted among Men, deriving their juſt Powers from the Conſent of the Governed, that whenever any Form of Government becomes deſtructive of theſe Ends, it is the Right of the People to alter or to aboliſh it, and to inſtitute new Government, laying its Foundation on ſuch Principles, and organizing its Powers in ſuch Form, as to them ſhall ſeem moſt likely to effect their Safety and Happineſs. Prudence, indeed, will dictate, that Governments long eſtabliſhed, ſhould not be changed for light and tranſient Cauſes; and accordingly all Experience hath ſhewn, that Mankind are more diſpoſed to ſuffer, while Evils are ſufferable, than to right themſelves by aboliſhing the Forms to which they are accuſtomed. But when a long Train of Abuſes and Uſurpations, purſuing invariably the ſame Object, evinces a Deſign to reduce them under abſolute Deſpotiſm, it is their Right, it is their Duty, to throw off ſuch Government, and to provide new Guards for their future Security. Such has been the patient Sufferance of theſe Colonies; and ſuch is now the Neceſſity which conſtrains them to alter their former Syſtems of Government. The Hiſtory of the preſent King of Great-Britain is a Hiſtory of repeated Injuries and Uſurpations, all having in direct Object the Eſtabliſhment of an abſolute Tyranny over theſe States. To prove this, let Facts be ſubmitted to a candid World.

He has refuſed his Aſſent to Laws, the moſt wholeſome and neceſſary for the public Good.

He has forbidden his Governors to paſs Laws of immediate and preſſing Importance, unleſs ſuſpended in their Operation till his Aſſent ſhould be obtained; and when ſo ſuſpended, he has utterly neglected to attend to them.

He has refuſed to paſs other Laws for the Accommodation of large Diſtricts of People, unleſs thoſe People would relinquiſh the Right of Repreſentation in the Legiſlature, a Right ineſtimable to them, and formidable to Tyrants only.

He has called together Legiſlative Bodies at Places unuſual, uncomfortable, and diſtant from the Depoſitory of their public Records, for the ſole Purpoſe of fatiguing them into Compliance with his Meaſures.

He has diſſolved Repreſentative Houſes repeatedly, for oppoſing with manly Firmneſs his Invaſions on the Rights of the People.

He has refuſed for a long Time, after ſuch Diſſolutions, to cauſe others to be elected; whereby the Legiſlative Powers, incapable of Annihilation, have returned to the People at large for their exerciſe; the State remaining, in the mean Time, expoſed to all the Dangers of Invaſion from without, and Convulſions within.

He has endeavoured to prevent the Population of theſe States; for that Purpoſe obſtructing the Laws for Naturalization of Foreigners; refuſing to paſs others to encourage their Migrations hither, and raiſing the Conditions of new Appropriations of Lands.

He has obſtructed the Adminiſtration of Juſtice, by refuſing his Aſſent to Laws for eſtabliſhing Judiciary Powers.

He has made Judges dependent on his Will alone, for the Tenure of their Offices, and the Amount and Payment of their Salaries.

He has erected a Multitude of new Offices, and ſent hither Swarms of Officers to harraſs our People, and eat out their Subſtance.

He has kept among us, in Times of Peace, Standing Armies, without the Conſent of our Legiſlatures.

He has affected to render the Military independent of and ſuperior to the Civil Power.

He has combined with others to ſubject us to a Juriſdiction foreign to our Conſtitution, and unacknowledged by our Laws; giving his Aſſent to their Acts of pretended Legiſlation:

For quartering large Bodies of Armed Troops among us:

For protecting them, by a mock Trial, from Puniſhment for any Murders which they ſhould commit on the Inhabitants of theſe States:

For cutting off our Trade with all Parts of the World:

For impoſing Taxes on us without our Conſent:

For depriving us, in many Caſes, of the Benefits of Trial by Jury:

For tranſporting us beyond Seas to be tried for pretended Offences:

For aboliſhing the free Syſtem of Engliſh Laws in a neighbouring Province, eſtabliſhing therein an arbitrary Government, and enlarging its Boundaries, ſo as to render it at once an Example and fit Inſtrument for introducing the ſame abſolute Rule into theſe Colonies:

For taking away our Charters, aboliſhing our moſt valuable Laws, and altering fundamentally the Forms of our Governments:

For ſuſpending our own Legiſlatures, and declaring themſelves inveſted with Power to legiſlate for us in all Caſes whatſoever.

He has abdicated Government here, by declaring us out of his Protection, and waging War againſt us.

He has plundered our Seas, ravaged our Coaſts, burnt our Towns, and deſtroyed the Lives of our People.

He is, at this Time, tranſporting large Armies of foreign Mercenaries to complete the Works of Death, Deſolation, and Tyranny, already begun with Circumſtances of Cruelty and Perfidy, ſcarcely paralleled in the moſt barbarous Ages, and totally unworthy the Head of a civilized Nation.

He has conſtrained our Fellow-Citizens, taken Captive on the high Seas, to bear Arms againſt their Country, to become the Executioners of their Friends and Brethren, or to fall themſelves by their Hands.

He has excited domeſtic Inſurrections amongſt us, and has endeavoured to bring on the Inhabitants of our Frontiers, the mercileſs Indian Savages, whoſe known Rule of Warfare, is an undiſtinguiſhed Deſtruction, of all Ages, Sexes, and Conditions.

In every Stage of theſe Oppreſſions we have Petitioned for Redreſs in the moſt humble Terms: Our repeated Petitions have been anſwered only by repeated Injury. A Prince, whoſe Character is thus marked by every Act which may define a Tyrant, is unfit to be the Ruler of a free People.

Nor have we been wanting in Attentions to our Britiſh Brethren. We have warned them, from Time to Time, of Attempts by their Legiſlature to extend an unwarrantable Juriſdiction over us. We have reminded them of the Circumſtances of our Emigration and Settlement here. We have appealed to their native Juſtice and Magnanimity, and we have conjured them by the Ties of our common Kindred to diſavow theſe Uſurpations, which would inevitably interrupt our Connexions and Correſpondence. They too have been deaf to the Voice of Juſtice and of Conſanguinity. We muſt, therefore, acquieſce in the Neceſſity, which denounces our Separation, and hold them, as we hold the Reſt of Mankind, Enemies in War, in Peace Friends.

We, therefore, the Repreſentatives of the UNITED STATES OF AMERICA, in GENERAL CONGRESS Aſſembled, appealing to the Supreme Judge of the World for the Rectitude of our Intentions, do, in the Name, and by Authority of the good People of theſe Colonies, ſolemnly Publiſh and Declare, That theſe United Colonies are, and of Right ought to be, FREE AND INDEPENDENT STATES; that they are abſolved from all Allegiance to the Britiſh Crown, and that all political Connexion between them and the State of Great-Britain, is, and ought to be, totally diſſolved; and that as FREE AND INDEPENDENT STATES, they have full Power to levy War, conclude Peace, contract Alliances, eſtabliſh Commerce, and to do all other Acts and Things which INDEPENDENT STATES may of Right do. And for the Support of this Declaration, with a firm Reliance on the Protection of DIVINE PROVIDENCE, we mutually pledge to each other our Lives, our Fortunes, and our ſacred Honour.

John Hancock.

GEORGIA,	Button Gwinnett, Lyman Hall, Geo. Walton.
NORTH-CAROLINA,	Wm. Hooper, Joseph Hewes, John Penn.
SOUTH-CAROLINA,	Edward Rutledge, Thos. Heyward, junr. Thomas Lynch, junr. Arthur Middleton.
MARYLAND,	Samuel Chaſe, Wm. Paca, Thos. Stone, Charles Carroll, of Carrollton.

| VIRGINIA, | George Wythe, Richard Henry Lee, Th. Jefferson, Benja. Harriſon, Thos. Nelſon, jr. Francis Lightfoot Lee, Carter Braxton. |
| PENNSYLVANIA, | Robt. Morris, Benjamin Ruſh, Benja. Franklin, John Morton, Geo. Clymer, Jas. Smith, Geo. Taylor, James Wilſon, Geo. Roſs. |

DELAWARE,	Cæſar Rodney, Geo. Read.
NEW-YORK,	Wm. Floyd, Phil. Livingſton, Frans. Lewis, Lewis Morris.
NEW-JERSEY,	Richd. Stockton, Jno. Witherſpoon, Fras. Hopkinſon, John Hart, Abra. Clark.
NEW-HAMPSHIRE,	Joſiah Bartlett, Wm. Whipple, Matthew Thornton.

MASSACHUSETTS-BAY.	Saml. Adams, John Adams, Robt. Treat Paine, Elbridge Gerry.
RHODE-ISLAND AND PROVIDENCE, &c.	Step. Hopkins, William Ellery.
CONNECTICUT,	Roger Sherman, Saml. Huntington, Wm. Williams, Oliver Wolcott.

IN CONGRESS, JANUARY 18, 1777.

ORDERED,

THAT an authenticated Copy of the DECLARATION OF INDEPENDENCY, with the Names of the MEMBERS of CONGRESS, ſubſcribing the ſame, be ſent to each of the UNITED STATES, and that they be deſired to have the ſame put on RECORD.

By Order of CONGRESS,

JOHN HANCOCK, Preſident.

Atteſt. Cha. Thomſon, Secy.   *A True Copy*

John Hancock, Presdt.

BALTIMORE, in MARYLAND: Printed by MARY KATHARINE GODDARD.

D

Daily Life, 1776

Colonists faced many hardships in the New World. In England, the economy was strong and many people were financially comfortable enough to work in cities and purchase consumable products, like flour, butter, and eggs, which they needed for daily use. Other consumables, such as candles, soap, and tea, were also readily available for purchase in vigorous centers of commerce.

Though hopeful for a better life overall in the colonies, those who braved the dangerous sea voyage to the New World were surprised to find the political and economic environments offered more freedom but less security than the society from which they fled. Family shelter must be built, rocky soil had to be cleared and prepared for planting. The economy was stable, but many items, like candles, soap, food, and cloth, had to be made at home because they were not available for purchase. Cooking implements, nails, salt, and tea were all fabricated in shops within the colonies or imported to the colonies from the mother country. Luckily, the colonists had a plethora of natural resources at their disposal and could either export them or use them in colonial endeavors.

THE COLONIAL FAMILY

The modern concept of a traditional family was not useful to the labor-intensive existence of the colonists. Most families consisted of parents and children, as well as extended relatives, apprentices, servants, and even slaves considered as a part of the family unit, regardless of relationship. In the colonial era, the individual's dependence on the family unit was the tie that bound.

The colonial family was patriarchal. Trades were generally divided by gender. A woman's primary responsibility was to the family and domestic environment. In addition to the daily domestic duties, female members of the family were responsible for nursing the ill and assisting with births, because medical care was scarce. When time permitted, women were also primarily responsible for the early education of the children. Women generally remained in the home, though there were some instances of circumstances when women could take a respectable trade. Female family members sometimes worked as educators, milliners, wig makers, weavers, and in some instances in the apothecary.

Men generally practiced a trade outside the household or farmed the family's land. Young males were sent to apprentice with a master craftsman in order to learn a trade. Common tradesmen of the period included basket makers, silver- and blacksmiths, wheelwrights, founders, carpenters, and brick makers. Each trade was labor-intensive and required uncounted hours of work to produce a quality product in an era when electricity and modern machinery were still more than 100 years into the future.

COLONIAL FARE

Most items were created by the family for family use. Likewise, most food products had to be grown at home and preserved to last through the harsh North American winters. Typical crops of the period were corn, grains, beans, and seasonal fruits. Crops for export were tobacco, cotton, and in one instance

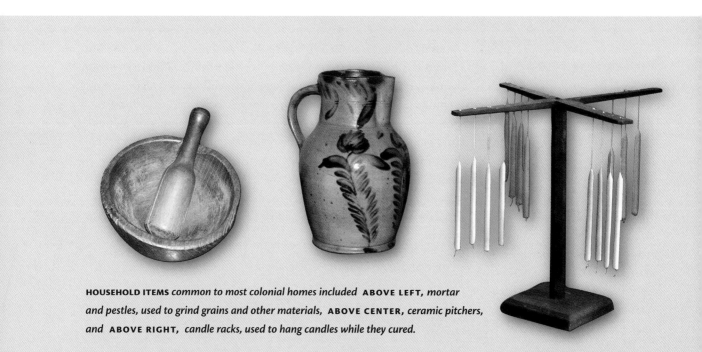

HOUSEHOLD ITEMS *common to most colonial homes included* **ABOVE LEFT,** *mortar and pestles, used to grind grains and other materials,* **ABOVE CENTER,** *ceramic pitchers, and* **ABOVE RIGHT,** *candle racks, used to hang candles while they cured.*

indigo. The majority of 18th-century fare was based on the season. In summer months the family was able to grow and eat a variety of fresh vegetables and collect wild berries, fruits, and hunt various game. Winter months offered any of the harvest that could be stored for a length of time, freshly hunted game, and winter vegetables. Breads and porridges were staples of the 18th-century diet because of their ability to be stored and because of their economical advantages, especially for poorer colonists.

Upper-class colonists were fond of foods with a French influence and had the best-equipped kitchens in the colony. Inventories from the governor's home in Williamsburg, Virginia, included many different copper pots and a charcoal-burning cookstove. Most middle-class families did not have those luxuries but did retain servants or slaves to do the cooking for the family. The less affluent members of society would not have been able to afford the luxury of cooks and would have generally possessed one cast-iron pot, which would have allowed for stews and porridges.

The acquisition and care of livestock were essential to the survival of the colonists. Sheep were used for wool for garments, and chickens not only provided a source of eggs, but also feathers for use in bedding. Cows provided the colonists with milk, which could then be made into butter and cheese. After slaughter, the cow was used for meat and leather.

SLAVES AND WOMEN

As fewer indentured servants were available, the demand for slaves increased. For those families who could afford the additional expense, slave labor was used to ensure the success of the crops, as well as assist the mistress of the house with the daily upkeep and cooking duties. Most slaves had been bru-

tally ripped from their homelands and families, and could expect to be sold to families and be held as captive laborers. Masters had complete control over the acquisition of, selling of, and treatment of those slaves in their homes.

Women were a minority subject to the rule of men. Women were not allowed governmental roles, voting rights, or the ability to inherit property. A woman could only hold property if she were widowed. She then had a choice of remarrying and allowing the property, as well as the security that went with it, to shift into the control of her husband, or remaining a single woman, attempting to care for herself, her family, and the land she now possessed.

THE CHURCH

Under the king's rule all white colonists were required to worship in the Church of England. Though many colonists fled to the New World to avoid religious oppression, they could not escape it permanently. Because of problems with administration and organization of the Anglican Church in the colonies, many colonists practiced their own conservative protestant religions. Initially, debates were held regarding the issue of separation of church and state, and finally in 1779, THOMAS JEFFERSON introduced a bill in Williamsburg, Virginia, which provided for free exercise of religion.

SCHOOLING AND HEALTH

Education in the colonies was primarily for the children of wealthy planters, generally male. Females learned to read, write, and do basic math only in order to facilitate the smooth running of their households. More densely populated areas in the northern colonies established community-funded schools by the late 17th century. Middle colonies offered poor, sporadic public education facilities, and wealthy citizens often found a suitable tutor for their children.

The less populated south had great amounts of distance between settlements and in some cases great distances between homes. This dispersion made forming a community school difficult. Wealthy citizens found tutors for their children and less fortunate families either taught their children what they knew, or simply did not educate the children at all.

Life in the colonies was not always pleasant. Many diseases such as yellow fever and typhus took their toll on the settlers. Unfortunately, medical care was primitive. Few remedies could be given for any diseases, much less viruses like influenza. Common ailments like headaches were viewed as coming from problems in the blood. Infections that are treated by antibiotics in modern America would have been fatal in the colonial era.

CLOTHING

The formal society of the colonists was not only apparent in their spiritual lives and social customs, but also in their clothing. Social situations called for various levels of dress or undress, the most formal being dress, and *undress* referring to daily clothing used for labor. Just as fashion is a driving force in the world economy today, it was also a driving force in the 18th century, when fine silks and linens were imported from Europe.

A woman required many layers of clothing before she was considered dressed in her most formal attire. Formal attire required the use of a stay—stays were much like corsets, but did not result in a smaller waist. A fashionable female form consisted of a slightly accented bosom which flowed to a tubular torso. Stays were made from layering lengths of fabric and inserting rigid or semi-rigid

Love Life

MARRIAGES OF the period were not based on romantic feelings and were rarely the sole decision of the couple. Relationships were matched to improve social standing, increase wealth, or provide financial security. Marriage was expected and though the age varied from colony to colony, women in their mid-20s who had not married were labeled as old maids. In most situations, the bride and groom and their parents must all have consented to the match, but in some cases—particularly in the south—the relationship was a business transaction arranged by the parents of the couple.

Courtship usually involved rare social functions, church meetings, and an occasional visit from the suitor to the woman's home. Once a suitor wished to take a wife, the father of the future wife was obligated to provide financial support in the form of a dowry. The function of the dowry was to provide a financial gift to the groom in return for taking on the added responsibility for his new dependent. Marriage was strictly forbidden among first and second cousins, but family ties that reached beyond that limit were not frowned upon for making a match.

material into the layers to form support. Stays were then topped by a shift, or knee-length undershirt. A petticoat or series of petticoats were set over the shift in preparation for the outer garments. Women's outer garments resembled open-front dresses, very robelike in nature, which were set over the shift and petticoats. The outer garments would then be secured with hook and eyes, pins, or laces. Stockings and appropriate shoes would complete the formal outfit.

Men's clothing was no less complicated. Like his female counterparts, he first donned a shift. Over the shift he would place a waistcoat, a vestlike garment that covered the chest and torso. Breeches were generally cropped just below the knee, and stockings that were made of silks, linens, or wool would cover the lower leg. Shoes were straight-soled and made of leather. The leather would conform to the wearer's feet as they were used. Men were not considered fully dressed without their coats. Coats were usually knee-length and were tailored to fit the individual very closely. Fashionable headwear of the period was a tricornered hat made of felt, and in the most formal situations rested on top of a highly styled wig. (See also CULTURE, 1776; FARM LIFE, 1776; PLANTATION LIFE AND SLAVERY, 1776; RECREATION AND LEISURE, 1776; RELIGION, 1776; SEAFARING, 1776; TAVERNS AND RESIDENCES, 1776; TRAVEL, 1776; WOMEN IN THE REVOLUTION.)

Further Reading: E. Bruun and J. Crosby, *Living History America* (Tess Press, 1999); E. Bruun and J. Crosby, *Our Nation's Archives Archive: A History of the United States in Documents* (Black Dog Publishers, 1999); Peter Copeland, *Life in Colonial America* (Dover Publications, 2002); Jerome Reich, *Colonial America* (Prentice Hall, 2000); Cokie Roberts, *Founding Mothers: The Women Who Raised Our Nation* (HarperCollins, 2005); James Schouler, *Americans of 1776: Daily Life in Revolutionary America* (Corner House, 1976).

—CARLISE E. WOMACK

Declaration House (Jacob Graff House)

On June 11, 1776, Congress appointed THOMAS JEFFERSON, JOHN ADAMS, BENJAMIN FRANKLIN, ROGER SHERMAN, and Robert R. Livingston to draft the statement that would become the initial draft of the DECLARATION OF INDEPENDENCE.

Jefferson's lodgings in Philadelphia proved to be too uncomfortable, and Jefferson wanted a more rural setting in which to focus on the task. He found that setting in the house of Jacob Graff. Jefferson rented two furnished rooms on the second floor of the house, and the Graff family continued to reside in the house while Jefferson worked on the first draft of the DECLARATION OF INDEPENDENCE. One of the rooms was a bedchamber, where Jefferson slept and could write at a desk.

The other was a sitting room, where he could entertain guests, such as fellow committee members Benjamin Franklin and John Adams, who helped him to revise his first draft of the Declaration. The three-story residence faced a stable across the road, and in the warmth of the summer, Jefferson noted that only the horseflies, which the stable attracted and which quickly traveled to the Graff house, marred his stay.

Further Reading: Independence Hall Association, "The Declaration House (Graff House)," www.ushistory.org/declaration/graff/index.htm (cited January 2006); Library of Congress, "Declaring Independence: Drafting the Documents," www.loc.gov/exhibits/declara/ (cited January 2006); Pauline Maier, Merritt Roe Smith, Alexander Keyssar, and Daniel J. Kevles, *Inventing America: A History of the United States* (W.W. Norton, 2003).

—AMY L. SOPCAK

From Past to Present: The Declaration House Today

PHILADELPHIA IS a much different city than it was in the 1770s, but many of the famous Revolutionary-era sites are still standing and host thousands of visitors each year. The Declaration House, located on the corner of 7th and Market Streets, is open year-round as a part of the Independence National Historic Park, and admission is free. The original house was torn down in 1883, but in 1975 the National Park Service rebuilt the structure based on photographs.

ABOVE *Jacob Graff's home on the corner of 7th and Market Streets in Philadelphia, where Thomas Jefferson penned the first draft of the Declaration in July 1776.*

Declaration of Independence

Today the Declaration of Independence is the founding doctrine of American society, a sacred text of freedom. "We hold these truths to be self-evident, that all men are created equal, that they are endowed by their creator with certain unalienable rights, that among these are Life, Liberty, and the pursuit of Happiness." No matter how many times it is repeated, whether in the hackneyed speech of political opportunists, or in the genuine aspirations of people living under tyranny, the opening sentence of the second paragraph of the preamble resonates. If there were ever the equivalent of the Lord's Prayer in the founding texts of the American dream, this is it. Whatever the specific political context, it is often on the basis of this universal creed that America has justified the defense, and even the "spreading" of freedom in other parts of the world.

But the main purpose of the Declaration of Independence was not the preamble, but the list of abuses by King GEORGE III that was most urgent to the Continental Congress (see CONTINENTAL CONGRESS, FIRST AND SECOND).

CLAUSES

The Declaration states "Prudence, indeed, will dictate that Governments long established should not be changed for light and transient causes. ..." The leaders of the American Revolution did not want to break away from or destroy every remnant of British society in the colonies. Their focus was the king and the government. Far from being a populist statement of absolute separation from 18th-century

British society and laws, the core grievances of the Declaration of Independence protest the uneven, unfair treatment of the American colonists, especially the American elite represented at the Continental Congress.

Congress wanted to show how the king and his government had perverted those laws and rights that were the foundations of colonial society and sought to establish "absolute Tyranny." The rhetoric of the preamble was a means to expressing these specific and frightful grievances heaped upon the colonists by the British king and government.

It was only after the passing of time and the gradual unfolding of American history that the ideals of the preamble seemed the ends more than the means. Whereas now it has become only a "Declaration of Independence" for all of humanity, on July 4, 1776, it was very much understood as a "Declaration of Independence" against the British.

The Declaration describes a long train of abuses. The king has "refused his Assent to Laws, the most wholesome and necessary for the public good." He has "dissolved Representative Houses repeatedly." He has "quartered large bodies of soldiers among us." He has "imposed taxes upon us without our consent." He has even "excited domestic insurrections among us" and "waged war against us."

But in a concluding section that was written more by Congress than by Jefferson, the Declaration also explains repeated attempts to "appeal to the native justice and magnanimity" of the "British brethren." It was not that the British did not know justice or that the entire British system was worth rejecting, but that they were "deaf to the voice of justice and consanguinity." It was only out of necessity that they must be held as "Enemies in War, in Peace Friends." If anything, the Continental Congress wanted to take the moral high ground, to show that it was the

The Signers

THE SIGNERS of the Declaration of Independence were among the most respected men in their various colonies. Over half were lawyers. Others were farmers, merchants, and manufacturers. Four representatives were physicians, and one was a minister. All were Protestant except for one Catholic. Most delegates were born in America and were of British descent. In 1776, the average age of the population was 40. Consequently, only seven signers were over 60. Three were in their 20s, and 18 were in their 30s. The rest were in their 40s and 50s. Overall, the signers were a long-lived group. Three of them died in their 90s, and 10 died in their 80s. The last surviving signer of the Declaration was Maryland's CHARLES CARROLL OF CARROLLTON, who died in 1832 at the age of 95.

king who truly rebelled against those freedoms the colonists had come to expect.

RESPONSES

Although it enraged the king and Parliament, the Declaration of Independence received no formal response from the British except the shipment of more redcoats and mercenaries to the colonies. Among writers who rejected the Declaration was British monarchist John Lind, whose pamphlet "An Answer to the Declaration of the American Congress" dismissed every point and branded the Americans as ungrateful rebels. Many writers, nationalists, and thinkers in France, Poland, and elsewhere in Europe responded positively to the document. The Declaration, after all, was not intended only for the British, but for the whole world to see.

Further Reading: Joseph Ellis, ed., *What Did the Declaration Declare?* (Bedford/St. Martin's, 1999); Pauline Maier, *American Scripture: Making the Declaration of Independence* (Knopf, 1997).

—**ALLEN FROMHERZ**

Declaration of Independence, August 2 Embossed

The Declaration was primarily written by THOMAS JEFFERSON, who entitled the document, "A Declaration by the Representatives of the United States of America, in General Congress Assembled." The Second Continental Congress (see CONTINENTAL CONGRESS, FIRST AND SECOND) immediately ordered copies printed to be sent to the 13 states. Printed by PHILADELPHIA printer John Dunlap on 18-by-15-inch paper (see DUNLAP'S BROADSIDES), these copies were designed for public readings in government buildings, pulpits, marketplaces, and military camps. The first public reading in Philadelphia took place on July 8 when the Liberty Bell summoned Philadelphians to the State House where Colonel John Nixon read the Declaration of Independence aloud. Immediately following the reading, patriots tore down and destroyed the King's Arms displayed in the courthouse.

On July 15, the New York delegation finally received permission from its legislature to vote for independence. Four days later, Congress approved a resolution to have the Declaration embossed on parchment, changing the title to "The Unanimous Declaration of the Thirteen United States of America." This version of the document, signed by 56 representatives from the 13 states, is historically accepted as the official Declaration.

The list of delegates who signed the Declaration on August 2, 1776, was kept secret for six months because in British hands the document would have provided grounds for accusations of treason, punishable by hanging. It was not until January 18, 1777, that the August 2 version of the Declaration of Independence was authenticated (see also DECLARATION OF INDEPENDENCE, DRAFTS AND COPIES).

The official signing of the Declaration of Independence was accomplished with excitement, resolution, and pride. The delegates came to the table and signed state-by-state. President John Hancock's signature was written at three times its normal size so that the British king could read it without spectacles. Hancock allegedly suggested that after reading it the British might be motivated to double the price on his head, which stood at £500. The signature of Stephen Hopkins of New Jersey, the oldest member of Congress after Benjamin Franklin of Pennsylvania, was almost unreadable because of ill health. Hopkins told his fellow delegates that even though his hand trembled, his heart did not. William Ellery of Rhode Island positioned himself so that he could see the faces of each delegate as he affixed his signature to the Declaration, fully aware that he might be signing his own death warrant.

Further Reading: The Declaration of Independence, www.thedeclaration ofindependence.org (cited January 2006); *Declaration of Independence: With Portraits of the Signers* (Applewood Books, 1997).

—**ELIZABETH PURDY, PH.D.**

Declaration of Independence, Drafts and Copies

When the delegates of the Second Continental Congress (see CONTINENTAL CONGRESS, FIRST AND SECOND) arrived in PHILADELPHIA in May 1776, their collective course of action remained uncertain. Some patriots, such as JOHN ADAMS and SAMUEL ADAMS of Massachusetts arrived fully persuaded of the legitimacy of independence. However, moderates, mostly from the middle colonies, hoped for a more amiable solution, endorsing action that might divert a full-scale rebellion.

The debate meandered on until RICHARD HENRY LEE arrived with a mandate forcing Congress into action. On Friday, June 7, Lee issued a formal resolution: "That these united colonies are, and of a right ought to be, free and independent States, that they are absolved from all allegiance to the British crown, and that all political connection between them and the state of Great Britain is, and ought to be totally dissolved." Congress argued over Lee's proposal, coming to resolution when the delegates from Pennsylvania acquiesced in favor of freedom.

On Tuesday, June 11, Congress appointed a Committee of Five (see DRAFTING COMMITTEE) consisting of Jefferson, Adams, BENJAMIN FRANKLIN, ROGER SHERMAN, and Robert R. Livingston to create an initial draft declaring independence. Years later, Adams recounted that Jefferson requested him to write the draft, though he refused, citing several reasons: "Reason 1: You are a Virginian and a Virginian ought to be at the head of this business. Reason 2: I am obnoxious, suspected, and unpopular; you are very much otherwise. Reason 3: You can write ten times better than I can." Apparently this convinced Jefferson.

The Declaration Today

IN THE 21st century, the Declaration of Independence is revered as the embodiment of American ideals of liberty and freedom. Along with the Constitution and the Bill of Rights, it is displayed at the rotunda in the National Archives in Washington, D.C. Since the Cold War, a 55-ton vault, impregnable to nuclear assault, holds these national monuments each night, safeguarding them from harm. Such fanfare likely would have amazed the Declaration's original composers who wrote it rather hastily during the exigencies of the moment, but one might suspect it would be an amazement mingled with satisfaction.

ABOVE *The Declaration of Independence is read to a crowd from the east balcony of the State House in Boston, 1776.*

Congress excised substantial portions of the draft, most especially Jefferson's lengthy discourse on slavery, believing perhaps that in a document endorsing natural rights the less said about the "peculiar institution" the better. By the time Congress finished its revision they had jettisoned nearly 25 percent of the original draft—an indignity Jefferson remembered for the rest of his life. They also made some minor additions, inserting the name of God twice, a name conspicuously absent in Jefferson's draft.

On July 4 Congress approved the Declaration, ordering that a formal parchment be produced beginning with the bold declaration "IN CONGRESS, JULY 4, 1776," and ending with the signature of JOHN HANCOCK, the President of the Continental Congress, in flowing script. The 55 other signatories appear in more modest lettering below (see DECLARATION OF INDEPENDENCE, SIGNERS). However, it is likely that many of these others did not register their names until August 2 or perhaps even as late as November.

Hancock acted quickly, sending broadsides to newspapers, state assemblies, and leaders of the army. Recipients reproduced the broadsides for mass circulation or printed them in local papers. In its first month, the Declaration appeared in dozens of newspapers in many key cities. Reading it aloud became another way to advance its message as GEORGE WASHINGTON did, announcing it to the army.

Widely celebrated, the Declaration was cheered with gun salutes, toasts, and jubilant celebrations. Ironically, during and immediately following the hostilities of war, such passionate embers cooled. While the principles of liberty remained vibrant, the text announcing that message nearly disappeared from view. Only well after the conflict did it reemerge as the quintessential expression of national sentiment regarding liberty.

In 1817, at the prodding of Jefferson, John Trumbull began work on a 12-by-18-foot painting commemorating the signing of the Declaration of Independence. Trumbull painted four scenes in tribute to the American Revolution, all of which were destined for the rotunda at the Capitol. Furthermore, the Federalists who had attempted to minimize both Jefferson and the Declaration were fading as a political force. In the Second Party System, both Whigs and Democrats claimed Jefferson as one of their important ancestors, vigorously endorsing the text of which he had served as principal architect.

Further Reading: Bernard Bailyn, *The Ideological Origins of the American Revolution* (Harvard University Press, 1992); James West Davidson and Mark Hamilton Lytle, *After the Fact: The Art of Historical Detection* (McGraw-Hill, 2005); Pauline Maier, *American Scripture: Making the Declaration of Independence* (Random House, 1998).

—RONALD F. SATTA, PH.D.

ABOVE *An E. A. Abbey drawing of the reading of the Declaration of Independence on July 8, 1776.*

Declaration of Independence, Signers

In the following thumbnail biographies, lawyers and merchants dominate, with a limited number of planters, physicians, and clergymen. The signers are grouped by state. (Some of the prominent signers of the Declaration are featured separately and alphabetically by last name in this volume: John Adams, Samuel Adams, Carter Braxton, Charles Carroll of Carrollton, Samuel Chase, Benjamin Franklin, Elbridge Gerry, John Hancock, Thomas Jefferson, Richard Henry Lee, Philip Livingston, Robert Morris, Caesar Rodney, Benjamin Rush, Edward Rutledge, Roger Sherman, and Richard Stockton.)

CONNECTICUT

SAMUEL HUNTINGTON (1731–96) of Windham, Connecticut, gained admittance to the bar in 1754. Huntington served as the president of Congress for two terms from 1779 to 1781 before he returned to Connecticut.

WILLIAM WILLIAMS (1731–1811) of Lebanon, Connecticut, graduated from Harvard College and became a merchant. He served as town clerk of Lebanon for 44 years and as a selectman for 25.

OLIVER WOLCOTT (1726–97) of Windsor, Connecticut, was a Yale graduate. He was sheriff of Litchfield County for 20 years. Wolcott eventually achieved the rank of brigadier general of the Connecticut army.

DELAWARE

THOMAS MCKEAN (1734–1817) of New London, Pennsylvania, was elected to the Delaware Assembly in 1762. His constituents reelected him for 17 years, even though he lived in Pennsylvania for six of those. A member of the committee that drafted the Articles of Confederation, he was elected president of the state of Delaware in 1776. The next year, he was appointed chief justice of Pennsylvania, a post he held until 1797. In 1781, he served as president of Congress.

GEORGE READ (1733–98) of New Castle, Delaware, served as attorney general before representing Delaware in the Continental Congress. He voted against RICHARD HENRY LEE's resolution because he thought it was a hasty move. Once the resolution passed, however, he worked for independence. Later in 1776, Read presided over the committee of Delaware's Constitutional Convention.

GEORGIA

BUTTON GWINNETT (1732–77) was born in England and traveled to the colonies in 1770. He first settled in Charleston, South Carolina, before purchasing a large tract of land in Georgia. He was elected to the Continental Congress in 1776.

LYMAN HALL (1731–90) was born in Connecticut and a Yale graduate. He moved to South Carolina and established a medical practice, then established a plantation in Georgia. He was elected to the Continental Congress in 1775, a post he held until 1780.

GEORGE WALTON (1740–1804) of Virginia was a carpenter's apprentice. Self-educated, he moved to Georgia to study law and was admitted to the bar in 1774. In 1778, Walton received a commission as colonel in the Continental Army.

MARYLAND

WILLIAM PACA (1740–99) of Maryland studied law in Annapolis. He was elected to the Continental Congress in 1774, where he served until 1778. He was appointed chief justice of Maryland the same year he retired from Congress and held that post until 1780, when he was advanced to chief judge of the court of appeals.

THOMAS STONE (1743–87) was born in Maryland, studied law, and was admitted to the bar in 1764. Stone joined the Continental Congress in 1775 and served until 1778, and again in 1783. Stone was a compelling orator, and his law practice became very successful.

MASSACHUSETTS

ROBERT TREAT PAINE (1731–1814) of Boston attended Harvard College in preparation to become a minister. He spent a few years as a merchant marine, then became a lawyer. Paine served as a delegate to the Continental Congress from 1774 to 1776, where he chaired a committee charged with encouraging the manufacture of arms for the defense of the colonies.

NEW HAMPSHIRE

JOSIAH BARTLETT (1729–95) of Amesbury, Massachusetts, trained to be a physician and established a practice in Kingston, New Hampshire. He was elected to the colonial legislature, and was particularly strong when pressured by the royal governor. Bartlett was elected to the Continental Congress in 1774. He signed the Declaration of Independence second, after John Hancock. Bartlett's signature can also be found on the Articles of Confederation.

MATTHEW THORNTON (1714–1803) was born in Ireland. His parents eventually settled in Worcester, Massachusetts, where Thornton received his education and became a physician. Thornton was elected to the Continental Congress in 1776 and 1777, but he declined to return because of his health. Though he was not a member of the Congress when the Declaration was voted on, he joined in time to sign it in August 1776.

WILLIAM WHIPPLE (1730–85) established himself as a merchant in Portsmouth in 1759. He was elected to lead the newly created patriot government in New Hampshire as well as the Continental Congress in 1776, and the next year he was commissioned as brigadier general of the New Hampshire militia.

NEW JERSEY

ABRAHAM CLARK (1725–94) of Elizabethtown, New Jersey, became a surveyor before educating himself in law. He was a popular lawyer because his familiarity with farming and generous nature allowed him to help his poorer neighbors. Clark was elected to the provincial assembly in 1775 and to the Continental Congress the next year.

JOHN HART (?–1779) was born sometime around 1710 in New Jersey, and inherited his father's successful farm. He served on the New Jersey Assembly from 1761 until its dissolution in 1771. In 1775 he became a member of the local committee of correspondence, and in 1776 he was elected to the Continental Congress.

FRANCIS HOPKINSON (1737–91) of PHILADELPHIA studied law and spent two years in England before receiving royal commissions in the colonies. He took up residence in New Jersey, joined the patriot cause, and joined the Continental Congress in 1776.

JOHN WITHERSPOON (1722–94) was a native of Scotland and attended the Universities of Edinburgh and St. Andrew's before becoming a minister. Recruited by RICHARD STOCKTON and BENJAMIN RUSH, Witherspoon moved to the colonies and took the position of president of the College of New Jersey (now Princeton) in 1768.

NEW YORK

WILLIAM FLOYD (1734–1821) was born into a wealthy family on Long Island. Naturally sociable, Floyd earned the confidence of fellow patriots and served on the Continental Congress from 1774 to 1776, long enough to sign the Declaration.

FRANCIS LEWIS (1713–1802) was an orphan from Wales. He immigrated to New York in 1735, where he set up shop as a merchant. In the early 1770s, Lewis made clear his feelings that the colonies could only be successful if they separated from Britain. He was unanimously elected to the Continental Congress in 1775 and served until 1779.

LEWIS MORRIS (1726–98) of Morrisiana, New York, was a Yale graduate who inherited a great deal of wealth from his father. He joined the Continental Congress in 1775, and he served on committees for the defense of New York, provisioning colonial forces, and Indian affairs. Also involved in the militia, Morris led as a brigadier general.

NORTH CAROLINA

JOSEPH HEWES (1730–79) of Princeton, New Jersey, moved to Edenton, North Carolina, to estab-

Thomas Jefferson, Author

ALTHOUGH JOHN Adams or Benjamin Franklin might have been expected to write the Declaration, by the age of 33 Thomas Jefferson had established a reputation as a scholar and as a writer of great literary skill.

In later years, the details of the decision to assign the writing of the Declaration of Independence to Jefferson varied according to whether Jefferson or Adams was recalling the event. Both agreed that the decision was based to some extent on the fact that Jefferson had not established a base of political enemies at this stage of his career, and the Declaration would be more likely to stand on its own merits if written by Jefferson. Adams recalled that he told Jefferson that in addition to writing 10 times better than he did, Jefferson, unlike himself, was not considered "obnoxious, suspected, and unpopular."

ABOVE *A color lithograph of Thomas Jefferson produced in the 1840s.*

lish a shipping business. He served on the provincial assembly from 1766 to the early 1770s. In 1774, he was elected to the local committee of correspondence and joined the Continental Congress. He became secretary of the Naval Affairs Committee, but he fell ill and died in 1779.

WILLIAM HOOPER (1742–90), a Boston native and Harvard graduate, set up a law practice in Wilmington, North Carolina, in 1767. Hooper served in the Continental Congress for two years, until his business affairs required him to relinquish his seat in 1777.

JOHN PENN (1741–88) was born in Virginia and received a common school education. With the help of neighbor Edmund Pendleton, Penn educated himself and became a lawyer. He moved to North Carolina in 1774 and was elected to the Continental Congress from 1775 to 1779.

PENNSYLVANIA

GEORGE CLYMER (1739–1813) was a Philadelphia native, raised by his uncle after being orphaned. He led fellow Philadelphians in resisting the Tea Act and the Stamp Act, and was elected to the Continental Congress in 1776. Most notably, he worked in conjunction with ROBERT MORRIS to strengthen the power of GEORGE WASHINGTON and to improve the provisions sent to the Continental Army.

JOHN MORTON (1724–77) of Ridley, Pennsylvania, was elected to the Provincial Assembly from 1756 until 1775 and participated in the Stamp Act Congress. A member of the Continental Congress, Morton chaired the committee, which reported the Articles of Confederation.

ABOVE *Carpenters' Hall, Philadelphia, meeting place of the First Continental Congress.*

Rodney Breaks the Deadlock

ON JULY 2, 1776, nine states voted in Congress to sever all ties with Great Britain. Pennsylvania and South Carolina refused to vote for independence, and the Delaware delegation deadlocked. After careful maneuvering and the removal of a controversial statement on slavery in the Declaration of Independence, Pennsylvania and South Carolina agreed to vote for independence. Because New York continued to abstain, Delaware became the only colony in the negative column with Thomas McKean in favor of independence and George Read, a close friend of John Dickinson's, opposed. In a last-ditch effort to achieve unanimity and protect Delaware's position on independence, McKean paid a messenger to rush to Delaware and summon Caesar Rodney back to Congress for the vote on July 4.

As a strong patriot, Rodney rightfully earned his place in American history for casting the vote that switched Delaware's vote for "Nay" to "Yea," cementing the unanimity of the vote for American independence.

GEORGE ROSS (1730–79) established his law office in Lancaster at the age of 20. He represented Pennsylvania in the Continental Congress in 1774 and from 1776 into 1777. During his second term, he was also a provincial legislator, a colonel in the Continental Army, and vice president of the first Constitutional Convention for Pennsylvania.

JAMES SMITH (?–1806) was born in Dublin, Ireland. He organized and led a volunteer militia group in York, served on the provincial convention in 1775, the state Constitutional Convention and the Continental Congress in 1776. In 1780, he served one term in the Pennsylvania Assembly.

GEORGE TAYLOR (c. 1716–81) was born and raised in Ireland, expected by his father to study medicine. Instead, Taylor came to the colonies and became a laborer at an ironworks. Taylor was elected to the provincial assembly in 1764. He joined the Continental Congress in the summer of 1776, and though he had not been a member long, he fully endorsed the Declaration of Independence.

JAMES WILSON (1742–98) was born in Scotland and educated at St. Andrews, Edinburgh, and Glasgow. He arrived in Philadelphia in 1766 and studied law with John Dickinson. In 1775 he was elected to the Continental Congress from Pennsylvania.

RHODE ISLAND

WILLIAM ELLERY (1727–1820) was a Rhode Island native and Harvard graduate. He was elected to the Continental Congress in 1776, and served until 1785. He signed both the Declaration of Independence and the Articles of Confederation.

STEPHEN HOPKINS (1707–85) of Rhode Island was the son of a farmer and became a successful surveyor. Hopkins served on the Rhode Island Assembly, was elected to the Continental Congress in 1774.

SOUTH CAROLINA

THOMAS HEYWARD JR. (1746–1809) was born into a wealthy planter family in South Carolina. Heyward was elected to the Continental Congress in 1775, an honor he initially declined. He returned to South Carolina to serve as a judge in 1778 and took a leave of absence to serve in the militia.

THOMAS LYNCH JR. (1749–79) was educated at Cambridge. He returned to the colonies around 1772, and in 1775 was appointed to command a company of South Carolina volunteers. Lynch fell ill after signing the Declaration, and his physician recommended a sea voyage. He and his wife departed in 1779, and the vessel was lost at sea.

ARTHUR MIDDLETON (1742–87) was a South Carolina native. He attended Cambridge and traveled through Europe. He served on the council of safety at Charleston in 1775 and was elected to the Continental Congress the next year.

VIRGINIA

BENJAMIN HARRISON (1726–91) attended the College of William and Mary. He was elected to the House of Burgesses and resisted a bribe from the governor; he served on the Continental Congress from 1774 to 1777. His son, William Henry, was the ninth president of the United States.

FRANCIS LIGHTFOOT LEE (1734–97) was born in Virginia, the younger brother of fellow patriot Richard Henry. He served in the House of Burgesses from

1765 to 1775, then in the Continental Congress from 1775 to 1779.

THOMAS NELSON, JR. (1738–1789) was born into a wealthy family and educated at Cambridge. He served on the House of Burgesses in 1774 before joining the Virginia militia and election to the Continental Congress in 1775. Nelson succeeded THOMAS JEFFERSON as governor of Virginia in 1781.

GEORGE WYTHE (1726–1806) of Virginia studied law and was admitted to the bar at age 20. Elected to the Continental Congress in 1775, he served until 1777, when he returned to Virginia to lead there. He died of poison administered by a beneficiary who hoped to earn his inheritance sooner.

Further Reading: Dennis Brindell Fradin, Michael McCurdy, *The Signers: The Fifty-Six Stories Behind the Declaration of Independence* (Walker, 2003); Independence Hall Association, Signers of the Declaration of Independence, www.ushistory.org/declaration/signers/index.htm (cited March 2006).

—AMY SOPCAK

Delaware in the Revolution

In 1609, Henry Hudson discovered Delaware and claimed it for the Dutch. Over the next six decades, groups of Dutch and Swedish settlers arrived in the colony, which was named after the Virginia governor, Baron de La Warr. When the English took control of Delaware in 1664, oversight of the colony was assigned to William Penn. Most of Delaware's trade was conducted with PHILADELPHIA, and young men were educated and apprenticed in that city. Philadelphia was the seat of government for both Pennsylvania and Delaware, with the governor visiting New Castle a couple of times a year.

Most of the population recognized strong ties to Great Britain and identified themselves as English citizens. The economy was based on agriculture and depended on a large slave population. Transportation was difficult and illiteracy was widespread. Delawareans were heavily influenced by public readings of the newspapers, pamphlets, and broadsides that arrived from Philadelphia. Loyalist support was initially thought to be particularly strong in Delaware, but recent studies suggest that this population was somewhere around 19 percent.

When the Stamp Act Congress was held in New York in October 1765, Delaware sent two delegates and joined in the cries of "No taxation without representation." When RICHARD HENRY LEE introduced the Virginia Resolution on the floor of the Second Continental Congress, the Delaware legislature was still ordering its delegates to attempt reconciliation with Britain. Those restrictions were lifted on June 15 at the urging of Speaker Caesar Rodney and Thomas McKean. The Delaware assembly then passed its own resolution of independence.

On July 4, when the final vote for independence was taken, Delaware cast the vote that made support for the sentiments expressed in the Declaration of Independence unanimous. At the official signing on August 2, all three delegates signed the Declaration.

Delawareans were well aware that the colony was incapable of adequately defending itself against the powerful British military and looked to the Continental Army and Navy for assistance. At the beginning of the war, Britain targeted New England and

ABOVE *An engraving of Caesar Rodney by artist Charles Saint-Mémin. Rodney urged that Delaware vote for independence.*

to return fire when the battle resumed at daylight. At New Castle, loyalists continued to supply British forces, while maintaining close ties with Virginia's governor, Lord Dunmore, who had fled to a British ship in the area.

By September 27, the British had captured both Wilmington and Philadelphia, and the legislature was forced to flee to Dover. Nonetheless, American forces maintained control of the Delaware River and thus were able to block supplies from reaching British forces in Philadelphia by placing obstructions in the water and locating small vessels around Fort Mifflin and Fort Mercer.

Further Reading: John A. Munroe, *History of Delaware* (University of Delaware Press, 2001); John A. Munroe, *The Philadelawareans and Other Essays Relating to Delaware* (University of Delaware Press, 2004); Jane Harrington Scott, *A Gentleman as Well as a Whig: Caesar Rodney and the American Revolution* (University of Delaware Press, 2000); Darren Staloff, *Hamilton, Adams, Jefferson: The Politics of Enlightenment and the American Founding* (Hill and Wang, 2005).

—ELIZABETH PURDY, PH.D.

the middle colonies, assuming that the pro-British South would be easier to subdue. As a result, Philadelphia via Delaware became an early target of British aggression. On March 27, 1776, the British man-of-war HMS *Roebuck* arrived on the Delaware River.

On Easter Sunday, April 17, 1776, American troops exchanged fire with the HMS *Roebuck*. Americans claimed victory because they damaged the ship so badly that it had to be towed for repairs. On May 8, a second battle ensued. The HMS *Roebuck*, which had run aground, was protected from American invasion only when another British ship, the HMS *Liverpool*, dropped anchor nearby. The grounded ship floated off the bar during the night and was ready

Disease and Medicine, 1776

Disease was a major factor in life in the American colonies. The low-lying areas with high water tables were conducive to the same unhealthy conditions that later plagued the port cities of PHILADELPHIA, New York, Boston, and Charles Town. Waste material from outdoor privies seeped into wells and polluted the water. Typhus first appeared in America at Jamestown. Internal infections caused by polluted water also led to general feelings of ill health and made early Americans more vulnerable to all diseases, resulting in low life expectancy. The most common diseases and conditions were dropsy, bilious colic, cramps, rheumatism, nosebleeds, eye problems, gout, infectious childhood diseases, circulatory problems, stroke, and cancers.

NUTRITION

By the mid-18th century colonists had begun to eat more balanced diets, consuming fish, pork, veal, chicken, goose, turkey, pigeon, and rabbit. Raw vegetables were rarely eaten because they were considered unhealthy. Cooked vegetables included white and sweet potatoes, turnips, parsnips, corn, beans, peas, asparagus, and cucumbers. Fruits, which were eaten raw, dried, and cooked, included apples, oranges, peaches, raisins, currants, and berries. Dairy products included milk, cheese, eggs, and butter.

HOSPITALS AND MEDICAL PERSONNEL

Britain did little to promote health care in the American colonies, leaving it up to each governor or proprietor to deal with the situation. The only hospitals that existed before the Revolution were a general hospital in New York and a Quaker hospital in

Immunizations

BY THE time the American Revolution began, smallpox immunizations had come to be generally accepted, partly because of the support of prominent Americans such as GEORGE WASHINGTON and BENJAMIN FRANKLIN. Washington had contracted smallpox, and Franklin had lost a young son to the disease. When smallpox appeared among the ranks of the Continental Army, Washington had special hospitals set up to inoculate all recruits. Although the epidemic continued to spread among British soldiers, the epidemic was checked among Americans. In 1796, British physician Edward Jenner discovered that humans vaccinated with cowpox built up immunity to smallpox. This discovery virtually wiped out smallpox around the world.

Washington understood the importance of sanitation in preventing the spread of diseases and knew that unchecked diseases could decimate his troops. In addition to inoculating soldiers, Washington issued orders that any soldier relieving himself outside latrine areas would be court-martialed. Other commanders, however, were not as diligent as Washington, and conditions at many camps led to the consumption of water that had been polluted by human and animal waste. Dysentery was the most common consequence of drinking such water. Respiratory illnesses, including tuberculosis, were the second most frequent cause of death in the military. Other common diseases included syphilis and other venereal diseases, scurvy (caused by vitamin deficiencies), and scabies (a parasitic condition). A major influenza epidemic that hit Europe in 1781–82 spread to America, where millions of people became ill and large numbers died. Because many recruits came from sparsely populated areas, they lacked immunities to diseases that other soldiers had developed. Of the 200,000 men who served in the Revolutionary War, approximately 7,174 were killed in battle. Another 8,500 died in enemy prisons, but most fatalities occurred in military camps, caused by diseases, malnutrition, and exposure to the elements because of inadequate clothing and shelter.

Philadelphia. Virginia established the first hospital for the mentally ill in 1772.

No medical training was available until the opening of medical schools at the College of Pennsylvania in 1765 and at King's College, New York, in 1767. Many American physicians still trained in Europe.

Apothecaries, barbers, ministers, plantation owners, magistrates, teachers, midwives, herbalists, and others with only a minimum of knowledge or access to medical books provided medical advice. Medications were often devised from family recipes, almanacs, newspapers, handbooks, and folklore. As a result, medicine was often a trial-and-error process, and there was almost no supervision of the medical community.

During the Revolution, medics assigned to care for American troops rarely had sufficient training. Even those who were trained suffered from a lack of medications and supplies. American soldiers paid a heavy price for the lack of proper medical care because scores of them died from wounds that qualified physicians would have taken in stride.

DISEASES

Smallpox had been of major concern to the American population since Europeans transported the disease to America in the mid-17th century. Major outbreaks occurred in all 13 colonies. The colonies were spared the chronic epidemics that plagued Europe, however, because the population was more spread out. Because of frequent contact from the outside world, residents of port cities were more vulnerable to epidemics than were other Americans. In the decade before the American Revolution, Pennsylvania, New York, New Jersey, and South Carolina all experienced major smallpox epidemics. Except for South Carolina, however, smallpox was rare in the South.

Once physicians learned that quarantines were effective tools in preventing the spread of infectious diseases, they began quarantining entire ships. After Boston minister Cotton Mather lost family members to the disease, he tried to convince local doctors to inoculate Bostonians. Most physicians distrusted inoculations, and only Zabdiel Boyston paid any attention to Mather. Boyston vaccinated his young son and two slaves and found that they became immune to the disease. Within a few months, 35 Bostonians had been immunized.

Typhus was endemic throughout Europe. Those who were most vulnerable to the disease included the poor, the undernourished, and those in the military, where men lived in close proximity to one another under less-than-sanitary conditions. Like typhus, typhoid could also spread quickly under unsanitary conditions and was particularly prone to transmission through contaminated water. Some scholars insist that more soldiers were killed by typhus than ever died in battle.

Contact with mosquitoes that bred in stagnant water resulted in outbreaks of yellow fever in America's port cities. From the beginning of the 18th century to the outbreak of the Revolutionary War, some 25 yellow fever epidemics occurred in America.

Malaria was most common in the Carolina low country where rice was the major export product. Particularly between June and October, the standing vats of water used to irrigate rice proved to be excellent breeding grounds for mosquitoes that spread the disease.

In the 21st century, dengue fever, which is known as *kidenga pepo* in Swahili, is known only in developing countries. In 1779, however, dengue surfaced among North Americans and Europeans who had come in contact with infected African slaves. The first American physician to pay substantial attention to the disease was BENJAMIN RUSH of Philadelphia, a signer of the DECLARATION OF INDEPENDENCE. In 1780, Rush noted that the disease appeared after several days of temperatures in the mid-to-high 90s.

Further Reading: James H. Cassedy, *Medicine in America: A Short History* (Johns Hopkins University Press, 1991); Gerald N. Grob, *The Deadly Truth: A History of Disease in America* (Harvard University Press, 2002); Kenneth F. Kiple and Stephen V. Beck, *Biological Consequences of European Expansion* (Ashgate, 1997); James Schouler, *Americans of 1776: Daily Life in Revolutionary America* (Heritage, 1990); Robert Wilkins, *The Fireside Book of Deadly Diseases* (Robert Hall, 1994).

—ELIZABETH PURDY, PH.D.

Drafting Committee

On June 7, 1776, RICHARD HENRY LEE introduced the Virginia Resolution on the floor of the Second Continental Congress (see CONTINENTAL CONGRESS, FIRST AND SECOND), stating that the American colonies "are and of a right ought to be, free and independent states," thereby establishing the political independence of the 13 colonies that joined together to create the United States of America. All delegates understood that if the Revolution failed, each of them could be put to death for treason. Therefore, it was essential that Americans as well as possible foreign allies understand the issues involved in the action.

On June 28, 1776, the Drafting Committee submitted its final draft to the Second Continental Congress. Jefferson had shown earlier drafts to Adams and Franklin, and both had made minor changes. On the floor of Congress, around one-fourth of the committee's draft was cut, with a total of 39 revisions. The most controversial pro-

Geographic Representation

THE DRAFTING committee was composed of Thomas Jefferson (Virginia), John Adams (Massachusetts), Benjamin Franklin (Pennsylvania), Roger Sherman (Connecticut), and Robert Livingston (New York). Except for Jefferson, these men were already well established in their respective states, both in their professions and as leaders of the patriot cause. Jefferson had only recently arrived in Congress as a replacement for the highly respected Peyton Randolph, who had returned to Virginia. Adams and Sherman were from New England, and Franklin and Livingston were from the middle colonies. Jefferson was the only southerner. Thus, the Drafting Committee was geographically representative of the 13 colonies.

vision would have abolished slavery in the United States. However, South Carolina refused to sign any document that abolished slavery, and in order to attain their goal of independence, Jefferson and other members of the Drafting Committee agreed to strike the provision.

The official copy of the Declaration of Independence was signed by 56 delegates on August 2, 1776. Today, Jefferson's draft with the corrections offered by John Adams and Benjamin Franklin is housed in the Library of Congress. This copy contains 19 corrections, additions, and erasures that were apparently made by Jefferson either of his own volition or in response to verbal suggestions made by Adams and Franklin. The draft also contains the handwritten changes made by Adams and Franklin. Adams's handwritten copy of the draft resides with the Massachusetts Historical Society.

Further Reading: Whitfield J. Bell Jr., *The Declaration of Independence: Four 1776 Versions* (American Philosophical Society, 1986); Allen Jayne, *Jefferson's Declaration of Independence: Origins, Philosophy, and Theology* (University of Kentucky Press, 1998).

—**ELIZABETH PURDY, PH.D.**

ABOVE *A Currier & Ives print of John Hancock signing the Declaration.*

Dunlap's Broadsides

On the morning of July 2, the delegates to the Second Continental Congress declared independence from Britain, and on the morning of July 4, the Congress adopted the DECLARATION OF INDEPENDENCE. The text of such an important document needed to be made public, and one of the easiest ways to spread the word was to print the Declaration for colonists to read for themselves. PHILADELPHIA printer John Dunlap, the official printer of the Continental Congress, produced a batch of printed copies of the Declaration that day, and these prints are now known as Dunlap's Broadsides.

The top of the document announces in large type, "In Congress, July 4, 1776, a Declaration by the Representatives of the United States of America, in General Congress Assembled." The text of the Declaration followed, and rather than listing all of the names of the delegates, the broadside was "Signed by Order and in Behalf of the Congress, John Hancock, President."

The broadside was first read publicly in Philadelphia on July 8. GEORGE WASHINGTON's copy was read to the American army, which was assembled in New York on July 9. As the broadside spread across the land, other printers produced copies, or included the Declaration in their newspapers. On July 19, Congress ordered an officially inscribed copy of the Declaration, and Congressional delegates began to sign it on August 2 (see DECLARATION OF INDEPENDENCE, AUGUST 2 EMBOSSED).

Today, 25 of these original Dunlap's Broadsides still exist, most of which are in the United States. Two copies are in the Public Record Office in the United Kingdom.

Further Reading: Frederick R. Goff, *The Dunlap Broadside: The First Printing of the Declaration of Independence* (Library of Congress, 1976); Library of Congress, Declaring Independence: Drafting the Documents, www.loc.gov/exhibits/declara/ (cited January 2006); Massachusetts Historical Society, Library Collections: Broadsides, www.masshist.org/library_collections/broadsides.cfm (cited January 2006).

F

Farm Life, 1776

Beginning in 1651, Parliament passed a series of Navigation Acts that heavily restricted the colonies' ability to trade with other countries. Although the partnership with Britain was generally viewed as beneficial, many farmers objected to being told where they could sell products and being denied the right to buy other products at cheaper prices. The trading partnership continued until America rebelled against arbitrary taxes. Most participants in the American Revolution were farmers, ranging from the subsistence farmers of the frontier to wealthy plantation owners of the South.

CROPS

Farming in the American colonies required constant vigilance and never-ending work, and many farmers lacked capital to plant and manage acreage sufficient to turn profits. After seeds were sown, weeds, droughts, and frost often destroyed crops. Animals were equally destructive, and rats sometimes destroyed harvested products stored in barns. During the war, crops were also vulnerable to enemy armies and to requisitioning from friendly armies.

Each family member had an assigned task. Boys were expected to help their fathers. Girls usually took on such tasks as churning, spinning, sewing, and child care around the age of five. By the age of ten, most girls also helped with milking, cooking, and laundry. Women in New York and Pennsylvania and in frontier areas regularly worked

ELFRETH'S ALLEY, AT LEFT, *in Philadelphia's Old City neighborhood is the oldest continuously occupied street in America. The first house in the alley was built in 1713, and all 33 homes are still private residences today. Ben Franklin once lived here, although which house he occupied is not documented.*

alongside their husbands in the field. Most women in New England worked only at harvest time, spending the remainder of their time on homemaking, gardening, dairying, and animal tending. Southern women on large plantations were essentially in charge of a small town, performing a variety of tasks that freed male owners to concentrate on production.

By the time of the American Revolution, some 90 percent of Americans were involved in agriculture, but the crops varied according to region. Maryland and Virginia produced tobacco for export. Frontier farmers grew corn, beans, squash, pumpkins, and hunted wild game and fowl. The middle colonies of New York, New Jersey, Pennsylvania, and Delaware produced large quantities of grain for both domestic and foreign consumption. While rye, oat, barley, and corn were important grains, wheat was the most significant grain for domestic use and for foreign trade.

Marine products were exported from all coastal areas. Sawmills appeared throughout America to prepare timber for export and for use in shipbuilding. Dairying was common in most colonies but was most successful in Pennsylvania. In New England, the infamous triangular trade developed in which cheap molasses was brought to New England from the West Indies and used to manufacture rum. The rum was exchanged for slaves along the African coast, and the slaves were transported to the West Indies, where they were traded for cheap molasses. New Englanders bought the molasses and turned it into rum, and the process repeated.

Virginia was the first state to officially recognize slavery in 1661 in response to the need for large numbers of workers to labor in the tobacco fields. North Carolina produced tobacco, as well as tar, pitch, turpentine, masts, and forest products. South Carolina and Georgia were the major rice producers, and Georgia also exported indigo and tropical fruits.

LIVESTOCK

The raising of livestock was restricted by Britain, and farmers were prevented from importing stock that would have allowed them to develop superior breeds. Draft horses, large workhorses suitable for heavy farm work, for instance, were generally banned from the United States until after the war.

While some American farmers enjoyed the trading partnership with Britain imposed by the Navigation Acts, others chafed at trading restrictions. A sheep farmer, for instance, was legally obligated to sell all wool to England, even though France would have paid twice as much as Britain for the wool. Subsequently, farmers were required to purchase woolen cloth from Britain that could have been bought at half the price from Italy.

For many farmers, smuggling became the only way to circumvent the restrictions. As more Americans rebelled against Britain, patriots began wearing clothing made from coarse homespun cloth and refused to buy English wool. After the war, American farmers were able to import superior breeding stock, and the quality of livestock production increased.

METHODS

In order to be self-sufficient, the American farmer needed a variety of tools and equipment. While human power was the essential commodity, horses and oxen were widely used. Most farmers owned a number of vehicles for farm work. The two-horse wagon was the most common; and on Sundays the family was transported to church in the wagon, which could be covered during inclement weather. These vehicles held six people and traveled around

Absent Farmers

SOME SCHOLARS insist that the American Revolution was a major setback for farmers because of the long years when males were fighting and their families were unable to keep farms producing at prewar levels. Nature took over fields; livestock was left without supervision. Pigs escaped into the woods, and many small farms went under. Battles took place on many farmlands, leaving them unsuitable for agriculture.

After the Revolution, some 75 percent of the population continued to labor in the agricultural sector and dedicated themselves to reclaiming the land. In 1790, Eli Whitney

Typical Colonial farm implements included wool cards, **BELOW,** *on which sheared wool was combed into loose strands that were then wound into threads and yarns on a spinning wheel,* **ABOVE RIGHT.** *Edged utensils were honed on the wheel of a sharpening stool, shown* **ABOVE LEFT.**

invented the cotton gin, and "King Cotton" became the primary export of the Deep South. Although production increased, the land was not completely restored until the 1830s. By that time, America's agricultural sector had expanded westward to Texas and California.

seven miles per hour. In 1750, the Conestoga wagon was invented in Pennsylvania. This heavy four-wheeled wagon was generally pulled by horses of the same name that had been bred for that purpose. These vehicles became the covered wagons of the 19th century that were used by families traveling westward. Sleds and sleighs were used for family and farm transport in cold winter climates. Many farmers also owned two-handed plows that were drawn by two to four oxen and a corn plow for tilling furrows.

Barns were shingled or clapboarded, and became gathering places for family tasks that ranged from threshing grain to weaving cloth. Smokehouses, root cellars, hog pens, henhouses, and workshops were also regular structures on American farms. Essential tools for farming in America included a plowshare, plow chains, scythes, sickles, a horse collar, harnesses, weeding hoes, grubbing hoes, a broad axe, a spade, a hatchet, a splitting tool, knives, flails, shingles, and cooper's timber. Most tools were hand made and ill-fitted to the tasks they were supposed to perform.

Agricultural technology made little progress in America until after the war because Britain controlled the export and import processes so rigidly that American farmers were prevented from employing new technologies. Also, Europeans jealously guarded their agricultural and industrial secrets for fear of competition.

MARKETING

Most colonial charters required New England's towns and cities to hold regular market days where products could be bought and sold. The first commercial building designed for that purpose was erected in Boston in 1742. Domestic trading was virtually destroyed in America as the focus of agriculture shifted to supporting rival armies. While most Americans preferred to direct their products to the Continental Army and local militias, a number of them, particularly those who remained loyal to the Crown, opted to sell to the British, who paid in cash rather than accepting the highly depreciated continental dollar from Americans. Both sides regularly commandeered the supplies of the other whenever possible. British soldiers also frequently destroyed American food and supplies whenever they invaded cities and towns, attempting to starve America into submission. British supply lines from Canada continued without disruption for most of the war.

In heavily agricultural areas, where food was plentiful, both armies were able to purchase sufficient food for their needs. At times, American soldiers sent food home to families who were unable to make farms productive while males were away at war.

The Royal Navy was largely successful at blockading American ports and disrupting foreign trade. However, privateering flourished throughout the war, and Americans continued to trade with France, Holland, Sweden, and Denmark. Regular trading of tobacco, wheat, and rice with foreign West Indies continued. Americans managed to obtain supplies from Spanish colonies, and the Dutch created a secure trading post on St. Eustaius Island. When the British captured the island in 1781, trading was relocated to the Danish islands of St. Thomas and St. Croix, ensuring that supplies and armaments would reach America. Since Europeans had come to depend on American tobacco and indigo, these products were regularly transported to Europe on the ships of neutral countries. When the war ended in 1783, many American farmers had amassed fortunes. (See also PLANTATION LIFE AND SLAVERY, 1776.)

Further Reading: Willard W. Cochrane, *The Development of American Agriculture: A Historical Analysis* (University of Minnesota Press, 1993); Stephanie Grauman Wolf, *As Various as Their Land: The Everyday Lives of Eighteenth-Century Americans* (HarperCollins, 1993).

—ELIZABETH PURDY, PH.D.

Flags of the Revolution

A ccording to legend, sometime late in the spring of 1776 a young PHILADELPHIA upholsterer and seamstress named Elizabeth Griscom Ross received three important visitors in her Arch Street shop: General GEORGE WASHINGTON, Colonel George Ross, and ROBERT MORRIS. They came as a committee of Congress, which was then meeting just a few blocks away at Independence Hall. They wanted to know if she could make them a flag.

Betsy Ross was 25 years old and recently widowed. "With her usual modesty and self-reliance," said her grandson many years later, she told them "that she did not know but she could try; she had never made one but if the pattern were shown to her, she had no doubt of her ability to do it."

She escorted them into her parlor and looked at their proposed design. Right away, she saw problems. It wasn't symmetrical or pleasing to the eye. She made some suggestions, which Washington noted on the sketch. And, she said, the stars should be five-pointed, not six-pointed. The general protested that it would take too long to make five-pointed stars. "Nothing easier," Betsy replied, picking up a piece of paper, folding it, and, with a single snip of her scissors, unfolding a perfect five-pointed star. With that, she won the honor of sewing the first American flag.

Betsy Ross House

ABOVE *The home of America's most famous flag maker, located at 239 Arch Street, Philadelphia, Pennsylvania, is now the American Flag House and Betsy Ross Memorial. Tours are self-guided or visitors may purchase an audio guide which brings to life the house and its occupants.*

Special daily programs are presented in the tree-lined courtyard from May through August, with additional programs around holidays and weekends.

The story of Ross and the flag has become one of the iconic tales of the American Revolution, albeit a myth. Most historians reject its accuracy. It was a story unknown to Americans until 1870, when her grandson, William J. Canby, delivered a speech to the Historical Society of Pennsylvania, repeating stories he had heard since childhood. But there is no documentary evidence of the event, either in the government archives or postwar memoirs or in Ross's own meticulous bookkeeping records. This lack of evidence is not surprising. The American veneration of the American flag did not begin until after the Civil War, and became a potent symbol of national unity around the time of the centennial in 1876.

Flag historians believe that the first true national flag was the Continental Colors, which flew mostly on navy ships beginning in late 1775. The Continental Colors used 13 alternating red and white stripes to represent the colonies, with the Union Jack in the upper left-hand corner.

Washington raised this flag over his Prospect Hill headquarters near Cambridge, Massachusetts, on New Year's Day 1776. Copies of a speech made by King GEORGE III in England months before, offering small concessions to the rebels, had just been sent to Washington, and the raising of a flag containing the Union Jack confused the enemy. "Behold!" Washington wrote, "It was received in Boston as a token of the deep Impression the Speech had made upon us, and as a signal of Submission … by this time I presume they begin to think it strange that we have not made a formal surrender of our Lines. …"

The Continental flag was the unofficial symbol of the new country for more than a year. On June 14, 1777, Congress approved a resolution that read: "Resolved, That the flag of the United States be thirteen stripes, alternating red and white; that the union be thirteen stars, white in a blue field representing a new constellation."

There is no record of debate on the issue, or a statement as to why that particular design was selected. And who came up with the final design? Many historians give the honor to Francis Hopkinson, a signer of the DECLARATION OF INDEPENDENCE and a prolific artist, writer, and composer. He was fond of designing seals and emblems and is known to have helped with the Great Seal of the United States. In 1780, he sent a bill to the U.S. Treasury asking for payment for designing, among other things, "the Flag of the United States of America."

Further Reading: Nancy Druckman, *American Flags: Designs for a Young Nation* (Harry N. Abrams, 2003); Mark Leepson, *Flag: An American Biography* (Thomas Dunne Books, 2005); Richard H. Schneider, *Stars and Stripes Forever: The History, Stories, and Memories of Our American Flag* (William Morrow, 2003).

—HEATHER MICHON

France, Reaction in

July 4, 1776, dawned in France over a troubled nation. Inexperienced, surrounded by advisors, and still having failed to produce an heir to his throne, the 22-year-old king, Louis XVI, faced crucial questions about the economy of France and its role in international affairs. In debt because of losses to Great Britain during the Seven Years' War (1754–63) and with an insufficient tax base, France's fiscal burdens fell increasingly on its peasantry. Riots engulfed Paris for three weeks in the spring of 1775, as rioters demanded food at fair prices. They were a portent of unrest in the years ahead and they would

Comte de Vergennes

CHARLES GRAVIER, Comte De Vergennes (1717–87), foreign secretary and chef du conseil royal (1774–87), was the architect of French policy on American independence. An established diplomat, Vergennes had risen to his position in spite of personal indiscretion: notably fathering two children with the French-born widow of a Turkish doctor, whom he had met when he was French ambassador in Constantinople. His subsequent marriage to her may have legitimized his children but her lowly birth kept her barred from Louis XVI's royal court. Vergennes's attention to French foreign policy was more astute. He took office with the primary intention of maintaining France's peace with Great Britain and allowing her time to rebuild her forces and her prestige while retaining France's remaining colonial possessions and rich trading posts.

While it has often been historically expedient to argue that France supported the American cause only to avenge their defeat to the British in 1763, Vergennes was motivated less by revenge and more by a desire to advance French interests in Europe. In America's efforts to secure independence, Vergennes saw an opportunity to develop a new balance of power, which had changed in 1772 when the Austrian, Russian, and Prussian powers partitioned Poland. Instead of checking each other's ambition, the three powers acted collectively to the detriment of a weaker state and had undermined a country that had been a traditional French bulwark against Russian advances from the east. They had been afforded this room to maneuver, argued Vergennes, because France's stature had been tarnished by the British in 1763.

The only solution would be to create a system where France and Britain were on equal footing and lesser states would not act without their tacit approval. Thus, his hopes for French security and ambition in the years ahead rested on the hope that Britain might be humbled through the loss of her American colonies and more willing to accede to French intentions. When the opportunity arose, Vergennes viewed the American War of Independence as a serendipitous means of facilitating the restoration of French power in Europe.

Vergennes's plans did not play out in the manner that he hoped. In fact, French involvement in the American war nearly bankrupted his nation and never produced any of the trade riches that Vergennes sought. France was in trade deficit with the United States by the close of the 18th century and, as Britain restored its trade links with the American nation, not only had the French not profited from the conflict, but the economic power of the British still reigned in Europe. France and Britain were at war again in 1793 although Vergennes did not live to see much of the consequences of his policies. He died in 1787 but his role in securing the independence of the United States cannot be underestimated.

ABOVE *Benjamin Franklin is shown at the Court of France in this photo of a painting by Hobens.*

be exacerbated by America's desire to throw off the yoke of a different monarch.

Louis XVI headed a nation that stood humiliated by its losses of 1763. France had ceded its North American colonies, some of the territories in the West Indies, and crucial trading posts in West Africa to Great Britain. After 1776, American calls for assistance in their war with Britain would prey on France's traditional enmity with its Atlantic neighbor and seek to draw France into the war for American independence. In 1778, France allied with the United States and, in 1783 when the Treaty of Paris formally ended the conflict, it was inescapably true that French aid, troops, and munitions secured American freedoms. Louis XVI helped America throw off monarchial rule only to see America's call for liberty echo through the bloody streets of revolutionary Paris in 1789 and end with the loss of his life and the fall of his absolute monarchy.

In December 1776, BENJAMIN FRANKLIN arrived in Paris to intensify America's lobbying for more than just intellectual affinity. The most famous American of his time, Franklin's presence in France, and the nature of the American fight, led some prominent individuals to involve themselves directly in the American cause. The Marquis de Lafayette (see LAFAYETTE, MARQUIS DE), a nobleman in the French army, volunteered for the American forces and was made a major general in the Continental Army in July 1777. A secret flow of arms to the American rebels also developed after Pierre-Augustin Caron de Beaumarchais created a dummy corporation to funnel materiel across the Atlantic. Louis XVI authorized the extension of loans to the Americans to fund the purchase of supplies. The purchases of Beaumarchais and appropriations by representatives of the Continental Congress in France constituted the majority of

the weapons and ammunition that the Continental forces used in 1777. A more sustained and overt commitment on behalf of the French crown remained elusive, however.

The loss of the Seven Years' War had done more than humiliate the French. It had also decimated its navy, left it with a debt burden of 50 million livres, and damaged its credibility in Europe. As a consequence of the Treaty of Paris, France was prohibited from harboring vessels belligerent to the British in its ports. Directly arming American rebels in France or protecting American vessels that had pirated on the British fleet would immediately drag the French into a conflict with the British that the French navy was in no position to fight. On the other hand, Vergennes felt that France could profit greatly from aiding America. With a weakened Great Britain,

ABOVE *A lithograph of Benjamin Franklin's first audience before King Louis XVI at Versailles. March 20, 1778.*

France's remaining colonial possessions—particularly the French Antilles—were more secure. Additionally, an independent United States suggested a future of new markets for French goods.

Evidence of military success on behalf of the ragtag American forces was necessary for France to fully commit. In August 1777, with the British capture of Philadelphia, it seemed as if America may capitulate too soon to the British for French ambition to be realized. But the British advances were nullified by the victory of the Americans at the Battle of Saratoga on October 17, 1777. Major General JOHN BURGOYNE's surrender was the impetus that the French required—albeit one that had been facilitated by their own munitions.

The French government declared its clear intention to aid the American rebels in early 1778 with the emergence of two treaties. The Treaty of Amity and Commerce established commercial relations between France and the "United States of North America" and outlined the parameters of open trade between the two nations. The Treaty of Alliance linked France and America against the common enemy, Great Britain. In effect, the military alliance was a secret one as it required war to break out between France and Great Britain to trigger the accord. Such an event occurred on June 17, 1778, when a British frigate fired on the French vessel *Belle Poule* and France committed a military force to the American theater. France was at war, Louis XVI wrote later that year to his uncle, Charles II of Spain, to "restore the honor of my oft-insulted banner, and ... assist an oppressed people who have come and thrown themselves in my arms."

In 1780, France committed 12,000 men to participate in the war of independence under the command of Admiral François-Joseph-Paul de Grasse, in command of French warships on the American coast, and General Jean Baptiste Donatien de Vimeur, Comte de Rochambeau (see ROCHAMBEAU, COMTE DE), who commanded the expeditionary force of soldiers. Along with the money that France had pledged to help supply American troops with clothing and material, the French troops helped to turn the course of battle in America's favor. They were crucial to the Battle of Yorktown in 1781 and the surrender of General Charles Cornwallis on October 17.

In the wake of Yorktown, France became the site of negotiations between American and British emissaries but the entangling of America's independence with European politics complicated the outcome. As the war wound down, France was committed to helping Spain force Great Britain into abandoning Gibraltar, after Spain entered the American war in 1779. Such demands were ultimately dropped, and after America and Britain reached their peace, Vergennes concluded French peace with Britain and secured the island of Tobago, several African trading posts, and the right to fortify Dunkirk. It is estimated that America's independence cost France more than 1.3 billion livres, the equivalent of $13 billion today. Moreover, France's monarchy carried an enormous fiscal deficit after 1783 because of its loans to the American cause, and Louis XVI's attempts to avoid bankruptcy triggered his summoning of the Estates General in 1788. France's own revolution had begun.

It was ultimately fitting that Paris, which in 1763 had given its name to a treaty that took France out of North America, performed a similar function for Great Britain in 1783. Undoubtedly, America's independence hinged on French military and financial succor. The acceptance of that historical reality, however, would be hard to bear for subsequent generations of Americans as they chafed against the suggestion that a republic's birth hinged on the generosity of a Catholic monarch. Yet, the reaction in France to America's Declaration of Independence only underscored the deep historical connection between the two nations: French munitions, money, and its imprimatur of legitimacy were essential to the success of the American Revolution; America's defeat of a monarchy and articulation of democratic principles were crucial in fostering similar sentiments in France and were indelibly knitted into the fabric of France's own revolution.

Further Reading: Frank W. Brecher, *Securing American Independence: John Jay and the French Alliance* (Praeger, 2003); John Hardman, *French Politics: 1774–89: From the Accession of Louis XVI to the Fall of the Bastille* (Longman, 1995); Stacy Schiff, *A Great Improvisation: Franklin, France, and the Birth of America* (Henry Holt, 2005); J. H. Shennan, *France before the Revolution* (Routledge, 1995).

—RICHARD J. GOWERS

Franklin, Benjamin (1706–90)

Benjamin Franklin would be the only Founding Father who signed the Declaration of Independence, the Treaty of Paris, and the Constitution.

Born in Boston, the 15th child of Josiah Franklin and Abia Folger, Franklin was apprenticed at the age of 12 to his older brother in the printing business, where he set type for the *New England Courant* newspaper and wrote his first anonymous essays known as the "Silence Dogood" letters. In 1723, he left Boston, going first to New York City, and then to PHILADELPHIA, where he arrived on October 6, 1723. He worked for the English printers Samuel Palmer and later John Watts until July

1726, when he returned to Philadelphia to work with his friend Thomas Denham in his mercantile store. Franklin started his own printing business in 1728 and became the official printer for Pennsylvania in 1730. Successfully publishing the *Pennsylvania Gazette* and *Poor Richard's Almanac* and creating several printing partnerships, Franklin was so successful that he was able to retire from his business in 1748. He began the Library Company of Philadelphia—the first subscription library in the colonies—the first fire department in the city, the American Philosophical Society, and a school that evolved into the University of Pennsylvania. He also became clerk for the General Assembly in 1736, and then post office master for Philadelphia in 1737.

From 1745 to 1747, Franklin conducted his electricity experiments that resulted in his book, *Experiments and Observations on Electricity Made at Philadelphia in America* (1751) that culminated in his famous kite experiment in 1752, proving that electricity was in nature. Franklin's scientific experiments propelled him into the most recognizable American in the world. He had wide correspondence with scientists throughout Europe, became a member of the Royal Society in England, one of only eight foreigners in the French Royal Academy of Sciences (1772), and received degrees from Harvard, Yale, the College of William and Mary, St. Andrews, Oxford, and Cambridge. It was his success as a scientist and writer that led to his success as the American minister in France. He also started the first insurance company and hospital in Philadelphia in 1751 and 1752, respectively.

It was not until the 1750s that he became active in politics as an opponent to the Penn family, who were the proprietors of Pennsylvania. He became a member of the General Assembly (1751–64) and

The Pennsylvania Constitution of 1776

THE PENNSYLVANIA constitution was the most radical, ultrademocratic constitution created by the first colonies in 1776. Written by George Bryan, James Cannon, and Thomas Young, it was divided into two parts: a Frame of Government and a Declaration of Rights. The Frame of Government did away with the concept of separation of powers. The constitution set up a single, unicameral legislature following Franklin's belief that it represented the sovereignty of the people. Proposed legislation had to be published "out of doors" for the population to review before it could be passed by the succeeding annual legislature. There was no governor, but an executive council. The people elected the executive council and the president of the council, thereby nullifying any separation of powers between legislative and executive branches. The electorate was the most liberal of all constitutions, providing for all freemen over the age of 21 who paid taxes.

The Declaration of Rights included freedom of religion, freedom of the press, the right to bear arms, and other rights eventually incorporated into the federal Bill of Rights. The Pennsylvania Declaration preceded the federal version by 15 years.

AT LEFT *A Currier & Ives color print of statesman Benjamin Franklin.*

postmaster general of North America (1753), and in 1754 he traveled to Albany to participate in the Albany Plan to join the colonies together. His plan of union, however, was rejected by both the colonists and the English Board of Trade. This early attempt at colonial union left a major impression upon Franklin and provided stimulus for similar proposals 20 years later at the time of the Continental Congresses (see CONTINENTAL CONGRESS, FIRST AND SECOND). He went to England as the colonial agent (1757 to 1762) to obtain Privy Council approval of taxation of proprietary estates in Pennsylvania. Later he supported the conversion of the proprietary colony to a royal colony, first writing several tracts and later, as an agent for Pennsylvania in England, attempted to obtain such status in the early 1770s, against the wishes of a majority of the people. He returned to Pennsylvania (1762–64) but lost a hotly contested election to the General Assembly in 1764. He then returned to England as Pennsylvania's agent, where he spent the next 10 years of his life.

His years in England were important because by his return he realized that the colonies had to become independent from the mother country if they were to remain viable. Although he did not oppose at first the Stamp Act tax of 1765, he later succeeded in obtaining its repeal by Parliament in 1767.

Franklin worked as a propagandist against the Stamp Act, attempted to obtain royal control of Pennsylvania, served as agent for four colonies, and, as a loyal Briton in the late 1760s and early 1770s, worked hard to maintain the relationship between the colonies and Britain. Although supporting the view that the colonies should be loyal to the monarchy, as early as 1768, he began to turn against the principle of parliamentary supremacy, writing against Parliament's role in determining how the relationship between mother country and colonies should be conducted.

Difficulties in England also helped shape Franklin's ideas. The Hillsborough government refused to recognize his appointment as Massachusetts agent (1771) and after the Boston Tea Party, in January 1774, Solicitor-General Alexander Wedderburn brought Franklin before the Privy Council and excoriated him over the release of the Hutchinson-Oliver correspondence, between the governor and lieutenant-governor of Massachusetts over events in Boston (see BOSTON IN THE REVOLUTION). Franklin's overall mission was a failure, leaving him to conclude that the English government did not consider the colonists as Englishmen but as a separate body to be ruled rather than integrated into the empire.

Returning to Philadelphia on May 5, 1775, he was appointed by the Pennsylvania Assembly to the Second Continental Congress the next day. He served on several committees over the next year. During the year 1776, at the age of 70, he joined three others in a failed mission to Canada to convince the Canadians to join with the American cause. He was on the DRAFTING COMMITTEE to write the Declaration of Independence, and made several changes in the text of Jefferson's draft before it was given final approval on July 4, 1776. Franklin, at 70, was the oldest signer of the Declaration.

Franklin's other major responsibility from July 15 to September 28, 1776, was serving as president of the convention to create a new constitution for Pennsylvania. As a member of the Continental Congress and the Pennsylvania Constitutional Convention, he attended both meetings in the same building. During the convention he signed four ordinances, five commissions, and contributed to the drafting of the constitution.

From December 1776 to 1784, Franklin served as the American plenipotentiary in France. Because of his natural philosophy writings and scientific experiments, he was honored by the nobility, and widely recognized as the most important American of his day. For nine years he served the United States in bringing the French into an alliance against England, obtaining more than 25 million livres in loans that funded the war. Although there were other representatives like Silas Deane and John Adams, the French wanted to deal only with Franklin.

Following his return from Paris to Philadelphia on September 14, 1785, Franklin was elected president of Pennsylvania. Franklin then became one of the Pennsylvania representatives to the Constitutional Convention of 1787. Two unsuccessful proposals in the convention were the recommendation of no pay for all members of the executive branch and the call for prayers at the beginning of each session. His most important contributions were his support for the Connecticut compromise for equal representation in the Senate and his defense of the work of the convention at its conclusion. In 1788, Congress failed to recognize Franklin's past contributions and denied him compensation or even recognition for his achievements and services to the government. Franklin also became president of the Society for Promoting the Abolition of Slavery (1787) and wrote the first remonstrance against slavery in 1789, and then presented a petition against slavery before Congress in 1790 that was not adopted. He died shortly after of pleurisy on April 17, 1790.

Further Reading: Walter Issacson, *Benjamin Franklin: An American Life* (Simon and Schuster, 2003); Leonard W. Labaree et al., eds., *The Papers of Benjamin Franklin* (Yale University Press, 1959); J.A. Leo Lemay, *Benjamin Franklin Writings* (Library of America, 1987); J.A. Leo Lemay and P.M. Zall, eds., *Benjamin Franklin's Autobiography: An Authoritative Text, Backgrounds, and Criticism* (Norton, 1986); Gordon S. Wood, *The Americanization of Benjamin Franklin* (Penguin Press, 2004).

—JOEL FISHMAN, PH.D.

Frontier in the American Revolution

The frontiersmen of the American Revolutionary War played a significant role in the victory that led to independence from Great Britain. When civil protests turned into open rebellion in 1775, nearly all colonies had open frontiers that were populated with white settlers and Native Americans that had been pushed westward during European colonization. As the war gained momentum, Britain focused most of its attention on securing major port cities such as New York City, Savannah, Georgia, and Charles Town, South Carolina. Both the Continental Army and state militias reacted by leaving protection of the frontiers to locals who formed groups

Pontiac Rebellion (1763–66)

IN MID-1763, over a decade before the American Revolution began, Pontiac, an Ottawa Indian, led three separate sieges against white settlers. Pontiac was the leader of a large group of tribes, which included the Ottawa, Delaware, Seneca, Chippewa, Miami, Potawatomi, and Huron. The uprising began when the Ottawa attacked a British garrison at Detroit. The surprise attack allowed the Ottawa to quickly overwhelm the small British force. When the British retaliated with a surprise attack against the fort on July 31, 1763, in the Battle of Bloody Run, they suffered heavy losses. Unchecked, Pontiac continued to conduct sieges over the following months.

In May, the Delaware and Mingo began attacking white settlers and destroying British posts. The Shawnee attacked settlers and destroyed homes and crops in western Virginia. More than 2,000 settlers were killed in the uprising, and hundreds more crowded into British garrisons for protection. The British dispatched General Thomas Gage to deal with the rebellion. Using a combination of threats and negotiations, peace was finally restored in late 1766.

of partisan solders. In some areas, particularly in the South, these partisan bands spent a good deal of time harassing the British by interfering with supply lines and releasing American prisoners. Many frontiersmen were also skilled trackers and were able to provide valuable logistical information to Continentals and militias.

ETHAN ALLEN

Ethan Allen formed the Green Mountain Boys in 1770 in New Hampshire and Vermont to stymie the efforts of New Yorkers to extend their boundaries northward. On May 10, 1775, he led a daring attempt to take Fort Ticonderoga from the surprised British. A number of weapons, including highly important cannon, were stored at the fort, and subsequently used against the British. After the capture of Ticonderoga the Green Mountain Rangers was formed under the command of Seth Warner as part of the northern army. This regiment was responsible for a victory at Bennington during the 1777 Saratoga campaign, which proved to be a turning point for the Americans during the Revolutionary War.

GEORGE ROGERS CLARK

Because a number of Native American tribes had allied themselves with American LOYALISTS and begun attacking settlers, GEORGE WASHINGTON asked American frontiersmen for help in quelling native attacks. A major campaign of this type occurred in the summer of 1778 when Lieutenant Colonel GEORGE ROGERS CLARK was asked to lead a campaign along the Ohio River. Clark agreed to attack British forts in the areas now known as Ohio, Michigan, Indiana, and Illinois. On June 26, Clark and his forces left what is now Louisville, Kentucky. Eight days later, the men arrived at a British garrison in Kaskaskia and took the fort without a shot being fired.

When Clark learned that the British had attacked Vincennes in Indiana City, he set out to retake it. The fort was under the command of the brutal British officer known as "Hair-Buyer Hamilton" because he enjoyed purchasing the scalps of women and children killed by Native Americans. Clark was accompanied by a Native American raiding party that had been captured along the way. When the loyalists inside the fort refused to surrender, Clark tomahawked one of the warriors in full view of the fort. Hamilton surrendered. By the time the campaign ended, he had laid claim to a large tract of land north of the Ohio River and east of the Mississippi River.

JOHN SULLIVAN

Around the same time, loyalists and Native Americans had also been conducting major raids against the Wyoming Valley. On July 3, 1778, in Wilkes-Barre, Pennsylvania, a group of Seneca people and 1,000 loyalists scalped 227 settlers and burned 1,000 houses. In November, a similar group attacked Cherry Valley, New York, and slaughtered 32 men, women, and children. Commander in chief George Washington dispatched 3,700 men under the command of General John Sullivan to make war against the Six Nations. By the time the American army finished destroying 40 settlements, 80 percent of Seneca land had been destroyed. Without food, hundreds of Seneca starved in the winter months, while others died from disease and exposure. To the natives, Washington became known as "the town destroyer."

ANTHONY WAYNE

In the spring of 1779, Sir Henry Clinton traveled down the Hudson River toward Manhattan Island with 6,000 men and 70 ships. On May 30, the British landed in New York at forts located at Stony and Verplancki Points. Clinton had no plans to attack; his only purpose was to extend the British supply line. Washington responded by dispatching Continentals under General Anthony Wayne to Stony Point. Wayne had learned the true value of surprise attack during the Paoli Massacre on September 21, 1777, when he was surprised by British who used bayonets but never fired a shot. Wayne redeemed himself at the Battle of Monmouth on June 28, 1778, when his troops turned the course of the battle and transformed a retreat into a decisive engagement. The British had fortified the fort at Stony Point by building a number of batteries, partially connected by trenches. They had also erected abatis formed by interlocking trunks and limbs of trees. Sharp points sticking out from the abatis were intended to stop Americans from trying to breech the defenses.

Wayne's attack force was made up of 1,350 men culled from the light infantry, with men on horseback posted at intervals to prevent observation by spies or reconnaissance agents. Wayne's plan was set into place on July 15, 1779. All men were warned that if they broke the order of absolute silence, they would be killed. All around the fort, volunteers chopped up the abatis to provide entry for teams made up of one lieutenant and 20 men. No muskets were used, only bayonets. In under two hours, the Americans captured the fort.

FRANCIS MARION

After the Battle of Camden in the summer of 1780, the participation of partisan soldiers became particularly important to the American military. FRANCIS MARION, affectionately known as the "Swamp Fox," was the best known of the partisans who roamed the southern frontier, harassing the British. Marion had been derailed by a broken ankle when Charles Town

ABOVE *A Currier & Ives print of General Francis Marion of South Carolina in his swamp encampment, inviting a British officer to share his dinner of sweet potatoes and cold water.*

was captured on May 12, 1780. His injury proved to be fortuitous because it kept him from being taken prisoner. Marion was largely responsible for maintaining the freedom of eastern South Carolina in the months following the fall of Charles Town. As commander of the South Carolina militia, Marion agreed to join Colonel Henry Lee in capturing all the British outposts along the Santee River, and he served under Nathanael Greene in the Southern Campaign that led to Yorktown and the surrender of the British army.

Further Reading: Colin G. Calloway, *The American Revolution in Indian Country: Crisis and Diversity in Native American Communities* (Cambridge University Press, 1995); David Dixon, *Never Come to Peace Again: Pontiac's Uprising and the Fate of the British Empire in North America* (University of Oklahoma Press, 2005).

—ELIZABETH PURDY, PH.D.

G

George III (1738–1820)

The American DECLARATION OF INDEPENDENCE directly points to King George as the source of colonial grievances. George III was born Prince George William Frederick of the House of Hanover on June 4, 1738, to Frederick, Prince of Wales, and Augusta of Saxe-Gotha, Princess of Wales. George III became king on October 25, 1760.

The king thought the colonists should be grateful that he had secured their victory in the French and Indian Wars, a view shared by the British Parliament. George III spent his first decade as king dealing with enormous political instability exacerbated by his inexperienced meddling in the affairs of government coupled with bad advice from his closest advisors. Many scholars allege that George III had willed himself to be an unyielding leader from the age of 12 when his father's premature death meant that he would ascend to the throne at a young age.

The Declaration of Independence blames King George for the unpopularity of the British in America and most lore surrounding the American Revolution holds George III, rather than the British Parliament, responsible for the state of affairs in the colonies. Part of this may stem from the failure of an initiative by the Continental Congress (see CONTINENTAL CONGRESS, FIRST AND SECOND) to seek redress for their grievances from the king. A formal document known as the Olive Branch Petition was passed on July 8, 1775. The document

GEORGE III, KING OF ENGLAND AT LEFT *The Declaration of Independence holds King George responsible for a long list of grievances. The king's refusal to read the Olive Branch Petition stood as the tipping point in the Continental Congress decision to declare independence.*

spoke of the "irksome variety of artifices practised by many of your Majesty's Ministers" and called upon King George, in an appeal to the sense of loyalty among many in the Congress, to provide a redress for these grievances. When no action was forthcoming, this slight became yet another grievance against the British, and the leaders of the revolutionary movement within the Congress used it as the basis for the Declaration.

King George encouraged the British to continue fighting the American Revolution for several years after it had become apparent that they could not prevail. Besides being a natural product of his obstinate nature, he wanted to see the war prolonged to further hinder France, after they joined the war on the side of the colonists. Keeping the French occupied with the American Revolution longer than some Britons thought necessary served a strategic function for the British.

George III had five prolonged episodes of insanity, including a particularly public one during the American Revolution, and this became a permanent condition in 1811. Authorities now believe that his insanity was the result of untreated organic conditions and possible arsenic poisoning, which may have resulted from remedies he was given for his various conditions. In many ways, George III is better remembered for his insanity than for anything else, because generations of Britons have known him as "the mad king" even if they knew little about the American Revolution.

While his legacy in the United States is consumed by his opposition to the American Revolution, some in Britain celebrate that it was while he

Quebec Act

THE QUEBEC Act was passed by the British Parliament in 1774 to provide for the governance of Quebec. It was essentially a compromise designed to accommodate the francophone (French-speaking) subjects conquered by Britain during the Seven Years' War. Essentially, Britain allowed the Quebecois to retain the French language for public purposes and the French civil law in their courts. The act also expanded the boundary of which British territory constituted Quebec, taking in the entire Ohio Valley as far west as the Mississippi River. This enraged the American colonists, who viewed the Ohio Valley as a natural extension of their colonies rather than of the Canadian colonies to the north. Of course, after the revolution, the Treaty of Paris of 1783 established the claim of the United States to the Ohio Valley, as far northwest as Minnesota.

The Quebec Act had the desired result of inhibiting participation by people in what is now Canada in the American Revolution. When the Revolution broke out, many thousands of LOYALISTS fled the American colonies for what are now the Canadian provinces of Ontario, Quebec, New Brunswick, and Nova Scotia. The Quebec Act is not completely responsible for the acquiescence of Canada to continued British rule—the British army and navy were based in what is now Canada, which also served to inhibit revolution. Nevertheless, the act served to simultaneously fuel the Revolution in the United States and quiet it in Canada.

was king that Britain emerged as a great power in Europe (through its role in the Napoleonic wars) and some of the greatest parliamentary leaders emerged. It was he who established the Royal Academy and the King's Library of the British Museum.

Further Reading: Stanley Ayling, *George the Third* (Knopf, 1972); John Brooke, *King George III* (McGraw-Hill, 1972); Christopher Hibbert, *George III: A Personal Biography* (Basic Books, 1998).

—TONY L. HILL

Georgia in the Revolution

Georgia was the last colony to be settled by English settlers coming directly from Europe. By 1752, the British Crown had taken control of Georgia, expecting the colony to be a major source of wine, olive oil, and silk for exports. Rice soon developed as the main export.

When the Revolutionary War began, Georgia was both the newest and poorest of the 13 colonies, still receiving a regular stipend from the British government. Although Georgia had established diplomatic relations with the Creek and Cherokee, hostile natives continued to be a problem. Outlaws roamed unchecked in the western frontier, and settlers were subject to attacks by marauders from Florida and South Carolina.

RISING TENSIONS

In Britain, Georgia's agent, William Knox, was given instructions to lodge a formal objection to the Stamp Act of 1865 but refused to do so. He was dismissed, and Georgia had no representative in Britain until 1768 when BENJAMIN FRANKLIN added Georgia to the list of colonies he rep-

resented. Unwilling to commit to what was still considered disloyalty to the king, Georgia sent an observer but no delegates to the Stamp Act Congress. James Wright, Georgia's last colonial governor, enforced the Stamp Act against the wishes of the legislature and the people, making Georgia the only colony in which the Stamp Act was enforced. When the legislature strongly expressed its opposition to the Townshend duties in 1767, the governor dissolved the legislature.

Although Georgians continued to hope for reconciliation with Britain, St. John's Parish sent Dr. Lyman Hall to the First Continental Congress (see CONTINENTAL CONGRESS, FIRST AND SECOND) as an observer. Without a mandate from the Georgia legislature, Hall was unable to represent the colony. By the beginning of the next year Georgia had acceded to the wishes of Congress and created its own provincial government. On July 4, 1775, the legislature met in Tondee's Tavern in Savannah and pledged its support for the political rights of America. When British troops arrived on the Georgia coast on January 18, 1776, Joseph Habersham arrested Wright, who later escaped to a British ship. The Georgia legislature named seven of Georgia's eight counties in honor of pro-American British statesmen. The other county was named Liberty. Georgia ratified the Articles of Confederation on February 26, 1778, anxious to solidify its position in the Union because South Carolina was more than willing to annex its neighbor.

On May 20, 1776, Button Gwinnett and George Walton joined Lyman Hall in PHILADELPHIA as Georgia's representatives to the Second Continental Congress with instructions to protect the interests of Georgia and America. Georgia's delegates joined those of eight other states in voting for independence on July 2 and contributed to the unanimous vote on July 4. All three Georgia delegates signed the embossed copy of the DECLARATION OF INDEPENDENCE on August 2. On August 10, a copy of the Declaration reached Georgia, where it was greeted with much celebration.

WAR

On January 18, 1775, five British ships arrived in the waters near Savannah in an attempt to purchase supplies and entice slaves to join in the fight against the revolutionaries. In what became known as the Battle of the Rice, local patriots managed to burn several rice boats that were waiting to dock, but the British stole the others. On November 3, Georgia's first troops joined the Continental Army. Other forces were needed at home to protect Georgia because the British were certain to attack. By the summer of 1776, the burden on local militia was mitigated by the arrival of Continental forces under Major General Charles Lee, whose army included several battalions of foot troops, a regiment of rangers, two artillery companies, and four row galleys that patrolled the coast.

Georgians knew from the beginning of the war that the state was vulnerable not only from the Atlantic Ocean but also from the Florida Territory to the south that remained under British control.

In the winter of 1777, General Henry Clinton led a force of several thousand British soldiers, German mercenaries (see HESSIANS), and loyalists from New York to Georgia. The British plan was to capture Georgia and South Carolina, then take out the remaining states one at a time. This force arrived at Tybee Island on December 23 and proceeded to take Savannah, maintaining control until the end of the war.

Throughout the war, two governments operated in Georgia. The first was the British civil govern-ment, and the other was Georgia's own provincial/state government. Both governments recognized the importance of property ownership to locals. The British assisted loyalists in acquiring patriot property through booty, plunder, and reward, frequently rewarding loyalists with the confiscated property of those who refused to profess loyalty to Britain. Consequently, many residents fled to the less settled areas of Georgia.

In the backcountry, residents often switched loyalties, then transferred back again, depending on circumstances. Georgia's government confiscated abandoned loyalist property and sold it to finance government activities and the war effort. Georgia's economy suffered through the years of British occupation, in part because of the impossibility of collecting taxes. Nevertheless, Georgia joined Delaware as the only two states that never issued unbacked currency during the Revolutionary War.

Helpless in a city where invaders outnumbered patriots three to one, eastern Georgia offered little resistance. The same was not true of the western area of the state, where Whig loyalties remained strong and enemy aggression was limited by a lack of activist loyalist support. By 1778, Elijah Clarke and John Dooley had organized a militia in western Georgia that continued to serve as an irritant to the British, particularly after the capture of Augusta later that year. This partisan activity was even more essential to the patriot cause when the British made the south the focus of their aggression.

The first major battle of western Georgia took place at Kettle Creek on February 13, 1779, when local forces, reinforced by Continental forces under the command of General Andrew Pickens, surrounded British troops and emerged victorious.

From September 23 to October 8, 1779, a French fleet under Count Charles D'Estaing laid siege to

Nancy Hart

ONE OF Georgia's most famed Revolutionary War residents was Nancy Morgan Hart (c.1735–1812), known as "Aunt Nancy" to the militia. Hart acted as a spy for the Georgia militia, and faced down the British, who controlled Augusta. On one occasion, Hart agreed to feed five British soldiers. While they were eating, Hart passed their guns outside to her daughter through a hole in the wall of her cabin. When she was discovered, Hart shot one of the soldiers and threatened to shoot them all if they did not surrender. They did. On another occasion, Hart poured boiling lye into the eye of a British soldier who was attempting to peek into her cabin.

When the Union cavalry arrived in the area on April 17, 1865, they were met by the Nancy Harts, an armed group of women determined to protect their town.

ABOVE *An illustration by A. I. Keller shows the October 8, 1779, attack on Savannah, Georgia, by a French fleet under Count Charles D'Estaing.*

Savannah, attempting to rout the British. The result was a devastating defeat for the American forces, in large part because a deserter gave the British details of the planned attack. Count Casimir Pulaski, a Prussian war hero who had come to America with the French Marquis de Lafayette (see LAFAYETTE, MARQUIS DE), led the attack at Spring Hill, the heaviest area of fighting, and was mortally wounded. Close to one-third of the American forces were killed or wounded in the siege of Savannah.

When General Elijah Clarke tried to free Augusta in September, he was likewise defeated. From May 22 to June 19, 1781, General Nathanael Greene of the Continental Army attempted to recover the Fort at 96 from the British but was forced to retreat. By the spring of 1783, the tables had turned against the British, and Clarke and the Continentals were successful in driving the British out of Augusta and back to Savannah. On July 3, the British abandoned the Fort at 96. Savannah remained in British hands until July. Once Georgians regained control of their homeland, laws were passed that allowed loyalists and slaves who had worked with the British to remain in Georgia only if they served in the Georgia military for two years. Most British supporters fled to Florida or Jamaica.

Further reading: Kenneth Coleman, *Colonial Georgia: A History* (Charles Scribner's Sons, 1976); Webb Garrison, *A Treasury of Georgia Tales: Unusual Stories of Georgia* (Rutledge Hill Press, 1987); Leslie Hall, *Land and Allegiance in Revolutionary Georgia* (University of Georgia Press, 2001); Hans W. Hannau, *Georgia* (Doubleday, 1994).

—ELIZABETH PURDY, PH.D.

Gerry, Elbridge (1744–1814)

Elbridge Gerry was a signer of the DECLARA-TION OF INDEPENDENCE and one of the leading advocates of independence in 1776. He was a delegate from Massachusetts to the Second Continental Congress (see CONTINENTAL CONGRESS, FIRST AND SECOND).

Gerry believed that the British people had become so corrupt and void of virtue that if America did not separate from Great Britain, they too would become like the vagrant British. The virtue of America was the primary goal of the Revolution, in Gerry's eyes.

Gerry took his seat in Congress on February 9, 1776. When asked where the matter of independence stood, he asked James Warren, speaker of the Massachusetts House, to obtain instructions from the Massachusetts legislature to the delegates in Congress expressing a solid position in favor of independence. Gerry hoped this move would provide the political leverage needed to turn the minds of some of those who were not as keen on independence. At the same time, he urged that American ports would be opened for foreign trade, another step toward independence.

Massachusetts lagged behind other colonies in the movement for independence, as the instructions Gerry requested failed to arrive. He took matters into his own hands and wrote again to Warren. As the months passed, he became more fervent about the need for American independence. In May, he wrote, "It appears to me that the eyes of every unbeliever are now open; that all are sensible of the perfidy of Great Britain, and are convinced there is no medium between unqualified submission and actual independency. The colonies are determined on the latter."

A Noted Career

ELBRIDGE GERRY was a member of the colonial House of Representatives, the Continental Congress, and was a delegate to the Constitutional Convention. However, he refused to sign the Constitution. When asked about his objections, he stated,

"My principal objections to the plan are, that there is no adequate provision for a representation of the people; that they have no security for the right of election; that some of the powers of the legislature are ambiguous, and others indefinite and dangerous; that the executive is blended with, and will have an undue influence over, the legislature; that the judicial department will be oppressive; that treaties of the highest importance may be formed by the president, with the advice of two thirds of a quorum of the senate; and that the system is without the security of a bill of rights. These are objections which are not local, but apply equally to all the states."

After the Constitutional Convention, Gerry was elected to two terms in the House of Representatives, served as governor of Massachusetts from 1810 to 1811, and served, until his death in November, 1814, as James Madison's vice president.

John Adams wrote that he was worried about the toll the fight for independence had taken on Gerry. He said, "…God grant he may recover it [his health], for he is a Man of immense Worth. If every Man here was a Gerry, the Liberties of America would be safe against the Gates of Earth and Hell."

For Gerry, the signing of the Declaration of Independence was the greatest single event of his life. The document created an identity in him that formed many of his subsequent ideas and actions. He was very confident that America could achieve independence, although he worried about supply shortages, lack of funds, and a lack of leadership, and worked to remedy those things. His optimism was rewarded when America finally achieved its independence from the British and became a nation of its own.

Further Reading: George Athan Billias, *Elbridge Gerry: Founding Father and Republican Statesman* (McGraw-Hill, 1976); Gary W. Cox and Jonathan N. Katz, *Elbridge Gerry's Salamander: The Electoral Consequences of the Reapportionment Revolution* (Cambridge University Press, 2002).

—JAMES E. SEELYE, JR.

Great Britain, Reaction in

The year 1776 proved to be a momentous one in British history. Political economist and rhetorician Adam Smith published *An Inquiry into the Nature and Causes of the Wealth of Nations*, which led to the rejection of mercantilism and the transformation of British economic thought. Political activist and social philosopher Jeremy Bentham anonymously published *Fragments on Government*, which launched the utilitarian movement that advocated "the greatest good for the greatest number." Most significantly, the 13 British colonies in North America declared themselves independent and broke off political ties with the mother country.

When Great Britain entered into the American Revolution, the mother country had no idea that the war would last years and drain Britain's economic and military resources. Up until April 19, 1775, when shots were fired at Lexington and Concord in Massachusetts, the rebellion had been more a matter of civil disobedience than open warfare. It soon became clear that significant numbers of the American population were willing to give their lives for what they saw as their inalienable right to be free.

Lord North, the prime minister of Great Britain from January 1770 to March 1782, convinced Parliament to throw the lion's share of Britain's military resources into demonstrating that Britain was mightier than its upstart colonies. Once it became clear that the colonies were united in their efforts to resist, the British government was forced to admit that the war would not be easily won.

In Britain, a public outcry against the war resulted from the economic toll that war exacted. From 1776 to 1783, the government's war expenses totaled some £120 million, roughly one and one-half times the country's annual gross national income. On a political level, Britain was strongly divided on the issue of American independence throughout the war. In the beginning, the British government believed the rebellion would be put down in record time and argued that the fleet would be able to blockade ports and put enough pressure on American tradesmen to force them to yield to the greater power.

As the tax burden rose by one-third and the national debt increased in response to government's heavy borrowing to finance the war, the conflict became increasingly divisive among the British public. Antiwar petitions were regularly circulated throughout Britain and may have numbered as high as 44,000. The Scottish people tended to support the war, but the Irish population was divided, with Protestants opposing the war, and Catholics supporting it. The impact of the American Revolution on life in Britain increased drastically after France (1778), Holland (1779), and Spain (1780) declared war on Britain and forced Britain to react defensively as well as offensively.

MOUNTING EXPEDITIONS

Since the British population was strongly divided on the issue of American independence, it made the task of recruiting military personnel even more difficult. Britain insisted America won the war because of foreign interference, particularly that of France, while troops from outside the British Isles made up the bulk of British military forces in North America. HESSIANS, hired German troops, formed an essential element of Britain's military might. By the end of the war, between 15,000 and 20,000 Hessians had participated in the Revolutionary War. When the war ended in 1783, several thousand opted to remain in the United States. Although Britain also made overtures to Holland and Russia about raising troops, it was unable to obtain support from either country.

When it first became clear that Britain would be forced to increase its military force in North America, King GEORGE III decided that it was more efficient to reinforce existing troops than create new units. However, he gave permission in 1775 to form Fraser's Highlanders, a two-battalion regiment, which was created by promising commissions to individuals who raised a stipulated number of recruits. No additional units were formed until 1777. As the war progressed, Parliament established new military quotas, and officials resorted to a variety of measures to increase enlistments. Parliament passed recruitment acts permitting the unemployed and those convicted of minor criminal offenses to be impressed for military duty. The government shortened terms of enlistment, provided bonuses, distributed blankets and winter coats, and provided benefits to families of those killed or incapacitated in service to the Crown, lowered the physical standards for recruits, and encouraged wealthy landowners to raise recruits from among their tenants.

Ultimately, King George also used his authority to recruit five regiments of Hanoverians and sent four of them to Minorca and Gibraltar to release the British troops there for service in America. Between September 1775 and September 1776, a total of 11,000 troops were raised to increase the size of the British military. Over the following months, some 7,000 additional recruits were added to the overall strength. Even with these additions, forces were still below the number needed to meet requirements, partly because the size of the prewar military had continued to decline, and desertion had always been a major problem.

The Royal Navy was particularly vulnerable to attrition. In 1776 alone, desertions rose by 13 percent. The death rate of the British seaman during this period was twice that of individuals who were not at sea. While impressments of civilians were unpopular and a potentially dangerous endeavor for the men who forced such service on an unwilling population, it was common practice.

A major obstacle in meeting the needs of an army to fight the American patriots was that the British overestimated the number of LOYALISTS willing to take up arms. Although loyalists were present in every colony and existed in large numbers in colonies such as New York, New Jersey, PHILADELPHIA, and South Carolina, patriots outnumbered loyalists in all colonies, and large numbers of Americans chose to remain neutral. Loyalists never reached the number that the British needed to stem the tide of the war, particularly after the alliance with France.

Overall, some 40 loyalist regiments were formed in America, including the Royal Greens, the Roman Catholic Volunteers, the Black Pioneers, Butler's Rangers, the Queen's Own Loyal Virginia Regiment, the Loyal Foresters, and the Royal Ethiopian Regiment.

The British government was also under the assumption that large numbers of slaves and Native Americans would join their ranks to fight the colonists. Slaves were promised their freedom if they fought for the British, and Native Americans were paid in cash and gifts for their participation in the war. Neither slaves nor Native Americans entered the fray in numbers large enough to satisfy British recruitment requirements.

BRITISH ARMY AND ROYAL NAVY

The upper echelons of the British military were generally members of the upper classes who had been given high-level military appointments, and those who had purchased commissions as colonels or other lower-ranking officers. The rank and file was made up of those who had chosen a military career for adventure or because no other career seemed feasible.

In 1775, neither the British army nor the Royal Navy were at full strength. The navy had decreased

Burgoyne's Strategy

BRITISH MILITARY officer General John Burgoyne was convinced that he could stamp out American resistance in a year's time with "one conclusive blow." Burgoyne bet 50 guineas on accomplishing this feat, equal to four years' pay for a regular soldier in the British army. He devised a strategy of divide and conquer, in which he planned to launch an attack on New York that would isolate New England from the rest of the colonies.

While in Canada in the summer of 1776, Burgoyne sent a diversionary force to the Mohawk Valley to recruit Native American allies. Together, these forces traveled 10 miles a day until they reached Fort Schuyler in New York. The ensuing attack on August 6, 1777, led to a loss of 160 American lives.

Burgoyne started his part of the Hudson Valley Campaign by bringing 11,000 soldiers and 2,000 camp followers into the area. He traveled rapidly, covering 100 miles in three weeks. Advised that the British were on the way, the Americans felled trees and knocked down bridges to delay Burgoyne's passage as he neared Albany. Meanwhile, local militias had reinforced the Continentals to 10 times their previous strength. The ensuing battle lasted only two hours; and when it was over, 200 Hessians were dead and another 700 were taken prisoner. Burgoyne had lost one-tenth of his forces but refused to surrender. At the Battle of Saratoga on October 16, 1777, Burgoyne was forced to surrender his entire army. This battle is considered to have marked the turning point of the Revolutionary War.

by 5,000 men over the previous year. Many ships were not seaworthy. Because many members of the crews had been impressed for service, they were not committed to the British military. A large number of British seamen were ill, either from disease or the harsh conditions of life at sea.

Prime Minister North was hesitant, early in the war, to launch the British fleet against the colonies because he believed such an action might serve to motivate France to join the war on the American side. The British placed their hopes for an early vic-

tory on the army, planning to use the Royal Navy mostly to blockade ports and prevent supplies from getting to the Americans. Once France joined the war, however, the British government began using its impressive fleet to full advantage.

Ostensibly, the British army of 49,646 men was comprised of 39,294 infantrymen, 7,868 cavalrymen, and 2,484 artillerymen. However, when the revolution began, this number was widely scattered, with 16,000 in England and Scotland and 12,000 in Ireland. Others were serving in India, Africa, Minorca, Gibraltar, and the West Indies. Only 8,000 were in America, serving under General Thomas Gage, who informed his superiors that some 20,000 additional troops were needed immediately. Although Prime Minister North believed such a large force was necessary, Parliament set a goal of sending 20,000 additional troops to America by the spring of 1776. Within two years, 12 additional infantry battalions had been formed. In 1779, 14 battalions and four regiments of light dragoons were added.

LEADERSHIP POSITIONS

According to his supporters, George III was well within his right to insist that the American colonies pay the taxes that Parliament had levied against them. They contended that the colonies had a responsibility to pay at least a portion of the cost of maintaining troops in America and for defraying the costs of the French and Indian Wars (1754–63). These supporters suggested that if colonial militias had defended the colonies, Britain would not have had to run up such a huge war debt.

Furthermore, they believed that if colonial legislatures would not raise money for this purpose, Parliament had a right to do so. The American colonists disagreed, claiming that "taxation without repre-

ABOVE *Four Continental Army soldiers stand in an informal group in this illustration depicting uniforms and weapons used during the Revolutionary War.*

sentation" was a violation of their rights as British citizens. Many Britons believed that the rebellion against the Stamp Act of 1663 involved only those elites who had been directly affected by the tax on paper and insisted that the average colonist remained loyal to the Crown.

The British were particularly bitter about the Franco-American alliance. With some justification, the British insisted that without the French fleet, the Americans would not have been able to successfully blockade British entry into the colonies and obstruct essential supply routes. While it is true that the French fleet was an essential element in determining the outcome of the war, the British military continued to underestimate American soldiers.

The issue of American independence became a major factor in British politics. While existing political divisions played a major role in positions taken on the issue, the situation was made more volatile by shifting political alliances. In 1775, the Duke of Grafton withdrew his support from Lord North and resigned his seat in Parliament, insisting that all taxes on the colonies should be repealed. His action launched a campaign of similar resignations, with many of them arising out of the belief that the war was an attack on British citizens rather than a war against a foreign enemy.

Prime Minister North worked closely with George III to promote the war even though he spent much of his time in office fighting with Parliament over his handling of the situation. North was harshly criticized for using large numbers of Highland Scots and Irish Catholics to fight the war in America. After Lord Cornwallis was forced to surrender his entire army to George Washington, the commander in chief of the American forces, at Yorktown, Virginia, in October 1781, the war was virtually over,

and dissatisfaction with North's leadership increased drastically.

On February 27, 1782, Parliament officially withdrew their support for the war. Less than a month later, North stepped down. His resignation paved the way for recognition of American independence, which was formalized at the Treaty of Paris on September 3, 1783. The Marquis of Rockingham had been one of the most vocal critics of the Crown's position, believing that American independence should be granted. When North resigned, George III was forced to appoint Rockingham as the new prime minister because his supporters were in the majority in Parliament. Rockingham immediately acknowledged American independence.

Prominent Britons opposed the War of American Independence for a number of reasons. English philosopher and statesman Edmund Burke insisted that no country could be truly free while keeping residents of another country in bondage, and accused British merchants of supporting the war in order to swell their profit margins. Like many Britons, Burke saw the American Revolution as the beginning of an attrition of political rights for all British citizens. The Earl of Denbigh, on the other hand, argued that the quickest way to put down the rebellion was to try the leaders of the revolution for treason. Many British citizens believed that allowing the American colonies to attain independence would destroy the British Empire and threaten Britain's place as the most powerful nation in the world.

Further Reading: Jeremy Black, *Eighteenth-Century Britain, 1688–1783* (Palgrave, 2001); Stephen Conway, *The British Isles and the War of American Independence* (Oxford University Press, 2000); Christopher Hibbert, *Redcoats and Rebels: The War for America, 1770–81* (Grafton, 1990); Denis Judd, *The British Imperial Experience from 1775 to the Present* (HarperCollins, 1996).

—ELIZABETH PURDY, PH.D.

H

Hamilton, Alexander (1755–1804)

Although he would play an important role in the early years of American government, Alexander Hamilton did not sign the DECLARATION OF INDEPENDENCE. On July 4, 1776, he commanded an artillery post in New York. On July 12, two British ships sailed up the Hudson River to Hamilton's position and opened fire on Manhattan. He returned fire until some of his own men accidentally blew up one of their cannons, killing six Continental soldiers. Hamilton served in the army until the end of the Revolutionary War and was appointed General GEORGE WASHINGTON's aide-de-camp in 1777, where he acquired a great reputation for bravery and writing.

Hamilton was responsible for handling information going to and from Washington, and as such was very much aware of the state of the war. He also saw the troubles the Continental Congress had with handling the war efforts, with their factionalism and emphasis on the states making their own decisions. This fueled his desire for a strong central government and translated into how he viewed the Constitution and the forthcoming Federalist Party.

Regarding independence and the way the British were governing the colonies, he wrote, "Since then, Americans have not by any act of theirs empowered the British Parliament to make laws for them, it follows that they can have no just authority to do it." This made a dispute over taxation into a question of the fundamental rights of man, which was a driving point behind the Declaration of Independence.

ALEXANDER HAMILTON, AT LEFT,
in a painting by John Trumbull. Hamilton was a strong advocate and certainly would have signed the Declaration of Independence had he been a delegate in PHILADELPHIA. *His work as the first secretary of the U.S. Treasury solidified American independence.*

ABOVE *The west face of the First Bank of the United States, formed by Alexander Hamilton, first secretary of the U.S. Treasury.*

Hamilton urged the recruitment of black soldiers, and eventually joined the New York Society for Promoting the Manumission of Slaves. Finance was also linked to independence and winning the revolution, and using the Federalist Papers, of which he wrote 51 of the 85 letters, he urged introducing order to American finances and restoring public credit. He felt a market-driven economy was best, and his economic vision was the alternative to mercantilism, which had resulted in the political tyranny the Declaration of Independence opposed.

Although Hamilton did not actually sign the Declaration of Independence, he was a strong advocate and certainly would have signed it had he been a delegate in PHILADELPHIA. His work as the first secretary of the U.S. Treasury solidified American independence, and the legacy he left behind is still felt today.

Further Reading: Richard Brookhiser, *Alexander Hamilton, American* (Free Press, 1999); Jacob Ernest Cooks, *Alexander Hamilton* (Scribner's, 1982); Stanley Elkins and Eric McKitrick, *The Age of Federalism: The Early American Republic, 1788–1800* (Oxford University Press, 1993); Alexander Hamilton, *Writings* (Library of America, 2001).

—JAMES E. SEELYE, JR.

The Life of a Patriot

LITTLE IS known for certain about Alexander Hamilton's earliest years. He was born on the island of Nevis in the British West Indies, the illegitimate son of Rachel Lavien. His mother had taken up residence with James Hamilton, whose last name Alexander took.

Hamilton had excellent penmanship, mathematical skill, and the capacity to express himself—skills noticed by the merchant firm of Beekman and Cruger, which employed him as a clerk at the age of 13. His employers sent him to Elizabethtown, New Jersey, to begin preparation for a college education. In 1773, he entered King's College in New York, where he remained for approximately two years. After college, he was appointed captain of the Provincial Artillery and fought in the battles of Long Island, Trenton, and White Plains. In 1777, he was appointed General Washington's aide-de-camp. He married Elizabeth Schuyler in 1780. He was a delegate to the Constitutional Convention of 1787. It was there that he wrote his share of the Federalist Papers. Hamilton became the first secretary of the U.S. Treasury, formed the first Bank of the United States, and helped Washington with his famous farewell address. On the morning of July 11, 1804, Hamilton met Aaron Burr at the dueling grounds in Weehawken, New Jersey, where he was mortally wounded.

Hancock, John (1737–93)

John Hancock was the only delegate at the Second Continental Congress (see CONTINENTAL CONGRESS, FIRST AND SECOND) to actually sign the DECLARATION OF INDEPENDENCE ON JULY 4, 1776. Other delegates signed on August 2.

His father died when Hancock was seven. He spent several years with his grandparents before being placed under the guardianship of a wealthy uncle, one of the leading merchants of Boston. This change of circumstance enabled Hancock to receive an excellent education at Boston Latin School and then Harvard. Hancock quickly revealed an aptitude for business, and his uncle sent him to England to observe that end of the business. He attended the funeral of King George II and the coronation of GEORGE III. Although George III appears to have granted the young colonial an audience, it did nothing to instill any great sense of loyalty to the Crown.

Far more important in Hancock's mind than any allegiance to the monarch was loyalty to the business class of Boston. This loyalty was cemented when he became his uncle's partner in 1763 and subsequently inherited the business. When the Stamp Act of 1765 was seen as a threat to the businessmen of Boston, Hancock quickly emerged as their leader and began a long career as a legislator.

He did not consider himself a patriot until he was arrested by customs agents and charged with smuggling. The seizure of one of his ships destroyed any residual sense of loyalty to the Crown, and when the resulting riots sent the customs agents fleeing to an island in the harbor, Hancock emerged from prison determined that the authority of the king's agents over the colonies must be reined in.

His rise to leadership of the Massachusetts patriots was furthered by the Adams cousins, John and Samuel (see JOHN ADAMS; SAMUEL ADAMS), who quickly saw the benefits of having such a wealthy businessman among their number.

During his presidency of the Continental Congress (see CONTINENTAL CONGRESS, FIRST AND SECOND), his ego alienated more than a few members, particularly when he proved blind to his own limitations. He fancied himself more suitable to command the Continental forces than GEORGE WASHINGTON, a seasoned military commander. As the president of the Continental Congress, Hancock was the first to affix his signature to the Declaration of Independence. He made a particular point of affixing his signature in large letters so that King George would have no difficulty whatsoever in knowing that he was a traitor.

Hancock stepped down as president of the Continental Congress, but continued to serve as a member of the Massachusetts delegation until 1780. He then served for many years as the first governor of the state of Massachusetts, with a brief interim between his two terms, during which he served in Congress. Although he took no part in the Constitutional Convention, he presided over the Massachusetts convention to ratify the Constitution, which he favored. In 1793, he died suddenly at the age of 56, still governor of Massachusetts.

Further Reading: Barbara A. Somervill, *John Hancock: Signer for Independence* (Capstone Press, 2005); Harlow Giles Unger, *John Hancock: Merchant King and American Patriot* (John Wiley, 2000); John Tebel, *Turning the World Upside Down: Inside the American Revolution* (Orion, 1993).

—LEIGH KIMMEL

The Sugar Smuggler

ONE OF the key factors propelling John Hancock to the forefront of the patriots' leadership was his arrest by royal tax collectors for sugar smuggling. Although a spirited and skilled defense by John Adams got him acquitted of the charges, the truth is far more complicated.

The official economic policy of Britain was mercantilism, a system in which the colonies were supposed to support the treasury of the mother country in two ways: first by providing raw materials at low prices, and second by purchasing finished goods from manufacturers in the mother country. Particularly after the economic strains created by the Seven Years' War (called the French and Indian Wars by the colonists), the British treasury was in perilous shape. As a result, King George III decided that it was time for the colonies to pay a greater proportion of the cost of their defense through taxes payable to the royal government.

While the principle might have been sound, George III could hardly have done worse if he had deliberately set about to do everything possible to alienate the colonists. Over the years, the colonists had become accustomed to seeing to many of their own needs through the acts of their own colonial legislatures and did not appreciate having royal agents horning in. The famous rallying cry "No Taxation without Representation" did not in fact refer to a lack of representation in Parliament. Rather, it represented a desire to keep the power of taxation in the hands of colonial legislatures, elected by the colonists.

AT RIGHT *A portrait of John Hancock, painted by John S. Copley. Hancock was the only delegate to sign the Declaration of Independence on July 4, 1776. Others signed on August 2.*

Furthermore, the colonial merchants had long enjoyed a relative freedom to trade as they wished. Now the king ordered that the mercantilist policies be strictly enforced. Suddenly the common practice by which Boston merchants bought sugar from the West Indies became the subject of harsh enforcement. Thus it can be said that Hancock was indeed a smuggler, in a technical sense of the word. But after such long neglect of the law, followed by sudden harsh enforcement, public opinion regarded him as the victim of arbitrary royal whim.

Henry, Patrick
(1736–99)

Patrick Henry is best remembered for his famous "Give me liberty or give me death" speech in the Virginia House of Burgesses, which is often credited with helping to ignite the fires of revolutionary sentiment. Though perhaps as influential as other leading revolutionaries, Henry played little or no role in the signing of the DECLARATION OF INDEPENDENCE.

He was raised on his family's plantation, and grew up surrounded by slaves and slavery. After a spotty education and several business failures, including the loss of a plantation received as part of his wife's dowry, he began to study law. In that rough-and-ready time, it was not necessary to obtain a law degree in order to sit for the bar examination, and although the examiners hesitated to certify a self-taught lawyer, they could not fault his knowledge of the law.

Henry soon built up a reputation as a skillful lawyer. He defended the colonists' rights against the growing encroachments of the Crown, and pressed for religious tolerance in a time when the Church of England was still the official church of Virginia and dissenters faced civil liabilities. In 1765 he was elected to the House of Burgesses, where he soon established a firm reputation for eloquence. He led the drafting of resolutions against the Stamp Act and saw to their publication in local newspapers, along with a warning that GEORGE III should look to the examples of Julius Caesar and Charles I. Accused of treason on the basis of this oblique statement, Henry answered that if it were indeed treason, his opponents should make the most of it.

Henry emerged as the leader of the radical faction and was soon regarded as more powerful than even the colonial governor. Henry called for a Virginia Convention and a Continental Congress. At the Virginia Convention he was named a delegate to the First Continental Congress (see CONTINENTAL CONGRESS, FIRST AND SECOND).

Even before the colonies as a whole declared their independence and formed the United States, Henry led Virginia in declaring its own independence on May 15, 1776. He was immediately elected Virginia's first governor, his new responsibilities precluding any possibility of his going to PHILADELPHIA and participating in the momentous events there.

Throughout the war, he did his best to keep Virginia active in the patriotic effort and was often dismayed when his fellow Virginians engaged in profiteering and speculation. More than once he compared them to the Israelites longing for the comforts of Egypt when they encountered privations in the wilderness.

After the Revolution he tried to retire from politics, until drawn back into it by the Constitutional Convention. He opposed the new Constitution, considering it to give too much power to the federal government, and was one of the leaders in the creation of the Bill of Rights.

Although there was some pressure for him to run as a candidate for president, he did not want to challenge George Washington. He did run for a seat in the Virginia legislature, but died of stomach cancer before he could take the oath of office.

Further Reading: Henry Mayer, *A Son of Thunder: Patrick Henry and the American Republic* (Grove/Atlantic 2001); John Tebel, *Turning the World Upside Down: Inside the American Revolution* (Orion, 1993).

—LEIGH KIMMEL

Hessians

One of the most fiercely hated troops that the British arrayed against the patriots were the Hessian mercenaries. Most of the Hessian mercenaries were little more than cannon fodder, warm bodies to fill the ranks and files of the formal squares of musketeers that were the common formation in the set-piece warfare of the 18th century.

They were loaned out to the British Crown by the rulers of their various German principalities in order to pay debts left over from the Seven Years' War. Had their various German principalities become embroiled in a war, they almost certainly would have been recalled to serve at home.

The largest number of Hessians were musketeers. There were also small numbers of elite troops known as Jaegers, literally "hunters." These were sharpshooters using rifled firearms somewhat shorter than the Brown Bess favored by the patriots, who were generally recruited from the families of gamekeepers and other trades in which marksmanship was at a premium. Many of the Jaegers were used in capacities similar to a modern sniper, to pick off selected leaders in a battle in order to destroy command cohesion.

The Hessians were generally regarded as barbaric in their conduct, and especially prone to atrocities. Stories of outrages committed by Hessian troops were circulated widely by patriot leaders even before the signing of the DECLARATION OF INDEPENDENCE, as a way of drumming up support for the patriot cause.

Many fence-sitters came to regard the importation of large numbers of German forces as a final cause to sever ties with the mother country, and the Declaration of Independence included a clause

Revolutionary Pedigree — Or Maybe Not

MANY WOMEN with ambitions to join the Daughters of the American Revolution have traced their genealogy back to the correct era and thought they had success in hand. However, on closer examination, efforts to identify the ancestor's unit prove difficult. More research reveals a most disquieting fact—the ancestor was not a patriot at all, but one of the German-speaking soldiers who fought on the British side.

The Hessian mercenaries were supposed to return to their German principalities after the British were finished with them. However, large numbers of them remained behind in the new United States to found families.

Once the patriots realized the lure of their country to these foreign soldiers, the foresighted among them encouraged such defections. Hessian soldiers who deserted their units were offered free land and protection from capture and prosecution. As a result, a significant number of Americans whose families go back to the Revolutionary era have at least one Hessian deserter among their ancestors.

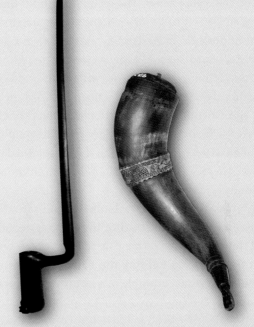

ABOVE LEFT *A French bayonet;* **ABOVE RIGHT** *a decorated powder horn.* **BELOW LEFT** *Surrender of the Hessian troops to General Washington after the Battle of Trenton; lithograph by Henry Hoff, 1850.* **BELOW RIGHT** *A Hessian officer's boot.*

specifically referring to the importation of foreign mercenaries, understood to be the German, or Hessian forces.

At the same time, the patriots might have been surprised to know that there was a significant opposition in Parliament to the use of German forces to suppress the American rebellion. Although many Members of Parliament opposed it primarily on grounds of the financial wisdom of the agreements, particularly the notorious "blood clause," which provided for money to be paid in compensation for each German soldier maimed or killed, there was significant opposition on moral grounds.

Many Members of Parliament still saw the American colonists as part of the English people, and thus the use of German auxiliaries, which was permissible when fighting the hated French, became utterly unacceptable. Many also held a low opinion of the German discipline and professionalism and anticipated massive atrocities of every imaginable sort.

One of the most famous missions of the Revolution, General GEORGE WASHINGTON's crossing of the Delaware River, was aimed against Hessian mercenaries. A large number of Hessians were encamped in Trenton, New Jersey, and were celebrating Christmas with traditional German observances, including Christmas trees, which were at that time unknown to English-speaking American settlers.

Although it is not true that the Hessians were all drunk, they were certainly relaxed enough that tactical surprise was achieved on the night of December 25, 1776, and Washington's forces were able to capture a large number of them. The British commanders subsequently relieved one Hessian officer of command and court-martialed a number of others. This defeat, along with the defeat at Redbank the following year, permanently demolished any and all myths of Hessian invincibility. The British would ultimately use them as a sort of scapegoat for their own failures, while the Americans reduced them to objects of ridicule.

Further Reading: Robert G. Ferris and Richard E. Morris, *The Signers of the Declaration of Independence* (Interpretive Publications, 1982); Edward Jackson Lowell, *The Hessians and the Other German Auxiliaries of Great Britain in the Revolutionary War* (Corner House, 1970).

—LEIGH KIMMEL

Howe, Richard (1725–99)

Lord Richard Howe led a failed British effort to avert war with the American colonies. In addition to serving in the British navy with distinction, Howe represented Dartmouth in Parliament.

The maneuverings that led to the appointment of a peace commission early in 1776 began late in 1774 with the death of the lieutenant general of the marines, Sir Charles Saunders. Prior to the death of Saunders, Prime Minister Frederick North promised the commissioner position to Howe. An uncomfortable situation arose when North, failing to remember the earlier conversation, agreed to the appointment of Admiral Hugh Palliser. North was placed in the position of finding a suitable command for Howe or deal with the political consequences resulting from the potential resignation of the Howe brothers from their respective military positions. Howe, believing that a negotiated settlement with the American colonies was both preferable and possible, offered to act as a mediator in December 1774.

George III formally proposed the creation of a peace commission in the October 1775 opening of Parliament. The peace commission, composed of Howe and two major-generals—William Howe and Henry Clinton—left for the colonies in May 1776. In addition to the peace commission, each man was given a military command. Lord Howe viewed the military commands as supportive to his role as peace commissioner. The British government viewed the commission as a political necessity that was unlikely to produce a positive result. Colonial secretary Lord George Germain had the terms constructed in such a way that the commission had no ability to negotiate; no pardons were to be granted until after the surrender of the rebellion, and Howe's naval orders called for him to blockade the Atlantic coast and to assist the army in putting down the rebellion.

The peace commission effectively came to an end with the DECLARATION OF INDEPENDENCE on July 4, 1776. The commission was ordered not to accept the declaration and the Continental Congress (see CONTINENTAL CONGRESS, FIRST AND SECOND) refused to withdraw the declaration. Howe made overtures to GEORGE WASHINGTON, the Continental Congress, and the American people urging them to renounce the rebellion and receive a pardon. In the end, the inability to offer terms attractive enough to permit serious negotiations doomed the commission from the start, and Howe concluded by late July 1776 that only a military solution would end the rebellion.

Further Reading: George A. Billias, *George Washington's Opponents* (William Morrow, 1969); Ira D. Gruber, *The Howe Brothers and the American Revolution* (Atheneum, 1972); Christopher Hibbert, *Redcoats and Rebels: The American Revolution through British Eyes* (W.W. Norton, 1990).

—ABBE ALLEN DEBOLT

Howe Siblings

LORD RICHARD Howe's preference for reconciliation between Great Britain and its American colonies can largely be explained by the connection between the Howe family and the American colonies on both a professional and personal level. Howe's older brother, George Augustus Howe (1724–58), third Viscount Howe, served as the commander of the 55th Infantry as a brigadier general during the French and Indian Wars. Viscount Howe was killed in action near Fort Ticonderoga on July 5, 1758. In recognition of his service, the colony of Massachusetts appropriated 250 pounds for the construction of a monument in Westminster Abbey. This personal connection to the colonies caused some in the British government to question whether the Howe brothers should receive military commands during the rebellion. In addition, Lord Howe's sister Caroline was a frequent chess opponent of BENJAMIN FRANKLIN while he was in London. Caroline introduced her brother to Franklin; Howe used the opportunity to put forth his own ideas concerning a peace commission to Franklin. Howe also encouraged Franklin to author a second peace plan to the British government. Both plans centered on American control of domestic issues and were soundly rejected.

I

Independence Hall

On May 10, 1775, the Second Continental Congress (see CONTI-NENTAL CONGRESS, FIRST AND SECOND) convened in PHILA-DELPHIA to discuss measures for dealing with the escalating situation with Britain. One of the first orders of business was to raise an army. GEORGE WASHINGTON was named commander in chief of the Continental Army on June 15.

When the meeting began, many delegates continued to believe that reconciliation with the mother country could still be achieved; however, a number of delegates had come to the conclusion that independence was the only way in which the colonies could maintain basic political rights. In the building that came to be known as Independence Hall, on July 4, 1776, delegates approved the DECLARATION OF INDE-PENDENCE without dissension.

Independence Hall was originally erected to house Pennsylvania's colonial legislature. After citizens enraged over the volatile issue of paper money had smashed the windows of their meeting place, legislators responded by building the State House in downtown Philadelphia.

The building was designed by lawyer Andrew Hamilton, and construction commenced under the watchful eye of master carpenter Edmund Wooley. The legislature moved into the State House in 1736, although the building was not fully completed for two decades.

INDEPENDENCE HALL AT LEFT

Originally built as the Pennsylvania State House, contruction on Independence Hall began in 1732. The building was completed in 1735, and was the most ambitious public building in the colonies at the time. Here the Declaration of Independence was adopted, and the Constitution debated, drafted, and signed. The basement once served as the city dog pound.

Liberty Bell

THE FAMOUS Liberty Bell, which weighs 2,080 pounds, was originally located in the south tower of the State House. The bell bears the inscription: "Proclaim liberty throughout all the land unto all the inhabitants thereof" from Leviticus 25:10. The bell was ordered from England in 1751 to mark the 50th anniversary of founder William Penn's Charter of Passage of 1701. When the bell was being tested, it cracked and was twice recast by skilled workers. The bell was moved in 1777 to protect it during the British invasion. On July 4, the bell rang out the news that Congress had approved the vote for independence.

In 1783, after the Treaty of Peace was ratified, the Liberty Bell informed Philadelphians that the long seven years of war had ended. Legend has it that the bell chimed for the last time in 1835 when it cracked while memorializing the death of the noted Supreme Court justice John Marshall. In 2003, the Liberty Bell was moved to the Liberty Bell Center on Market Street located to the west of Independence Hall.

In 1774, the First Continental Congress chose to meet in the newly erected Carpenter's Hall a block away. However, because the Georgian-style, two-and-one-half-story brick State House was protected by a gate, the Second Continental Congress considered it less accessible to the public. Well aware that they could be arrested as traitors, Congress was adamant about preserving privacy.

Congress fled to York, Pennsylvania, in June 1777 when the British occupied Philadelphia. They remained in York until the British evacuated Philadelphia in June 1778. During the occupation, the British used Independence Hall both as a barracks for soldiers and as a hospital for American prisoners. Congress continued to meet in Philadelphia until 1783, when the capital of the United States was moved to New York. In 1787, a convention was held in Independence Hall that led to the creation of the United States Constitution. On September 17, 1787, the delegates signed that document in the same building in which the Declaration had been signed 11 years before. In 1789, the Bill of Rights was also approved in Independence Hall because Philadelphia was again serving as the capital of the United States.

Beginning in the late 1780s, the area around Independence Hall, known as Independence Square, began to expand. In 1787, the County Court House was built on the western side of the square. Three years later, the American Philosophical Society Hall was erected in an area southeast of Independence Hall. In 1791, City Hall was built on the eastern side of the historic building.

When the national government returned to Philadelphia in 1790, congressional meetings took place in the County Court House, which subsequently became known as Congress Hall. In 1793, George Washington's second inauguration took place in Independence Hall, followed by the inauguration of JOHN ADAMS in 1799.

Independence Hall has been restored to approximate its original state, but the only original furniture is the "Rising Sun" chair and the silver inkstand with the quill that was used to sign the Declaration of Independence. (See also INDEPENDENCE NATIONAL HISTORIC PARK.)

Further Reading: Robert G. Ferris, National Park Service, "Signers of the Declaration: Historic Places Commemorating the Signing of the Declaration of Independence," www.nps.gov/inde/ (cited March 2006); Independence Visitor Center, www.independencevisitorcenter .com (cited January 2006); Liberty Bell Virtual Museum, www. liberty bellmuseum.com (cited March 2006); National Constitution Center, www.constitutioncenter.org (cited January 2006).

—ELIZABETH PURDY, PH.D.

Independence National Historic Park

ANY MODERN-DAY patriot looking to soak up Revolutionary-era sites should visit Independence National Historic Park. Located in downtown PHILADELPHIA, the park includes approximately 20 buildings spanning 45 acres.

At the Liberty Bell Center, visitors can see the bell encased in glass, a video presentation, and exhibits about the bell as an icon of freedom. INDEPENDENCE HALL, the meeting place of the Second Continental Congress (see CONTINENTAL CONGRESS, FIRST AND SECOND), requires a free ticket for entrance. Carpenter's Hall served as the meeting place of the First Continental Congress, and later in the war was a hospital and an arsenal for the Continental Army. The DECLARATION HOUSE (JACOB GRAFF HOUSE) was where THOMAS JEFFERSON drafted the DECLARATION OF INDEPENDENCE in June 1776. Congress Hall was built to serve as the meeting place of the U.S. Congress from 1790 to 1800. The Second Bank of the United States was a powerful financial institution from 1816 to 1832, and it now exhibits paintings of colonial and federal leaders, military officers, explorers, and scientists.

—AMY L. SOPCAK

J

Jefferson, Thomas (1743–1826)

According to Thomas Jefferson's Account Book, it was 68 degrees Fahrenheit at 6 A.M. on July 4, 1776. Jefferson recorded this temperature using a newfangled thermometer. As a scientist or natural philosopher he was concerned with observing the details of nature as exactly as possible. Jefferson took serious care in making records of weather and temperature throughout the day and days afterward. Although it may seem a trifling matter to modern readers, this simple observation and Jefferson's obsession with the weather was perhaps not that much out of step with the historical events that were to happen later in the day.

Jefferson lived in an age when the greatest minds believed that observing nature and natural processes was the best way to understand the truth of humanity. An Enlightenment statesman, Jefferson believed in natural law and humanity's ability to understand "Nature's God." It was this inherent ability that explained humanity's right to declare independence from arbitrary power. If there are natural, inherent rights for man to be free, then there was no divine right for tyrannical kings. Thus, the difference between this seemingly mundane temperature observation at 6 A.M. and Jefferson's eloquent demand for the "separate and equal station to which the Laws of Nature and Nature's God entitle…" is not perhaps so great. This was a universal demand for the equality bestowed by nature, the beating heart of the Declaration of Independence, the justification that circulates throughout the entire document, giving it life and power. It was no mistake that the "Laws of Nature" was capitalized in Jefferson's Declaration and that God was not simply God. He was "Nature's God."

Yet even as Jefferson the thinker and the writer could see the world in clear, universal, and natural terms, Jefferson the man was full of all too human contradictions, evident even on July 4, 1776. For many modern historians the most glaring contradiction in Jefferson's life was the fact that he owned slaves even as he advocated for freedom.

In Jefferson's submitted draft of the DECLARATION OF INDEPENDENCE he described how the king "has waged cruel war against human nature itself, violating its most sacred rights of life and liberty in the persons of a distant people who never offended him, captivating and carrying them into slavery. ... Determined to keep open a market where *Men* should be bought and sold." Was Jefferson aware of the contradiction? It is impossible to really know the answer; however, it does say something about the man, and his desire to transcend contradictions to defend universal ideals. It also perhaps says something about the struggle and contradiction between realities and ideals that later defined the history of the country he would help to create.

A genius of the pen but not a man of rhetorical skill, Jefferson sat anxiously and refrained from speaking even as the Congress cut out a third of his original Declaration over the course of July 1 to 3. When he did speak, he did so softly and without the confidence or clarity of his writing. This would be yet another personal contradiction for a man more comfortable with the finality of words and thoughts on paper than with the potential flaws of words spoken and acted. Jefferson was especially anxious about losing the section on the slave trade when the Congress edited his draft, which was reported

to the house on June 28. He had already made some minor changes in the DRAFTING COMMITTEE with BENJAMIN FRANKLIN, JOHN ADAMS, ROGER SHERMAN, and Robert Livingston, but he was most anxious about what the Congress would delete.

Jefferson wrote in his autobiography how "the clause reprobating the enslaving of the inhabitants of Africa, was struck out in complaisance to South Carolina and Georgia, who had never attempted to restrain the importation of slaves. ..." Even the "northern brethren felt tender under those censures; for tho' their people have very few slaves themselves yet they had been pretty considerable carriers of them to others." Thus, Thomas Jefferson, a beneficiary of the slave trade, was also radically against it, even by northern standards. He was also concerned, however, that the Congress was being too lenient on the British. The section of his draft that refers to the wrongs of the British people, not merely the king, was excised from the document. With strong and biting language Jefferson said the British people, not merely the king, "have given the last stab to agonizing affection." Those, like John Dickinson, with the "pusillanimous idea that we had friends in England worth keeping," convinced the Congress to delete this section of the Declaration and focus on the wrongs of King GEORGE III.

While Jefferson sat silently and agonized over the editing of his masterwork, Franklin told him that "I have made it a rule to avoid becoming the draftsman of papers to be reviewed by a public body."

On July 4, 1776, Thomas Jefferson and his servant Bob were staying at the house of a newlywed bricklayer named Graff, on the corner of 7th and Market Streets. He rented the second floor of the Graff house for 35 shillings a week. The room was already furnished except for the legendary writing desk on which he wrote the Declaration of Independence

Declaration Deletions

TWO DELETED sections from Thomas Jefferson's original version of the Declaration of Independence included one passage in which the original accused the king of first, supporting the slave trade, and then, second, encouraging those very slaves to rise in rebellion and join with the loyalists. The original language pointed out that by this call to arms, the king was asking slaves "to purchase that liberty of which he has deprived them, by murdering" their owners and others. Thus, in the original language, the king was "paying off former crimes committed against the liberties of one people, with crimes which he urges them to commit against the lives of another. ..." Since this whole passage raised the difficult question of whether or not slavery itself was legitimate, it was deleted from the original version of the Declaration because it tended to offend the sensibilities of slaveholders.

The fact that Jefferson, a slaveholder himself, had suggested stronger language against the institution of slavery in the original declaration than the language accepted in the final, has been a subject of great interest to Jefferson biographers. Some have concluded that Jefferson was quite ambivalent about slavery, believing that it contradicted American principles of freedom, liberty, and equality, but that he had no clear view of what should be done about it.

Another deleted and altered passage strengthened the language that Jefferson had used in the original when accusing the British parliament and "our British brethren" of betraying the affection that bound the colonies to Britain. Although the changes were slight in this passage, they apparently derived from the fact that Congress was less willing to place most of the blame for the grievances of the colonies on the king than was Jefferson, and that many members of Congress believed that Parliament and the British public should more clearly share the blame for sending mercenaries, and for other offenses against the colonies. Thus the British people, the final version pointed out, would be regarded like "the rest of mankind, enemies in war, in peace friends."

Study of these altered passages has suggested some of the issues that divided the patriot camp. Slavery was clearly an issue that divided the colonists, with some clearly opposed to it, while others, like Jefferson, were willing to admit that it was wrong, but not quite willing to abandon it. Others would rather simply avoid the issue and postpone any decisions regarding slavery. Similarly, colonists were divided over whether they conducted their Revolution against Britain as British subjects distressed over abuses of the monarch, or whether they were truly an independent people, conducting a war against not just against the monarchy, but against the British government more generally and against the British people. That ambivalence, like the ambivalence over slavery, would remain part of the American cultural and political landscape for decades.

ABOVE *A side view of the Graff House, where Thomas Jefferson wrote the first draft of the Declaration of Independence.*

(see DECLARATION HOUSE [JACOB GRAFF HOUSE]). Decades later in 1825 Jefferson was aware of the potential value of this desk when he gave it to a granddaughter who had lost her possessions at sea and who was to marry Joseph Coolidge. This message was attached to the desk:

"Thomas Jefferson gives this writing desk to Joseph Coolidge, Jr. as a memorial of affection. It was from a drawing of his own by Ben Randolph, cabinetmaker of Philadelphia, with whom he first lodged on his arrival in that city, in May 1776, and is the identical one on which he wrote the Declaration of Independence. Politics, as well as religion, has its superstitions. These gaining strength with time may one day give imaginary value to this relic, for its association with the birth of the Great Charter of our Independence."

Although it was written almost entirely by Thomas Jefferson, the Declaration soon became the proud property of a people, a nation. In modern times, and in places as far away as Tiananmen Square where the Declaration was repeatedly quoted, it has been transformed into an inspiration for human struggles for freedom.

Jefferson's Library

THOMAS JEFFERSON's appetite for learning was rarely satiated and his pursuit of higher levels of self-enlightenment seemed endless. Books allowed the sage of Monticello to study the latest theories in mathematics, philosophy, physics, botany, and zoology, among other disciplines. By the time America declared independence from its sovereign, and as a result of his trips to Europe, Jefferson had more books for his personal library than any other American collector in his day. When the British burned the nation's capitol in 1814, the newly established Library of Congress, with roughly 3,000 books, was lost in the flames. Upon hearing the news, Jefferson sold his personal library, doubling the size of the original library, to Congress for $23,950. He catalogued each book and arranged them by subject. Unfortunately, a majority of the library was destroyed in a second fire in 1851.

ABOVE *The library at Monticello, Thomas Jefferson's home. In 1814, Jefferson sold his private collection of books to the government to form the nucleus of the Library of Congress.*

Further Reading: Joseph Ellis, *American Sphinx: The Character of Thomas Jefferson* (Knopf, 1997); Joseph Ellis, ed., *What Did the Declaration Declare?* (Bedford/St. Martin's 1999); Thomas Jefferson, *Autobiography* (Literary Classics of the United States, 1984); Pauline Maier, *American Scripture: Making the Declaration of Independence* (Knopf, 1997); Garry Wills, *Inventing America: Jefferson's Declaration of Independence* (Doubleday, 1978).

—ALLEN FROMHERZ

Jefferson's Sources

A detailed analysis of the DECLARATION OF INDEPENDENCE reveals the extensive intellectual influences of its author. Thomas Jefferson voraciously read, copiously annotated, and at times regularly socialized with leading European and American thinkers of his day. Jefferson's sources for the Declaration came from a virtual "who's who" of the Enlightenment. Historian Christopher Hitchens has labeled America's third president as the "author" of the United States. If such a label is accurate, then we need to acknowledge the many "editors" who contributed to Jefferson's *magnum opus.*

In 1760, at the age of 16, Jefferson enrolled in the College of William and Mary in Williamsburg, Virginia. The first professor to whet the young student's mind was William Small, the only faculty member of the college who was not an Anglican clergyman. Jefferson was attracted to Small's ability to synthesize mathematics with moral and natural philosophy, combining, in essence, both head and heart. As the two immersed themselves in the works of Euclid and Isaac Newton, they developed a friendship that would last for years.

Small introduced Jefferson to George Wythe, the first to become professor of law at William and Mary

Enlightenment Theory of the State

SIXTEENTH- AND 17th-century thinkers, mainly in Britain and France, argued against the traditional assumption that society was ordered according to a static hierarchy in which individuals were permanently situated in a particular rank or caste, and that those at the top ruled those at the bottom by divine right. Enlightenment intellectuals such as Thomas Hobbes, John Locke, and Jean-Jacques Rousseau believed that nature provided each individual common or universal civil rights that could not be usurped by any individual or institution. They popularized, in particular, a political theory known as the social contract. Accordingly, each individual in a distinct community agreed on standards that regulated the actions of the state and its people. In other words, they contracted or made a covenant with the governing authorities that delineated how society should function. The philosophy that government was formed by the consent of the governed became a galvanizing motto for patriots in the American Revolution.

in 1779. Born in Elizabeth County, Virginia, in 1726, Wythe was a self-made enlightened citizen. During his academic years, Wythe dropped out of college because of his inability to pay the tuition. Despite the fact that he never received a formal degree, Wythe studied law and was admitted to the bar in Spottsylvania County in the late 1740s. A little less than 20 years later, after securing a career in politics and law, Wythe was elected to the board of William and Mary. A former alderman who became mayor of Williamsburg, Wythe was not only an important member of the Virginia House of Burgesses and the Continental Congress (see CONTINENTAL CONGRESS, FIRST AND SECOND), but also an architect of the U.S. Constitution. This juridical sage tutored Jefferson in the minutiae of legal discourse and, along with Small, became one of Jefferson's best friends. As a result of his interaction with Wythe, Jefferson became a member of the Virginia bar in 1767. Wythe enthusiastically signed the Declaration of Independence, the first among Old Dominion's political elites.

It was through Wythe that Jefferson met Virginia's lieutenant governor, Francis Fauquier. Fauquier, a student of economics, physics, and religion, became governor in 1758. He discussed with Jefferson contemporary politics, both foreign and domestic.

The regular interaction with Small, Wythe, and Fauquier and the experience at William and Mary ushered Jefferson into the modern age. A variety of revolutionary thinkers underwrote Jefferson's own revolutionary experiment. From Francis Bacon and Newton, Jefferson learned to apply the tools of the inductive method, rejecting classical Aristotelian categories for experiential examination of nature's patterns in order to formulate general concepts.

In the realm of politics and civil government, Jefferson was indebted to Francis Hutcheson, the "Father of the Scottish Enlightenment" and John Locke, famed author of *Two Treatises on Civil Government.* Hutcheson was a pioneer in formulating the notion of the "moral sense," an internal appetite whereby an individual recognizes the morality of action and is compelled to act accordingly. Locke opened up discussions about the spheres of sovereignty between the government and the governed.

As Hutcheson argued, humanity retained an inner sense of true morality. Nature cultivated such inner morality, and freedom was necessary to plumb the depths of this moral sense. Freedom meant to live and thrive in nature and by nature's God. This was the key to national peace. Jefferson's religious crusade was to fight those who would suppress humanity's duty to live in accordance with nature and, therefore, to be free. Political despots and ecclesiastical tyrants, especially those who reinforced their status by appealing to their extraordinary connection to the divine, were the focus of Jefferson's invectives. In a letter written to BENJAMIN RUSH in 1800, Jefferson wrote, "I have sworn on the altar of God, eternal hostility against every form of tyranny over the mind of man." This religious confession guided Jefferson's pen in 1776.

Further Reading: Joyce Appleby, *Thomas Jefferson* (Times Books, 2003); Joseph Ellis, *American Sphinx: The Character of Thomas Jefferson* (Albert A. Knopf, 1997); Edwin Gaustad, *Sworn on the Altar of God: A Religious Biography of Thomas Jefferson* (Eerdmans Publications, 1996); Christopher Hitchens, *Thomas Jefferson: Author of America* (HarperCollins Publishers, 2005).

— **RYAN MCILHENNY**

Jones, John Paul (1747–92)

The man who would become the greatest early hero in the history of the U.S. Navy was the fourth of seven children born to the family of John Paul, a Scottish estate gardener. At the age of 13 he signed on as a seaman's apprentice with a ship bound for Virginia and the Caribbean. Four years later he secured a berth as third mate on a slave trader. Jones eventually rose to the rank of first mate on a ship plying the notorious middle passage from Africa to the Americas, but left it to become a captain of an ordinary trading vessel. He was 21 at the time he assumed his first command.

The young captain accumulated a small fortune, which enabled him to adopt the dress and manners of a gentleman. When the First Continental Congress (see CONTINENTAL CONGRESS, FIRST AND SECOND) authorized an American navy in 1775, John Paul, calling himself John Paul Jones, applied for and received a commission. Over the next several months he served on board the *Alfred*, a merchantman converted into a warship, and later obtained command of the *Providence*, a nimble, lightly armed sloop. His mission was to escort cargo vessels safely along the Atlantic coast, and on July 4, 1776, he was very likely at sea, shepherding a convoy to either New York, Boston, Newport, Rhode Island, or PHILADELPHIA.

Although Jones made considerable profit from the seizure and sale of enemy ships, he maintained always that it was a lust for glory that stoked his aggressiveness. By 1779 his skills and aggressive nature earned him the command of the 40-gun *Bonhomme Richard*, the ship on which he would earn lasting fame, gaining the most impressive American naval victory of the Revolution, with his capture of the British 44-gun HMS *Serapis*.

Jones first sighted the HMS *Serapis* near Flamborough Head off the Yorkshire coast on September 23, 1779. No American warship had yet defeated a large-size British man-of-war, and the *Bonhomme Richard*'s captain was determined to be the first to do so. The two ships both unleashed tremendous broadsides from their heaviest guns. In due course the British struck their colors, and Jones had his victory.

Jones was lionized in France and America for his triumph, but the heroic aura quickly dimmed. When the Revolutionary War ended in 1783, his

How John Paul Became John Paul Jones

IN 1773, Captain John Paul sailed from London with a cargo of butter and wine. When he arrived in Tobago late in the year, the butter had turned rancid and was unsaleable, which meant he could not obtain enough cash to provide advances on the wages he owed his men. At least one member of the crew, described by the captain as a "prodigious brute of thrice my strength," took matters into his own hands. Wielding a belaying pin, he advanced on his commander, who then drew a sword and ran him through. Fearing he would receive no justice if tried locally for murder, the captain fled Tobago. As a fugitive from justice, he first called himself John Jones to escape detection, and by the time he arrived safely in Virginia, he was using the name under which he would become famous, John Paul Jones.

ABOVE LEFT *An engraving of John Paul Jones by J. B. Fosseyeus, 1781.* **ABOVE RIGHT** *John Paul Jones capturing the HMS Serapis, from a painting by Alonzo Chappel.*

fortunes took a downward turn. He then went to Paris, where he secured only a small portion of the money he thought was owed to him and his men for the capture of the HMS *Serapis*. In 1788, he obtained an appointment as an admiral in the Russian navy, but eventually returned to Paris and died July 18, 1792.

Further Reading: William Gilkerson, *The Ships of John Paul Jones* (Naval Institute Press, 1987); Nathan Miller, *Broadsides: The Age of Fighting Sail, 1775–1815* (Wiley, 2000); Evan Thomas, *John Paul Jones: Sailor, Hero, Father of the American Navy* (Simon and Schuster, 2003).

—B. R. BURG, PH.D.

July 2 Vote

On June 7, 1776, RICHARD HENRY LEE of Virginia introduced a resolution in the Second Continental Congress (see CONTINENTAL CONGRESS, FIRST AND SECOND) with the intention of declaring the 13 American colonies free of Great Britain and initiating the formation of a confederation to serve as a national government for the new states. Conservatives, who were worried that having a state outside New England introduce the resolution on independence would give the argument more weight, attempted to table the issue. To prevent this, radicals managed to postpone debate by appointing the Committee of Five to draft a statement of independence explaining why the colonies found the move necessary. Thomas Jefferson agreed to write the statement, which became known as the DECLARATION OF INDEPENDENCE.

The committee presented the Declaration to Congress on June 28. A tally of potential votes on July 1 indicated that New Hampshire, Connecticut, Massachusetts, Rhode Island, New Jersey, Maryland, Virginia, North Carolina, and Georgia favored independence. All of the members of Congress understood the importance of presenting a united front

The Events of July 2, 1776

INFORMATION ON the events of July 2 come from a variety of sources. The congressional journal entry for July 2, 1776, states that Congress, acting as a committee of the whole, adopted the resolution on independence. Thomas Jefferson's notes refer to South Carolina's decision to join the vote for independence in order to ensure unanimity and mention that Caesar Rodney's arrival in PHILADELPHIA swung Delaware's vote in favor of independence. Jefferson was mistaken in his assumption that Pennsylvania's vote had changed because of a new delegation in Congress. New delegates were not elected until July 20.

In a letter to his wife, Abigail, John Adams wrote on July 3 that the vote taken the day before had been on the "greatest Question" ever debated in America and assured her that the break with the mother country was the "will of Heaven." In a second letter, written later that day, John told Abigail that July 2 would be the "most memorable Epocha in the History of America," expecting that the day on which the 12 colonies declared themselves independent would be celebrated as the birth date of the United States. Instead, early Americans chose to celebrate Independence Day on July 4, the date on which the Declaration of Independence was formally approved by Congress.

to potential foreign allies and were well aware that any colony not declaring independence might take up arms against her sister colonies.

During the three days of debate on the Declaration of Independence that followed its introduction, John Adams became the staunchest defender of the document. According to protocol, Jefferson took no part in the debate. Instead, Adams served as what Jefferson called "our colossus on the floor." On July 1, South Carolina and Pennsylvania continued to express opposition to independence. After asserting that they and the people of New York personally favored independence, delegates from New York abstained because they had no authority to vote for independence. Delaware's delegation was split, with one member voting for independence and the other opposed to separation from the mother country. CAESAR RODNEY, the third member of the delegation, was in Delaware attempting to stamp out a loyalist uprising. The vote was postponed until the following day, giving pro-independence members the opportunity to continue lobbying delegates who were still opposed to breaking ties with Britain.

By July 2, unanimity had been achieved. In addition to the nine colonies that had voted for independence on the preceding day, South Carolina agreed to support independence in exchange for Jefferson's agreeing to remove a section in the Declaration that condemned slavery. Benjamin Franklin convinced a reluctant James Wilson to vote for independence, and John Dickinson and Robert Morris agreed to absent themselves from Congress. Thus, the majority of the Pennsylvania delegation was willing to vote for independence. As a result, only Delaware and New York prevented unanimity. In response to a cry for help, Caesar Rodney arrived in Congress after riding 80 miles in a thunderstorm. His presence swung Delaware's vote toward independence. When the official vote tally was taken, 12 states voted to declare the colonies free and independent. Consequently, JOHN HANCOCK, the president of the Second Continental Congress, signed the Declaration to indicate congressional acceptance of the document. By the time the official copy of the Declaration of Independence was signed on August 2 (see DECLARATION OF INDEPENDENCE, AUGUST 2 EMBOSSED), New York also favored independence.

Further Reading: L.H. Butterfield, ed., *The Book of Abigail and John: Selected Letters of the Adams Family, 1762–84* (Harvard University Press, 1975); Thomas Jefferson, *Notes on the State of Virginia* (Prentice-Hall, 1988); "Journals of the Continental Congress," http://rs6.loc.gov/ammem/amlaw/lwjc.html (cited March 2006).

—ELIZABETH PURDY, PH.D.

July 4 Celebrations

Because of the federal nature of its government, the United States does not have any mandatory national holidays. The federal government can only impose holidays upon federal institutions and employees. State governments may choose to follow suit and establish those same days as holidays, but the federal government cannot compel them to do so.

However, virtually every single unit of government in the United States has observed the 4th of July as Independence Day every year. From the very beginning, Americans recognized the significance of the day and the importance of commemorating it on a regular basis. The first officially sanctioned celebration did not take place until 1781, when the Massachusetts legislature formally authorized a celebration.

ABOVE *Spectacular fireworks displays have become a much-anticipated tradition in the celebration of Independence Day in cities across America.*

On July 4, 1776, there were some spontaneous celebrations in PHILADELPHIA. As news spread of the DECLARATION OF INDEPENDENCE through the new states, there were celebrations over the next few weeks. Most of them involved public readings of the full text of the Declaration. The year 1777 saw more elaborate observances of the first anniversary of the Declaration of Independence, including the captain of one Continental frigate inviting some of the leading members of the town in which he had docked to come and dine aboard. However, the first anniversary of independence was also marred with violence against those perceived to be less than patriotic. Because Quakers were pacifists, it was not their custom to celebrate holidays that commemorated military victories. As a result, a number of patriots vandalized the homes of Quakers in retaliation for their perceived lack of patriotism.

Philadelphia had the prototypical 4th of July celebration, complete with parades, speeches by public officials, picnics, and even some fireworks. A Hessian band captured at Trenton the previous December played stirring tunes for the crowd, and a number of British deserters publicly professed their new loyalty. The people of Philadelphia also established the custom of drinking a toast for each of the states in the union.

As the Revolutionary War progressed, the celebrations began to take on aspects of custom and tradition, simply because they were repeated year after year. After independence was firmly won, the custom of celebrating the adoption of the Declaration of Independence was deeply set into the public mind as an immovable custom.

After the adoption of the Constitution created a strong federal government, there was new opportunity for formal pomp and pageantry in the national capital. Although GEORGE WASHINGTON kept his own participation in such ceremonies relatively modest, later presidents developed a custom of presenting public speeches in honor of the nation's birthday. Particularly during times of strife, the holiday became a time for self-reflection. Leading abolitionist orator Frederick Douglass once delivered a stinging speech on the 4th of July, seeing the nation through the eyes of a black slave, making plain the hypocrisy of celebrating freedom in a nation in which a significant portion of the populace was chattel. Over a century later, during the demonstrations against the Vietnam War, the 4th of July became a flashpoint between the two sides that regarded each other as betraying the ideals upon which America was founded.

Further Reading: Ray Raphael, *Founding Myths: Stories That Hide Our Patriotic Past* (The New Press, 2004); John Tebel, *Turning the World Upside Down: Inside the American Revolution* (Orion, 1993).

—LEIGH KIMMEL

July 8 Proclamations

On July 4, 1776, the DECLARATION OF INDEPENDENCE was accepted by the Continental Congress (see CONTINENTAL CONGRESS, FIRST AND SECOND). The broadsides of the document, bearing only the signatures of congressional president JOHN HANCOCK and secretary Charles Thomson, were hurriedly sent to local printers for copy and distribution to the rest of the 13 American colonies (see DUNLAP'S BROADSIDES).

Though a "leaked" copy of the Declaration was read beforehand, the first official reading and celebration of the Declaration of Independence took place on July 8, 1776, at the State House (eventually renamed Liberty Hall) in PHILADELPHIA. The date was chosen in order to give town officials throughout the colonies time to prepare for the celebrations that would follow.

To ensure that the people of the colonies were "universally informed" of the Declaration and its contents, Hancock had asked the colonies' provincial officials to devise methods to guarantee the circulation of the news to those living in the rural countryside. As well as sending copies to the local assemblies, committees, and leaders to inform the general public and gain their support, a copy was also sent to the head of the Continental Army, GEORGE WASHINGTON, to have read aloud to his soldiers.

On July 8, the bells rang out in Philadelphia to call the general public to come to the State House. There, at the appointed time, Colonel John Nixon, a member of the Committee of Public Safety, read the Declaration aloud to the gathered crowd from a platform in the State House yard.

When he finished, the crowd gave three loud huzzas and the town's celebrations began. JOHN ADAMS later recalled how the "bells rang all day and almost all night" and how the houses were lit by candles in every window and bonfires burned throughout the city.

Everywhere, symbols of the English monarchy were taken down and publicly destroyed. After Nixon's reading in Philadelphia, soldiers removed the King's Arms from above the entrance to the State House and later that evening burned them in front of the London Coffee House—an unmistakably symbolic gesture of America's independence from Britain. In New York City, crowds pulled down a gilded statue of GEORGE III erected in 1770 and cut the head from the statue's body.

Further Reading: Scott Douglas Gerber, ed., *Declaration of Independence: Origin and Impact* (Congressional Quarterly, 2002); Rod Gragg, *Declaration of Independence: The Story Behind America's Founding Document and the Men Who Created It* (Rutledge Hill Press, 2005); Pauline Maier, *American Scripture: Making the Declaration of Independence* (Alfred A. Knopf, 1997).

—VICTORIA EASTES

K

Kosciusko, Thaddeus (1746–1817)

Called by his good friend THOMAS JEFFERSON "the purest son of liberty," Thaddeus Kosciusko embodied America's revolutionary struggle for independence even though he was a foreigner who resided in America for a relatively short time. The son of a minor nobleman, Kosciusko (in Polish Tadeusz Andrzej Bonawentura Kosciuszko) was born on February 4, 1746, in Siechnowica in eastern Poland and was educated at the Cadet School in Warsaw and later in Paris. While in France he studied the writings of the great thinkers of the Enlightenment and especially took to heart their ideas concerning natural rights and personal liberty for all men.

Deeply moved when the Americans declared their independence in July 1776, Kosciusko traveled to North America to offer the colonies his services in their struggle. Kosciusko received a commission in the Continental Army as a colonel, and served with distinction. He took part in the Saratoga Campaign and helped fortify West Point before moving south to serve under Nathanael Greene during his campaign through the Carolinas. Kosciusko earned high praise from many American officers, including GEORGE WASHINGTON, and was promoted to brigadier general. Kosciusko accompanied Washington on his triumphant march into New York City in November 1783 and was reportedly in attendance when Washington gave his farewell address to his officers.

After helping the United States win its independence, Kosciusko returned to his homeland and became part of another great struggle.

THADDEUS KOSCIUSKO *lived in this house,* AT LEFT, *in Philadelphia for a brief time. The house was also the birthplace of Colonel John Nixon (1733–1808), an ancestor of President Richard Nixon. Colonel John Nixon first read the Declaration of Independence publicly in the State House Yard on July 8, 1776.*

During the early 1790s he led several attempts to free Poland from the control of its more powerful neighbors. Though ultimately unsuccessful in fending off Russian and Prussian troops, the uprisings in Poland made Kosciusko a national icon.

Wounded during the fighting and imprisoned in tsarist Russia for a time, he was eventually freed and in 1796 returned to the United States where he was welcomed as a conquering hero. He rented a small room in a PHILADELPHIA boarding house and there engaged in conversations about issues of the past and present with frequent visitor Jefferson.

In 1797, when he joined the Society of Cincinnati, an organization of Revolutionary War officers, Washington presented the Polish patriot with a saber and a set of engraved pistols. Before he returned to Europe in 1798, Congress granted Kosciusko $15,000 in back pay for wartime services and 500 acres of land in Ohio.

Kosciusko continued to work for Polish independence, although his dream of an autonomous Polish state would not be realized during his lifetime. He lived in Paris for more than a decade where he tried to convince French authorities to aid the cause of his homeland. He later turned down an invitation by Napoleon to accompany the French army on an invasion of Poland, doubting the dictator's motives and assurances.

After Napoleon's final defeat in 1815, Kosciusko traveled to the Congress of Vienna and made one last unsuccessful attempt to convince the major nations represented there to create a new, independent Poland. Two years later, on October 5, 1817, Kosciusko died while in Switzerland and his body was brought back to Krakow. The people there gave him a funeral deserving of a national hero and laid his remains to rest in the royal crypt at Wawel Castle. In his will Kosciusko made provisions for his prop-

Legacy in America

THADDEUS KOSCIUSKO'S contributions to the United States's fight for independence are still celebrated. There are major monuments to the Polish general in Washington, D.C., Boston, Philadelphia, Chicago, and the U.S. Military Academy at West Point, and statues in many cities. Kosciusko County, Indiana, was named in his honor, with local citizens paying further tribute to the Polish general's heritage by naming their county seat Warsaw. In Mississippi, Attala County residents named their county seat Kosciusko upon its founding in 1836. Two bridges in New York State are also named for Kosciusko as is a major thoroughfare in downtown Los Angeles. The brick house in Philadelphia where the general briefly lived is now administered by the National Park Service as a museum.

erty in the United States to be sold, and for all of the money from the sale to be used to purchase the freedom for slaves in America and also to provide for their education. Funds from the sale eventually helped found a school for former slaves in Newark, New Jersey.

Further Reading: Miecislaus Haiman, *Kosciuszko in the American Revolution* (Kosciuszko Foundation, 1975); Francis C. Kajencki, *Thaddeus Kosciuszko: Military Engineer of the American Revolution* (Southwest Polonia Press, 1998); Robert M. Ketchum, *Saratoga: Turning Point of America's Revolutionary War* (Owl Books, 1999); James S. Pula, *Thaddeus Kosciuszko: The Purest Son of Liberty* (Hippocrene Press, 1998).

—BEN WYNNE, PH.D.

L

Lafayette, Marquis de (1757–1834)

Marie-Joseph-Paul-Yves-Roch-Gilbert du Motier, the Marquis de Lafayette, was one of the most loved heroes of the American Revolution, although he never received his due in France, where many still consider him a traitor. Lafayette was born into a wealthy French family, which had historically been involved in the political, financial, and social worlds of Europe. As a youth of 19, backed up by four years of minor military experience, Lafayette acted on his belief that liberty was worth fighting for and traveled to the United States with the Baron De Kalb and several other French officers. Upon arrival, Lafayette volunteered to serve under GEORGE WASHINGTON at his own expense.

Ironically, both Lafayette's departure from Europe and his arrival in America were occasions for dismay. France was outraged that such an important individual had left the country without official permission, and England began seizing all foreign vessels with the intention of arresting Lafayette and his party. When the group arrived in America on January 13, 1777, they found themselves in Charles Town, South Carolina. Drawing on his membership in the international fellowship of the Masonic Lodge, Lafayette made friends with the locals who entertained him lavishly.

He later wrote in his diary that he was astonished that all Americans had the same political rights, regardless of social class. To repay the kindness of the South Carolinians, Lafayette donated equipment

After the War

RETURNING TO France after the American Revolution, Lafayette became embroiled in events surrounding the French Revolution and the overthrow of the French monarchy. He escaped death by fleeing to Belgium when a plot to overthrow the government was discovered, was subsequently arrested by Austrian forces, and imprisoned in a dungeon. American officials smuggled his son, the 14-year-old Georges-Washington, out of France to the safety of George Washington at Mount Vernon. The marquis was freed by Napoleon's troops when the French Reign of Terror ended in 1794. Although Lafayette was offered the presidency of the new republic, he refused the position.

In 1824, President James Monroe invited Lafayette to spend a year touring the United States. To Americans, Lafayette remained "the Marquis" who had fought for their freedom. Hundreds of cities, streets, mountains, lakes, rivers, and buildings have been named after him, most called Lafayette or Fayetteville. According to legend, when General Pershing's troops arrived in France during World War I, an aide planted an American flag on Lafayette's tomb, shouting, "Lafayette, we are here!"

ABOVE RIGHT *The Marquis de Lafayette in his military uniform, in an engraving by George E. Perine.* BELOW RIGHT *Lafayette in the conclusion of the campaign of 1781, in an engraving by Noel Le Mire. Lafayette was part of the force that crossed the frozen Delaware River on Christmas night, 1776, to launch the Battle of Trenton.*

and arms to the local militia and began his 800-mile journey to PHILADELPHIA.

Congress initially refused to entertain Lafayette's request for a commission because the war was not going well. Additionally, legislators were tired of dealing with similar requests from French officers who saw the revolution only as an opportunity for adventure and military advancement. Some Americans mistakenly believed that Lafayette had been involved in a plot to seize control of the emergent government by proclaiming Frenchman Comte de Broglie the king of the United States. After verifying his credentials and acting on a recommendation by George Washington, who immediately accepted the Frenchman as a friend, Congress gave Lafayette the honorary title of Major General of the Continental Army.

However, Lafayette had no intention of being an honorary officer. He began sitting in on war councils and soon took an active role in the fighting. Lafayette was present during the harsh winter of Valley Forge and was part of the force that crossed the frozen Delaware River on Christmas night in 1776 to launch the Battle of Trenton.

On September 11, 1777, Lafayette took part in his first battle. During the Battle of Brandywine, the wounded marquis managed to distinguish himself by twice rallying American troops. He subsequently took part in a number of significant skirmishes and distinguished himself at the Battles of Monmouth and Saratoga.

Lafayette knew that America was in dire need of foreign aid if the new country was to repel the powerful British military. As a result, he returned to France in 1779 to help convince the French government to come to America's aid. When Washington announced to the troops that a Franco-American treaty had been signed, the troops celebrated with a 13-gun salute, a sermon by the army chaplain, and cheers for the American States and the king of France. On the journey home, the seasick Lafayette had been forced to put down a threatened mutiny from crewmen who were interested in claiming a reward from the British. He was saved by an American who informed him of the plot.

When a son was born to Lafayette in 1779, he named him Georges-Washington Lafayette after the commander in chief, whom he called his "adopted father." Washington had no children, and Lafayette had been orphaned at the age of 13. After returning to America, Lafayette was privileged to be present with his Virginia troops when Lord Cornwallis surrendered in October 1781. The surrender signaled the end of the war except for mopping up activities designed to drive the British out of southern strongholds. The marquis was in France again raising money for America when the Treaty of Peace was signed in 1783. He returned for a celebrated farewell tour the following year. Throughout his life, Lafayette served as an unofficial American ambassador.

Further Reading: Oliver Bernier, *Lafayette: Hero of Two Worlds* (E.P. Dutton, 1983); Peter Buckman, *Lafayette: A Biography* (Paddington Press, 1977); James Thomas Flexner, *Washington: The Indispensable Man* (Little, Brown, 1974); Harlowe Giles Unger, *Lafayette* (Wiley, 2002).

—ELIZABETH PURDY, PH.D.

Lee, Richard Henry
(1732–94)

Despite his substantial contributions to the independence movement, Virginia statesman Richard Henry Lee has often been overlooked by scholars who study the Revolutionary War period, partly because Lee made a number of powerful enemies who accused him of putting his own financial interests above the political interests of the United States. Some modern scholars contend that earlier historians discredited Lee because they accepted two inaccurate assessments perpetuated by his enemies. The first of these was that Lee was involved in the probably mythical Conway Cabal, a secret group that supposedly tried to have GEORGE WASHINGTON removed as commander in chief of the Continental Army. Second, Lee's detractors insisted that he wrote a series of letters, collectively known as *Letters from the Federal Farmer to the Republican*, that were designed to discredit the U.S. Constitution during the ratification period. Historians J. Kent McGaughy and Gordon S. Wood have stated that there is no real evidence to support the notion that Lee was the author of those letters.

As a member of the prominent Lees of Virginia, Richard Henry served as a member of the Virginia House of Burgesses from 1758 until 1775. When the British Parliament passed the Stamp Act in 1765, levying taxes on all legal documents in America, Lee was in the vanguard of those who organized associations to ban the importation of British products throughout the colonies. When it became clear that the colonies needed to develop a way to remain in close contact during the tax crisis, Lee served on the Virginia Committee of Correspondence (see COMMITTEES OF CORRESPONDENCE) and pressured residents of other colonies to resist "taxation without representation."

By the spring of 1776, Lee was solidly in the camp of independence advocates. He was close friends with JOHN ADAMS of Massachusetts, the strongest advocate for independence in Congress. In May, Lee and Adams pushed through a resolution that directed all states in which royal governments had ceased to operate to form their own governments. In essence, this served as a declaration of war against Britain.

Lee's most direct influence on the issue of independence came with his introduction of the Virginia Resolution of June 7, 1776, which had unanimously passed the Virginia Convention on May 6. The resolution proposed that the Second Continental Congress declare that "these United Colonies are, and of right ought to be, free and independent states." The Virginia Resolution also sought to dissolve the political bonds with Britain and paved the way for the creation of a confederation of states in which the 13 colonies could become self-governing while maintaining state sovereignty. Because Britain was the most powerful nation in the world in 1776, the resolution also called for plans to develop foreign alliances with countries that would be willing to provide revenue, troops, and general support to America during the fight for independence and afterward.

Lee served in both the First and Second Continental Congresses (see CONTINENTAL CONGRESS, FIRST AND SECOND), serving for most of the period from 1774 to 1780. He returned to Virginia on June 13, and was therefore not present on July 2 or July 4, 1776, when the DECLARATION OF INDEPENDENCE was approved by Congress. However, he returned to PHILADELPHIA and signed the Declaration in August. Lee was also involved in making foreign policy for the new nation and served on a committee that maintained close contact with American allies in Britain and Ireland. Lee introduced a proclamation that established a national Thanksgiving Day to express national gratitude for the American victory at Saratoga, New York, on October 17, 1777, in

Political Career

AFTER THE Revolutionary War, Richard Henry Lee continued to play a major role in Virginia and national politics. From November 30, 1784, until November 24, 1785, Lee served as the 12th president of Congress. In the late 1880s, when the U.S. Constitution was being approved, Lee was criticized for not supporting the document as did most of his allies of the revolutionary period. However, Lee was afraid that a strong central government would trample on state rights. He also publicly expressed his objections to the fact that the Constitution, as written in 1787, had no Bill of Rights. Lee was mollified when the Federalists, the supporters of the Constitution, agreed to add the Bill of Rights, which became the first ten amendments to the Constitution. Virginia ratified the Constitution on July 25, 1788, and Lee served in Virginia's first senatorial delegation from 1789–94. He died at Chantilly, his Virginia plantation, on June 19, 1794.

ABOVE *Photo of a portrait of Richard Henry Lee painted by C. W. Peale.*

which General JOHN BURGOYNE surrendered his entire army and turned the tide of the American Revolution. It was after this victory that France signed the alliance with America.

Expansion was a major issue to those states that had western frontiers during the colonial and revolutionary periods, and Virginians were adamant about laying claim to the Ohio River Valley. Thus, many of Lee's political decisions were made to protect Virginia's interests. Because of this, he was heavily involved in the formation of territorial governments after the war. Lee was also a realistic businessman who made self-interested decisions when it was necessary. However, he echoed PATRICK HENRY in asserting that he was "not a Virginian, but an American."

When the British moved the war to the South, Richard Henry Lee was the commanding officer of the Westmoreland County Militia. He organized the protection of the 1,000 miles of navigable waters off the Virginia coast, placing vessels at strategic points to prevent British vessels from entering the Chesapeake Bay. Lee also engaged the British in battle on April 9, 1781, when his militiamen prevented the British from disembarking at Stratford Landing. Unfortunately, Lee was not able to protect his state when BENEDICT ARNOLD arrived with a fleet and 1,600 soldiers in December 1780. He had his revenge, however, when Washington and the Marquis de Lafayette (see LAFAYETTE, MARQUIS DE) joined General Nathanael Greene and his troops the following spring. With American troops surrounding him, Lord Cornwallis was forced to surrender his entire army. The Revolutionary War was essentially over, although sporadic fighting continued until the Treaty of Peace was signed on September 3, 1783.

Further Reading: Alf J. Mapp, Jr., *The Virginia Experiment: The Old Dominion's Role in the Making of America, 1607–1781* (Hamilton Press, 1987); J. Kent McGaughy, *Richard Henry Lee: A Portrait of an American Revolutionary* (Rowman and Littlefield, 2004).

—ELIZABETH PURDY, PH.D.

Livingston, Philip (1716–78)

JOHN ADAMS described Philip Livingston as "a great, rough, rapid mortal. There is no holding any conversation with him. He blusters away; says, if England should turn us adrift, we should instantly go into civil war among ourselves." Other contemporaries portrayed him as an aristocratic figure, austere in his appearance and with an irritable temper; though most often silent and reserved, Livingston could be scathingly blunt toward those he saw as failing in morality or patriotic fervor.

Born to one of New York's wealthiest landowning merchant families, Livingston was positioned to take a prominent role in the social and political realms of his state. He began his political career in 1754 with his election as one of the seven aldermen of New York City, where he served for nine years, during which he helped found Columbia College and the New York City Public Library. As a member of the First Continental Congress (see CONTINENTAL CONGRESS, FIRST AND SECOND), Livingston proved an invaluable source through his wide range of knowledge on topics from finance and trade to Native American affairs. However, as a conservative patriot and a prosperous merchant he disapproved of total independence from England. He, along with many others, feared that the resulting disruption of trade would severely harm colonial merchants, weaken the new nation's economy, and lead to civil war among the colonies for primary control of the nation. Due to his sentiments and his unwillingness to listen to the proposals of extreme patriots, Livingston's actions led several of his fellow congressional leaders to say that patriotism had taken only a shallow hold in New York.

Absent from PHILADELPHIA for the months of June and July 1776 because of the demands of his own colony, Livingston was not present in Philadelphia on July 4 when the revised DECLARATION OF INDEPENDENCE was read to and approved by Congress. He was, however, present on August 2 when the first embossed copy was signed by the delegates. Though he had long disapproved of the idea of independence, Livingston was a true patriot at heart and when the decision was made by Congress to accept the Declaration, he did not hesitate in adding his signature.

Unfortunately, Livingston did not live to see the surrender of British General Cornwallis at Yorktown and the realization of American independence. Ater the war began, he found his presence in constant demand both at home and in Congress. In 1777, he was chosen to serve as a senator to the New York legislature, while still fulfilling his duties as a delegate to the Continental Congress. The constant demands on his time and the financial burdens placed on his estate by the war eventually proved too much for Livingston's already failing health. Despite the pleas of his family to remain home, Livingston returned one last time to Congress where it met in York,

A Family Affair

PHILIP LIVINGSTON was not the only Livingston family member who played an important role in the founding of the United States. His brother William and his cousin Robert R. both served as members of Congress and shared similar conservative viewpoints toward independence. Torn between the desire to remain under the security of British control and the desire to secure the colonies' right to self-rule, the Livingston family hoped for reconciliation to occur between the two positions. Robert R. Livingston once said: "Every good man wishes that America might remain free, in this I heartily join; at the same time I do not desire she should be wholly independent of the mother country. How to reconcile their jarring principles, I profess I am altogether at a loss."

Pennsylvania (the British having occupied Philadelphia). Succumbing to exhaustion, Livingston died at the age of 62 on June 12, 1778, in a small tavern room, attended only by his son Henry. His funeral took place on the same day and was attended by all the members of Congress.

Further Reading: Rod Gragg, *Declaration of Independence: The Story Behind America's Founding Document and the Men Who Created It* (Rutledge Hill Press, 2005); National Park Service Museum Collections, www.cr.nps.gov/museum (cited January 2006).

—VICTORIA EASTES

Loyalists

The loyalists were those colonists from North America who supported the British Crown during the American Revolution. In the 18th century, the American Revolutionary War was known as a war of revolution or rebellion. A closer look from later social scientists opened the view to a new perspective. These historians described the Revolutionary War as a civil war. On the one hand, American loyalists, or as they were called by their opponents "Tories" or "the King's Men," subtended the revolution.

On the other hand, there were the patriots, Americans, or rebels, as the loyalists called the revolutionary party that was resisting British rule and promoting the Revolution and independence of the 13 colonies. During the Revolutionary War, loyalists suffered little from their views. However, a minority, up to about 50,000 loyalists, armed and supplied by the British, fought in the conflict.

Historians estimate that about 15 to 20 percent of the adult white male population of the 13 colonies were loyalists. From the perspective of the patriots, the loyalists betrayed the movement in order to gain independence, because they associated with the British forces. From the perspective of the British, the loyalists were backing the crown and serving it and the British Empire. In their opinion, the American patriots were rebels and traitors.

After the DECLARATION OF INDEPENDENCE on July 4, 1776, the patriots, who represented the majority in the Second Continental Congress (see CONTINENTAL CONGRESS, FIRST AND SECOND), held the power in the newly declared 13 states. They ordered the residents to be loyal to the new temporary government and not to support the British. Although open fighting continued, the

United States controlled from that day on nearly 90 percent of the population. As a result the British called back their governors and forbade the remaining loyalists to set up new governments or to re-create old ones.

Loyalists recruited their followers, for the most part, from small farmers, artisans, and shopkeepers. Most British officials, as it could be assumed, remained loyal to the Crown. Wealthy merchants tended to remain loyal, as well as Anglican ministers, especially in Puritan New England. Some African Americans, believing the British promise that they would get their freedom in exchange for loyalty, indentured servants, and German immigrants supported the loyalist cause. Those Germans stood on the side of the Crown because the English king was of German origin.

New York City and Long Island had the largest concentration of loyalists of all colonies. This was because the British army controlled the area until the evacuation in late 1783. Also many loyalist families from elsewhere fled to New York. In North and South Carolina, the farmers in the countryside were loyalist, while the planters were more inclined to support the Revolution. In Georgia, loyalists supported the reestablishment of British colonial government. In none of the other colonies did the British launch an attempt to restore colonial government that included loyalist participation. The British preferred a strong military rule after the troubles had ended.

Loyalists were casually associated with the Anglican Church. Many prominent Anglicans supported the king, because he was the supreme head of their church. Overall, loyalists tended to be older, more likely wealthier and better educated than their patriot opponents, but there were also many loyalists of humble means.

Joseph Brant Thayendenegea
1742–1807

JOSEPH BRANT Thayendenegea, commander of Iroquois forces, was a Mohawk leader and British military officer during the American Revolutionary War. Brant was perhaps the most well-known North American Indian of his generation—people now generally called Native Americans in the United States and First Nations in Canada. He met many of the most significant people of the age, including GEORGE WASHINGTON and King GEORGE III. During the American Revolution, Brant led warriors of the four Iroquois nations that had sided with Britain (the Mohawk, Onondaga, Cayuga, and Seneca), along with a number of white loyalists, who preferred serving under him to enlistment in the regular army. Brant was made a captain in the British army. He was defeated by General John Sullivan on August 29, 1779, in the Battle of Newtown.

On October 6, 1775, Congress passed a resolution calling for the arrest of all loyalists who were considered dangerous to "the liberties of America." In most of the colonies loyalist property was confiscated by the patriots. Where the patriots held the majority, loyalist behavior was subject to heavy sanctions. Cheers for the king might have led to tar and feathering. Loyalists commonly were arrested, threatened, and even attacked by mobs fighting for the revolutionary cause and against their former neighbors.

At first supporters of the British rarely formed any political organization and generally remained passive in the fighting. Only after British army units arrived in loyalist areas did they try to mobilize. About 50 military companies or regiments were made up of loyalists during the war. In numbers of 30,000 to 35,000, men enrolled in regularly organized British corps. These numbers do not include the small groups that engaged the patriots in guerrilla warfare in South Carolina and elsewhere.

After the fighting, the Treaty of Paris restored all property to the loyalists, who were previously dispossessed by the revolutionaries. Despite this ruling many of the loyalists still had to abandon substantial parts of their property. In the Carolinas the animosity between the patriots and the supporters of the king was hard to overcome and only a few loyalists regained their property. Both in New York and in the Carolinas, officials parceled out most of the confiscated land to yeoman farmers and did not return it to its previous proprietors.

When supporting the king turned into a political provocation, about 100,000 loyalists left the United States as political refugees. Altogether nearly 3 percent of the population of the 13 British colonies that declared independence left for Nova Scotia, Canada, Britain, and the Caribbean. The émigrés included William Franklin, the illegitimate son of BENJAMIN FRANKLIN and last royal governor of New Jersey, and John Singleton Copley, who was considered the greatest American painter of his time.

Nova Scotia and Canada, still colonies of the British Empire, provided a new home under British rule for most of the displaced Americans. Nova Sco-

ABOVE *A "Virginian loyalist" is forced to sign a document by a club-wielding mob of "liberty men." On the left, a man is being led toward a gallows standing in the background on the right and from which hangs a sack of feathers and a barrel of tar.*

tia alone received about 32,000 and Canada received 10,000 of the refugees. Main areas of loyalist settlements were New Brunswick, the eastern townships, and in what is modern-day Ontario.

Further Reading: Francis D. Cogliano, *Revolutionary America, 1763–1815* (Routledge, 1999); Sheila L. Skemp, *Benjamin and William Franklin: Father and Son, Patriot and Loyalist* (St. Martin's Press, 1994); Gordon S. Wood, *The Radicalism of the American Revolution* (Alfred A. Knopf, 1992).

—ALEXANDER EMMERICH

M

Marion, Francis (c. 1731–95)

Little is known of Francis Marion's early life. He grew to manhood near Georgetown, South Carolina, and gained his first military experience in campaigns against the Cherokees in 1759 and 1761. As war with Britain approached in 1775, the South Carolina Provincial Congress began forming military units, and Marion was made a captain in the Second Regiment. The following year he was promoted to major and given command of the Second, which was assigned to construct fortifications on Sullivan's Island to protect the port of Charleston from an attack that had been anticipated for months (see CHARLESTON IN THE REVOLUTION). On June 28, a British fleet dropped anchor off the island and began shooting broadside cannons into the partially completed fort. Marion fired at the enemy slowly and deliberately to conserve his limited supply of gunpowder. After several hours it became clear that the Americans were getting the better of the exchange. By evening the battle was over, and the severely battered British ships moved out of range.

On June 30 Marion participated in a celebratory parade, and he was surely present several days later at a ceremony on July 4 when John Rutledge, president of the South Carolina Provincial Congress, inspected the fort and presented a sword to one of the garrison, Sergeant William Jasper, for heroism during the engagement.

The Second Regiment once again helped defend Charleston when the British attacked in 1780, but this time they could not repel the

THE FLINTLOCK *mechanism* AT LEFT *was the first reliable and economically priced gun, and was hugely popular in colonial America.*

invaders as they had done four years earlier. They surrendered the city on May 12. The situation of the American forces in South Carolina was precarious after the fall of Charleston, but it became untenable later in the year when the British army soundly pummeled patriot forces at the Battle of Camden, killing or wounding over 1,000 men and taking another 1,000 prisoner. The two catastrophic defeats ended resistance in the state by regular military units (see SOUTH CAROLINA IN THE REVOLUTION).

Marion avoided capture after the debacles at Charleston and Camden, but was persuaded that opposing the British by standard military means was no longer possible in South Carolina. The only re-

course, he decided, was to form a guerrilla band and operate against the enemy from the state's extensive swamps. Once organized, his 150 irregulars proved to be an effective force. Because of their ability to move rapidly over difficult terrain and gain the element of surprise, they were able to harass the British continually, and from time to time they actually defeated small units.

The British supremacy in South Carolina was only temporary. When a powerful American force under the command of Major General Nathanael Greene moved into the state in 1781, Marion abandoned his insurgent style of warfare for more conventional tactics. During the final years of the war,

The Legend of "The Swamp Fox"

MASON LOCKE Weems, an itinerant book peddler, ordained cleric, and quondam biographer, is today remembered as the man who concocted the story of GEORGE WASHINGTON and the cherry tree. In 1807, however, when his name was well known and his writings much admired, he sent a letter to Colonel Peter Horry, who had served under Francis Marion and had written a biography of him. Weems asked to use Horry's account as a base for a biography of Marion he hoped to publish. Horry agreed to let him to use his manuscript, but when he received a copy of the printed book some months later, with his name on the title

page as a coauthor, he lashed out at Weems, saying "You have carved and mutilated [my account] with so many erroneous statements...embellishments, observation[s] and remarks. ...Can you suppose I can be pleased with reading particulars (though so elevated, by you) of Marion and myself, when I know such never existed." Despite Horry's outrage, subsequent 19th-century chroniclers embraced Weems's rendition of Marion as the "Swamp Fox," and the nickname and the legend became the stuff of American history.

AT LEFT *Francis Marion, the legendary "Swamp Fox."*

he took leave of his military duties to serve in the South Carolina senate, and some years after peace was secured he retired to his plantation, where he died in 1795.

Further Reading: John W. Gordon, *South Carolina and the American Revolution: A Battlefield History* (University of South Carolina Press, 2003); Peter Horry and Mason Locke Weems, *The Life of Gen. Francis Marion, A Celebrated Partisan Officer in the Revolutionary War* (John F. Blair, 2000).

—B.R. BURG, PH.D.

Maryland in the Revolution

During the Revolutionary War, Maryland saw little fighting. Consequently, Elk Landing, an inland waterway used to travel between the American north and south, served as a major shipping and supply site for the Continental Army.

A large number of German immigrants began arriving in Maryland in 1734, and their influence prompted Maryland to look for commonalities with Pennsylvania, rather than with its southern neighbors. The German contingent was also instrumental in swelling the population of Baltimore and turning the city into a significant commercial center. Annapolis became the political, legal, and cultural capital of the colony. Maryland had some of the best legal minds in the country, and the Maryland bar was respected throughout the 13 colonies.

Colonial Maryland's economy was heavily dependent on tobacco. In the years immediately preceding the Revolutionary War, the colony suffered through a period of political, economic, and religious upheaval that almost destroyed it. During the war, the legislature was forced to borrow money to finance its own activities as well as those of the military. The debt was somewhat reduced by the seizure of British and Tory property and the release of un-backed paper money, but Maryland was deeply in debt at the end of the Revolutionary War.

RISING TENSIONS

When the British Parliament passed the Stamp Act in 1765, Maryland reacted to the proposed taxes with outrage because the colony had been in the midst of a depression for a year and was neither willing nor able to take on new financial burdens. Consequently, the demonstrations that followed news of the Stamp Act were particularly violent in Maryland. Because of the large German population, which had no direct links to Britain, Marylanders joined the patriot cause much more rapidly than residents of other states, where loyalties to the mother country eroded over a period of years.

In Maryland, LOYALISTS tended to concentrate among the plantation owners, poor farmers, and fishermen of Maryland's eastern shore. Their loyalty was to a large extent due to the influence of Anglican and Episcopal ministers who were required to take loyalty oaths to the king.

The Country Party was instrumental in winning support for the revolutionary movement in Maryland. The group had begun as an antiproprietary movement that strenuously objected to the vast sums collected by the colony's proprietors in the decade before the Revolutionary War. These sums included a payment of £12,500 sterling each year directly to the proprietors, a yearly tax of £12,000 that supported the proprietors' revenue system, and £8,000 earmarked for the salaries of the Anglican clergy. Only half of that amount was used for local services. In the House of Delegates, the Country Party began trying to transfer powers to the legislature and away from the proprietors' representatives, but they were generally blocked by loyalists. In response, the Country Party joined ranks with local merchants to promote the interests of Marylanders over those of the proprietors.

Maryland reacted to the Boston Port Act by passing a nonimportation agreement, registering official protests, organizing a military, sending relief to Boston, and appointing delegates to Congress. The Country Party took on the responsibility for enforcing the nonimportation agreement and for raising a militia. In response to these events, Governor Robert Eden left Maryland and returned to England. The council of safety assumed the role of coordinating Maryland's revolutionary activities, and Matthew Tilghman became the moving force in organizing the colony for war. When Maryland chose delegates to the First Continental Congress (see CONTINENTAL CONGRESS, FIRST AND SECOND) that met in PHILADELPHIA in the autumn of 1774, delegates included Matthew Tilghman, Thomas Johnson, William Pace, and SAMUEL CHASE.

INDEPENDENCE

On May 23, 1774, two months after the Boston Tea Party, Marylanders had their own encounter with the British when the ship HMS *Geddes* arrived with a shipment of tea. In an event known as the Chestertown Tea Party, locals boarded the ship and threw tea into the Chester River. On October 15, the HMS *Peggy Stewart* arrived in Annapolis carrying 2,320 pounds of tea. The brig was owned by Anthony Stewart, who offered to publicly burn the tea after assuring his angry neighbors that he had not known the tea was part of the brig's cargo. Ultimately, Stewart chose to burn the entire boat publicly.

In the winter of 1775–76, hopes for reconciliation with England were dashed when Marylanders

learned of the burning of Norfolk, Virginia, by Governor John Murray, Earl of Dunmore. Chase, William Paca, and Robert Alexander represented Maryland in the Second Continental Congress in 1776. Alexander, although a member of Maryland's committee of correspondence (see COMMITTEES OF CORRESPONDENCE) and the council of safety, became disillusioned with the patriot cause and resigned from Congress. Despite this move, Alexander continued to pay for cartridge paper for the militia out of his own pocket. He was replaced in Congress by Thomas Stone.

On July 3, the Maryland legislature declared that the colony was free of all political ties with Britain and authorized its congressional delegation to vote for independence. Marylanders Carroll, Chase, Paca, and Stone added their signatures to the DECLARATION OF INDEPENDENCE on August 2, 1776.

As Maryland began establishing its own government independent of British influence, the founders designed a system of government intended to retain the political base of the small group of planters, lawyers, and merchants that already governed the colony. This was accomplished in part by requiring a high property qualification for all office holders and permitting only those who owned at least 50 acres of land valued at £40 sterling or more to vote.

The property qualification was later dropped to £30 sterling and all religious qualifications for suffrage were removed. The framers of Maryland's constitution gave the upper house of Maryland's bicameral legislature the power to veto any legislation that threatened property or positions. From the beginning, this provision led to heated battles between the two houses of the legislature. The more liberal lower house attempted to be responsive to the popular will and was less respectful of

ABOVE *In this painting by John Trumbull, General George Washington resigns his commission at Annapolis on December 23, 1783. Standing 6'2" tall and weighing over 200 pounds, Washington was in his mid-40s when the war began. At the time of his resignation, he intended to retire to Mount Vernon. Instead, he served two terms as the first president of the United States.*

property rights. In protest, the people of Maryland were frequently on the verge of rebelling against their own government.

Once war was inevitable, the Country Party set itself to raising troops, and the ranks of Maryland's militia grew rapidly. In August 1775, the first battalion of Marylanders joined the Continental Army. In general, the only Marylanders who refused to join the military effort were Quakers, Mennonites, and Dunkers. The war in Maryland began at the Head of the Elk River in late July 1777 when the British landed a 265-ship fleet carrying 17,000 soldiers under the command of General William Howe. When one

of the boats ventured out to buy milk, it was captured by the Maryland militia, which claimed the boat's crew as prisoners of war. When the Americans came within sight of a British galley, the vessels exchanged fire. The Americans returned to the shore without incurring damage.

The town of Elkton had emptied before the British arrived, so they set up headquarters at Elkton Tavern. On August 29, the militia skirmished with General Charles Cornwallis, who captured the iron works. Although they were not averse to such skirmishes, the ultimate British goal was to capture Philadelphia.

Further Reading: Charles McLean Andrews, *The Colonial Background of the American Revolution: Four Essays in American Colonial History* (Yale University Press, 2001); Aubrey C. Land, *Colonial Maryland: A History* (KTO Press, 1981); M. Christopher New, *Maryland Loyalists in the American Revolution* (Tidewater Publications, 1996).

—ELIZABETH PURDY, PH.D.

Massachusetts in the Revolution

While the first English settlement in the American colonies had been established in Jamestown, Virginia, in 1607, it was the arrival of the Pilgrims on the HMS *Mayflower* in 1620 that led to the settlement of the Massachusetts Bay Colony and, subsequently, to the colonization of what became the United States. From the time these Pilgrims signed the Mayflower Compact, attesting to their belief that civil law was essential to their security in the new land, the people of Massachusetts began developing an independent spirit that came to be identified as uniquely American.

In the years preceding the American Revolution, Boston grew into one of the largest cities in America. In this city, with its enormous respect for political rights, the revolutionary spirit began to take hold (see BOSTON IN THE REVOLUTION). The revolutionary spirit was born in reaction to arbitrary acts by Britain under GEORGE III that led Parliament to pass legislation taxing the colonies to pay for debts incurred during the French and Indian Wars (1754–63).

The people of Massachusetts responded to the passage of the Stamp Act of 1765 with such wrath that they agreed to send representatives to the Stamp Act Congress, which met in New York in October 1766. This Congress adopted resolutions urging all colonies to pass nonimportation laws, preventing British goods from entering the colonies. Although Parliament repealed the Stamp Act, it was followed by other taxes.

In colonial Massachusetts, an acrimonious battle for power raged between the Court Party, which remained loyal to Great Britain, and the Country Party, which represented local interests. The Country Party focused on checking the widespread corruption of the patronage system and keeping the merchant society that controlled Boston from overwhelming the rights of the working class. To plot strategy, the Country Party began holding regular meetings of the Caucus Club. Under the leadership of SAMUEL ADAMS, the Country Party gained in popularity, and Adams's second cousin, JOHN ADAMS, a rising young lawyer, was drawn into the activities of the Caucus Club. This experience helped John Adams prepare for a substantial role in the founding of the United States. As Massachusetts moved toward revolution, the older parties were merged into the Whigs (patriots) and the Tories (LOYALISTS), between whom the acrimonious debate continued.

INDEPENDENCE

Unlike most other colonies, Massachusetts's radicals generated a strong following early in the pre-Revolutionary course of events. Bostonians had reacted to the passage of the Stamp Act of 1765 with demonstrations that forced the tax collector to resign out of fear for his own safety. In Braintree, the protest statement written by John Adams became a model for protest statements generated in other colonies, as well as in other towns of Massachusetts. Adams accused Britain of reducing the colonists to beggary,

John Adams, 1735–1826

WHEN THE revolutionary spirit was awakened in Massachusetts, John Adams (1735–1826) became a major voice in expressing outrage that the colonists were being denied the basic rights due to all English citizens under the English Bill of Rights of 1689. Because he believed so strongly in his cause, Adams was willing to be considered, in his own words, "obnoxious, suspected, and unpopular." While THOMAS JEFFERSON had written the Declaration of Independence, it was Adams who convinced the other delegates that independence from Britain had become their only course. Adams later negotiated loans and support from crucial allies that helped America to win the Revolutionary War. He played a major role in negotiating the Treaty of Paris that officially ended the war in 1783. Adams also penned the first draft of the Massachusetts constitution after in-depth research on various forms of government. The Massachusetts constitution served as one of the models for the U.S. Constitution in 1787.

In one of the most well-known love stories of American history, Abigail Adams acted as an equal partner to her husband throughout the 54 years of their marriage. Their rich correspondence has provided scholars with a first-hand view of major events in the founding of the United States. On March 31, 1776, in what became the most famous letter to her husband, Abigail chided John, imploring the delegates to the Second Continental Congress to "Remember the Ladies, and be more generous and favourable to them than your ancestors." After the war, John Adams represented the United States as an ambassador in London (1785–88).

When the Constitution created a three-branch government, George Washington became the first president, and John Adams served as the first vice president. When Washington left office after two terms, Adams was elected as the second president of the new country. In the bitterly contested election of 1800, Adams lost to Jefferson, and the two men who had once been close friends did not speak for 10 years. Afterward, they began corresponding and continued to do so until they both died on July 4, 1826.

ABOVE LEFT *General George Washington takes command of the American army at Cambridge, 1775, in an engraving by C. Rogers, from a painting by M. A. Wageman.* **ABOVE RIGHT** *The attack on Bunker Hill with the burning of Charlestown, June 17, 1775, in an engraving by Lodge.*

violating the constitutional principles of the Magna Carta, and violating the right to trial by jury.

The people of Massachusetts celebrated the repeal of the Stamp Act with bonfires. However, when Britain levied additional taxes on the colonies, the Massachusetts SONS OF LIBERTY began organizing a protest designed to make Britain understand the enormity of "taxation without representation." The result was the Boston Tea Party (1773), which led to Britain's tacit declaration of war on Massachusetts. The newspapers of Massachusetts accused Britain of attempting to enslave the colonists, while they railed against British tyranny.

By the summer of 1776, the situation with Britain had convinced patriots throughout the colonies that reconciliation with the mother country was no longer possible. On June 28, the Massachusetts delegation to the Second Continental Congress (see CONTINENTAL CONGRESS, FIRST AND SECOND) voted in favor of the Virginia Resolution, which declared the colonies independent of Britain. The delegation again voted for independence on July 4 when the DECLARATION OF INDEPENDENCE was unanimously accepted by Congress.

WAR

In 1768, the Massachusetts militia intensified its organization and training after word reached the colony that a contingent of British soldiers was arriving in Boston—ostensibly to protect the colony from invasion by France. Hostility rose to an unprecedented level on March 5, 1770, when, by some accounts, Brit-

The Boston Tea Party

ON THE night of December 16, 1773, 200 Bostonians dressed themselves as Mohawk warriors and descended on three ships carrying heavily taxed British tea. In a few hours, they dumped an estimated 90,000 pounds of tea into the harbor. In 1834, George Hewes remembered the scene:

"...In about three hours from the time we went onboard, we had thus broken and thrown overboard every tea chest to be found in the ship, while those in the other ships were disposing of the tea in the same way at the same time. We were surrounded by British armed ships, but no attempt was made to resist us...we then quietly retired to our several places of residence, without having any conversation with each other, or taking any measure to discover who were our associates..."

ABOVE *Three cargoes of tea are destroyed at the Boston Tea Party in an engraving by D. Berger in 1784.*

ish soldiers broke curfew and roamed the streets of Boston with clubs, looking for fights. Becoming frightened when a crowd converged on them, the soldiers indiscriminately shot into a crowd and killed five civilians. Bostonians demanded that the soldiers be tried for murder. Other accounts say that drunken sailors in the pub began to harass the British soldiers who felt compelled to defend themselves. Defended by John Adams, who insisted the soldiers had a right to a fair trial with competent counsel, two soldiers were convicted of manslaughter, while eight others were acquitted of all charges. As a result of the Boston Massacre, the spirit of revolution spread from Boston to other areas of the state.

Outraged that Britain was importing nontaxed tea into Massachusetts, a group of Bostonians dressed as Mohawk warriors on December 16, 1773, and dumped the cargo of three British ships into Boston Harbor. Britain reacted to the Boston Tea Party by passing the Intolerable Acts, designed to subdue the revolutionary spirit in Massachusetts. The Boston Port Act prevented the passage of all ships into the harbor, and 10,000 soldiers joined those already in Boston to enforce the new laws. In response, other colonies sent direct aid to Boston and began raising troops. Colonies and towns created COMMITTEES OF CORRESPONDENCE to facilitate the exchange of information. The situation in Boston steadily worsened with the passage of the Administration of Justice Act of 1774, which provided for Americans to be tried in Britain for alleged violations of British laws and allowed British soldiers accused of crimes to be tried in England or in other colonies, usurping the authority of the Massachusetts justice system. The British followed these outrages by destroying gunpowder belonging to the Massachusetts militia on September 1, 1774.

Congress was still in session on the night of April 18, 1775, when Paul Revere made his famous ride to warn the Minutemen of Massachusetts that the British were headed toward Concord by boat. Because of this advance warning, the militia was waiting at Lexington for the British, who were on their way to destroy the arms stored at Concord. British officers warned the soldiers not to fire, and Captain John Parker ordered the militia to disperse. In the ensuing skirmish, eight militiamen were killed and others were wounded. The British returned to Boston after destroying the arms but were forced to deal with skirmishes all along the way. Within two months, the colonies had formed the Continental Army and named GEORGE WASHINGTON as commander in chief.

The first major battle of the Revolutionary War took place on June 17, 1775, at Breed's Hill, south of Bunker Hill in Charlestown. The battle pitted 1,500 Americans against 2,400 British. The Continentals held their own until they ran out of gunpowder, giving the British a tacit victory.

Washington spent months plotting strategy for the eviction of British troops from Boston. He ordered the retrieval of cannons 300 miles away in Fort Ticonderoga, New York. By March 4, 1776, the Continentals had fortified Dorchester Heights, and 59 cannons encircled Boston. Because of a storm, British General William Howe lost the opportunity to attack the American forces and decided to evacuate Boston. On March 17, 1776, one of the largest fleets ever seen in America sailed out of Boston and headed for Halifax, Nova Scotia.

Further Reading: John Adams, *The Letters of John and Abigail Adams* (Penguin, 2004); Richard D. Brown and Jack Tager, *Massachusetts: A Concise History* (University of Massachusetts Press, 2000); Janice Potter, *The Liberty We Seek: Loyalist Ideology in Colonial New York and Massachusetts* (Harvard University Press, 1983); Peter D.G. Thomas, *Tea Party to Independence: The Third Phase of the American Revolution* (Clarendon Press, 1991).

—ELIZABETH PURDY, PH.D.

Memoirs of the Revolution

Forty-five years after the fact, remembering the week the DECLARATION OF INDEPENDENCE was approved still had the power to aggravate THOMAS JEFFERSON:

> Congress proceeded the same day to consider the declaration of Independance which had been reported & lain on the table the Friday preceding, and on Monday referred to a commee of the whole. The pusillanimous idea that we had friends in England worth keeping terms with, still haunted the minds of many. For this reason those passages which conveyed censures on the people of England were struck out, lest they should give them offence.
>
> The clause too, reprobating the enslaving the inhabitants of Africa, was struck out in complaisance to South Carolina and Georgia, who had never attempted to restrain the importation of slaves, and who on the contrary still wished to continue it. Our northern brethren also I believe felt a little tender under those censures; for tho' their people have very few slaves themselves yet they had been pretty considerable carriers of them to others. The debates having taken up the greater parts of the 2d 3d & 4th days of July were, in the evening of the last, closed the declaration was reported by the commee, agreed to by the house and signed by every member present except Mr. Dickinson.

Jefferson's recollections of 1776 are just a few pages out of a large library of memoirs written between the 1790s and the 1840s. People realized they had lived through extraordinary times, had won a war against all odds, and created an entirely new nation. Memoirs, unlike letters or diaries, involve a conscious shaping of a storyline, and this was very appealing to the veterans of that era. It was an opportunity to write part of the creation myth of the United States.

And there was an audience for their stories, be they multivolume accounts or slim pamphlets. Even before the Revolution, literacy rates in America were among the highest in the world. Although books were expensive and, outside the cities, difficult to get, people still found ways to feed their reading habits, joining subscription lending libraries, forming reading clubs, and subscribing to journals and newspapers.

The greatest of the Founders—Jefferson, JOHN ADAMS, BENJAMIN FRANKLIN—all wrote memoirs, but not for publication. Adams and Franklin wrote for their immediate families and Jefferson at the request of a friend. Jefferson was the only one of the three to write about the passage of the Declaration of Independence. Adams skipped over it almost entirely.

And Franklin, whose *Memories of a Private Life* is perhaps the finest colonial-era autobiography, stopped his narrative around 1760, even though he didn't write it until he was minister to France in the 1780s. GEORGE WASHINGTON, a prolific diarist and letter-writer, never wrote a memoir. For the military perspective of the Continental Army, one has to turn to the recollections of junior officers or foreign participants.

Several British officers wrote of their experiences in North America, and as might be expected, their narratives had a slightly defensive tone. In 1777, General JOHN BURGOYNE—called "Gentleman Johnny" for his vanity and arrogance—had to surrender his army after a disatrous defeat at Saratoga. Just three years later, he published a defense of his actions that at least partially rehabilitated him in the eyes of his countrymen. Charles Cornwallis, who made the final surrender to Washington in 1781, wrote an account of his war experiences largely to refute the claims made against him by another officer, Banistre Tarelton, in *his* memoir.

Thousands of rank-and-file Continental soldiers wrote what might be called "accidental" memoirs after Congress passed the first military pension bills in 1789. Ex-soldiers who thought they deserved a pension petitioned the government with a sworn affidavit, describing their service. Often, the affidavits would be accompanied by journals or other documentary evidence to prove that they served in the army during those years. While often short on colorful details or anecdotes, these pension files are a good source of basic information on the average Revolution veteran.

Valley Forge

WASHINGTON'S TROOPS spent the miserable winter of 1777 in Valley Forge, outside **PHILADELPHIA**. A French officer, the Chevalier de Pontgibaud, joined them in December, and published this account of his arrival:

"Soon I came in sight of the camp. My imagination had pictured an army with uniforms, the glitter of arms, standards, etc., in short, military pomp of all sorts; Instead of the imposing spectacle I expected, I saw, grouped together or standing alone, a few militiamen, poorly clad, and for the most part without shoes—many of them badly armed, but all well supplied with provisions, and I noticed that tea and sugar formed part of their rations ...Such, in strict truth, was, at the time I came amongst them, the appearance of this armed mob, the leader of whom was the man who has rendered the name of Washington famous; such were the colonists—unskilled warriors who learned in a few years how to conquer the finest troops that England could send against them..."

ABOVE RIGHT *George Washington's quarters at Valley Forge.* **BELOW RIGHT** *Replicated cabins of quarters used by Washington's troops in the winter of 1777.*

Some common soldiers did pen formal memoirs in the decades after the War. One of the best known was Joseph Plumb Martin. Martin enlisted in the Connecticut militia in 1776 at the age of 16 and fought until the surrender at Yorktown in 1781.

He fought in some of the major battles of the war, including Brooklyn, White Plains, and Monmouth. After Yorktown he moved to Maine, married, and had a family.

While one Maine historian described him as "a poet, a writer, and an artist," other records indicate that by 1818, he was practically destitute, supporting his family on his military pension of $96 and his small salary as a town clerk. His memoir, *A Narrative of Some of the Adventures, Dangers and Sufferings of a Revolutionary Soldier,* was published in 1830, when Martin was 70 years old.

It was an entertaining tale, funny and opinionated. Martin didn't shy away from talking about the rougher aspects of 18th-century soldiering, whether he was describing action on the battlefield or his actions against officers' stockpiles of liquor. He also had an eye for the females. Describing a march through Princeton in 1778, he said "I declare that I never before nor since saw more beauty...than I saw at that time; they were *all* beautiful. New-Jersey and Pennsylvania ladies are, in my opinion, collectively handsome, more so than any in the United States."

Martin's narrative has problems in terms of its historical accuracy. He describes events that, logically speaking, he could not have seen; the passage of time and the desire to tell a good story undoubtedly trumped strict adherence to fact. Most historians believe that he used a journal kept during the war, but that journal has not been found, making it impossible to check his original sources.

Martin died in 1850 at the age of 90. His book did not sell well and quickly faded into obscurity. It was rediscovered—and republished—in the 1960s and has since become one of the most popular memoirs of the Revolution.

One *uncommon* soldier wrote a memoir in 1797. *The Female Review; or, Memoirs of a American Young Lady* told the story of Deborah Sampson, a.k.a. Robert Shurtliff. Disguising herself as a teenage boy, Sampson enlisted in May 1782 and managed to keep her identity secret until October 1783. Twice wounded, she managed to stay away from doctors who might uncover her deception—until she came down with a fever in the fall of 1783. She was honorably discharged that month, and returned to her home in Massachusetts.

Sampson married a farmer named Benjamin Gannett in 1784 and had three children. The Gannett family fell on hard times in the 1790s, and in 1797, Deborah Sampson agreed to cooperate with a local publisher named Herman Mann. Mann penned her memoirs for her. She followed publication of the book up with a speaking tour around New England, where she gave lectures dressed in her old Continental uniform. All of this was to support her petition for a federal pension. In 1802, her request was granted, and she was given a pension of $4 a month. Without her memoir, Sampson might well have been forgotten by history. Instead, in 1983, she was named the Official Heroine of the Commonwealth of Massachusetts.

Further Reading: Thomas S. Abler, *Chainbreaker: The Revolutionary War Memoirs of Governor Blacksnake as Told to Benjamin Williams* (Bison Books, 2005); Henry Steele Commager, ed., *The Spirit of '76: The Story of the American Revolution as Told by Its Participants* (Da Capo Press, 1968); Joseph Plumb Martin, *A Narrative of a Revolutionary Soldier* (Signet Classics, 2001).

—HEATHER K. MICHON

Morris, Robert (1734–1806)

As a delegate from Pennsylvania, Robert Morris did not initially support the DECLARATION OF INDEPENDENCE. He felt the colonies were not ready for such a step and did not vote for the Declaration on July 4.

Morris was born in Liverpool, England. His father, the American tobacco agent for a Liverpool firm, brought his son to PHILADELPHIA to be educated in 1747. A few years later, Morris became an apprentice in the mercantile house of Charles Willing. Proving to be an excellent businessman, Morris became a partner with Thomas Willing in 1757 and quickly established himself as a leading merchant.

He became active in public affairs following the passage of the Stamp Act. He was a signer of the nonimportation agreement of 1765 and later served as a member of the Pennsylvania Council of Safety. In 1775 he was elected to the Continental Congress (see CONTINENTAL CONGRESS, FIRST AND SECOND), where he served until 1778. During his time in Congress, as a member of the Secret Committee of Commerce, Morris worked tirelessly to procure and distribute supplies for the Continental Army. In view of these activities it is perhaps surprising that Morris did not initially support the Declaration. Nevertheless, once the decision was made, Robert supported it and signed the Declaration of Independence on August 2.

Following his term in Congress, Morris became a member of the Pennsylvania State Assembly. In 1781 he became the first superintendent of finance. He was selected as a delegate to the Constitutional Convention in 1787 and offered the post of secretary of treasury under President GEORGE WASHINGTON. He turned down this position but did become one of Pennsylvania's first senators, serving in the U.S. Senate until 1795. Following his retirement from public life, Morris was forced to confront the enormous debt he and his partners had amassed while speculating in land. In the end, it proved too much even for the great financier and he was taken to debtor's prison in 1798. Morris remained in prison until 1801 and died bankrupt on May 8, 1806.

Further Reading: Robert Morris, *Confidential Correspondence of Robert Morris, the Great Financier of the Revolution* (Kessinger Publishing, 2003); Clarence Ver Steeg, *Robert Morris: Revolutionary Financier* (Octagon Books, 1972); Eleanor May Young, *Forgotten Patriot: Robert Morris* (Macmillan, 1950).

—JOSHUA P. SCHIER

ABOVE *Photo of a painting of Robert Morris by C. W. Peale. Morris did not initally support the Declaration, but signed it on August 2.*

N

National Archives

The original signed and embossed copy of the DECLARATION OF INDEPENDENCE is carefully preserved today at the National Archives in Washington, D.C., where it is viewed daily by tourists from all over the world. Officially sanctioned in 1926 by Congress, the concept of an official hall of records became a reality for the American people. But it was not until 1933 that construction finally began on the facility, with Herbert Hoover laying the cornerstone of the building. The concept of a centralized location in which to preserve and protect historical records that were of great value was not a new one.

The realization that the government needed a specialized location in which to preserve documents of great legal and historical value came in the year 1800. A fire destroyed or damaged many records housed in the War and Treasury departments. This was the first inkling that the nation would need a more structured method of preservation and holdings.

By the late 19th century the land holdings and population had begun to boom. This boom caused a surge in the various types of records that needed to be preserved. By 1877 the need for a national hall of records was again confirmed, when a fire destroyed the upper floor of the patent office and a fireproof location seemed the ideal remedy. Founded to organize the preservation and archival structures of a hall of records, the American Historical Association went

THE NATIONAL ARCHIVES AT LEFT
Each year more than one million people visit the National Archives building in Washington, D.C., where the Declaration of Independence, the Constitution, and the Bill of Rights are on display. Built in the neoclassical revival style, the National Archives building is located halfway between the White House and the Capitol, on Pennsylvania Avenue, and occupies two full city blocks.

Charters of Freedom

THE MOST famous of the exhibits in the rotunda of the National Archives building is the Charters of Freedom. The Declaration of Independence and the Constitution of the United States were installed into protective glass cases to preserve the documents for as long as possible. Each encasement is filled with helium and is at a controlled 25 to 30 percent humidity at all times. To prevent fluctuations in gases and humidity the case was sealed with a thin strip of lead soldered to the copper frame. The only way to open the case is to break the seal. The Charters move on a system of remote conveyors when they are not on display. Security surrounding the documents is so tight that neither the government nor Diebold, the company responsible for the construction of the vaults as well as the conveyors, will discuss specifics. The location, distance the documents travel, positions of rest inside the National Archives Building, and direction of travel are all closely guarded secrets. When the documents reach their separate locations within the building each rests in a sealed reinforced concrete vault that is strategically placed within the Archives. Each set of documents that constitute the Charters of Freedom has a vault in which it is secured.

on record in support of the concept. Though a study of European archival systems was conducted, Congress voted down the bill recommending that funding be allocated in 1898. By 1899 a commission was developed to study the need for a hall of records. The years between 1900 and 1917 brought much collaboration between government agencies to create the holdings of the archives.

Fire again brought the issue of a centralized holdings facility to the forefront when a majority of the New York State archives was destroyed. President William Howard Taft brought the issue before Congress. Again, no action was taken and in 1921 another fire, this time in the Commerce Department, destroyed the records from the census of 1890. After a long and embattled journey that spanned over 100 years, the Congress finally appropriated $6.9 million in 1926, but that was later increased to $8.5 million. By 1931 ground had been broken and just two years later, the building was under construction. The first staff of the National Archives moved into the buildings as the construction was being completed, and in 1936 Barry Faulkner's murals were installed in the rotunda.

The role of the National Archives has been one of change and adaptation over the years. By the 1950s the National Archives name had changed to the National Archives and Records Service. The organization was now responsible for not only archives of historical materials, but current records of historical significance.

The building is constructed of pale gray granite as well as limestone. The massive structure has the capacity to house 757,000 square feet of storage space and occupies a space equivalent to two city blocks. Originally, plans for construction included the inclusion of an interior courtyard in the center of the archives. Immediately, the need for more archival space was recognized and the courtyard was filled in to create double the storage space of the original design. The courtyard only allowed for 374,000 square feet of storage space. The original design severely underestimated the amount of storage space that would be needed for the archives and records, and storage and administration space was rented in various locations in the Washington, D.C., area. In 1984 the name of the organization was again changed to the National Archives and Records Administration (NARA) and for the second time in its history, it was an independent governmental administration.

The National Archives and Records Administration has jurisdiction over the original archives building as well as several facilities throughout the country. Included under the auspices of the NARA are the National Archives at College Park, Maryland, all presidential libraries, and all regional records services facilities.

Further Reading: E. Bruun and J. Crosby, *Our Nation's Archives Archive: A History of the United States in Documents* (Black Dog Publishers, 1999); R. Conrad Stein, *The National Archives* (Watts Library, 2002); Robert Warner, *Diary of a Dream: A History of the National Archives Independence Movement, 1980–85* (Scarecrow Press, 1995).

—**CARLISE E. WOMACK**

Native Americans

M any people think of the momentous events of July 4, 1776, as the official beginning of a struggle between Great Britain and its North American subjects over the issue of independence. But the American Revolution involved many other peoples and affected their independence as well. Among those most affected by the American Revolution were the Native American tribes that inhabited the territories claimed by Britain and its American colonists. Native Americans played an important role in the Revolution and had been involved in European politics in North America long before July 4, 1776.

Many Native American tribes inhabited and claimed for themselves the territories settled by British colonists. In the north, the Iroquois and various Algonquian tribes, such as the Montagnais, the Abenaki, the Mahican, the Massachusett, the Mohegan, the Wampanoag, and the Narragansett, held sway over the land. In the middle colonies of Pennsylvania and Delaware, tribes such as the Lenni Lenape—also called the Delaware—dominated. In the south, a variety of tribes, including the Cherokee, the Choctaw, the Chickasaw, the Creek, and the Catawbas, controlled the land.

THE IROQUOIS FEDERATION

The Iroquois were the most powerful. The Iroquois were a large tribe that controlled territory in Canada, in the Great Lakes region, and in New York. The Iroquois consisted of five separate tribes: the Mohawks, the Onondagas, the Cayugas, the Senecas, and the Oneidas. Together, these tribes formed the Five Nations of the Iroquois, also known as the Iroquois League or the Iroquois Federation. Each tribe inhabited and governed its own villages but met regularly with the others at the main town of the Onondagas, who occupied the center of the Federation's territory, to discuss matters of importance to the Five Nations. The Iroquois Federation's central purpose was to maintain peace and unity among the various Iroquois tribes. The federation, however, had no authority to compel the member Nations to act in any particular way. The unity that the federation brought to the Five Nations gave them the ability to function as a powerful military unit, and the Iroquois were famous for conducting brutal attacks on the villages of neighboring tribes.

In 1715, the Iroquois Federation was enlarged, and the Iroquois became known as the Six Nations, when the Tuscaroras, a southern tribe forced out of their homeland by American settlers, sought refuge among them. As European settlement spread, the Shawnees, the Miamis, and the Delawares also turned to the Iroquois for help. The Iroquois allowed these tribes to settle on their lands and granted them protection, but, unlike the Tuscaroras, they were not made part of the federation, and the Iroquois treated them as subject peoples.

WHITE–NATIVE AMERICAN RELATIONS

In the beginning, relationships between European settlers and traders and the native peoples were varied and complex. Many tribes, both in the north and south, aided the initial European settlers, often keeping them alive by bringing them gifts of food. In New England, some Puritan ministers eagerly undertook the conversion of Native Americans and encouraged them to settle in missionary villages near British settlements.

Friendly relations quickly deteriorated, however. As European colonists continued to arrive, settlers began to push into the interior looking for unoccupied land. Often the land claimed by settlers was used as traditional hunting areas or seasonal campsites by Native American tribes. As Europeans fenced off their newly acquired property, many tribes found themselves denied access to woods and meadows that they had made use of for generations. Conflict over control of the land quickly arose be-

Native American Rebellion

ALTHOUGH THE war between Britain and France formally ended in 1763, the British war in North America continued against a new enemy. In 1763, a prophet among the Delawares proclaimed that the native tribes of North America were the natural rulers of the land and that if they abandoned European ways and ceased their consumption of alcohol, the "Great Spirit" would give them the strength needed to drive the Europeans from their territory. In April 1763, at a meeting of various Ohio Valley tribes, Pontiac, an Ottawa leader, encouraged the warriors present to destroy the European settlers. The Ottawas, Shawnees, Delawares, Wyandots, Potawatomis, and other tribes began to attack British forts and kill American settlers, sometimes by burning them alive. Finally, in October of 1763, Pontiac received a message from the French informing him that France would not assist him in his fight with the British. Realizing that he could not succeed without the aid of his former European ally, Pontiac offered to make peace with the British on November 1, 1763.

ABOVE *A British cartoon, ca. 1780, critcizing the king's use of Indians in the Revolutionary War.*

tween eastern tribes and European settlers. All too often, conflicts ended in violence. Many tribes, no longer able to hunt in their traditional areas, moved westward in search of new territory.

The ability of the British colonists and their French and Dutch counterparts in Canada and New York to control the land and force out the Native American inhabitants was aided greatly by smallpox. Epidemics that struck North America in the 1630s decimated Native American tribes in Canada, New England, and the Great Lakes region. The death toll was high. Of those Native Americans living in the Connecticut Valley who contracted the disease in an outbreak in 1633–34, approximately 95 percent died. The Iroquois took advantage of the situation and increased their attacks on neighboring tribes that had been ravaged by the disease. As tribe after tribe fell before the might of the Iroquois Federation, the Iroquois extended their territory and their control farther to the south.

Smallpox epidemics were a recurring problem among the native population of North America, and northern tribes were not the only ones affected. Outbreaks of smallpox in South Carolina in 1698 and 1699 killed countless natives and so badly destroyed one band that fewer than 10 people survived. An outbreak in South Carolina in 1759–60, this time in the Cherokee town of Keowee, took countless lives.

As the living abandoned their dead and dying relatives and sought refuge in other Cherokee towns, they brought the highly contagious disease with them. By the time of the American Revolution, smallpox and numerous other European diseases, including influenza, measles, mumps, whooping cough, diphtheria, typhus, and scarlet fever, had taken a heavy toll on the native population of North America.

Smallpox was not the only source of death brought by Europeans to North America. The depopulation of the land was hastened by the European fur trade as well. As English, French, and Dutch settlers offered high prices for beaver pelts and other furs, Native American tribes competed to gain control of the fur trade. Many European traders readily exchanged guns and ammunition for furs. The presence of guns made tribal conflicts much bloodier. Several small tribes were destroyed by their more powerful neighbors, and other tribes abandoned their traditional territories. Fleeing westward, eastern woodlands tribes came into conflict with tribes who lived beyond the Appalacian Mountains.

Another result of the fur trade was that each of the Native American tribes began to sell their pelts almost exclusively to the traders of one European nation. Many Algonquian tribes traded exclusively with the French. Other Algonquian tribes, such as the Mahicans, traded with the Dutch. The Mohawks, jealous of Algonquian success, attacked the Mahicans and assumed the role of fur suppliers to the Dutch. The other members of the Iroquois Federation followed the Mohawks' example and also began to trade with the Dutch. When New Amsterdam gave way to British might, tribes that had traded with the Dutch often switched their allegiance to the English. Thus, by default, the powerful Iroquois Federation became linked to England and to British aspirations in North America.

THE FRENCH AND INDIAN WARS

Algonquian ties to the French and Iroquois ties to the English soon led to their involvement in a series of long and bloody conflicts such as King William's War, Queen Anne's War, and King George's War, that were tied to European power struggles in other parts of the world. In 1754, the last major conflict between the French and the British for the control of North America, the French and Indian Wars (1754–63), broke out. This conflict was the natural result of the earlier colonial wars. Following the British victory in Queen Anne's war (1702–13), American colonists headed to the Ohio Valley, previously claimed by France, to lay title to land there. Virginians in particular wished to claim land in the Ohio Country in order to cut off French trade. Fearing English encroachment on their lucrative trade with the Native American tribes of the region, France sent 200 soldiers into the Ohio Valley. In response, Virginia's Governor, Robert Dinwiddie, sent an expedition led by a young GEORGE WASHINGTON to the Ohio Country to order the French to leave.

The French refused and subsequently attacked a party sent by Governor Dinwiddie to construct a fort at the forks of the Ohio and Monongahela rivers. The French established their own fort on the spot instead. Learning of the attack on the Virginia party, Dinwiddie sent another military expedition, including some Iroquois warriors, to rout the French. The French fort, Fort Duquesne, was seized by the colonial forces led by George Washington. The French, however, counter-attacked, defeating Washington and forcing him to return to Virginia.

In retaliation, in 1755, the British government sent a force of 2,500 colonial militia and 1,000 British soldiers under the command of General Edward Braddock to capture Fort Duquesne. Braddock's forces were attacked en route by 300 French soldiers and 600 Native Americans. The British forces were decisively defeated, and Braddock was killed. Part of the reason for Braddock's defeat was that while the French were ably assisted by warriors from the local tribes, Braddock had no Native American allies to come to his aid. Earlier, in 1753, when the Iroquois

had expressed discontent over colonial encroachment on their territory, the governor of New York refused to recognize their grievances. Braddock himself further antagonized his potential Delaware and Mingo allies by treating them, in the words of one Native American, "like dogs."

At the same time that Braddock's forces were failing in their attempt to recapture the forks of the Ohio for the British, France's Native American allies were attacking farms and villages in New England and New York. Witnessing Braddock's defeat, the attacks on American settlements, and other British failures, the Iroquois Federation, disgusted at the inability of their trading partners to hold their own against the French, informed the British that they would receive no support from them in the conflict.

Instead of appealing to other tribes for help, British and American actions seemed designed to antagonize and alienate all of their potential allies. Colonial "rangers," ordered "to distress the French and their allies," committed atrocities against Native American communities, at one point attacking and destroying a village of 200 people, including women and children. The French, however, had no difficulty attracting Native American allies. Following Braddock's defeat in 1755, Delaware, Mingo, and Shawnee warriors initiated a series of deadly attacks on American settlements in Pennsylvania.

British fortunes did not change until 1759 when the Iroquois, in exchange for a British promise that American colonists would not be allowed to encroach further upon their territory, resumed their traditional alliance with the British. With support from the Iroquois, who convinced many of the Native Americans assisting the French to desert, the French Fort Niagara fell to the British. Following British orders, the Iroquois subsequently destroyed over 1,000 farms and killed Canadian settlers in an

King William's War, Queen Anne's War, King George's War

KING WILLIAM'S War, Queen Anne's War, and King George's War were a series of colonial wars fought in North America among the European powers, their colonists, and their Native American allies. The causes of these wars were political and/or economic conflicts among the great nations of Europe.

The first of these conflicts was King William's War (1689–97), which, in the colonies, consisted mainly of attacks along the frontiers of British and French territory. The French had numerous Native American allies and used them to attack British settlements, such as Schenectady, along the New York frontier.

When other colonies delayed in sending aid to New York, New York's governor called upon Britain's Iroquois allies to defend Britain's northern frontier. The Iroquois proved loyal to their British allies; for eight years they fought to defend Britain's territorial claims in North America and lost approximately one-third of their adult male population in the process. Although the British had the support of Iroquois, British actions alienated many other tribes. American colonist and famed Indian fighter Benjamin Church earned the undying enmity of Canadian tribes by attacking a Native American settlement in New Brunswick while the men were gone and killing the women and children.

ABOVE *Colonel George Rogers Clark's conference with the Indians at Cahokia, in a photo of a painting by Ezra Winter.*

Following close on the heels of King William's War, which ended without a clear winner, came Queen Anne's War (1702–13). Once again, the French and the Native American tribes who sided with them attacked British settlements on the northern frontier. In the attack on Deerfield, Massachusetts, 47 people were killed and 100 were taken prisoner. Many of the captives were marched into Canada. Some died on the way; others were killed when they proved unable to keep up. Once in Canada, some of the prisoners were returned to the British. Others remained, often for years, with the tribes who had captured them. Attacks by the Spanish (France's ally) along the southern frontier were not as successful. The Yemasee tribe, in allegiance with the governor of South Carolina, attacked Spanish missions in Georgia and Florida. Native American Christian converts were captured and sold as slaves to the English. Spanish priests and soldiers who were unlucky enough to fall into Yemasee hands were burned alive.

Queen Anne's War was followed by yet another conflict fought in North America over issues that were related to greater European concerns. King George's War (1744–48) once again set loose a series of devastating attacks on northern frontier settlements in which, once again, the European forces were supported by Native American allies, and atrocities took place on both sides.

effort to lure the French army out of their stronghold at Quebec. Although France did not come to the defense of its settlers, Quebec nevertheless fell to the British after a daring attack in September 1759. In 1760, the French, largely deserted by their Native American allies, surrendered their North American possessions to the British. The larger war ended two years later, and the treaty signed in 1763 left Britain in control of North America.

The outcome of the various European conflicts fought in North America with the aid of Native American allies had a profound impact on both the American colonists and on those tribes who had cast their lot with the French or the British. Britain's triumph in Queen Anne's War and later in the French and Indian Wars gave it claim to the lands of the Ohio Valley; American colonists assumed that the region was open to settlement and land speculation. Conflicts broke out between American settlers and surveyors and the tribes of the Ohio Valley. The Shawnees and Delawares began to attack American settlements.

TAKING SIDES IN THE REVOLUTION

In an effort to maintain peace in the volatile region, and in keeping with the agreement made with their Iroquois allies, the British government issued the Proclamation of 1763, which forbade settlement west of the Appalachians and ordered those settlers already established in the region to leave. This decision caused great anger among American colonists who believed that their participation in the war had given them the right to occupy the land. The Proclamation of 1763 also cut off land speculation in the Ohio Valley. This angered many prominent American colonists who desired to enrich themselves by investing in the land. Among those colonists who found their entrepreneurial dreams thwarted were

GEORGE WASHINGTON, BENJAMIN FRANKLIN, PATRICK HENRY, and the father of THOMAS JEFFERSON. American colonists were affected by the French and Indian Wars in yet other ways. The need to repay the enormous cost of the war induced the British government to institute new taxes in the colonies, which the Americans resented.

Some tribes decided long before the official DECLARATION OF INDEPENDENCE on July 4, 1776, which side they would favor in the conflict. Most Native American tribes sided with the British. The British government's issuance of the Proclamation of 1763 had led other tribes to hope that a British victory over the Americans would prevent settlement of the Ohio Valley. Thus, tribes such as the Shawnees, the Delawares, the Mingoes, the Miamis, the Ottawas, the Potawatomis, and the Wyandots willingly fought for the British cause.

Nearly all of the southern tribes, including the Cherokees, the Choctaws, the Chickasaws, the Creeks, and the Seminoles, allied themselves with Britain as well. The memory of brutal colonial assaults upon tribal villages also played a role in leading most Native American groups to turn against the Americans. The British were valuable trading partners who were more generous in their gift-giving than were the Americans.

In New England, however, many tribes did side with the American cause. The tribes of New England had been in close contact with European settlers for generations. Many had been Christianized, adopted English names, and settled in villages established by missionaries to house "praying Indians." Men from these tribes eagerly joined the Continental Army.

Some tribes, such as the Iroquois, split over the decision of which side to support. The Mohawks and Senecas pledged their loyalty to the British, as did many members of the Cayuga and Onondaga tribes. The Oneidas and the Tuscaroras, however, favored the American side. The allegiance of the Oneidas and the Tuscaroras with the American colonists made them the target of fierce attacks by those Iroquois who had remained loyal to the British.

Regardless of the side they chose, Native American tribes would ultimately discover that the message of freedom and equality proclaimed on July 4, 1776, was not intended for them.

Further Reading: Colin G. Calloway, *The American Revolution in Indian Country: Crisis and Diversity in Native American Communities* (Cambridge University Press, 1995); Gregory Evans Dowd, *War under Heaven: Pontiac, the Indian Nations, and the British Empire* (Johns Hopkins University Press, 2002); Elizabeth A. Fenn, *Pox America: The Great Smallpox Epidemic of 1775–82* (Hill and Wang, 2001).

—ANN KORDAS, PH.D.

Navigation Acts

O ne of the underlying causes of the American Revolution and the DECLARATION OF INDEPENDENCE was British enforcement of trade restrictions. Many of the prominent colonial merchants who supported the move for independence were well-known violators of those restrictions, and JOHN HANCOCK proudly regarded himself as the leading sugar smuggler in the British colonies. Trade restrictions were embodied in the Navigation Acts, enacted between 1651 and the eve of the Revolution. Between the 16th and 18th centuries, British mercantilists were in control of the decision-making process in London. Consequently, the emphasis remained on profits rather than on fair play. The expansion of the British Empire provided the country with new resources that became even

American Response

FACING ARBITRARY and oppressive taxes, Americans began formulating responses that ultimately provided a basis for the right of rebellion. The first response, known as the Fairfax Resolution, did not totally reject the Navigation Acts, but protested the right of Parliament to create monopolies that infringed on America's right to act in her own interests. GEORGE WASHINGTON carried the document to the Virginia Convention, where it became a major influence on Virginia's ban on the importation of British goods.

At the same time, THOMAS JEFFERSON believed the colonies should pass both nonimportation and nonexportation laws and accused Parliament of infringing on the "natural rights" of the American colonists. Although Jefferson tacitly accepted Britain's right to regulate American trade, his draft articulated the growing resentment against the arbitrary actions of the king and Parliament. In "Considerations on the Nature and Extent of the Legal Authority of the British Parliament," James Wilson went even further, arguing that all regulations on trade were detrimental. British mercantilism ended with the 1775 congressional vote to close the British customs houses in the colonies and open American ports to *all* commerce.

more important with the advent of the Industrial Revolution in the mid-18th century.

The American colonies were thus viewed as a vast area of untapped natural resources capable of providing British manufacturers with the raw materials needed to increase profits. Initially, the colonies profited from the passage of the series of Navigation Acts because the colonists were classified as "English" and given trading advantages that opened markets to American traders. However, as trade restrictions led to colonial taxes levied by Parliament, the American colonies rebelled.

Mercantilists believed the most practical way to enhance British economic power was to control exports and imports. Consequently, Parliament passed the British Acts of Trade, placing the colonies in the role of enriching Britain's government and industries.

The first of the Navigation Acts was passed in 1651, restricting the import of enumerated items from Asia, Africa, and America to those transported on English ships, vessels owned by English citizens, or ships transporting items from countries in which the products originated. Certain enumerated items such as sugar, tobacco, cotton, and indigo could only be exported to England. The 1663 version of the Navigation Acts required all foreign imports bound for America to be channeled through England. In return, the British provided monopolies for certain American products such as tobacco.

In 1733, Parliament passed the Molasses Act, which placed high tariffs on foreign West Indies molasses. Since New England was dependent on cheap molasses to turn out its rum, smuggling became common, and its practitioners became creative. When the vessels of American smugglers were seized by the British, resentment in the colonies expanded.

With the Act to Prevent Frauds and Abuses in 1696, Britain created admiralty courts that were charged with hearing cases concerning smuggling. Any ship sailing from England to the American colonies was required to post a bond with British customs officials who were authorized to board any ship to conduct searches for smuggled goods. Any ship carrying enumerated goods was required to prove that the goods had actually reached their destination. In 1673, the Plantation Duty Act further tightened enforcement of the Navigation Acts.

The Sugar Act of 1733 gave Lord Grenville's administration the power to close loopholes that had allowed smuggling to continue. In addition to products restricted by earlier Navigation Acts, the Sugar Act restricted the export and import of cacao, coffee, and whale fins and increased tariffs on foreign cloth. Subsequently, the passage of such acts as the Stamp Act of 1665 and the Tea Act of 1773 were met with open rebellion in America.

When residents of Boston responded to the passage of the Tea Act by dumping the taxed tea into Boston Harbor on December 16, 1773, Parliament reacted by closing Boston Harbor and blocking all trade in and out of Massachusetts (see BOSTON IN THE REVOLUTION). The other colonies rallied to Boston's aid and presented a united front of resentment. Nevertheless, Britain followed the Boston Port Act with the passage of the Intolerable Acts and sent 10,000 soldiers to Boston to enforce the acts. Thus, the stage was set for the American Revolution. (See also AMERICAN REVOLUTION, CAUSES OF.)

Further Reading: Thomas C. Barrow, *Trade and Empire: The British Customs Service in Colonial America, 1660–1775* (iUniverse, 1999); Jeremy Black, *Eighteenth-Century Britain, 1688–1783* (Palgrave, 2001); John E. Crowley, *The Privileges of Independence: Neo-mercantilism and the American Revolution* (Johns Hopkins University Press, 1993).

—ELIZABETH PURDY, PH.D.

New Hampshire and Vermont in the Revolution

In some ways New Hampshire and Vermont were progenitors of the American Revolution. Paul Revere's first ride and call to arms took place in New Hampshire, as did the first truly military action on behalf of the colonies. New Hampshire also ratified the first state constitution independent of the British Crown. In Vermont, which was not recognized as a colony, Ethan Allen's Green Mountain Boys were the first militia to be beholden to no one save the people of Vermont, or the Grants, as the land was then called.

By the onset of the Revolutionary War, New Hampshire was a well-established colony. The coastal regions had a profitable shipbuilding enterprise, ample fisheries, a logging trade, and no small amount of smuggling. Further inshore, the land was hard, but no harder than the people. The Scotch-Irish immigrants grew apples and potatoes, made cider and beer, and sent masts south and east for ships of both North America and England. Vermont was subject to dispute between New York and New Hampshire over ownership, or at least the right to cede land.

The affairs of the colonies' grievances had their strident voice in Boston. However, the nearby colony of New Hampshire, whose roads seemed always to have a terminus in Boston, had a citizenry sympathetic to the growing dissatisfaction with the English way of rule. Moreover, Portsmouth, New Hampshire, was separated from Boston only by Cape Ann.

Portsmouth, New Hampshire

PORTSMOUTH WAS a shipbuilding center. In addition to outfitting many privateers, several ships of the Continental Navy were built there. Among these was the USS *Ranger*, which was commanded by JOHN PAUL JONES. The USS *Ranger*, under Jones's command, became the first commissioned ship ever to be rendered honors by a foreign power. It also landed the first armed force in England in over 700 years, when Jones led his raids on English shores. Jones's residence in Portsmouth still stands and is a museum of his life. Jones insisted on having a fast ship, for he said he intended to go "in Harm's way."

AT RIGHT *An artist's rendering of the second New Hampshire flag. The field was yellow, and the triangles in the upper right corner were red and blue.*

Revere made his first ride summoning action in December 1774 in New Hampshire, over four months before his famous ride to call the Minutemen to action at Lexington and Concord. Proceeding north to warn his New Hampshire compatriots of the deteriorating situation in Boston, his message found a willing audience. Shortly after the conference, John Sullivan, later a Continental Army general, led a group of New Hampshire militiamen and volunteers to Fort William and Mary in Portsmouth Harbor to secure arms and ammunition, should armed revolt become necessary. Some of the seized weaponry would later be used at the Battle of Bunker Hill.

After the Battles of Lexington and Concord, the Massachusetts legislature sent a summons to all New England states to mobilize their militia. New Hampshire men proceeded south and fought at Bunker Hill. The New Hampshire troops were led by John Stark of Londonderry. Stark had been a member of the famous Rogers' Rangers during the French and Indian Wars. Robert Rogers himself hailed from New Hampshire, but cast his lot with the British.

Stark, best remembered for his "Live Free or Die" statement, which is New Hampshire's motto, continued to prove a most capable soldier. After the crossing of the Delaware River on Christmas night 1776, he commanded the Continental Army's right wing in the assault on Trenton. Stark would also command at the Battle of Bennington, Vermont, in the summer of 1777.

Another general from New Hampshire was John Sullivan, so appointed by the Continental Congress (see CONTINENTAL CONGRESS, FIRST AND SECOND) at the outset of the war. Sullivan could fight well; however, when not fighting he tended toward acrimony with his fellow officers. General GEORGE WASHINGTON became a bit irritated at times with Sullivan's propensity to feel slighted for apparently no reason.

The last royal governor of New Hampshire, John Wentworth, fled the state early in the war, seeking refuge on board a Royal Navy man-of-war in Portsmouth Harbor. He had been a capable governor and not pleased with the Townshend and Tea Acts. Yet he tried to straddle a middle road when none was available. He eventually fled to England.

The Grants, or Vermont, is best remembered for Ethan Allen and his Green Mountain Boys. The abiding passion of Allen's life—and he was a large and outspoken man of passion—was that Vermont should be a state. Allen had been declared an outlaw by the royal governor of New York, and organized his militia of Vermonters to defy and harass the royal agents well before Lexington and Concord.

When war broke out in April 1775 at Lexington and Concord, Allen and his troops, assisted by Connecticut's BENEDICT ARNOLD, seized British forts Crown Point and Ticonderoga. Asked by the surrendering British commander of Ticonderoga about his authority, Allen replied, "In the name of the Great Jehovah and the Continental Congress."

Allen and his Green Mountain Boys also took part in the ill-fated assault on Canada in December 1776 and he became a prisoner of war. Exchanged, he returned to Vermont, which would declare itself an independent commonwealth. While Allen was imprisoned in England, the Green Mountain Boys fought under New Hampshire's Stark at the Battle of Bennington.

Allen's service and reputation earned him an appearance before the Continental Congress to appeal for Vermont's admission as a separate state. Vermont was eventually granted statehood in 1791, the first state added to the union after the 13 original colonies.

Further Reading: Jere R. Daniel, *Experiment in Republicanism: New Hampshire Politics and the American Revolution, 1741–94* (Harvard University Press, 1970); Patricia K. Kummer, *New Hampshire* (Capstone Press, 2002); Paul W. Wilderson, *Governor John Wentworth and the American Revolution: The English Connection* (University Press of New England, 2004).

—RAY BROWN

New Jersey in the Revolution

New Jersey was frequently referred to as "the cockpit of the Revolution" because of its strategic location between New York and PHILADELPHIA. In 1664, Jersey had become a British colony when the Duke of York, the brother of Charles II, was granted the plot of land between the Connecticut and Delaware rivers that encompasses portions of modern day Connecticut, New York, and New Jersey. In 1676, the land was divided between Governor Philip Carteret and a group of English Quakers, becoming East and West Jersey. The area was prosperous, and by 1760 the Jerseys claimed a population of over 100,000 people. Some New Jerseyans believed that the British had decided during the French and Indian Wars that the colonists were incapable of realizing their great wealth and determined to take advantage of the situation by claiming the wealth for themselves and the British Crown.

In 1702, the two Jerseys reunited into New Jersey, and a royal governor replaced the proprietors. Inherent political, religious, and ethnic differences continued to hinder the integration of the colony, and intensive rivalry between patriots and LOYALISTS flourished for most of the Revolutionary War. Suffrage had been granted to all male freeholders

New Jersey Legend

ALTHOUGH THE Battle of Monmouth was not taken lightly by either side, the location of the battle was the site of a humorous New Jersey legend. The battle took place on land that had once belonged to the Revered William Tennent, who was known locally as the man who died and went to heaven and came back to New Jersey. The minister had passed out during a conversation with his brother and been assumed dead. However, the local physician stated that Tennent was still warm and prevented the burial. When a fellow minister returned after three days, he attempted to continue the service but ran away in fright after Reverend Tennent rose up and rejoined the living. Although Tennent ostensibly had no memory at all of his past life, he later miraculously returned to normal, and began regaling his family and friends with descriptions of the afterlife.

ABOVE *George Washington at Monmouth, June 28, 1778, in an engraving by G. R. Hall in 1858.*

who owned at least 100 acres of land or who could claim at least £50 of real and personal property. At the time of the Revolution, New Jersey was made up chiefly of small farms, and most farmers were eligible to vote.

Wheat was the major moneymaker, although the colony had come to be known as "the garden of America" because of the production of a wide variety of truck garden crops, marketed in both New York and Philadelphia. William Franklin, the son of patriot BENJAMIN FRANKLIN of Pennsylvania, was the royal governor of New Jersey when the hostilities with Britain began. The younger Franklin lived in great style at Perth Amboy surrounded by a cadre of loyalists.

Overshadowed by New York and Pennsylvania, New Jersey has frequently been overlooked when considering the American Revolution, even by its own historians. This is partly because New Jersey did not have a newspaper during the revolutionary period, and documentation of its role in the Revolutionary War has been dependent on letters, diaries, and sources outside the state.

INDEPENDENCE

At the end of the French and Indian Wars, New Jersey was considered a royal subject of the British Crown. When most of the other colonies rebelled against the passage of the Stamp Act of 1765, New Jersey initially refused to send representatives to the Stamp Act Congress that met in New York in 1766. Once convinced of the need to resist the British trend toward arbitrary taxes, New Jersey appointed delegates and joined with her sister colonies in rejecting Parliament's right to tax the American colonies. After the act was repealed the following year, New Jerseyans toasted the king's health. However, jubilation was short-lived because Parliament fol-

lowed the repeal of the Stamp Act with the even more onerous Townshend Acts. New Jersey fully supported the SONS OF LIBERTY, who dumped British tea in Boston Harbor on December 16, 1773. Two months after the Boston Tea Party, New Jersey created a committee of correspondence (see COMMITTEES OF CORRESPONDENCE) charged with remaining in close contact with similar committees in other colonies.

When the First Continental Congress (see CONTINENTAL CONGRESS, FIRST AND SECOND) urged all colonies to pass nonexportation laws, the deep divisions within New Jersey were revealed. Some New Jerseyans chose to remain loyal to the Crown, but others simply resisted what they saw as the highhanded tactics of the New Jersey revolutionary element. A good deal of the division arose over the issue of the paper money that New Jersey had been liberally printing until Governor Franklin instructed them to stop. Without the paper money, New Jerseyans were thrown into jail because they could not pay their debts.

PROVINCIAL LEGISLATURE

Subsequently, the provincial legislature met in Trenton from May to September 1775 and attempted to devise a course for protecting the financial interests of the colony. The legislature passed laws mandating jail sentences for all merchants who refused to comply with the nonexportation ban.

Several months after shots were fired at Lexington and Concord, a second provincial legislature met in New Brunswick and complied with a congressional request to raise a battalion of troops for the Continental Army. However, New Jersey had no guns to equip the soldiers, nor did it have money to pay them. To deal with this problem, the legislature approved $50,000 in bills of credit, which served to put new paper money in circulation and to raise taxes.

When the election for a new provincial legislature was held on May 28, 1776, a major upheaval occurred. With only one-third of the electorate voting, radicals gained a majority. They set about creating a state government, even though the royal government was technically still in operation. The following month, Governor Franklin was arrested and brought to Burlington for a hearing. He refused to acknowledge the legislature's authority to act and chose not to answer questions. He was exiled to Connecticut where he remained until the following year when he won his freedom in exchange for the patriot governor of Delaware. Franklin died in England in 1813.

On June 23, 1777, the New Jersey legislature agreed to draft a new constitution and appointed RICHARD STOCKTON, John Hart, Francis Hopkinson, Abraham Clark, and the Reverend John Witherspoon as new delegates to the Second Constitutional Convention and instructed them to vote for independence. On July 2, 1776, the same day that THOMAS JEFFERSON'S DECLARATION OF INDEPENDENCE was first approved in Congress, the New Jersey legislature approved a new constitution. Support was not overwhelming; the constitution passed by a vote of 26–9, with 30 legislators abstaining.

Loyalist support in New Jersey was strong. The strongest loyalists were those who had been in positions of power under New Jersey's royal government, the Anglican clergy, lawyers, and some physicians. Most Quakers attempted to remain neutral.

The most active participants in the loyalist militias were farmers and workers, and they became known for looting and plundering their way through the war. Those most loyal to the patriot cause were

ABOVE TOP *George Washington at the Battle of Trenton, in an engraving by Illman Brothers.*
ABOVE BOTTOM *Washington inspecting the captured flags after the Battle of Trenton, in a lithograph of a painting by Percy Moran.*

Episcopalians, Presbyterians, those of New England and Scotch-Irish descent, and the wealthy.

WAR

The war began for New Jersey on July 1, 1776, when observers identified a fleet of British ships off Sandy Hook. The fleet, under General William

Howe, was carrying 30,000 men. Lieutenant Colonel Nathaniel Sudder became known as "New Jersey's Paul Revere" after he rode to Burlington to warn the New Jersey legislature. The legislators, in turn, informed Congress that the British were on the way. British troops subsequently landed unopposed at Staten Island and set off overland. By this time, New Jersey had sent her required battalion to join GEORGE WASHINGTON's Continentals and had raised 21 regiments and nine battalions for home defense.

As the war progressed, however, many soldiers became disillusioned and returned home. In order to maintain the local defense force, the New Jersey legislature created a system by which soldiers served in alternate months. However, a large number of militiamen refused to return to battle when their furloughs were over. As a result, only 100 men answered the call to protect New Jersey from British invasion.

Because of the lack of support among locals, reclaiming New Jersey from the British became the sole responsibility of the Continental Army. While the British were in control of the state, loyalists waged their own war against patriots. For instance, Richard Stockton, one of the signers of the Declaration of Independence, witnessed the destruction of his home and property. He agreed to sign a loyalty oath in response to brutal treatment from loyalists. Stockton never fully recovered from the ill treatment he received from his neighbors.

Between August 27 and December 25, 1776, the Americans lost approximately 2,000 men, but General Washington learned from each mistake he made. After the British took Fort Washington, Washington led his troops across New Jersey. On December 25, 1776, General Washington returned, leading American forces across the fro-

The Traitor

GENERAL CHARLES Lee (1732–82), an Irishman, was labeled a traitor by many New Jerseyans. Because of his prior military experience with the British army—he had served in Portugal, Poland, Turkey, and Romania, as well as in the French and Indian Wars—Lee believed that he was the only American qualified to lead America to victory. Lee was convinced that as a resident of Virginia, he would be named commander in chief of the Continental Army. Instead, that honor went to fellow Virginian, George Washington.

Lee's hatred of Washington set the stage for subsequent insubordination that culminated with his being dismissed from the army after a court-martial on January 10, 1780, following his refusal to obey a direct order from Washington during the Battle of Monmouth. In New Jersey, Lee had already been severely ridiculed for his failure to follow orders and reinforce Washington with a force of 4,000 men during the campaign to recapture New Jersey. Instead, after leaving, his men camped out, and Lee retired to a nearby tavern to spend the night. He was reportedly arrested by the British the following morning in his nightclothes.

zen Delaware River from Valley Forge into Trenton. Taking Hessian troops by surprise, Washington scored a major victory and boosted American morale. By January 2, 1777, a force of 5,000 Americans was poised on the banks of Assanpink Creek facing Lord Cornwallis's troops. The Americans repelled three separate British attempts to take the bridge, losing 130 men.

During the battle, Washington proceeded to Princeton where he regained control of the town and captured the Hessian soldiers who had been left to guard it. During the Battle of Saratoga on October 17, 1777, the British were again defeated when General JOHN BURGOYNE surrendered his entire army. On October 22, 1777, Count Carl Emil Kurt von Donop led his band of HESSIANS against Fort Mercer. His troops were crushed, and Donop was fatally wounded. The tide turned for the Americans, and the French joined the United States in an alliance that provided much-needed revenue, troops, and supplies.

In New Jersey, the battle between loyalists and patriots gathered new momentum, with loyalists kidnapping judges, sheriffs, and constables to keep the courts from operating and terrorizing the population. With the government of New Jersey in shambles, William Livingston took charge and restored order. Although some loyalists were hanged, Livingston granted clemency to many.

After the British occupied the city of Philadelphia, General William Howe sent about 2,000 Hessian soldiers to Red Bank in Gloucester County, on the Delaware River. Their mission was to destroy the American fort which was defended by 400 patriot troops. After an overland march through local communities, on October 22, 1777, the British attacked, but the patriots repulsed them in a short and violent battle. The American forces served under the command of Christopher Greene while the Hessians were led by Count von Donop. The Hessians sustained some 200 casualties, including wounded and captured, while the Americans lost 37.

Other engagements in South Jersey included a massacre of patriot militia holed up in a house at Hancock's Bridge by British troops on March 18, 1778. Skirmishes and battles between patriot and loyalist militias, and the tendency of many New Jerseyans not to declare for either side, troubled the commanders on both sides.

In June 1780, the British determined to capture Morristown, where the American troops had established headquarters. Twice, the Americans repelled the British. The first attempt in June 1780 was led by Baron Wilhelm Knyphausen, who was convinced that he could coerce the starving American troops, some of whom had mutinied, to desert to the British. Knyphausen had handbills distributed among the American troops that were designed to scare the Americans into committing treason rather than face his invading army.

At the battle of Connecticut Farms on June 6, Knyphausen was defeated. The second unsuccessful attempt to take Morristown took place at Springfield on June 23, under the command of General Henry Clinton. The battle resulted in British losses of 150 men. The Americans lost only 15 men, and another 61 were wounded. Neither Knyphausen nor Clinton discovered any Americans who were willing to desert.

Further Reading: Thomas Fleming, *New Jersey: A Bicentennial History* (W.W. Norton, 1977); Marc Mappen and Maxine N. Lurie, eds., *Encyclopedia of New Jersey* (Rutgers University Press, 2004); Barbara J. Mitnick, *New Jersey in the American Revolution* (Rivergate Books, 2005).

—ELIZABETH PURDY, PH.D.

New York in the Revolution

When the Second Continental Congress voted on the DECLARATION OF INDEPENDENCE that severed all political ties with Britain on July 4, 1776, New York was the only colony to abstain. The congressional delegation had caught revolutionary fever, but the provincial legislature continued to withhold permission that would have allowed delegates to vote for independence. The reluctance to endorse independence was due in part to the fact that New York had a large loyalist population concentrated on western Long Island and in New York City, which led to a divided legislature. Scholars have disagreed about the exact percentage of New York's LOYALISTS, but recent research has suggested that 10 to 15 percent of the population may have been loyal to the king, with an indeterminate number opting for neutrality.

New York Bay was discovered in 1524 by Giovanni da Verrazano, an Italian whose voyage had been financed by the French government. Englishman Henry Hudson arrived in the area in 1524, but it was not until 100 years later that the first permanent settlement was established by the Dutch at what is now Albany. The following year, Peter Minuit bought what is now New York City from Native Americans. The British took control of the colony in 1664 as a result of a decisive victory in the Third Anglo-Dutch War. With the best harbor on the Atlantic coast, New York City emerged as the commercial and political capital of New York and as one of the major cities of the American colonies. The city was also serving as the military headquarters of the British military in America.

Despite close political and economic ties to Britain, New Yorkers reacted to the passage of the Stamp Act in 1765 with anger. New York City hosted the Stamp Act Congress in the fall of 1766, which led to the passage of nonimportation measures throughout the colonies. New York's SONS OF LIBERTY were active in lodging protests against British tyranny. However, New York was the first colony to lift the boycott of British goods imposed in response to Britain's Townshend Acts. By 1775, as the call for independence grew louder, New York remained ambivalent on the issue of independence, honoring the royal governor and GEORGE WASHINGTON on the same day.

WAR

Control of New York's ports was essential to Britain's plan to subdue the colonies, and by July 2, 1776, British forces had taken Staten Island. With this port secured, General William Howe began landing troops. When the full expeditionary force was gathered on August 22, it became the largest force that Britain had ever employed, with 427 ships, 1,200 cannon, and 35,000 men prepared to wage war against the American colonies. Five days later, in the largest battle of the Revolutionary War, the British were victorious at the Battle of Brooklyn Heights on Long Island and came close to capturing Washington's entire army. Although he lost 1,500 men in the attack, Washington managed to escape with his remaining troops in the middle of a storm.

Within two weeks, the British had captured New York City, where they remained for seven years. A fire that broke out on September 21 encompassed the entire area between Whitehall and Broad Streets. Because Washington had removed the city's bells to be melted down into bullets, it was impossible to raise an alarm. British soldiers tried to control the fire, but approximately a fourth of all homes in New York City were destroyed by the fire.

Eventually, the British occupied Manhattan, Staten Island, and western Long Island. However,

Legislative Reconciliation

BECAUSE LOYALIST sentiment remained high in New York, members of the provincial legislature were reluctant to give up their hopes that reconciliation with Britain could be achieved. The legislature was made up of both radicals and conservatives, and these factions were engaged in a bitter battle for control of the legislature. In June 1775, the legislature drew up a plan of reconciliation and dispatched it to the New York delegation in PHILADELPHIA. By the time it arrived, New York's delegates were aware that it was useless to introduce the plan because the issue of reconciliation had already been tabled.

When the vote on the Declaration of Independence was taken on July 4, 1776, in the Second Continental Congress, New York was the only colony that did not vote for independence. The New York delegation had been expressly forbidden to vote in favor of drastic action of any kind. Anxious to make the vote for independence truly unanimous, the delegation continued to await new instructions from the legislature. On July 9, the New York legislature bowed to inevitability and declared independence. The congressional delegates were subsequently given permission to approve the Declaration.

On July 19, Congress voted to change the title of the Declaration from "A Declaration by the Representatives of the United States of America," which THOMAS JEFFERSON had given it in his first draft, to "The Unanimous Declaration of the Thirteen States of America." Congress then ordered an embossed copy of the Declaration to be printed (see DECLARATION OF INDEPENDENCE, AUGUST 2 EMBOSSED). When delegates signed this official copy on August 2, William Floyd, PHILIP LIVINGSTON, Francis Lewis, and Lewis Morris signed for New York. Robert Livingston, who had served on the DRAFTING COMMITTEE that prepared the declaration, was no longer in Congress and was not eligible to sign.

ABOVE TOP *The Battle of Long Island in a photo of a painting by Alonzo Chappel.* ABOVE MIDDLE *The Retreat at Long Island in a photo of a painting by M. A. Wageman.* ABOVE BOTTOM *The Triumph of Patriotism: General George Washington entering New York on November 25, 1783, in an engraving by A. H. Ritchie.*

Washington maintained control of mainland New York. In three separate battles, Howe failed to encircle Washington's troops. Instead, the Continentals escaped to New Jersey. Periodically, Washington made attempts to retake New York City but was never successful. On May 10, 1775, in what many thought to be a foolhardy attempt, Ethan Allen of Vermont led his Green Mountain Boys to Fort Ticonderoga in upstate New York. The British had paid a heavy price to win the fort from France in the French and Indian Wars, but because the British were not expecting a strike, Allen's forces basically walked into the fort and ordered the British to surrender with only one shot fired. The fort was significant because it was a major trade route and because of the cannon and other weapons that were stored there. The Battle of Fort Ticonderoga was the first colonial victory of the Revolutionary War and was a severe embarrassment to Britain.

In the autumn of 1776, it became clear that the British planned to retake Fort Ticonderoga. BENEDICT ARNOLD, who had been with Allen's forces, was still reeling from his embarrassing failure to capture Quebec. He was determined to delay the British if he could not stop them. Arnold put together a navy comprised of 15 boats and 800 men. He sailed behind Valcour Bay and waited for the British to arrive. The Battle of Valcour Bay, which took place at noon on October 11, 1776, decimated the small American navy. One-third of the men were killed and all of the boats were damaged. Nevertheless, Arnold had accomplished his goal. He managed to escape during the night, and the British settled in for the winter without retaking Fort Ticonderoga. The following summer, Americans abandoned the fort to avoid bombardment, and the British reoccupied it.

On October 28, the American forces under Washington faced Howe's forces in the Battle of White Plains. Outnumbered and outflanked, the Americans were again forced to retreat. Washington arrived in Trenton, New Jersey, with only 3,000 men. By November 1776, Fort Washington at Harlem Heights was the only area of Manhattan still in American hands. When the battle for the fort began on November 16, 2,900 Americans faced off against an army of 8,000 British and HESSIANS. The Americans refused to surrender the fort, and Howe responded by storming it.

Although New York's legislature had held on to the notion that reconciliation with Britain was still possible, that hope was lost on July 4, 1776, when the Second Continental Congress (see CONTINENTAL CONGRESS, FIRST AND SECOND) declared that the American colonies had become independent states. Throughout the debate on independence, the New York delegation had been forced to abstain because they had not been given the freedom to exercise their own judgment. Finally, recognizing that there was no turning back after the Declaration of Independence had been approved by Congress, the New York legislature followed suit and declared New York independent on July 9. The focus of the legislature then shifted to creating a state government. The first New York constitution, adopted on April 20, 1777, was clearly an attempt to protect the interests of the state's elites. However, the document also established popular sovereignty and provided for secret ballots and annual elections.

THE TIDE TURNS

By the fall of 1777, the American cause had suffered so many setbacks that victory seemed impossible. The tables turned on October 17, 1777, when a force of 12,000 to 14,000 Americans under Generals BENEDICT ARNOLD and Horatio Gates faced a force of 5,000 British, Brunswickers, Canadians, and Native Americans under the command of General JOHN BURGOYNE at the Battle of Saratoga, New York, on the Hudson River. The British had intended for the battle to deal the Americans a crushing blow that would isolate New England from the other colonies. The plan failed when the Americans overwhelmed Burgoyne and forced him to surrender his entire army.

The implications of the Battle of Saratoga went far beyond the actual victory. It served to energize the entire American army and convinced France and Spain that America could win the war. Both countries declared war on Britain. On February 6, 1778, America and France signed a treaty of alliance, and the French forces and supplies greatly strengthened American chances for victory. Although New York had been an ideal base for the British while facing the tiny American fleet, the arrival of the French fleet demonstrated the danger of the numerous sandbars and other obstacles. British ships were frequently stranded and unable to respond adequately to attacks from the French fleet.

On October 19, 1781, after being encircled by American and French forces, General Charles Cornwallis surrendered his entire army to Washington in Yorktown, Virginia. It was the beginning of the end of the Revolutionary War. By July of the following year, news arrived in America that the king was ready to recognize the independence of his former colonies. The "Cessation of Arms" was read at New York's City Hall on April 8, 1783. Subsequently, all prisoners of war were released. Despite previous hostilities, British vessels carried many American prisoners close to their homes to save them from walking long distances. Some residents reported that a number of loyalists were so devastated by news of the American victory that they shot or hanged themselves.

On September 3, the Treaty of Paris was signed, officially ending the Revolutionary War. Some two years after Cornwallis surrendered at Yorktown, the last British soldier sailed out of New York. Around 28,000 loyalists also left America, many of them headed for the area that became Canada and for the West Indies. On November 26, the American flag was hoisted in New York for the first time in seven years. The evacuation of New York meant that the 13 separate colonies had forged a new and independent nation. The American Revolution continued to inspire people around the world to fight against tyranny.

Further Reading: James MacGregor Burns and Susan Dunn, *George Washington* (Henry Holt, 2004); Barnet Schecter, *The Battle for New York: The City at the Heart of the American Revolution* (Walker and Company, 2002); Joseph S. Tiedmann, *Reluctant Revolutionaries: New York City and the Road to Independence, 1763–76* (Cornell University Press, 1997); Judith L. Van Buskirk, *Generous Enemies: Patriots and Loyalists in Revolutionary New York* (University of Philadelphia Press, 2002).

—ELIZABETH PURDY, PH.D.

ABOVE *An interior view of the re-created cabins that the soldiers under General George Washington used for winter quarters in Valley Forge.*

North Carolina in the Revolution

The passage of the Stamp Act in 1765 changed North Carolina's attitude toward England from affection to hostility. On August 25, 1774, the First Provisional Congress met in New Bern and issued harsh statements against the colonial tax policies of Parliament and elected William Hooper, Joseph Hewes, and Richard Caswell as delegates to the First Continental Congress in PHILADELPHIA, and appointed them the following year to the Second Continental Congress (see CONTINENTAL CONGRESS, FIRST AND SECOND). The three delegates urged support for independence in June 1775.

Military action began on July 19, 1775, when 500 militiamen seized and burned Fort Johnston on the Lower Cape Fear. The following month, Governor Josiah Martin issued a warning to the people not to support the rebels or the Third Provincial Congress, but despite the governor's opposition the 184 members of the body met on August 20, 1775, in Hillsborough, and though they professed loyalty to the Crown they also denied the right of Parliament to tax the colonies. Fearing the loss of possible reconciliation, they rejected BENJAMIN FRANKLIN's call for a unified colonial governing body.

Despite the hope for reconciliation expressed at the Third Provisional Congress, the delegates sent mixed signals. When Virginia asked the North Carolinians for help against Lord Dunmore, who plundered plantations and promised slaves freedom in exchange for loyalty to the mother country, the North Carolinians responded by sending troops to Norfolk and defeating the British at Great Bridge. Likewise in South Carolina, the North Carolina Line came to the aid of the patriot cause and helped crush the LOYALISTS there on December 22, 1775.

All this is not to say that Tories did not exist in North Carolina. Rather, the Tories were numerous and were often a greater danger for the Whigs than the Redcoats. Governor Martin tried to play on the patriotic sentiments of Highland Scots, Regulators, and Tories in the colony, but the Whigs, anticipating such a move, prepared for armed struggle. By the middle of February 1776, tensions rose to fever pitch, and the patriot forces acted. Militia from Dobbs, Johnston, Pitt, and Craven counties and two regiments of the North Carolina Line led by Robert Howe and James Moore made plans for battle. Quickly, Wilmington was put under martial law and 20 suspected Tories were detained.

Shortly after, 1,600 Highland Scots led by Donald McDonald reached Cross Creek, but Colonel Robert Moore, determined to keep the Tories and the Scots out of Wilmington, deployed 1,100 troops at Moore's Creek Bridge led by Colonels Richard Caswell and Alexander Lillington. The armies clashed in an engagement that lasted three minutes. The colonials lost one man and another was wounded. The British lost 50 men and 850 were captured. In addition, they lost all their weapons and stores along with £1,500. The colony remained free of British invasion for another four years, but its troops fought in other areas.

The victory at Moore's Creek resulted in a call for a Fourth Provisional Congress, which met at Halifax from April 4 to May 15, 1776, in which the conveners called on the Continental Congress to declare for independence. While the Provisional Congress met, British General Henry Clinton organized raids on the Lower Cape Fear area, but the North Carolinians did not give in. By July 22, the colony received news of the DECLARATION OF INDEPENDENCE and three days later the Provisional Council of Safety declared the colony absolved from all allegiance to the British Crown. The Fifth Provisional Congress drafted a state constitution, bill of rights, and Declaration of Rights based on English legal precedents, and it elected Richard Caswell first governor of the state. The new assembly voted to send North Carolina's Continental Line north to aid General GEORGE WASHINGTON. North Carolina troops served valiantly at Brandywine, Germantown, Monmouth, and Valley Forge.

Horatio Gates, assuming command of the Southern Department at Hillsborough on July 25, 1780, had among his troops 1,200 North Carolina militiamen under the command of Richard Caswell and Griffith Rutherford. Gates engaged the British at Camden, South Carolina, on August 16 and lost 800 men killed and 1,000 captured—including General Rutherford. Half of the dead were North Carolinians. Gates lost his command as a result of the debacle, and Caswell was removed from command of the North Carolina militia.

After the disaster at Camden, the British occupied Charlotte, but found that loyalist support was nearly nonexistent. On October 7, 1780, frontiersmen met the British about a mile and a half from the North Carolina border at King's Mountain. The Americans captured the mountain and inflicted heavy losses on the British, forcing General Charles Cornwallis, now distrustful of loyalist support in Charlotte, to retreat into nearby Winnsboro, South Carolina.

By December 1780, Nathanael Greene took command of the Southern Department at Charlotte. Daniel Morgan, with an army of 1,000 men (300 from North Carolina) defeated Colonel Banastre Tarleton at Cowpens on the Broad River. Cornwallis set out in hot pursuit of Morgan, who retreated toward Charlotte. Greene, upon hearing of Cornwallis's pursuit, took control of Morgan's forces and retreated deep into Virginia. Greene's retreat resulted in Cornwallis finding his troops deep in patriot territory in the middle of winter, 230 miles from his base of supply. Greene returned to North Carolina to face Cornwallis, and the two armies fought at Guilford Courthouse on March 15, 1781. North Carolina militia formed the first two lines of defense against the British and suffered great losses during the battle, and though Cornwallis could claim victory, his army was weakened. Cornwallis then marched to Wilmington and arrived there on April 7, but then left for Virginia April 25, where he surrendered at Yorktown on October 19, 1781.

Further Reading: John Buchanan, *Road to Guilford Courthouse: The American Revolution in the Carolinas* (Wiley, 1999); Walter B. Edgar, *Partisans and Redcoats: The Southern Conflict That Turned the Tide of the American Revolution* (HarperCollins, 2003); Hugh F. Rankin, *North Carolina in the American Revolution* (North Carolina Division of Archives and History, 1996).

—JAMES BAUGESS

ABOVE *Soldiers in the Continental Army carried water in barrel canteens, such as the one shown above.*

P

Pennsylvania in the Revolution

Dutch and Swedish settlers originally settled Pennsylvania, but with the capture of New York in 1664 during the Third Anglo-Dutch War, Britain gained control of the area. In 1681, in order to discharge a debt to the Penn family, King Charles II granted a charter to Quaker William Penn, who laid out a plan to build the city of PHILADELPHIA over the next year. During the colonial period, each of the 13 colonies had its own legislature, and the royal colonies had governors appointed by the king. As a proprietary colony, Pennsylvania exercised a good deal of control over its own government. In 1776, the population of Philadelphia was around 300,000 and the colony was home to 11,000 slaves. As the largest city in America, Philadelphia became the political, financial, and cultural hub of the British colonies in North America.

The Pennsylvania colony was sharply divided over the issue of independence. The city was home to a large contingent of Tories. Quakers, also called Friends, were a significant factor in Philadelphia politics, and they tended to oppose independence because of their pacifist tendencies (see SOCIETY OF FRIENDS). Many Quakers also had strong economic ties to Britain and ongoing disagreements with the Presbyterians, who were mostly Whigs. This made it unlikely that the Quakers would join Whigs in supporting the patriot cause.

In the mid-1760s when Britain began levying taxes on the colonies to pay for debts incurred in the French and Indian Wars (1754–63),

CANNON FIRE *Historical societies and other organizations across America keep the stories and lessons of the Revolutionary War alive with special presentations and battle reenactments, such as the one shown* AT LEFT, *in which smoke and spray give clear indication of the power of cannons from the 1770s.*

Pennsylvania joined the other colonies in protest. Pennsylvania sent representatives to the Stamp Act Congress that met in New York in October 1766, and complied with the request to pass nonimportation agreements that banned all trade with Britain until the Stamp Act was repealed. As Pennsylvania and Delaware, which had come under Penn's control in 1664, began to formulate a response to Britain's "taxation without representation," John Dickinson rose to the forefront of the debate with a series of letters that appeared in the Philadelphia newspapers in the final months of 1767 and the early months of 1768. The letters were later republished as "The Farmer's Letters" and read throughout the colonies and Europe. Although he remained loyal to the Crown, Dickinson theoreti-

cally supported the right for people to rebel against tyranny. By 1773, Britain had repealed taxes on all products except tea. In response, Dickinson urged the colonists to use restraint and seek reconciliation with the mother country.

INDEPENDENCE

After Britain removed the taxes imposed on the colonies under the Townshend Acts that had followed the repeal of the Stamp Act, they retained the tax on tea. Britain further compounded this aggravation by granting the East India Company the right to export tea to America without paying the required taxes. Colonial merchants were furious, and Massachusetts retaliated by dumping the cargo of three British ships in Boston Harbor on December 16, 1773

The Pennsylvania Delegation

BY THE time the Second Continental Congress met in Philadelphia in the winter of 1776, America was already at war. When the Virginia Resolution was introduced, the Pennsylvanian delegation was split on the issue of independence. John Dickinson, a nonpracticing Quaker, argued fervently that independence was not in the best interests of the colonies.

Each colony had only one vote in Congress, decided according to the majority of the members in its delegation. If the delegation tied, the vote was thrown out. Pennsylvania's delegation was composed of seven members.

When Congress voted on THOMAS JEFFERSON's Declaration of Independence, BENJAMIN FRANKLIN, John Morton, and James Wilson supported independence. John Dickinson, Robert Morris, Charles Humphreys, and Thomas Willing opposed it. The delegates understood that unanimity was essential. Ultimately, John Dickinson and Robert Morris agreed to absent themselves from Congress

ABOVE *An encounter between Captain Allan McLane and a British dragoon at Frankfort, near Philadelphia, is shown in this photo of a painting by James Peale.*

so that the majority vote would place Pennsylvania on record as voting for independence.

(see BOSTON IN THE REVOLUTION). Parliament subsequently passed a series of acts, which the colonists called Intolerable Acts, that blocked the ports of Massachusetts and severely limited the colony's ability to govern itself. Some 8,000 Pennsylvanians gathered at the State House and demanded action. Various towns had already created COMMITTEES OF CORRESPONDENCE to serve as clearinghouses for information, but a new committee of correspondence was established to interact with those of other colonies. The colonies began choosing delegates to a national meeting to discuss a unified reaction to Britain's tyranny.

PROVINCIAL LEGISLATURE

The First Continental Congress (see CONTINENTAL CONGRESS, FIRST AND SECOND) met from September 5 to October 26, 1774, in Carpenter's Hall in Philadelphia and developed plans to convince Britain that the Parliament in which America had no representation had no right to tax the colonies. They did not go so far as to declare themselves independent. Philadelphia received word of an impending British attack in Massachusetts directly from Paul Revere on April 18, 1775. When the first shots of the Revolutionary War were fired at Lexington and Concord the next day, public opinion in Pennsylvania shifted toward independence, just as it did in the other colonies.

The Second Continental Congress convened in Philadelphia on May 10, 1775. Following the dictates of public opinion, a number of delegates were more inclined to support independence than reconciliation as the earlier Congress had done. They were responding in large part to the actions of Britain in closing the ports of Boston and the dispatch of troops with orders to enforce the series of acts that had been designed to punish Massachusetts for the Boston Tea Party. On June 28, RICHARD HENRY LEE introduced the Virginia Resolution in Congress. After Congress agreed to debate the issue, the delegates were forced to take a position on the issue of independence. Through compromises and capitulations, the DECLARATION OF INDEPENDENCE was unanimously approved on July 4. The 13 colonies had become the United States of America. That night, Philadelphians heard the Liberty Bell ring out, signaling that independence had been approved. Patriots responded with celebrations that lasted through the night.

Following the proclamation of independence, Philadelphia served as the official seat of the national government until it was moved to New York City after a new national government was created by the constitution written in 1787. From July 4, 1776, to March 4, 1777, however, Pennsylvania virtually had no state government. When the legislature refused to declare Pennsylvania independent from Britain, as most provincial legislatures had done, the Committee of Privates declared the government vacant and set about establishing a government for the new state.

The drafting process for the new constitution was dominated by lesser-known radicals and inexperienced newcomers who ignored the interests of the elite power bloc. As a result, property and financial restrictions on suffrage were removed, and all white males over 21 were permitted to vote. Quakers were disenfranchised by a stipulation in the constitution that required voters to swear that they believed in the Holy Trinity. Opponents to the constitution, led by James Wilson and ROBERT MORRIS, objected to the fact that the document had been ratified by the legislature rather than by the people of Pennsylvania. For years, the operation of Pennsylvania's government was hampered by the battle over the constitution.

In June 1777, the Pennsylvania legislature passed the Test Act, requiring all adult males to sign loyalty oaths and renounce allegiance to the king. Divisions between Whigs and Tories became even more pronounced when Tories were forced to pay special taxes and a number of prominent Tories were arrested. A law was passed stipulating that any Tory accused of treason who did not appear for trial would be delcared guilty.

On June 11, General Thomas Mifflin received word from GEORGE WASHINGTON that the British were planning to attack Philadelphia. Congress moved to Yorktown, and the Pennsylvania government moved to Lancaster. In August, British ships arrived at the Head of Elk in Delaware and began unloading the troops. After the Battle of Brandywine on September 11, in which American forces were badly defeated, the British headed for Philadelphia.

By September 26, the British controlled Philadelphia, and divisions between Whigs and Tories became even more pronounced. Many Tories sided openly with the British, and three Philadelphia newspapers took a pro-British stance. In an effort to convince locals to join the British army, officials offered noncommissioned officers 200 acres and privates 50 acres. The British also began printing their own paper money.

General George Washington's forces confronted the British at Germantown, five miles north of Philadelphia on October 4, with Washington's force of 11,000 facing off against 8,000 British soldiers and HESSIANS. Although the Americans lost 152 lives and 921 soldiers were wounded or captured, they managed to inflict 537 casualties on the British and capture 14 prisoners. Washington retreated to Whitemarsh, and Howe lost his advantage by failing to follow up on his success.

While the Philadelphia militia was blocked by the British occupation, Pennsylvanians continued to serve with the Continentals. The Pennsylvania navy, which had been created six month before the Continental Navy was established in October 1775, was involved in patrolling the Delaware River and protecting supply routes for the Continental Army.

After the British evacuated Philadelphia on June 18, 1788, and moved to Halifax, Nova Scotia, relations between the Whigs and Tories grew even more intense. Several dissidents were tried, and two Quakers were executed. In 1781, several Tories were charged with theft after it was discovered they had stolen money from local governments. Groups of Tory highwaymen established regular routes along which they robbed residents and interfered with supplies to the Continental Army. When several of these highwaymen were arrested, they admitted that they were on the British payroll.

Further Reading: John B. Frantz and William Pencak, eds., *Beyond Philadelphia: The American Revolution in the Pennsylvania Hinterland* (Pennsylvania State University Press, 1998); Joseph E. Illick, *Colonial Pennsylvania: A History* (Charles Scribner's Sons, 1976).

—ELIZABETH PURDY, PH.D.

Philadelphia

Philadelphia was the leading city of colonial America and the site of the key events of early July 1776. It was also the first capital of the United States. Philadelphia was a planned city, founded by William Penn as a haven for persecuted Quakers (see SOCIETY OF FRIENDS). The name is Greek for "brotherly love." But Philadelphia's status as the primary American city was in decline by the end of the 18th century. It soon relinquished its function as U.S. capital to Washington, D.C., which was developed to serve as the capital of the growing country. It ceded its role as the capital of Pennsylvania to Lancaster in 1799. Its role as the leading business center declined with the growth of New York, which unlike Philadephia was also a leading port. New York also benefited as an economic center as the country progressed westward. Philadelphia was disadvantaged by the cumbersome Appalachian Mountains, which hinder the route to the west only a few hundred miles beyond the city. Boston and Baltimore were similarly disadvantaged. New York, meanwhile, prospered by its easy route northward along the Hudson River, which was later developed westward by means of the Erie Canal.

Capitalists who charted the economic growth of cities found it easier to function in New York with its marketplace ethos than in either Philadelphia or Boston, which had been founded with a religious ethos in mind. Philadelphia has continued to decline in stature as a national business center into the 21st century, hindered by the presence of other large business centers nearby. While Boston can claim to be the leading center for all of New England (except a few places in Connecticut adjacent to New York) and Atlanta is the leading business center for a large part of the South, Philadelphia's area of economic dominance does not even extend to all of Pennsylvania, with the rise in the 19th century of Pittsburgh as the leading economic center for the western part of the state. Thus, as an economic center, Philadelphia has contracted from being the leading business city of the nation to being the leading business city for eastern Pennsylvania, southern New Jersey, and Delaware.

In 1790, Philadelphia had a population of 28,522, making it the second-largest city in the United States after New York, which then consisted of Manhattan and Bronx, with 33,131. By 1820, Philadelphia had 63,802 people, making it about half the size of New York and bigger than Baltimore by only about 1,000 people.

Penn laid Philadelphia out on a grid. Pennsylvania—literally "Penn's woods"—was named for him, and was the first city in the world to be laid out on a grid. A grid is more suitable for the relatively flat land that lies

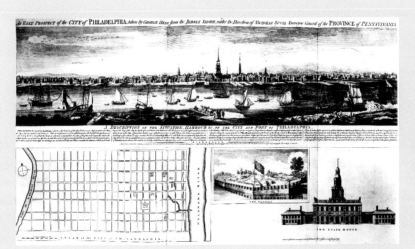

AT LEFT *A prospect of the city of Philadelphia, engraved and published according to an act of Parliament by T. Jeffreys, 1768.*

under Philadelphia and most U.S. cities developed afterward than for Old World cities and the earliest U.S. cities. A grid is also more harmonious with the ideals of orderliness and simplicity embodied in Quakerism. City Hall sits at the center of the grid, obliterating the intersection of Broad and Market streets, with a 37-foot statue of William Penn atop it.

Philadelphia was chosen as the capital of the United States under the Articles of Confederation because of its central location and superior transportation access.

The Continental Congress (see CONTINENTAL CONGRESS, FIRST AND SECOND) met at the Pennsylvania State House, now known as INDEPENDENCE HALL, and it was here that the DECLARATION OF INDEPENDENCE was approved on July 4, 1776. In the eastern part of Philadelphia's downtown can be found the most historic square mile in the United States, and it is now constituted as Independence National Historical Park. In this space, bounded by 7th Street, Locust Street, Vine Street, and the Delaware River, are contained Independence Hall, Carpenters' Hall, the DECLARATION HOUSE (JACOB GRAFF HOUSE), the ruins of BENJAMIN FRANKLIN'S house and his grave, the Liberty Bell, the Betsy Ross house, the tomb of the unknown soldier of the Revolutionary War, the first U.S. Mint, and several historic churches.

Philadelphia hosted the Centennial Exposition in 1876. It was the first world's fair in the United States. Philadelphia was also one of the focal points of the American Revolution BICENTENNIAL in 1976. The centennial and bicentennial of the U.S. Constitution received much less attention than the respective anniversaries of the Declaration of Independence, but those were focused on Philadelphia also.

Further Reading: Edwin Wolf II, *Philadelphia: Portrait of an American City: A Bicentennial History* (Stackpole, 1975); Robert E. Wright, *The*

First Wall Street: Chestnut Street, Philadelphia, and the Birth of American Finance (University of Chicago Press, 2005).

—TONY L. HILL

Plantation Life and Slavery, 1776

The institution of slavery had been a point of contention in Philadelphia. Northern colonies were beginning to abolish the practice and free their few remaining slaves. But in the South, slavery had developed into an important part of the economy and culture, and white southerners could see no alternatives. Many of the men who signed the Declaration of Independence were themselves slave owners, including its primary author, THOMAS JEFFERSON.

Estimates of the number of Africans brought across the Atlantic between 1680 and the early 1800s vary, but 600,000 to 650,000 seems a reasonable figure. Native-born African Americans reduced the need for imported slaves by the 1760s in Virginia, but demand remained high in the Carolinas and Georgia until the turn of the 19th century. Captured from all over western Africa, men, women, and children were herded onto overcrowded slave ships for the five- to six-week journey to America. Mortality rates on these trips ranged from 5 to 20 percent.

Those who survived found themselves herded into slave auctions, poked and prodded by prospective buyers, purchased, sometimes branded with a hot iron, and renamed by their owners. The majority of slaves worked as common field hands. The staple crops of the colonial South—tobacco, rice, indigo—were labor-intensive, required endless hoeing, weeding, and irrigation. Soil depletion meant there was always more land that required clearing. Because plantations were large, self-sustaining farms, work constantly needed to be done just to keep the community running smoothly. Slaves worked from dawn to dusk, six days a week, with Sundays and some holidays free.

Women served in the fields performing labor as demanding as that done by the men. Most worked through their pregnancies and returned within a couple of days of birth. Children, until they were 6 or 7, were cared for by older slaves who could no longer work the crops, then given light work. By the time they were 10 or 11, they were laboring full time.

The larger estates generally had a hired overseer who managed the field hands on the owner's behalf. Overseers were commonly hired on a one-year contract, and at the end of that year, an owner would assess the crops' quality and yield to decide whether the contract would be extended or ended. Some overseers chose to motivate field hands with the whip, but this could be a self-defeating method. Slaves were valuable property, and if they were permanently injured or killed by overzealous punishment, it created a huge financial loss. Most overseers had the assistance of an enslaved "driver," who relayed, and sometimes enforced, their orders.

In the Chesapeake colonies, slaves would work the fields in small groups. In the Carolinas and Georgia, they preferred the task system, where each slave had a specific job he or she had to finish during the day. Once the task was completed to the satisfaction of the overseer, the slave would have the rest of the day free.

Colonial plantations were small compared to those of the 19th century. The largest colonial-era plantations had between 10 and 50 slaves. House

---

Slave-Owning Signers

AT LEAST 18 of the 56 men who signed the Declaration of Independence owned slaves: Button Gwinnett, George Walton, RICHARD HENRY LEE, Francis Lightfoot Lee, CARTER BRAXTON, THOMAS JEFFERSON, George Wythe, Benjamin Harrison, Thomas Nelson, Jr., Edward Rutledge, William Hooper, Thomas Lynch, Jr., Arthur Middleton, Thomas Heyward, Jr., CHARLES CARROLL OF CARROLLTON, SAMUEL CHASE, Thomas Stone, and William Paca.

---

slaves were as much status symbols as servants, and received better food and clothing than field hands, but round-the-clock service to demanding masters made their lives no easier.

During the War for Independence, slaves in Virginia were invited by loyalist governor Lord Dunmore to flee their plantations and to join the loyalist cause. It is estimated that between 30,000 and 100,000 fled to British lines. Some 3,500 men and their families who had actively fought on the Loyalist side were evacuated to Nova Scotia after the war. In the New England colonies, African Americans volunteered on the patriot side. After independence, the New England states abolished slavery, while the states from Maryland through Georgia retained slavery. This division between the regions would divide the new nation for 89 years.

Further Reading: Andrew Levy, *The First Emancipator: The Forgotten Story of Robert Carter, the Founding Father Who Freed His Slaves* (Random House, 2005); Kenneth Morgan, *Slavery and Servitude in Colonial North America* (New York University Press, 2001); Betty Wood, *Slavery in Colonial America, 1619–1776* (Rowman and Littlefield, 2005).

—HEATHER K. MICHON

R

Recreation and Leisure, 1776

In colonial America, people pursued many of the same recreation and leisure activities that they or their ancestors had enjoyed in their mother countries. Consequently, leisure activities in America varied according to region and culture. In New England, where the Puritan ethic was strong, recreational activities were sometimes seen as frivolous. On the frontier, families were often too busy to take time away from their work. Combining leisure with work or religion was one way to have fun without feeling guilty. Camp meetings, quilting bees, and barn raisings were popular on the frontier. In the South, along the eastern seaboard, and in large cities, Americans had few scruples about enjoying themselves.

Leisure time was often spent with families. Talking, singing, reading aloud, and walking were pursuits that could be enjoyed by family members of all ages. Many families also enjoyed taking rides together to observe the surrounding countryside. On journeys of over 15 miles, entire families might drop in on friends or other family members to break the journey. Weddings and funerals gave all Americans a chance to socialize. Another popular diversion was dining out at local inns.

ARTS AND LITERATURE

Music was very much a part of the lives of colonial and revolutionary Americans. Even in the military, those who were musically inclined

THE CRIME OF GOSSIP AT LEFT
A modern interpreter, at a colonial reenactment event, demonstrating a somewhat unusual form of punishment for the "crime" of gossiping. The face-mask contraption, called the gossip's bridle or brank in England, was not the only form of punishment for gossiping, but was perhaps the cruelest.

joined the Fife and Drum Corps, which called the troops to arms and entertained the public on ceremonial occasions. In homes, pianos, violins, flutes, and guitars were regularly used to entertain guests or while away leisure hours. Wealthy Americans supported subscription concerts that were held over a period of several weeks. Attendees could buy a season's ticket or choose to attend a single performance for half a dollar. Concerts featured solo vocalists who sang to the accompaniment of violins, French horns, hautboys, and harpsichords. Handel was America's favorite composer, and "Acis and Galatea," the "Coronation Anthem," and the "Messiah" were popular requests.

Americans enjoyed going to the theater in areas where opportunities existed. The first dramatic performance in America was a presentation of William Shakespeare's *Merchant of Venice* in Williamsburg on September 5, 1752, featuring Lewis Hallem's America Company. New York built its first theater in 1766, but a mob led by Presbyterians demolished it. One of the most popular playwrights of the revolutionary period was Mercy Otis Warren, author of *The Group* and *The Blockheads*. Warren was a strong patriot and generally used her pen to point out the shortcomings of her loyalist neighbors. She was not above poking fun at leading patriots, as she did in *Upper Servia*.

Reading was a popular pastime among educated Americans, and most towns had circulating libraries. For the highly moralistic, reading matter was likely to include *Jonathan Edwards' Sermons* or *Witherspoon on the Gospels*. Most families owned a copy of *Domestic Medicine, Johnson's Standard Dictionary*, and *The Frugal Housewife*. BENJAMIN FRANKLIN's *Poor Richard's Almanac* was a perennial favorite. In 1775 in *Philadelphia Magazine*, Thomas Paine wrote the first article on wom-

en's rights ever published in America and followed it up the following year with "Common Sense," which was instrumental in moving the colonies toward independence. *Night Thoughts* by the Reverend Edward Young (1683–1765) was the best-selling book of 1777, and Americans continued to read books by English authors such as John Milton, whose *Paradise Lost* was a best-seller during the Revolution. The first museum in the colonies opened on January 12, 1773, in Charleston, South Carolina. Other popular forms of entertainment included lectures and wax-works shows.

GAMES AND OUTDOOR ACTIVITIES

While Americans played all kinds of games, many religions were opposed to games that included any form of gambling. Board games, including backgammon, draughts (a form of checkers), and chess were popular in colonial and revolutionary America. While the upper classes had more time to play, people of all classes played games, and board and card games were favorite pastimes. While most women played at home or in the homes of friends or family, men engaged in regular card games at local taverns, coffee houses, and private clubs. Popular card games included whist (a precursor of bridge), loo, piquet, and *vingt-un* (twenty-one).

Edmond Hoyle's book of rules had been brought to America in 1742 and continued to provide instruction for playing whist, quadrille, piquet, backgammon, chess, billiards, and tennis. Benjamin Franklin's printing press regularly printed decks of cards. Card decks of the colonial and revolutionary periods were vastly different from modern versions. Cards had no numbers in the corners, which made it difficult to man them out while playing. The backs were plain. Designs were later added to enhance fairness since astute players could

Sundays in Colonial America

MOST AMERICANS, even slaves, were not required to work on Sundays. On Saturday nights, slaves generally celebrated the end of the work week with singing and dancing. During Sunday services, most Americans were required to focus entirely on worship. Seating varied among different religions, assigned or claimed according to family membership or sex. Some churches placed restrictions on behavior even outside formal services. In Connecticut, for instance, boys and girls were not allowed to interact between the morning and evening services.

After morning services, social interaction was acceptable in most churches and was often a time of feasting, with food enjoyed communally. In some communities, families retreated to small dwellings built on church property where they ate picnic meals and rested until it was time for the evening service to begin. In Massachusetts, such dwellings were known as "noon houses." Since most churches were not heated, church members were glad to return to these houses, where fires had been started before morning services. In those areas where Puritan beliefs were still a great influence, Sunday afternoon activity might be limited to reading edifying books aloud. In other towns, however, the time after church was used to entertain family and friends and to consume elaborate meals. In Sheldon, South Carolina, one wealthy planter entertained his whole congregation after morning services. Wealthy families were invited into his home, but lesser individuals became the responsibility of the overseer.

Leisure-time activities in the colonial period sometimes involved items such as a ball-and-cup toy, **ABOVE LEFT,** *tic-tac-toe boards made of twigs and small tree branches,* **ABOVE TOP,** *and decks of playing cards such as those shown* **ABOVE BOTTOM.**

memorize marks on the backs of certain cards of familiar playing decks.

In addition to playing some of the same games as their elders, young people in America played marbles and flew kites. Organized games for young people of the period included blind man's bluff, still palm, and various games that included forfeits and kissing. Outdoor recreation was an important part of colonial life, with activities differing according to region. In New York, for instance, bull baiting was a regular part of Thursday afternoons. In other areas, the practice was rare, and bull running was never a leisure activity in America as it was in Europe. Southerners particularly enjoyed horse racing and cockfighting.

Many outdoor activities emphasized physical activity, including early forms of hockey and bowling, wrestling, boxing, cudgeling, fencing, ice skating, and swimming. Fishing and hunting spanned the fields of work and leisure. Some individuals fished or trapped to provide their families with basic necessities, while others engaged in such activities simply for sport.

Outdoor festivals were common, frequently featuring competitions such as shooting contests, greased pig contests, and contests to climb a greased pole to capture a prize at the top. Gambling was an integral part of gaming and in the 18th century, the Great Awakening gave rise to organized efforts by the Methodists and Presbyterians to bring an end to gambling, drinking, hurling, wrestling, bull baiting, cockfighting, and other forms of public entertainment that were considered immoral. In 1774, with the Revolution looming, the First Continental Congress (see CONTINENTAL CONGRESS, FIRST AND SECOND) temporarily put an end to such activities by banning them for the duration of the crisis with Britain.

PARTIES AND FEASTS

In colonial America, parties and feasts ranged from informal events such as quilting bees or turkey shoots to elaborate balls and concerts, all providing entertainment and forging bonds among those of similar interests or backgrounds. Since distances between family and friends were often great and communication was difficult, extended visits were a regular part of life.

Visitors were entertained with picnics, parties, excursions, and expeditions. Food and drink were an essential part of entertaining in America, as they were elsewhere. Consequently, lavish menus and expensive wines and liquors were essential to formal gatherings. According to legend, the first American cocktail was mixed in 1776 by Betsy Flanagan, a barmaid at Hall's Corners in Elmsford, New York.

During the harsh northern winters, leisure activities were of necessity moved indoors. In cities such as Philadelphia and Boston, a major form of winter entertainment was the subscription ball or assembly. Activities were held in public halls and were attended by political and social leaders. Before the Revolution, such festivities were also attended by English officials and military officers. Most colonies had dancing schools, and Americans prided themselves on their social skills. During the Revolution, the names of dances took on a patriotic flavor, and such names as "Burgoyne's Surrender," "The Campaign Success," and "Clinton's Retreat" were common.

Dancing was suspended at midnight for a supper but resumed afterward, continuing until the early morning hours. In Williamsburg, Virginians mixed politics and recreation by holding lavish balls at the Raleigh Tavern, attended by prominent Virginians. Many American political and military leaders were also members of the Masonic Lodge, which frequently combined pleasure with other activities.

Young people throughout America enjoyed getting together to socialize. In the middle colonies and New England, bundling, the practice of opposite sexes sharing a bed while still dressed, was common. In other areas, bundling was seen as promiscuous. In New York, young people attended candle-dipping frolics. While the purpose of the gathering was to make candles for the winter months, couples socialized and romanced one another over kettles of hot tallow, and during the traditional "fire dance," which followed the candle making and feasting.

At formal dinners, women generally retired to the parlor for tea while men enjoyed brandy, smoking, and male companionship. Philadelphia's Quaker community (see SOCIETY OF FRIENDS) also segregated the sexes during wedding celebrations in which family and friends visited the newlyweds for a week.

Benjamin Franklin

IN HIS *Autobiography*, Benjamin Franklin announced that he had no time for taverns, games, or other foolishness. Nevertheless, Franklin was not above frivolity and had invented the harmonica. From the time he retired at the age of 42 until his death at age 86, Franklin's daily schedule at home followed the pattern laid out in his *Autobiography*:

5:00–6:00 A.M.	Begin the day with a bath
6:00–7:00 A.M.	Plan activities for the day
7:00–9:00 A.M.	Eat breakfast and examine course of the study for the day
9:00 A.M.–Noon	Work
12:00–3:00 P.M.	Eat lunch, read, and look over accounts
3:00–6:00 P.M.	Work
6:00–7:00 P.M.	Put things in their proper places
7:00–8:00 P.M.	Dine and enjoy music or diversion
8:00 P.M.–Midnight	Engage in conversation and consider events of the day
1:00–5:00 A.M.	Sleep

ABOVE TOP *Benjamin Franklin's return to Philadelphia in 1785, in a painting by Jean Ferris.* **ABOVE BOTTOM** *Franklin opening the nation's first subscription library in Philadelphia, in a photo of a painting by Charles E. Mills.*

Newport, Rhode Island, became a tourist mecca. Americans swarmed to the area for picnics, parties, card games, and balls. In the South, the upper classes gathered at Williamsburg, Charleston, and Annapolis to attend balls and plays.

HOLIDAYS

Americans came from cultures where holidays had frequently been associated with agricultural off-seasons. Many European holidays became an integral part of American culture, but they often developed an American twist. New Year's Day, for instance, was a time for wild celebrating in the 1770s, just as it is in contemporary times. The custom had been brought to the United States by the Dutch, who celebrated the day by visiting and exchanging gifts. The English continued to celebrate the holiday but added an annual turkey shoot to the festivities. In 1773, a celebration in New York turned so riotous that the provincial legislature banned public discharge of guns and explosives. Christmas and May Day were celebrated throughout America in much the same ways they had been experienced in the mother countries.

Thanksgiving was a distinctly American holiday. It had begun in 1621 in Plymouth, Massachusetts, as a celebration of a plentiful harvest. All 13 colonies continued to celebrate Thanksgiving, but until October 1777, there was no effort to make the holiday a unified time of national celebration. RICHARD HENRY LEE of Virginia proposed to Congress that a national day of Thanksgiving be celebrated as a way of expressing gratitude for the American victory at the Battle of Saratoga in New York on October 17, 1777. When GEORGE WASHINGTON became the first president of the United States, he designated November 26, 1789, as a day of national thanksgiving. In 1777, Americans also began celebrating the 4th of July as Independence Day. Many American holidays occurred in conjunction with elections and militia training, and people came together to buy and sell products, feast, and frolic. Public punishments were also scheduled for such days to make the humiliation more public. (See also CULTURE, 1776; DAILY LIFE, 1776.)

Further Reading: Donna R. Braden, *Leisure and Entertainment in America* (Henry Ford Museum of Greenfield Village, 1988); Gary Cross, *A Social History of Leisure Since 1600* (Ventura, 1990); Benjamin Franklin, *The Autobiography and Other Writings* (Penguin, 1986); James Schouler, *Americans of 1776: Daily Life in Revolutionary America* (Heritage Books, 1990); Stephanie Grauman Wolf, *As Various as Their Land: The Everyday Lives of Eighteenth-Century Americans* (HarperCollins, 1993).

—ELIZABETH PURDY, PH.D.

Religion, 1776

Some historians have remarked that the American Revolution is the most significant event in the history of the United States. Such a statement is particularly applicable to the study of religion in the United States. While the Revolution brought sweeping changes politically, economically, and socially, it also indelibly affected the shape of religion in the United States. Many of the freedoms that modern practitioners enjoy were crafted in early America.

Religion was not only affected by the Revolution, however. It also played an important part in shaping the culture that brought forth the Revolution in the first place. Political, economic, and social rhetoric were couched in religious terms. The war itself was envisioned through religious lenses. Revolution and religion came together on July 4, 1776, in ways that have left their mark on American society since.

Millennialism

ONE WAY that religious people thought about the American Revolution was through the lens of millennialism. Millennialism, in a Christian context, is the belief that there would be apocalyptic events preceding the Second Coming of Christ. Drawing on statements from New Testament writers (particularly Matthew 24 and the book of Revelation), Christians have looked for "wars and rumors of wars" (Matthew 24:6) to precede Christ's return. When Christ returned, he would set up a kingdom on earth where he would rule in peace for a thousand years (the Millennium). Millennial thought, however, is not limited to Christianity, as other religious groups have looked for an age of peace and prosperity to come. Individuals during the Revolution were no different.

Many religious people in the revolutionary age looked upon the conflict as the precursor to a millennial period of peace. Even secular individuals throughout the 18th and 19th century looked upon the founding of the new republic as the dawn of the millennial age (although they would have divorced the concept from the Second Coming of Christ). By viewing the Revolution through the concept of millennialism, many individuals brimmed with religious optimism over the fate of America and its people. It is important to note, however, that each war since the Revolution has also been given millennial significance by a variety of religious individuals.

ABOVE TOP The 600-year-old baptismal font in the back of Christ Church was sent to Philadelphia in 1697 from All Hallow's Church Barking-by-the-Tower, London. It is the font in which William Penn was baptized. ABOVE BOTTOM The Palladian window in Christ Church, Philadelphia.

Colonial America at the time of the Revolution was a religious mixture. Most of that diversity, however, was made up of varieties of Protestant Christian denominations. There were small numbers of Jews and Catholics in the colonies, but the majority of religious people were Protestant. The Church of England—the Anglican Church—was the legally established church in the colonies, but had a majority only in the colony of Virginia. In the Carolinas and Georgia there were groups of Quakers (see SOCIETY OF FRIENDS), Scots-Irish Presbyterians, Lutherans, and Moravians. Maryland had been created as a colony of toleration, where many Catholics settled, although they remained a minority.

In the New England colonies, many of the denominations were heirs of the Puritan legacy. Congregationalists and Presbyterians were among the larger groups. Baptists found some adherents in places like Rhode Island. Quakers and other smaller religious groups who were subject to persecution joined the Baptists in the colony of Rhode Island.

The middle colonies were also extremely diverse. Large populations of Dutch and German Reformed churches were in colonies such as New York. Quakers made their homes in middle colonies like Pennsylvania. Mennonites, Amish, Baptists, Lutherans, and others also settled in the middle colonies. The diversity of American religion in the colonial period fostered conflict between religious groups in many places. By the time of the Revolution, however, many came to agreement on the cause of liberty. Despite significant differences, religious indiviuals supported the Revolution, sometimes for religious reasons.

CLERGY AS REVOLUTIONARIES

The colonists had many religious reasons for chafing against English rule. Those who had chosen to be members of churches other than the Church of England, called Dissentors, still suffered persecution from the government in certain colonies. In 1689 William and Mary, joint sovereigns of England, passed the Act of Toleration. The act gave freedom from persecution to those who chose to worship with nonestablished churches. The toleration, however, was only extended to Protestants. Catholics and other dissenters could still be legally persecuted.

Of concern as well was the Quebec Act (1774), which gave state protection to Catholics in Canada. For colonists who had observed or heard about the shifting religious beliefs of English monarchs for almost two centuries, there was genuine concern among Protestants that the monarchy would be in Catholic hands again. They feared that such a shift in leadership would lead to renewed persecution of Protestants, even in the colonies.

Some of the leaders in expressing this religious dissatisfaction were clergy. Ministers would preach sermons decrying the immorality of British society and its leaders. As the war drew closer, clergy became political activists arguing for the separation of the colonies from England. While many clergy were fearful of revolutionary ferment, some were outspoken supporters of the patriot cause.

One patriot clergyman was John Witherspoon, who stoked the fires of the Revolution as president of the College of New Jersey. He encouraged his students to support the patriot cause, and wrote prolifically for revolution. He eventually served as a member of the Continental Congress (see CONTINENTAL CONGRESS, FIRST AND SECOND) and was the only cleric or minister who signed the DECLARATION OF INDEPENDENCE.

SIGNERS OF THE DECLARATION

When those 56 men gathered in PHILADELPHIA to sign the Declaration of Independence, they came from diverse religious backgrounds. Some were Anglican, or at least had a connection to Anglicanism, even if in name only. There was at least one Catholic signer, CHARLES CARROLL OF CARROLLTON. Several of the signers were also probably deist, whether explicitly or implicitly. Jefferson and JOHN ADAMS were known to have deist leanings.

Deists tended to look at the universe as the product of a deity who had created the universe then left it to its own devices. Deists broke from traditional religion, specifically Christianity, over questions of the supernatural. Deists were often anticlerical and rejected tradition and other types of religious authority. They did, however, believe in transcendent values and immortality.

Despite the religious diversity, however, nearly all the founders had imbibed ideas from Enlighten-ment thinking. Optimism in the powers of humanity and history along with emphasis on reason in approaching everything, including religion, helped shape the views of many of the signers. Ideas of tolerance also rose out of Enlightenment thinking and shaped the way the founders looked at religious liberty.

FREEDOM OF RELIGION

Freedom of religion as an American ideal has a varied legacy. There is no one particular source. Toleration had been an established system in England since 1689, but was extended only to Protestants and often overlooked in the colonies. The theory, however, was still in the ideology of the colonists. Surrounding the ideology of religious toleration was the thought of John Locke. Locke's

John Carroll: From "Sermon on Gratitude for Independence"

GOD HAS visited you in particular by a signal instance of his mercy in removing obstacles which heretofore cramped the free exercise of our Religious functions. ... In the events, to which I allude, they who attribute nothing in the affairs of Mankind to the government of providence; will only discover the result of human councel [sic] & passions, but they whose enlightened faith beholds in the history of Mankind the traces of a divine & overruling wisdom, will acknowledge the power of God continually exerted for the preservation of Religion. We particularly, dear Brethren, must feel a tender sentiment of gratitude towards the bestower of every good gift for the favours we now enjoy. ...The Holy Ghost has so worked upon & tutored the minds of men, that now, agreeably to the dictates of our own consciences, we may sing canticles of praise to the Lord in a Country no longer foreign or unfriendly to us, but in a Country now become our own & taking us into her protection. In return for so great a blessing, your first duty was & I trust you forget it not, to render to Alm[ighty] God the tribute of thankfulness due above all to him, & next to hear in your hearts, gratitude, respect & veneration for them, whose benevolence was the instrument of God's favour & mercy towards us. Let your earnest supplications be addressed to the throne of grace, that every blessing, temporal & eternal may descend on your fellow Citizens, your brethren in Jesus Christ.

A Letter Concerning Toleration had shaped English thought on religious freedom and was influential on colonial thought. Locke himself was indebted to an early American, Roger Williams, a Puritan, for his thought on religious toleration.

Locke's ideas on government, particularly equality and consent of the governed, shaped not only colonial political thought but religious thought as well. If people were equal, then they had the ability and the right to make choices concerning religious beliefs in accordance with their own consciences. Individuals had the right to join or leave any religious group that they wanted.

In later crafting the First Amendment to the U.S. Constitution, the authors drew on these revolutionary ideals to institute a policy of religious freedom. Despite the First Amendment, however, there remained a *de facto* established religion in many colonies' constitutions until the 1830s.

After the Revolution many religious groups found themselves in a new situation. Living in a nation with democratic ideals, churches and other religious organizations had to make significant changes to the way they practiced religion to keep up with the spirit of the times. In the revolutionary and post-revolutionary era, many churches became focused on the voice of the people. Hierarchies were rearranged and new hierarchies were created, especially within those denominations whose leaders were based in foreign lands.

In the years leading up to the Revolution, the Presbyterians were divided among patriot and loyalist ties. Gradually, the loyalist support decreased and the Presbyterians became patriots. While there were differences among Presbyterians over how to best approach relations with England, many felt that the colonies needed at least a measure of autonomy from the British Crown.

After the Revolution, Presbyterians were faced with the challenge of developing a Presbyterianism that interacted with the ideal of the Revolution and the new national spirit. While holding onto much of traditional Presbyterian doctrines, the Presbyterians made institutional changes to encounter the new American pathos. Among those changes was moving authority to more local authoritative groups, while also establishing a national General Assembly.

The Revolution, however, had a greater effect on American Catholics. Prior to the Revolution, Catholics were not allowed to vote, run for office, or worship publicly in many colonies. They were not allowed to participate fully in the social structure of the colonies. Because of the anti-Catholicism of many English colonists, American Catholicism had to adapt to difficult situations unlike what Roman Catholicism had faced in Europe. There were few priests in the colonies, leading to the development of a type of Catholicism that centered around the home and domesticity instead of priest and church.

With the onset of the Revolution, Catholics became almost wholesale supporters of a break from English rule. In the ideals of the patriots, Catholics saw the opportunity to enter public life in levels they had previously been denied, without fear of legal consequences.

The freedom that American Catholics experienced also led to tensions between the church in America and the Vatican. The doctrines, theology, and canon law of the Catholic Church were not designed to deal with democracy. The new theological situation in America, plus the Vatican's focus on European concerns (like the French Revolution), left Catholics in the United States to shape a post-Revolution Catholic Church. John Carroll, cousin of Charles Carroll of Carrollton and friend of

ABOVE *Abraham Baldwin, a chaplain in the American army, was also the founder of the University of Georgia.*

BENJAMIN FRANKLIN, was one of the most prominent priests to attempt to re-create a Catholicism compatible with the American situation. Renewed attention from authorities in Rome and the arrival of foreign (specifically French) priests caused the American experiment in Catholicism to be short-lived.

Arguably the greatest changes were within the Anglican Church. The Church of England had enjoyed favored status in most of the colonies simply because it was the official religious body of England. After the war Anglicans found themselves in a unique situation. The doctrines and liturgies of the Church required them to pray for the monarchy. Priests were ordained in the Church of England pledging allegiance to the king. Such facets of Anglicanism were not welcome in the new American

nation. In the end, out of the ashes of English Anglicanism arose American Episcopalianism.

Further Reading: Ruth Bloch, *Visionary Republic: Millennial Themes in American Thought* (Cambridge University Press, 1985); Ronald Hoffman and Peter J. Albert, eds., *Religion in a Revolutionary Age* (University Press of Virginia, 1994); Frank Lambert, *The Founding Fathers and the Place of Religion in America* (Princeton University Press, 2003); Mark A. Noll, *America's God: From Jonathan Edwards to Abraham Lincoln* (Oxford University Press, 2002); Nancy L. Rhoden, *Revolutionary Anglicanism: The Colonial Church of England Clergy during the American Revolution* (New York University Press, 1999).

—TODD M. BRENNEMAN

Revolution, Theory of

Before the Revolutionary War began in 1775, the majority of colonists considered themselves English citizens with all the political rights assigned to that position. However, acceptance of an innate right of people to rebel against tyranny had begun with the works of English philosopher John Locke (1632–1704), who had discarded the divine rights theory of government in favor of contract theory, which allowed people to retain their "natural rights" of life, liberty, and the right to own property. According to Locke, those rights could not be taken away by any government because they were bestowed on humankind by their Creator. For Locke, the moment that the people determined that sovereigns were acting beyond their rightful powers, governments were dissolved. At that point, power reverted back to the people who then had the right to create new governments of their own choosing.

A number of influential people in Great Britain favored granting independence to the American colonies. Those supporters included Prime Minister

Secession

THE PATRIOTS in Congress were well aware that the same theory of secession that allowed America as a whole to free itself from British tyranny also applied to sovereign states, because they also had the right to create new governments of their own choosing. At the same time that the Second Continental Congress appointed a DRAFTING COMMITTEE to write the Declaration of Independence, they appointed a committee composed of members from each colony charged with developing a plan whereby a confederacy would be formed among the 13 states. As a confederation, the states could each maintain individual sovereignty, while authorizing a weak form of central power. The result of their deliberations was the Articles of Confederation.

William Pitt and the "Father of Conservatism," Edmund Burke. Pitt informed Parliament after the passage of the Stamp Act in 1765 that they had charged him with giving birth to sedition in America, because the colonies had expressed their dissatisfaction with the act without giving them a voice in the passage of such acts. Like Pitt, Burke believed that GEORGE III and the British Parliament had laid the grounds for rebellion by the colonies because of their arbitrary exercise of authority. On the floor of Parliament, Burke accused the British government of attempting to starve 300,000 Americans by the arbitrary actions of the king who had banned imports to the colonies.

As late as 1775, many colonists remained loyal to the king. Other loyalties were assigned to individual colonies or regions, and the concept of what it meant to be an American was unclear. However, as George III continued to deny the rights of the colonies, a body of literature on basic human rights and the inherent right of rebellion accelerated a move toward nationalism. American revolutionary literature included such polemics as Thomas Paine's "Common Sense" (1776), John Dickinson's series of "Farmer's Letters," and the works of Philadelphian James Wilson. Written in 1768 but not published until 1774 because of its "radical" tone, Wilson's "Considerations on the Nature and Extent of the Legislative Authority of the British Parliament" was based on the Lockean belief that the ultimate authority for government resided with the people. Wilson insisted that in the face of the king's actions, the colonists had an innate right to rebel against arbitrary claims of authority. Jefferson later acknowledged that Wilson's work had also influenced the language of the Declaration of Independence.

By 1775, 38 newspapers were regularly printed and distributed in the United States. Broadsides, printed in three or four columns in small print to cram as much information as possible on a single sheet, were widely distributed. Gathering to read the broadsides in crowds in taverns, public squares, homes, and meeting houses, the colonists were exposed to current treatments of the theory of revolution and learned about their inherent rights as human beings and as English citizens.

By the time the delegates of the Second Continental Congress arrived in PHILADELPHIA in May 1775, Parliament had passed the Prohibitory Act that banned all trade with the American colonies. When the King granted the Royal Navy permission to attack American ships, many Americans considered it a tacit declaration of war. The move toward nationalism was, thus, much in evidence in the language of the Declaration of Independence, which lists specific incidences in which the king had denied the rights of the colonists. In the Declaration, Jefferson contended that the king's actions justified the right of the colonies to declare themselves free of tyranny because "Governments are instituted among Men, deriving their just powers from the consent of the governed. That whenever any Form of Government becomes destructive of those ends, it is the Right of the People to alter or abolish it, and institute new governments."

Further Reading: John Ferling, *A Leap in the Dark: The Struggle to Create the American Republic* (Oxford University Press, 2003); Jerome Hayler, *Locke in America: The Moral Philosophy of the Founding Era* (University Press of Kansas, 1995); Darren Staloff, *Hamilton, Adams, Jefferson: The Politics of Enlightenment and the American Founding* (Farrar, Straus and Giroux, 2005).

—ELIZABETH PURDY, PH.D.

Rhode Island in the Revolution

Rhode Island had the most independent of all colonial governments and remained in the vanguard of the independence movement as events accelerated the likelihood of war. The colony had begun its march toward independence in 1764 and became more determined to free itself from Britain as GEORGE III and Parliament continued to alienate the colonies. Rhode Island's main exports were rum and molasses, and most of the rum manufactured in the colony was derived from illegal sources. Initially, Britain turned a blind eye to such activities because most of the profits from the manufacture of rum were spent on British goods. However, with the passage of the Sugar Act in 1764, the British began enforcing import restrictions and sent the HMS *Liberty* and the HMS *Gaspee* to patrol Narragansett Bay with authority to try those who ignored the law in Halifax, Nova Scotia, without benefit of jury.

In the summer of 1764, the crew of a British naval vessel, the HMS *St. John*, was assigned the task of arresting a smuggler in the waters around Newport. Governor Stephen Hopkins ordered local gunmen to fire on the ship, leading to an exchange of fire in which the vessel was damaged. Hopkins's insistence that Britain had no right to tax the colonies served to ignite revolutionary fervor in Rhode Island.

In 1765, the crew of the HMS *Maidstone* was sent to impress men from Newport into royal service. When Hopkins demanded the release of all Rhode Islanders, the captain refused. In retaliation, an angry mob burned a British boat. In June, an exchange of fire between Rhode Islanders and a British sloop, the HMS *Rose*, occurred. After the encounter, Rhode Island raised what is thought to be the first navy of the American colonies. Governor Hopkins convinced the legislature to outfit 13 armed vessels and commission them for military service. Four years later, a crowd from Newport attacked and burned the HMS *Liberty*. The presence of the British patrol boats eventually forced the legislature to move the capital from Newport to the more sheltered city of Providence.

Rhode Island continued to move even further toward independence and away from reconciliation. In September 1765, the Rhode Island legislature passed a set of resolutions modeled on those introduced by PATRICK HENRY in the Virginia legislature declaring the Stamp Act invalid. The following month, Rhode Island sent two representatives to the Stamp Act Congress in New York. The Rhode Island delegation voted in favor of all resolutions that were proposed to deal with resisting British taxes. Tensions often flared between patriots and LOYALISTS, and the homes of Martin Howard, Jr., and Dr. Thomas Moffat, Rhode Island's leading loyalists, were partially destroyed by angry crowds. It was common practice in Rhode Island to tar and feather local Tories.

Stephen Hopkins and Samuel Ward, Rhode Island's delegates to the First Continental Congress (see CONTINENTAL CONGRESS, FIRST AND SECOND), joined their colleagues in Congress in adopting a Declaration of Rights for the 13 colonies and developing a list of grievances against the British government. While the colonies were not prepared at this time to break all bonds with Britain, the delegates promised to encourage their legislatures to pass nonimportation agreements to protest British taxes. Although Rhode Island merchants tacitly agreed to abide by the nonimportation measures passed in PHILADELPHIA, many continued to trade with Britain. When other colonies responded by refusing to trade with Rhode Island, the merchants stopped trading with Britain.

In April 1775, Rhode Island's legislature responded to the news of battle in Lexington and Concord by raising an army of 1,500 to defend the colony. Britain responded by sending additional patrol boats to Narragansett Bay and threatened to bombard Rhode Island when locals refused to sell them supplies. Frightened residents fled from the coast. In May, Rhode Island sent 1,000 troops to Massachusetts to take part in the Siege of Boston.

When Rhode Island chose delegates to the Second Continental Congress, they again selected Stephen Hopkins and Samuel Ward, the leaders of Rhode Island's chief political factions, and gave them instructions to vote for any measures that were deemed necessary to protect the liberty and security of Rhode Island. The Virginia Resolution was introduced in

Congress by RICHARD HENRY LEE on June 7, 1776. Rhode Island had declared its own independence from Britain the month before.

Congress appointed a DRAFTING COMMITTEE to write a document explaining the rationale for declaring independence. This document became the DECLARATION OF INDEPENDENCE, and Stephen Hopkins and William Ellert signed the Declaration for Rhode Island on August 2, 1776.

In December 1776, the British occupied Newport with little resistance, blockading Rhode Island's navy and preventing them from taking any further part in the war. During the three years that the British controlled the city, the once thriving port was almost deserted as people fled inland. Residents who remained in Newport were subjected to a severe food shortage and to harsh treatment. Without relief from Connecticut, many residents would have starved in those first months of British occupation.

Further Reading: Patrick T. Conley, *Album of Rhode Island History, 1636–1986* (Donning Company, 1986); Charles Rappleye, *Sons of Providence: The Brown Brothers, the Slave Trade, and the American Revolution* (Simon and Schuster, 2006); David Watters and Burt Feintuch, *The Encyclopedia of New England* (Yale University Press, 2005).

—ELIZABETH PURDY, PH.D.

Rochambeau, Comte de (1725–1807)

On July 4, 1776, the Comte de Rochambeau sat at his estate in the French countryside contemplating his desire to retire from military service and enjoy his final years in the quiet company of his beloved wife. At the age of 52, still suffering from numerous wounds received during nearly four decades of military service, Rochambeau was considered by both his countrymen and his enemies as one of the ablest military minds in France.

In 1779, Louis XVI took serious interest in the plight of the American colonies. The king turned to Rochambeau to lead an expeditionary force of nearly 5,000 men to aid the Americans in their fight against the British. As a veteran of the Seven Years' War, Rochambeau had long desired to pay back the British for France's humiliating loss of its colonies in Canada. Though unable to speak English, Rochambeau agreed to his new appointment and set off across the Atlantic.

Before leaving, Rochambeau was instructed by Louis XVI to place his forces fully under the command of General GEORGE WASHINGTON. By doing so, the French forces would serve only as reinforcements for the Continental Army and thus prevent the war from becoming a wholly French affair. For the French king it was important that the Americans should receive the most credit for gaining their own independence.

Rochambeau did not find a ready welcome from the inhabitants of Newport, Rhode Island. The only thing that the average colonist knew was that from 1778 to 1780, the French fleet had failed to drive the British from American shores. Prejudice against the French as ineffectual interlopers ran high. With his stocky figure, open face, and friendly air, Rochambeau quickly convinced the colonists of France's desire and ability to help them in their struggle and received the welcome of Newport's residents.

Rochambeau sent back to France a report on the meager living conditions of the colonists and the assurance that although every effort at frugality would be made, the expense of French involvement would be high. Subsequent reports related the heavy reliance of Washington's army on French troops and support. A long year after his landing, Rochambeau joined with Washington and Lafayette on the Hudson River and marched toward Yorktown.

With his tactical skill and administrative knowledge, Rochambeau proved an indispensable aide to Washington and contributed significantly to the American victory at Yorktown in 1781. Two years later, Rochambeau returned to France, where he was given command of the Northern Armies for the remaining years of Louis XVI's reign. Shortly after his retirement in 1792, he was arrested by revolutionaries, but avoided execution and was restored to his position by Napoleon Bonaparte.

Further Reading: National Park Service Museum Collections, www.cr.nps.gov/museum (cited January 2006); Comte de Rochambeau, *Memoirs of the Marshal Comte de Rochambeau Relative to the War of Independence of the United States*, trans. M. W. E. Wright, Esq. (Arno Press, 1971).

—VICTORIA EASTES

Rodney, Caesar (1728–84)

JOHN ADAMS observed that Caesar Rodney, a fellow pro-independence delegate at the Second Continental Congress (see CONTINENTAL CONGRESS, FIRST AND SECOND), "is the oddest looking man in the world; he is tall, thin and slender as a reed, pale; his face not bigger than a large apple, yet there is a sense and fire, spirit, wit and humor in his countenance." Everyone liked and admired the strange, sickly delegate from Delaware with the commanding name. Nevertheless, he rarely attended sessions of Congress, and in late June and early July of 1776, while the delegates struggled with the burning issue of independence, Rodney was off in Delaware investigating loyalist military activities. Therefore, few could expect that Rodney would provide the most dramatic moment as the issue of independence came to a vote in PHILADELPHIA.

Rodney was a true patrician, born on October 7, 1728, near Dover. Except for briefly attending a parson's school, he received no formal education. In 1745, his father died, and the 17-year-old eldest son inherited the grand estate. His guardian, a local court clerk, introduced Rodney to politics. At 22, he was appointed high sheriff of Kent County and went on to serve as justice of the peace, captain of the militia, clerk of court, and was elected to the Delaware assembly at 30.

With his characteristic determination, Rodney threw himself behind the patriot cause. He took part in the Stamp Act Congress in 1765, served on the Delaware Committee of Correspondence, helped to draft a protest of the Townshend Acts, and in 1774, he illegally called a special session of the legislature in response to the closure of Boston Harbor. Although a member of the Continental Congress, his

Remembering Rodney's Ride

CAESAR RODNEY'S desperate ride to the Continental Congress to secure Delaware's vote for independence has been commemorated in many ways since 1776. It has been reenacted, and his arrival at INDEPENDENCE HALL in the nick of time was portrayed in the Broadway musical and film *1776*, although the productions incorrectly have Rodney leaving his deathbed to save the day. In 1998, the Delaware 25-cent coin was first minted depicting Rodney on his horse galloping to the rescue of liberty. But perhaps the most enduring tribute was the stirring poem "Rodney's Ride" by an unknown author, which was recited by schoolchildren of the 19th and early 20th centuries. The last verse reads:

> At Tyranny's feet was the gauntlet flung;
> "We are free!" all the bells through
> the colonies rung,
> And the sons of the free may
> recall with pride,
> The day of Delegate Rodney's ride.

duties in the legislature and as brigadier general of the militia kept him away from much of the Philadelphia proceedings.

Yet on the night of July 1, 1776, while in Sussex County, Delaware, Rodney received urgent word from a fellow Delaware delegate, Thomas McKean, that he was immediately needed in Congress to break a tie in the three-member Delaware delegation, for delegate George Read had declared against the resolution for independence.

The frail Rodney rode through the night in a thunderstorm, an 80-mile journey, stopping only to change horses. Mud-splattered and wearing spurs, Rodney was anxiously greeted by McKean at the door of the hall and barely entered the conference room in time to cast the tie-breaking vote that swung his colony onto the side of independence. Almost anticlimactically, on July 4, Rodney, McKean, and Read voted to confirm the DECLARATION OF INDEPENDENCE.

Although conservatives defeated Rodney for reelection to the Congress and the legislature, he went on to fight in the Revolution, became a close associate of GEORGE WASHINGTON, and served as president of Delaware and admiralty judge. In 1782 and 1783, he was triumphantly reelected to Congress under the Articles of Confederation, but his failing health prevented him from serving. Of July 4, 1776, Rodney later recalled, "No one was either Tory or Whig; it was either dependence or independence."

Further Reading: Jan Cheripko and Gary Lippincott, *Caesar Rodney's Ride: The Story of an American Patriot* (Boyds Mill Press, 2004); Robert G. Ferris and Richard E. Morris, *The Signers of the Declaration of Independence* (Interpretive Publications, 1982).

—RUSSELL FOWLER, J.D.

Rush, Benjamin (1745–1813)

B enjamin Rush, signer of the DECLARATION OF INDEPENDENCE, joined ROBERT MORRIS, BENJAMIN FRANKLIN, John Morton, George Clymer, James Smith, George Taylor, James Wilson, and George Ross as delegates from Pennsylvania to the Second Continental Congress (see CONTINENTAL CONGRESS, FIRST AND SECOND).

Before the calling of the Second Continental Congress, Rush divided time between circulating among the delegates and treating his medical patients. However, once news of the battle at Lexington reached Rush, he decided it was time to act. He stated that the news of the battle, "gave a new tone to my feelings, and I now resolved to bear my share of the duties and burdens of the approaching revolution." From then on he favored independence and designed his publications to convince the public of the worthiness of the American cause.

Rush hosted many of the delegates in his home, including GEORGE WASHINGTON, SAMUEL ADAMS, and JOHN ADAMS. By the time the Second Continental Congress was called in May 1775, he was known as a patriot and advocate of independence. He began his service to the Continental Army as a fleet surgeon on gunboats protecting the Delaware River entrance to PHILADELPHIA.

Many radicals in Philadelphia began to question the conservatives in Congress who opposed independence and even questioned their Americanism. Rush and other liberals were in the thick of the fight. On June 23, he offered a motion to draft an address in favor of American independence, and was immediately made chairman of the committee appointed for the task. This report, submitted to Congress on June 25, foreshadowed many of the points set forth in the Declaration of Independence, which Rush signed with great pride and satisfaction.

Further Reading: David Barton, *Benjamin Rush: Signer of the Declaration of Independence* (Wallbuilders, 1999); Alyn Brodsky, *Benjamin Rush: Patriot and Physician* (St. Martin's Press, 2004).

—JAMES E. SEELYE JR.

Dr. Rush

BENJAMIN RUSH was born on December 24, 1745, near Philadelphia. He was educated at the Nottingham Academy in Maryland, then at Princeton, where he received his bachelor of arts before he turned 15. He then returned to Philadelphia where he spent six years before attending the university in Edinburgh, Scotland, and received his M.D. in 1768.

Soon after his return home Rush was appointed to a position as professor of chemistry at the College of Philadelphia's medical department, thus becoming at the age of 23 the first professor of chemistry in America. He built up a large private practice, at first among the poor. He published a pamphlet on the iniquity of the slave trade and helped organize the Pennsylvania Society for Promoting the Abolition of Slavery and the Relief of Free Negroes Unlawfully Held in Bondage, the first antislavery society in America, and later became its president. After serving in the Continental Congress, he stayed in Philadelphia, continuing his medical practice. Rush died in 1813.

ABOVE *Dr. Benjamin Rush in a painting attributed to John Neagle, from a painting by Thomas Sully.*

Rutledge, Edward
(1749–1800)

The public proclamation of the DECLARATION OF INDEPENDENCE on July 4, 1776, was something of an anticlimax for Edward Rutledge, whose significant participation in its passage had occurred on June 29, when he filibustered to force the removal of sections criticizing slavery, and again on July 2, when, against the instructions of the South Carolina legislature and his own inclinations, he persuaded the South Carolina delegation to vote for the Declaration.

Born in November 1749, Edward received a classical education in South Carolina, and then legal training in London's Middle Temple, which connected him to England's political decision makers.

After passing the English bar in 1772, he returned to a colony increasingly shaken by protests against British taxation and royal government. He made his name as a young lawyer by successfully defending printer Thomas Powell, who was being prosecuted for printing proceedings of the legislature.

Although a victory against the governor, Rutledge was wary of provoking the British crown or moving too far for reconciliation. The intricate network of social connections into which he had married in 1774 tied him to planters with substantial fortunes and political futures at stake. Edward and his brothers supported economic protests against British policy, but promoted the Galloway plan for a compromise relationship with Great Britain.

As a young delegate to the First Continental Congress (see CONTINENTAL CONGRESS, FIRST AND SECOND), Rutledge proved an able conciliator, serving on the panel that drafted GEORGE WASHINGTON's military commission in June 1775. He played a crucial role in placating southerners anxious about the enlistment of African American soldiers by insisting Washington refuse to accept further black volunteers. In January 1776, he moved in Congress that a War Office be created and served as a member of the Board of War. In February 1776, Rutledge was on an important committee, drafting a message to the states that demanded the creation of viable state governments. Rutledge was also deeply concerned with the fate of South Carolina's economy, since its staples, indigo and rice, were enumerated goods, with developed markets only in the British Isles.

Rutledge saw the state governments as vital to independence, a position he now cautiously considered in the face of the failure of the Galloway plan. However, while the revolutionaries suffered military defeats, Rutledge feared that a declaration in the spring of 1776 might erase any chance of reconciliation and tip the colonists' hand to the British authorities. Although he opposed RICHARD HENRY LEE's May 15 proposal for a declaration, Rutledge helped to draft the Articles of Confederation, an obvious step after the formation of state government.

THOMAS JEFFERSON's submission of the draft Declaration of Independence on June 28 provoked Rutledge to lead a filibuster through the night, demanding the removal of sections criticizing the slave trade. Rutledge was keenly aware that the South would not sign on to any proposal that threatened their economic system and successfully forced the confrontation to occur in the draft stage rather than in the final document. Rutledge and his fellow delegates had instructions from Charleston to oppose the Declaration, but in the face of nine other colonies' support, Rutledge realized the importance of unanimous voting and on July 1 stalled the final vote to secure the cooperation of Thomas Lynch, Thomas Heyward, Jr., and Arthur Middleton. News from home reporting victory against the British navy at Sullivan's Island buoyed morale, and on the following day, South Carolina joined in voting for the Declaration of Independence.

Further Reading: James Haw, *John and Edward Rutledge of South Carolina* (University of Georgia Press, 1997); David K. Wilson, *The Southern Strategy: Britain's Conquest of South Carolina and Georgia, 1775–1780* (University of South Carolina Press, 2005).

—MARGARET SANKEY

AT LEFT *Edward Rutledge aided in drafting the Articles of Confederation.*

S

Seafaring, 1776

In 1776 the new nation had been dependent upon seafaring since the first impermanent settlements. By the time of the DECLARATION OF INDEPENDENCE, Boston and PHILADELPHIA were among the busiest ports of the British Empire, ranking in tonnage behind only London and Bristol. Fishing, commerce, and shipbuilding were essential elements of life in all 13 colonies. Ninety percent of all residents of the 13 colonies lived within 50 miles of the Atlantic Ocean.

The waters of North America's continental shelf had been used by fishermen for well over two centuries by the time America became an independent nation. Cape Cod is so named for a most appropriate reason. All colonies engaged in fishing, but New England was then, as now, identified as a place where fishing was a way of life. Stocks of cod, haddock, flounder, lobster, halibut, and scallops abounded.

Captain John Smith of the Virginia Company described the New England coastal fishery: "Here should be no landlords to rack us with high rents, or extorted fines to consume us. Here every man may be a master of his own labor and land in a short time. The sea there is the strangest pond I ever saw. What sport doth yield a more pleasant content and less hurt or charge than angling with a hook, and crossing the sweet air from isle to isle over the silent streams of a calm sea?"

Actually, fishing was always hard work. The weather could be capricious, with summer fog and winter storms. The most highly prized stocks were groundfish, which required deeper sets of hooks, nets, or trawls. The earliest settlers did their fishing close to shore in small boats. However, by 1720 ships with a fore and aft rig, later called schooners, became common. It was always a dangerous, if lucrative, profession.

Losses of life at sea were a way of life. Homes often had a widow's walk, a platform high on a house to see if a ship might be homeward bound. Fishing created early urban centers in New England, built around fishing.

New England fishermen fought in the French and Indian Wars in part to keep French fishermen and privateers out of the Gulf of Maine and off Georges Bank. The taking of Louisbourg on Cape Breton in 1745, a feat considered to be a near military impossibility, was undertaken by some irate Yankee fishermen. The colonies were often exasperated by British treaty terms concerning fishing rights, or failure to enforce terms in the many negotiated peaces with France during almost a century of intermittent conflict. Great Britain's attempts to restrict New England fisheries, as hostilities were breaking out, were anathema to coastal communities.

Whaling was also an important industry. Plymouth, Salem, and Nantucket in Massachusetts, New London in Connecticut, and Greenport in New York were all whaling ports. Hundreds of vessels ventured forth for spermaceti, sperm oil, ambergris, and whalebone.

By 1776 the 13 colonies were an integral part of the Triangular Trade. This commercial pattern was based upon supply and demand, and prevailing winds in the Atlantic. Manufactured items proceeded from Europe to Africa and the American colonies. From Africa to the New World came slaves, gold, and pepper, flowing mostly to the West Indies and South and Central America. Molasses and sugar were sailed from the West Indies to North America and Europe. From North America ships carried to Europe lumber, indigo, tobacco, furs, and fish. To Africa was shipped rum, made from the molasses of the Caribbean.

The prevailing winds favored these routes, thus coining the name "trade winds" for the air flow across the Atlantic from the northeast toward the West Indies. Similarly, the prevailing westerly winds farther north in the Atlantic hastened passage. Ships could often run "full and bye" with a following wind, while sailing for the Old World. North from the Caribbean, the Gulf Stream pushed ships filled with molasses, sugar, and rum. In 1769 BENJAMIN FRANKLIN, long a student of the sea, actually had a chart of the Gulf Stream printed that was remarkable for its accuracy.

The coastal trade also flourished. It is easier and cheaper to move goods by water, and never more so when roads are few. Goods and passengers often traveled by sea. The fore- and aft-rigged schooner was invented in New England for that purpose. Lumber, flour, wood staves, livestock, grain, coal, sugar, bricks, lime, hay, fruits and vegetables, and firewood were moved to small urban centers and to large shipping centers by the many coastal packet ships that worked the waterfronts. Sailing craft also proceeded up rivers until narrows or shoals made passage improbable. Thereafter keelboats were employed—shallow draft and flat-bottomed, propelled by push poles. Similarly, maritime trade much like that on the coast existed in strength on Lake George, Lake Champlain, and Lake Winnepesaukee.

Shipbuilding as an industry began in America in the 1640s. Lumber was abundant and was the main reason certain roads were created. New England began as the major shipbuilding region, but was eventually challenged by other growing merchant communities. In the South, slave labor eased expenses. Colonial America's economy was export-driven and this required that ships be built. However, ships themselves became an export, and vessels built in America were as good or better than any others in the world. Most shipyards were small, and accidents were common. Yet, by 1775, 40 percent of Britain's oceangoing tonnage came from the 13 colonies.

By 1776 a nautical almanac had been published for nine years, used for celestial observations and position-fixing. Coastal waters were fairly well charted. In ocean passage, latitude was easily calculated by the sun and the North Star. Longitude was harder. Captain James Cook's discoveries were not yet in the public domain, so dead reckoning was necessary. A transatlantic voyage usually took six to eight weeks.

In coastal waters, a lead line for soundings had to be used. The depths of many places in the Caribbean Sea were simply unknown. Local knowledge was always a valuable commodity. Navigational charts were a good deal less than perfect.

The *Turtle*

IN 1776 the first submarine was invented in America by David Bushnell. The four-by-seven-foot *Turtle* was built in Saybrook, Connecticut. This submersible looked like two gigantic tortoise shells joined together. The watertight hull was made of six-inch-thick oak timbers coated with tar. On July 7, 1776, the *Turtle* targeted the HMS *Eagle*, flagship of the British fleet, in the approaches to New York. The submarine was supposed to secure a cask of gunpowder to the hull of the *Eagle* and sneak away before it exploded. Unfortunately, the *Turtle* got entangled with the *Eagle's* rudder bar, lost ballast, and surfaced before the gunpowder could be planted. Subsequently, there was a second attempt on a British frigate, which was also unsuccessful. General George Washington encouraged future attempts and gave Bushnell a commission as an engineer officer. While there were no more attacks by the *Turtle*, Bushnell did design sea mines.

ABOVE *David Bushnell's* Turtle *was used to attach explosives to British ships in 1776.*

Privateers in the American Revolution

WHEN THE American colonies declared their independence from Great Britain, the infant nation was in no position to defy British rule of the seas. States individually outfitted vessels of war and Congress established a navy, but it was a slow beginning. At no point in the conflict did the American naval forces have adequate resources to confront the Royal Navy on its own terms. The Royal Navy—once the protector of American shipping—now made every effort to suppress and destroy it. The Americans responded to the situation with the time-honored practice of privateering. American privateering activity during the American Revolution became an industry born of necessity that encouraged patriotic private citizens to harass British shipping, while risking their lives and resources for financial gain.

Privateering encompassed two levels of participation. A Letter of Marque authorized armed merchant ships to challenge any likely enemy vessel that crossed its path during the course of a commercial voyage. A Privateer Commission was issued to vessels, called privateers or cruisers, whose primary objective was to disrupt enemy shipping. The ideal target was an unarmed, or lightly armed, commercial ship. With the passage of an act on March 23, 1776, the Continental Congress formalized the commissioning process, and uniform rules of conduct were established. Owners of privateers had to post monetary bonds to ensure their proper conduct under the regulations. Although the documentation is incomplete, about 1,700 Letters of Marque, issued on a per-voyage basis, were granted during the American Revolution. Nearly 800 vessels were commissioned as privateers and are credited with capturing or destroying about 600 British ships.

Vessels of every size and description were pressed into service as privateers. At the upper end of the scale was the 600-ton, 26-gun ship USS *Caesar* of Boston. At the

ABOVE *The USS* Lexington, *in a photo of a painting by F. Muller.*

other end was the 8-ton boat USS *Defense* of Falmouth, Massachusetts. Crews ranged from a few men in a whaleboat to more than 200 aboard a large, fully equipped privateer. Two-masted schooners and brigantines were most often used in privateering, reflecting the kind of vessels available to American seamen.

Privateers achieved the best results if they could bluff an opponent into believing opposition was futile. When this failed the result was often vicious combat with unpredictable results. Many privateers were captured or sunk when the odds were against them. In spite of all the risks and hazards, the overall effort to cripple Britain's commercial fleet was highly effective, and fortunes destined to finance the new republic were made. It is estimated that the total damage to British shipping by American privateers was about $18 million by the end of the war, or just over $302 million in today's dollars.

—JOHN FRAYLER, SALEM

A most respectable business with official laws and international recognition was privateering, involving privately owned ships that in time of war would seize the vessels and cargoes of enemy nations.

The Continental Congress (see CONTINENTAL CONGRESS, FIRST AND SECOND) authorized the practice in May 1776 and also provided means of becoming armed and other incentives. There were hundreds of American privateers. It was not a new industry, and was practiced during the many wars against the French up until 1763. Privateers made fortunes and did great damage to British trade. Lord Horatio Nelson's first naval operations were on patrol against American privateers in the Caribbean Sea. The American Congress also encouraged French and Irish privateers.

Until hostilities broke out, American ships were English ships by law, with all the attendant rights and protections. The Royal Navy was the strongest and best naval force in the world. The Union Jack flag was known and feared and generally welcomed into any port in the world.

That security was sundered by the rebellion. However, American trade continued, as the coast was long and shipbuilding well established. It was a big ocean, and the Royal Navy could not be everywhere. Moreover, though trade was more difficult during the war, privateering in some locales more than compensated.

Further Reading: Bernard Bailyn, *Atlantic History: Concept and Contours* (Harvard University Press, 2005); Paul A. Gilje, *Liberty on the Waterfront* (University of Pennsylvania Press, 2003); Benjamin W. Laberee et al., *America at Sea: A Maritime History* (Mystic Seaport Museum, 1998); Peter Linebaugh, *The Many Headed Hydra* (Beacon Press, 2001); Marcus Rediker, *Between the Devil and the Deep Blue Sea* (Cambridge University Press, 1987).

—RAY BROWN

Self-Evident Truths

On July 4, 1776, the delegates in PHILADELPHIA voted on the DECLARATION OF INDEPENDENCE and pledged to one another "our Lives, our Fortunes, and our Sacred Honor." Contained in the document, authored by THOMAS JEFFERSON, was not only the new nation's official pronouncement that it was no longer part of the British Empire but also a concise explanation of the American colonists' decision to take this momentous step.

Jefferson begins the Declaration of Independence with a basic premise, a "self-evident" truth, "that all men are created equal, that they are endowed by their Creator with certain unalienable Rights, that among these are Life, Liberty and the Pursuit of Happiness." The acceptance of this premise, Jefferson's reasons, must lead to the acceptance of other "self-evident" truths: People create governments to protect these rights. The power of governments is awarded to them by "the consent of the governed." People may withdraw their consent when the government they created fails to do that for which it was designed or when it proves "destructive" of the people's rights. Once consent is withdrawn, people may then alter that government, or, if need be, "abolish it" and create a new government better able to protect their "Safety and Happiness."

These ideas were not original to Thomas Jefferson. These truths, which had not always been quite so "self-evident," are usually credited to John Locke, a British writer and philosopher of the Enlightenment. Locke was a revolutionary and a political activist who had supported Britain's Glorious Revolution of 1688. Unlike some of his contemporaries, Locke rejected the theory of divine monarchy, which held that kings had been appointed to their positions by God. Divine monarchs ruled—or so they told themselves—at the will of God and were thus responsible to no one but Him for their actions. Locke opposed the very idea of divine monarchs and also rejected the belief, deeply held by the Stuarts, as well as by many other European rulers, that monarchs should have absolute authority over their subjects and did not need the permission of others before putting their will into action.

Locke instead posited a different basis for government, one that was postulated on the existence of what he termed "natural rights." According to the theory of natural rights, all people possessed rights that had been given to them by God simply because they were human. These "rights" were those that allowed people to ensure their survival: life, liberty, and the property needed to maintain life. Because these rights were given to people by God, not by a monarch, they could not be taken from them. They were thus "unalienable."

All men were equal in their possession of these basic rights. God had denied them to no human being. All men, Locke also stated, were born free to do what they desired, so long as one man's actions did not interfere with another person's right to his own life, liberty, and property. In order to protect their "natural rights" from those who might attempt to deprive them of these rights, people, according to Locke, formed governments. This government was the result of a "social contract" in which people relinquished a portion of their rights to a government, which would then protect the life, liberty, and property of those who had created it. People thus sacrificed some of their rights in exchange for greater security.

Because governments had been created by people to protect their natural rights, governments that failed to do so, or that themselves deprived people of these rights, were illegitimate. Locke, however, did not believe that revolutions to alter or abolish governments would be common occurrences. In Locke's view, people could and would endure endless suffering rather than attempt to dismantle their government. Only long-standing, constant, unendurable oppression, Locke believed, would be able to move most people to revolution. It is perhaps for this reason that Thomas Jefferson emphasized GEORGE III's "history of repeated injuries and usurpations" and appended a long list of grievances as "proof" of the king's perfidy.

Although Jefferson was undoubtedly heavily influenced by Locke, there were also elements of English history and tradition that stressed that English kings should not be allowed to oppress their subjects. In 1215, King John of England had sealed the Magna Carta, a document designed to limit the power of the English monarch and to ensure basic protections for people's lives, freedom, and property. These rights, dubbed the "rights of Englishmen," included the right to a trial by a jury, compensation for property taken by the government, and the need of "the realm" to consent to taxation.

Despite its grounding in British tradition, there was also something profoundly American in Jefferson's declaration that the colonies should be free and independent. Freedom, independence, and self-government were key elements of the Puritan tradition. Puritan churches made their own laws, chose their own ministers, and governed themselves. Puritan churches did not form part of a hierarchy, such as that which existed within the Anglican Church. Traditions of church government affected civil government in Puritan communities in New England. Puritan settlements were largely self-governing. In Massachusetts, for example, property requirements for voting were fairly low, and more men were able to vote in Puritan Massachusetts than in Anglican Virginia or in England.

Although Jefferson, in his Declaration, proved to be a faithful copyist of Locke, there is one significant way in which Jefferson's conception of "unalienable rights" differed. While Locke asserts that one's natural rights consist of life, liberty, and property, Jefferson omits any reference to property and instead proclaims that people have a right to life, liberty, and *the pursuit of happiness*. This change, many scholars believe, was made to indicate that in a nation built upon the concept of freedom, the protection of slave property would not be considered a fundamental right and would not be among the foremost concerns of the new nation.

Further Reading: F. Forester Church, *The American Creed: A Spiritual and Patriotic Primer* (St. Martin's Press, 2002); John R. Howe, Jr., *The Role of Ideology in the American Revolution* (Holt, Rinehart, and Winston, 1976); "John Locke," *Stanford Encyclopedia of Philosophy*, September 2001, http//plato.stanford.edu/ entries/locke (cited March 2006).

—ANN KORDAS, PH.D.

The Glorious Revolution

IN THE Glorious Revolution of 1688, King James II of England was bloodlessly removed from his throne in favor of his daughter, Mary, and her husband, William, a prince of the Dutch House of Orange. James was a Catholic in a country that for over 100 years had been ruled by Protestant monarchs. Mary and William were staunch Protestants. James's far greater fault was that he was descended from the Stuart line of kings, who believed in divine right, had repeatedly balked at submitting their requests for funds to Parliament, and rejected the idea that their actions should be subject to the scrutiny of Parliament. The Stuart kings were also welcoming to the Catholic faith and friendly to the Catholic nation of France.

Sherman, Roger (1721–93)

With hostilities against Britain already under way, the delegates to the Second Continental Congress (see CONTINENTAL CONGRESS, FIRST AND SECOND) had a lot to deal with. Roger Sherman, delegate from Connecticut, had very little faith in the possibility of reconciliation with Britain. He felt the Congress was doing all it could by balancing support for the American cause, while at the same time keeping a possibility of reconciliation open. Sherman felt that reconciliation would only be possible if the colonies submitted to the British mercantile system. Sherman served along with Samuel Huntington, William Williams, and Oliver Wolcott as a delegate from Connecticut to the Second Continental Congress.

By late 1775, GEORGE III had made reconciliation nearly impossible. Parliament passed the Prohibitory Act, which made trade with the colonies illegal. Many delegates felt the next steps should be the assertion of American independence, cultivation of foreign trade, and negotiated treaties with foreign powers. However, Sherman was a shrewd

ABOVE *Roger Sherman in a photo of a miniature painting by John Trumbull*

The Life of Roger Sherman

ROGER SHERMAN was born on April 19, 1721, in Newton, Massachusetts. He had a limited, informal education. In 1743 he was appointed surveyor of New Haven County, Connecticut. By the age of 21, he was busy in both the civic and religious affairs of New Milford, Connecticut.

Sherman was admitted to the bar of Litchfield in 1754, and the following year was chosen to represent New Milford in the state assembly. After a successful legal career, he became a delegate to the Continental Congress. In addition to signing the Declaration of Independence, he was a member of the Constitutional Convention, renowned for being one of the most vocal and persistent members. Sherman died on July 23, 1793.

politician. While some of his fellow delegates strenuously argued for the opening of American ports to commerce of all foreign nations, Sherman noted the impossibility of carrying on successful trade with enemies taking ships at will. To counter this, he argued that a treaty with a foreign power for, among other things, protection should be signed first.

Sherman was reconciled to independence early. By 1775, he was ready for each colony to do what was necessary to make the war successful. He was selected in October of that year to a committee to write instructions to New Hampshire on the administration of civil justice. The committee was happy to discuss the subject and urged all the states to call conventions and institute regular governments. Although out of town for the first part of the independence debate, Sherman's feelings were well known, and when the Congress finally decided to act upon the question of a declaration, Sherman was picked for that committee as well (see DRAFTING COMMITTEE).

Further Reading: Sherman Boardman, *Roger Sherman: Signer and Statesman* (Da Capo Press, 1971); Christopher Collier, *Roger Sherman's Connecticut: Yankee Politics and the American Revolution* (Wesleyan University Press, 1971); Ann Malaspina, *Primary Source History of the Colony of Connecticut* (Rosen Central, 2005).

—JAMES E. SEELYE JR.

Society of Friends

The Society of Friends, also known as the Quakers, emerged in England during the Puritan Revolution in the 1640s. Quaker theology revolved around the organic connection an individual had with God. This direct experience with the Divine confirmed the essence of true religion and instilled an ethic in the believer's mind to work for the peace and stability of society.

William Penn joined the society in 1666. He was incarcerated in the Tower of London at the close of the 1660s after writing a tract that criticized the doctrines of the Anglican Church. While in prison, he wrote the now popular *No Cross, No Crown*, recognized as a primary source for Quaker piety. *No Cross* is a treatise that emphasizes the importance of Christ's suffering on the cross as an example of self-denial for believers. Without the cross—without suffering—there is no crown.

For a long time, Quakers sought refuge from religious persecution. Many Friends in England were fined, imprisoned, or exiled. North America was just as hostile. Between 1659 and 1661, four Friends were hanged for disturbing the peace by offering a blasphemous religion.

Eventually the Quakers found a secure foothold in North America, settling in an area that bore the name of its proprietor. In 1681, Penn acquired a tract of land in North America in settlement of a debt owed to his father by Charles II. Pennsylvania, meaning "Penn's woods," immediately became a place that protected the freedom of religion. This was radical in an era fractured by religious fighting.

By 1682, the Quakers organized PHILADELPHIA, the city of brotherly love. The Society of Friends contributed to making the city one of the wealthiest and most influential centers in North America. Pennsylvania's political stability rested on the freedom of religion and republican constitutionalism.

Early Quakers were marked by their commitment to pacifism. While colonial Quakers agreed that the Bible sanctioned a form of state power to maintain peace, they opposed involvement in supporting vi-olence, which included the paying of war taxes and participating in military conscription. Violence, whether committed in the name of the Lord or not, conflicted with the Inner Light. Quakers were critical of the rising patriotism in the months prior to the outbreak of war against Britain. At the yearly Meeting in Philadelphia in 1775, Quakers encouraged society members to obey the civil magistrate, not to entangle themselves in military conflicts, and to do good to all men.

While a majority of Quakers rejected both loyalist and patriot participation in the war, a small group called Free Quakers participated in the war against Britain. Free Quakers believed that a defensive war was not a violation of the Christian's calling. Many Friends sympathetic to the Free Quakers united in 1781 and established the Free Quaker Monthly Meeting of Philadelphia. They differed from the older Society in that they did not rely on theological distinctions and sought participation in civic affairs. While many Friends attempted to protect their religious commitments without undermining the cause of independence, they opposed taxes that went directly to the war effort and the imposition of fines and imprisonment for conscientious objectors.

The Friends were outspoken enemies of the established order. Even before the Revolution, they were pioneers in the cause of antislavery. The war for the cause of "liberty" exacerbated the contradiction of slavery and freedom. Anthony Benezet, a Philadelphia Quaker, used the rhetoric of American patriotism to expose the errors of slavery. War and slavery were linked in that they stemmed from an insatiable desire for power over another's property. The arguments used against British tyranny could be easily applied to the tyranny of slavery. Benezet's quick and deadly polemical writings had a profound effect on Benjamin Franklin, who, in 1787, helped organize the Pennsylvania Society for Promoting the Abolition of Slavery.

Further reading: Thane Elswyth, *The Fighting Quaker: Nathanael Greene* (Aeonian Press, 1972); William C. Kashatus, *Conflict of Conviction: A Reappraisal of Quaker Involvement in the American Revolution* (University Press of America, 1990).

—RYAN MCILHENNY

Soldiers, American

The patriot soldiers who fought in the War of American Independence generally fell into three groups. Members of the Continental Army served under Commander in Chief GEORGE WASHINGTON and were assigned to duty wherever they were needed. The Continentals included soldiers from all 13 colonies. Additionally, each colony had its own militia that was charged with protecting the home front. In the South, militias also frequently came to the defense of neighboring colonies. In the western, less-settled areas of the country, partisan frontiersmen, sometimes loosely attached to local militias, waged constant war against the British and their loyalist and Native American allies. Continentals were away from home for long periods, but militias and frontiersmen were sometimes able to return home between periods of fighting. Their enlistment terms were also shorter, varying from three to six months. Each group of soldiers was necessary to the defense of the country, and all experienced both victory and defeat in the long years of battle between 1776 and 1783.

The Continental Army was created by the Second Continental Congress (see CONTINENTAL CONGRESS, FIRST AND SECOND) on June 7, 1775. The following week, Washington was chosen as commander in chief. Each colony was asked to contribute a specified number of troops, and determined their own responses to the call. In areas where the fighting was heaviest, Continentals bore the brunt of battles. In other places, Continentals fought alongside militias and frontiersmen.

State legislatures were responsible for appointing all officers below the rank of colonel. Congress appointed officers above this rank. Initially, four major generals were appointed: Artemas Ward, Charles Lee, Philip Schuyler, and Israel Putnam. The eight brigadier generals chosen by Congress were Seth Pomeroy, Richard Montgomery, David Wooster, William Heath, Joseph Spencer, John Thomas, John Sullivan, and Nathanael Greene. Horatio Gates was appointed as an adjutant general. Of these men, Greene and Gates were chosen by Washington for particular commands. Greene served throughout the war with distinction, but Gates disgraced himself and retired from the battlefield.

DAILY LIFE

One of the most difficult aspects of serving in the Continental Army was leaving families behind to fend for themselves. Because Congress had no power to levy taxes, there was a chronic shortage of revenue. Soldiers were often unpaid for months. Consequently, the families of the poorest soldiers frequently suffered from a shortage of food, clothing, and fuel. Even when pay was forthcoming, it was likely to be in unbacked currency, which merchants were reluctant to accept. Pay was prorated, with privates earning less than $7 a month. Life was also difficult for more affluent families as prices rose. Between 1779 and 1780, the price of beef in

Mutiny

ON JANUARY 1, 1781, the fact that they had not been paid for an entire year led a group of Pennsylvania Continentals stationed in Morristown, New Jersey, to mutiny. The soldiers had learned that Congress was offering a bonus of $81 to each convict who would enlist in the army while they served without pay. Some 1,500 soldiers commandeered artillery, gunpowder, and cannonballs and set out for Philadelphia to confront Congress and the Pennsylvania legislature.

The British army sent a loyalist to entice them into the British army. The mutineers responded by hanging the loyalist and his guide. On January 6, the group met with Congress, negotiated terms, and returned to duty. Subsequently, 200 Continentals in New Jersey decided to proceed along the same lines. Washington determined that such rebellions were not in the best interest of the army, and ordered the men arrested. Three of the sergeants who had led the mutiny were chosen by lots to face a firing squad, and Washington ordered the remaining mutineers to serve as the firing squad.

ABOVE *The commanders and line officers of the Continental Army.*

PHILADELPHIA increased fifteen-fold and the price for a horse rose to $20,000.

The day-to-day life of soldiers was often unbearably hard because supply lines were cut off, and resources had been drained or destroyed by the British and LOYALISTS. Even when supplies were available, merchants sometimes preferred to sell to the British, who paid with gold sovereigns.

Whenever the American army moved to a new location, they set up camps. Temporary camps were a good deal more primitive than those used as winter headquarters. Officers were frequently housed in local homes, but regular soldiers lived in tents or shoddily built huts. In addition to providing shelter, each camp set up improvised cooking and medical facilities and dug latrines. Washington was well aware that unsanitary conditions could lead to the spread of diseases such as typhus. He announced that any soldier relieving himself outside designated latrine areas would be court-martialed. When they were on the move, soldiers slept on the ground, with or without blankets, often after marching for days without proper food or clothing. In camp, each soldier was assigned to particular duties that ranged from cutting trees to roofing huts to digging ditches. Southern soldiers found such tasks particularly onerous because they believed no white person should perform such labor. During periods of inactivity, soldiers sang and told stories. Books were always prized, and many of them passed from hand to hand or were read aloud for all to enjoy.

At Valley Forge, Baron von Steuben, whom Washington had designated as the inspector general, employed his training as a Prussian officer under Frederick the Great of Prussia to turn Washington's Continentals into a formidable army. Von Steuben, who could curse in three languages, knew little English. He wrote his training instructions in German. They were translated into French and then delivered to the soldiers by a French-speaking American. Von Steuben was so successful in his task that Washington ignored the fact that he may not have been a true Prussian noble and promoted him to general.

DISCIPLINE

At the beginning of the war, patriotic Americans were eager to join in battle. However, as the years passed, enthusiasm waned. Congress resorted to cutting terms of enlistment and offering bonuses to meet quotas. Continentals were allowed to sign up for three-year terms but were encouraged to sign up for the duration of the war. Because of the need to keep men from deserting, the discipline of American soldiers was more lenient than the punishment meted out by their British counterparts. Nevertheless, discipline was a fact of army life in American camps, and much of it would be considered harsh by 21st-century standards. Deserters who were caught received 100 lashes for the first offense. The punishment was meted out over a period of days. Congress passed a law requiring soldiers to carry passes when they left camp and rewards were offered to anyone who turned in deserters. Members of the militia could be court-martialed for crimes ranging from murder to minor theft. Like the British, Americans could be forced to run a gauntlet in which they were switched, or they could be placed on wooden horses with weights tied to their feet.

In both the Continental Army and militias, Americans were sometimes able to select their own lower-level officers. An American officer could be court-martialed for fraternizing with soldiers, forgetting his status, or performing tasks assigned to soldiers.

While discipline was always necessary in the American army, it was particularly important on the battlefield. In early 1781, Washington dispatched General Nathanael Greene to attempt recovery of South Carolina from the British. Greene was joined by Daniel Morgan, who had recently been promoted to brigadier general in return for his coming out of retirement to take a place in the Southern Campaign. On January 17, 1781, Morgan's forces met British Colonel Banastre Tarleton's men at the Battle of Cowpens. Morgan knew that his inexperienced troops were likely to cut and run in the face of charging cavalry, so he gave them permission to run after firing two rounds. After the militia fell back, the more experienced Continentals launched their attack. Tarleton escaped, but he suffered 100 fatalities and had 830 men taken prisoner. This strategy of requiring the militia to fire before falling back would continue to be used for the rest of the war.

UNIFORMS AND EQUIPMENT

As the war continued, it became more difficult to keep soldiers outfitted. Many American soldiers wore hunting shirts that had been dyed brown and decorated with fringe. The British derisively called the Americans "shirtmen." Washington used this disdain to his advantage, believing that the British underestimated Americans by thinking they were not "real" soldiers. Washington suggested that all states adopt the hunting shirt with woolen or linen trousers. Facings and buttons of particular colors were used to identify particular regiments. In 1779,

Congress recommended that all soldiers wear blue coats with facings to denote regiments, but most soldiers continued to dress in the hunting shirts.

Essential equipment for American soldiers included weapons, artillery, food, medicine, tents, blankets, cooking implements, and all sorts of personal items needed to maintain a basic standard of living whenever possible. Regular soldiers had few luxuries, but officers generally carried personal items to ensure that they could live as gentlemen. Supplies were generally transported on wagons and by pack horses. Soldiers also carried their own weapons and personal supplies on their persons.

Americans used the standard smoothbore muzzle-loading cannon that had been in use for the past two centuries. It was loaded with a prepared cartridge of paper or cloth in which gunpowder had been wrapped and ignited by inserting a goose-quill tube of quick-match into the vent. Choices of ordnance included gun, howitzer, and mortar.

Further Reading: Wayne Bodle, *Valley Forge: Winter Civilians and Soldiers in War* (Pennsylvania State Press, 2002); John Buchanan, *The Road to Valley Forge: How Washington Built the Army That Won the Revolution* (John Wiley and Sons, 2004); Caroline Cox, *A Proper Sense of Honor: Service and Sacrifice in George Washington's Army* (University of North Carolina Press, 2004); Benton Rain Patterson, *Washington and Cornwallis: The Battle for America, 1775–83* (Taylor Trade Publishing, 2004).

—ELIZABETH PURDY, PH.D.

Soldiers, British

When Great Britain sent soldiers to the American colonies to stamp out the rebellion of the mid-18th century, they were able to send a number of veterans who had already served in America during the French and Indian Wars. This experience had given them a firsthand knowledge of the American landscape and allowed them to develop an understanding of the American people. Despite this knowledge and their superior military might, the British drastically underestimated the American soldier who refused to give in and who was often unaware of the protocol for fighting wars. The embarrassment of being outmaneuvered by Americans frequently led the British to impose harsh treatment whenever they were in the position of victor.

It was understood from the moment of enlistment that British soldiers retained no human rights. Military law was absolute, and soldiers were enlisted for the duration of the war. Contrarily, officers served at their own discretion. Unlike the Americans who often had a voice in choosing their immediate commanders, British soldiers below the rank of colonel were allowed to purchase their ranks. All higher-ranking officers were appointed

ABOVE LEFT *Uniform of the British 48th Regiment.*
ABOVE RIGHT *The death of Major André, October 2, 1780. Engraving by Goldar, 1783.*

to their positions. Because the lines between officer and regular soldier were distinctly drawn, there were rigid rules about interaction between officers and troops.

American LOYALISTS joined British and Hessian soldiers (see HESSIANS) in waging war against the patriots of the United States. In the South, a good deal of the war was fought between patriots and loyalists and not between the Americans and the British. Virginia loyalist forces included the Queen's Own Loyal Virginia Regiment, the Loyal Foresters, and the Royal Ethiopian Regiment. Some regiments were ultimately merged into the British army. Those that operated on their own tended to be loosely organized and poorly led. William Franklin, the Governor of New Jersey and the son of patriot BENJAMIN FRANKLIN, was the nominal head of American loyalists.

DAILY LIFE

British soldiers were precisely trained according to accepted military standards. Because they were so rigidly controlled in their military lives, British soldiers were given a certain leeway in how they behaved when they were off duty. Swearing and drinking were considered their right, as was the free access to the prostitutes found among camp followers. British soldiers frequently socialized with American loyalists and neutrals when they were encamped.

Unlike American soldiers, British soldiers were paid regularly, in two categories. Subsistence pay was intended to cover food, shoes, clothing, firearms, and other personal items. A portion of the subsistence pay was also set aside to remunerate the surgeon and the paymaster. The rest of the pay was used to pay the salaries of the Paymaster General, the regimental agent, and to support the Chelsea Hospital for Veterans.

DISCIPLINE

Discipline was often swift and harsh, with a different set of rules for officers and regular soldiers. British soldiers were highly trained to follow each command to the letter, even if it meant immediate death. Forms of punishment included incarcerating soldiers in dark, cold, cramped cells for hours or making them run the gauntlet in which other soldiers hit them with sticks or belts as they ran down a line. One particularly uncomfortable punishment involved placing the individual to be punished on a wooden hump-backed horse with weights tied to his feet. The lash was the most frequent form of physical punishment and was used for even minor infractions. Using a cat-of-nine-tails, drummers were assigned to flog recalcitrant soldiers. The number of lashes varied from 100 to 2,000 and was usually levied at a rate of 250 at a time, with an interval in between for the lacerations to heal. Each session ended with the drummer pouring water on the wounds to prevent infection. The Americans began calling the British "bloody backs" and "lobsters" because of this horrendous practice.

UNIFORMS AND EQUIPMENT

At the beginning of the war, all British soldiers arrived in their designated uniforms designed to indicate rank and regiment. The uniforms were tight-fitting and tended to be particularly unbearable during American summers. The basic uniform consisted of a thick red coat with button-back lapels. Each soldier also wore stocks and garters and boots. They wore their hair greased and powdered and pulled back at the neck in a style known as "clubbing." Hats, facings, lining, waistcoats, and various forms of decoration varied according to regiment and rank.

British soldiers generally used the flintlock rifle known as Brown Bess, which had a barrel measuring three feet eight inches long. The rifle, which was most effective at 300 yards, was highly inaccurate at distances under 100 yards. Therefore, bayonets or even swords were used in hand-to-hand combat. Instead of bayonets, some sergeants carried halberds, which combined the properties of a sword and a battle-axe. A number of British officers preferred spontoons, a shorter version of the halberd.

The Brown Bess was loaded by pouring powder into a priming pan and ramming the ball and cartridge into the muzzle with an iron rod. In inclement weather, the rifles were often unusable because rain washed the powder out before the gun could be primed. Some regiments rejected the Brown Bess and carried fusils, which were lighter flintlock muskets. Because of the problems with their weapons, the British often opted to sit out storms, and the Americans learned to use such occasions to their own advantage.

While the British usually found it less difficult than Americans to obtain supplies, their supply system was so complicated that it led to major deficiencies in equipment and food supplies. Shipments of supplies could not always get through because the activities of the American army, privateers, and weather conditions frequently interfered. Technically, each soldier was supposed to receive a pound of beef a day, but this promise was often impossible to fulfill.

Further Reading: Stephen Brumwell, *Redcoats: The British Soldier and War in the Americas, 1755–63* (Cambridge University Press, 2002); Caroline Cox, *A Proper Sense of Honor: Service and Sacrifice in George Washington's Army* (University of North Carolina Press, 2004); Christopher Hibbert, *Redcoats and Rebels: The War for America, 1770–81* (Grafton, 1990).

—ELIZABETH PURDY, PH.D.

ABOVE *The Boston Tea Party, as it is known today, was an action of the Sons of Liberty. Some members of the group disguised themselves as Mohawk Indians, as shown in this lithograph by Sarony and Major, 1846.*

Sons of Liberty

The actual origin of the Sons of Liberty is disputed. Both New York and Boston claim the movement began in early 1765 in their cities. Most likely, both cities had chapters that developed simultaneously. No matter which city they actually started in, the Sons of Liberty groups began for the same reasons and pursued the same results.

The roots of the Sons of Liberty began with the COMMITTEES OF CORRESPONDENCE, which had as their goal formally organizing public opinion and actions against Great Britain. Once the British passed the Stamp Act of 1765, the Sons of Liberty took over where the committees of correspondence left off.

The Stamp Act was levied by the British as a means of maintaining troops in the American colonies. The items taxed included customs documents, newspapers, legal documents, licenses, and playing cards. The British felt this was justified because of the protection provided by their troops, and it was also seen as a way to pay off the national debt from the Seven Years' War. The colonists saw it differently. To many of them, especially those active in the Sons of Liberty, this was another example of Parliament curtailing the colonists' right to tax themselves. This led to the famous slogan "no taxation without representation."

The Sons of Liberty declared that they would do whatever was necessary to prevent the Stamp Act from being enforced. By 1766, the New York Sons of Liberty had already confiscated, unpacked, and burned stamped documents. Other actions turned more violent. Some members of the group would tar and feather LOYALISTS and royal officials, in addition to burning their homes and businesses.

From New York and Boston, the Sons of Liberty spread to include groups throughout New England, the Carolinas, Virginia, and Georgia. The average member was a male from the middle and upper class. SAMUEL ADAMS and Paul Revere were among the organization's most historically well-known members. The movement had a tradition to preserve anonymity and safety, but did all it could to build a strong base of public support. While British officials accused the group of trying to overthrow the government in the colonies, the Sons of Liberty strenuously asserted that their organization's purpose was organizing opposition to the illegal Stamp Act.

The repeal of the Stamp Act in 1766 led to a waning of the activities of the Sons of Liberty. However, other acts, including the Townshend Acts, led to a revival, and the group maintained active correspondence throughout the colonies until it disbanded in 1783. Their work had a significant impact in the independence movement, and many members were not only delegates to the First and Second Continental Congress (see CONTINENTAL CONGRESS, FIRST AND SECOND), but also signed the DECLARATION OF INDEPENDENCE. The group gave colonists a chance to actively participate in the politics and history going on around them.

Further Reading: Henry B. Dawson, *The Sons of Liberty in New York* (Arno Press, 1969); William M. Fowler Jr., *Samuel Adams, Radical Puritan* (Longman Press, 1997); Adam Rutledge, *Sons of Liberty* (Bantam Books, 1992); Richard Walsh, *Charleston's Sons of Liberty* (University of South Carolina Press, 1959).

—JAMES E. SEELYE, JR.

South Carolina in the Revolution

The first colony in the Carolinas was established in 1670 at Albemarle Point on the Ashley River. Gradually, settlers moved to the city of Charles Town (now Charleston). In 1719, in a bloodless revolt, the colony rebelled against the Lord Proprietor, and the Carolinas were designated as a royal colony. In 1729, the colony split into North and South Carolina. As a thriving British colony, South Carolina had few problems with the Crown. With a coast easily accessible to foreign invaders and privateers and a frontier that was home to hostile Indians, the colony depended on the mother country for protection. As a result, South Carolina was initially reluctant to challenge royal authority as other colonies began to chafe under what they considered British tyranny.

When Britain began taxing the American colonies, South Carolina was outraged. Thus, the Stamp

Act of 1765 was a turning point for South Carolina, as it was for the other 12 colonies. Upon being informed of its passage, 2,000 patriots marched under the slogan, "Liberty and no Stamp Act." Subsequently, volunteers prevented the British vessels carrying stamped paper from entering Charles Town. Instead, the paper was stored at Fort Johnson, a royal fort on James Island.

A committee was selected to organize resistance, and three companies of armed volunteers summarily took possession of Fort Johnson and the paper. To show that the city was not afraid to fight if necessary, Charles Town loaded every cannon and informed the British that if they fired on the fort, their vessel would be sunk. The British left, carrying the stamped paper.

When Britain instituted a tax on tea, South Carolinians confiscated the tea. On November 17, 1774, a second shipment of taxed tea arrived in Charles Town. Without waiting for darkness, Charlestonians climbed aboard and threw the tea into the Cooper River. Because South Carolina had renounced her loyalty to the Crown and decided to throw in her lot with her sister colonies, the British marked the colony for particularly harsh treatment. By the end of the Revolutionary War, South Carolina had lost more men than any other colony/state.

The news of the confrontations at Lexington and Concord on April 19, 1775, spurred South Carolinians into open rebellion. William Campbell, the royal governor of South Carolina, believed he could stymie the rebellion by ordering the Assembly to meet in Beaufort, 75 miles away from Charles Town. Members blocked his strategy by making the day's drive to attend the session. South Carolina cemented the rebellion by forming a provincial government in March 1776, two months before the Declaration of Independence was signed. Four Charles-

Isaac Hayne (1745–81)

DURING THE British occupation of Charles Town, Colonel Isaac Hayne paid for his loyalty to the American cause with his life. Hayne had been paroled along with other members of the South Carolina militia after the surrender of Charles Town. Under terms of surrender, Hayne was not required to join the British military, yet Sir Henry Clinton demanded that he sign an oath of loyalty to Britain or be imprisoned. Because his wife was fatally ill and his children were sick, he signed the oath. Clinton ordered Hayne into the British military. Hayne refused and began actively fighting the British. He was captured on July 8, 1781, and without benefit of a trial was sentenced to hang. Even local Tories pleaded for Hayne's life, and his young children begged for mercy. The pleas went unheeded, and Hayne was hanged as a traitor to Britain on August 4, 1781. The event convinced a number of Tories to become patriots.

ABOVE *The Battle of Camden and death of DeKalb, in an engraving from a painting by Alonzo Chappel.*

tonians signed the Declaration for South Carolina: EDWARD RUTLEDGE, Thomas Heyward, Jr., Thomas Lynch, and Arthur Miller.

The provincial congress dispensed with the Commons House Assembly, a vestige of royal authority, on March 26, 1776, and on September 15, 1776, the royal governor fled to the British warship, the HMS *Tamar*. For most South Carolinians, Campbell's flight was viewed as the final break with Britain. Subsequently, South Carolina elected its own governor and established the Privy Council, a board of advisors made up of the lieutenant governor and eight members chosen by the legislature.

By September 1775, locals had reclaimed Fort Johnson and begun preparing for battle. On November 11, 1775, South Carolina's first shots of the revolution were fired in a battle between the British war sloops, the HMS *Tamar* and the HMS *Cherokee*, and South Carolina's sloop, the USS *Defense*. The shots fired from Fort Johnson during that battle were the first of the war that were fired from a permanent fortification. The first shot of the Civil War was also fired from this same fort, which had been renamed Fort Sumter.

The British fleet that arrived in South Carolina on June 28, 1776, consisted of two 50-gun ships, five 28-gun ships, and two eight-gun ships. British troops numbered 3,000 under the command of Sir Henry Clinton and Lord Charles Cornwallis. Between the two forts, the Carolinians had 780 men and 31 guns. Nevertheless, they managed to repel the British. When a second attack was made in June 1776, South Carolinians were even more successful in driving the British out of Charles Town.

For the next three years, the British basically left South Carolina to its own devices, with the exception of minor contact with the tiny South Carolina navy. The years were spent manufacturing weap-

ons and fortifying defenses. When the British returned to South Carolina in 1779, they chose to attack overland, traveling northward from the British-controlled Florida Territory. These land forces were reinforced by the return of Sir Henry Clinton with a fleet and 13,500 men on February 11, 1780. The siege, which began on April 13, lasted for a month. Local politicians were determined to fight as long as possible and threatened to cut up Lieutenant General Henry Lincoln's boats and open the gates to the enemy if he tried to evacuate the forts.

By May 12, Charles Town had no option other than surrender. The terms were harsh, and the British refused to let the soldiers march out according to protocol. Prominent politicians and members of the Continental Army were imprisoned. Historical records indicate that at least one-third of those imprisoned died in the hands of the British. The South Carolina militia was allowed to return home as long as members agreed to refrain from taking up arms against the British. Later, the British reneged and tried to force some of the patriots into the British army. Loyalist activity in South Carolina increased significantly, and some 200 residents who were convinced that the war was over signed the British loyalty oath. Most Charlestonians refused and, consequently, suffered the indignities of British occupation for the rest of the war. During this period, Colonel Banastre Tarleton continued to terrorize the population.

Despite the devastating loss of Charles Town, frontier partisans continued to wage war against the British. This continued resistance proved to be instrumental when the Continental Army returned to South Carolina to fight the British. While Charlestonians could no longer fight the British directly, they contributed to the partisan effort by smuggling food and clothing to the soldiers. By 1780, General

GEORGE WASHINGTON had determined to reclaim the areas of the South that had been lost and dispatched troops under General Horatio Gates. In the summer of 1780, with only 700 men, Gates marched his troops through barren country from which they were unable to replenish their dwindling supplies. The men mixed stringy beef and corn with hair powder to make stew. When Gates provided them with molasses rather than the food and rum he had promised, debilitating dysentery further weakened the soldiers.

Gates met the British on the night of August 15 at Camden, and the exhausted Americans suffered another devastating loss. From beginning to end, the battle was a disaster. Inexperienced militiamen fled without discharging a single shot, and veterans under the Baron De Kalb held too long. After De Kalb was mortally wounded, his troops fled with "Bloody" Tarleton's cavalry in pursuit. In one of the most shameful episodes of the war, General Gates ran away and was never allowed to command another army. Many South Carolinians believed the entire war had been lost at Camden. To retaliate for the treatment they had suffered from the patriots, LOYALISTS commandeered patriot homes and forced entire families into the woods.

By the next month, however, the tide had started to turn. On October 7, 1780, at the Battle of King's Mountain, frontiersmen faced troops of loyalists under the command of Major Patrick Ferguson. To his dismay, Ferguson, who had chosen to launch his attack from the high ground, discovered that bullets were sailing over the heads of the patriots, inflicting no damage. When the loyalists called for "quarter," the patriots responded with "Tarleton's quarter" and continued fighting. At battle's end, 150 loyalists were dead and 700 were captured. Devastated loyalists who realized that the new turn of events meant that

ABOVE *Colonel William Augustine Washington at the Battle of Cowpens, in an engraving by S.H. Gimber for Graham's Magazine.*

Christopher Gadsden (1724–1805)

ALTHOUGH HE had been educated in Britain, Christopher Gadsden was considered the foremost anti-British agitator in South Carolina during the revolutionary period. As the owner of the Gadsden Wharf and an active member of the SONS OF LIBERTY, Gadsden was in an ideal place to influence his fellow South Carolinians to resist British tyranny. These agitators generally consisted of mechanics and young lawyers and planters who gathered at local taverns and at Charles Town's Liberty Tree. Gadsden served as a member of South Carolina's delegation to the Stamp Act Congress in 1766 and was a delegate to the First Continental Congress in 1775. During the Revolutionary War, Gadsden served in the military, achieving the rank of Brigadier General.

America was likely to win the war laid down their arms. Many of them subsequently fled the area.

The victory at King's Mountain was reinforced on January 17, 1781, when patriots faced British and loyalist troops at Cowpens on the North Carolina border. Brigadier General Daniel Morgan joined General Nathanael Greene of the Continental Army. When Greene separated his army, Lord Cornwallis ordered "Bloody" Tarleton to go after Morgan and annihilate him. Instead, aided by reinforcements from Colonel William Washington, Morgan succeeded in decimating Tarleton's forces. Tarleton fled when his cavalry refused to continue the battle.

On December 14, 1782, 300 British ships sailed out of Charles Town, and South Carolina was free of British rule. Ignoring the terms of surrender, the British carried most of the plunder that had been stolen from Charlestonians during the occupation. (See also CHARLESTON IN THE REVOLUTION.)

Further Reading: Walter B. Edgar, *South Carolina: A History* (University of South Carolina Press, 1998); Michael C. Scoggins, *Day It Rained Militia: Huck's Defeat and the Revolution in the South Carolina Backcountry, May–July 1780* (The History Press, 2005); Peter H. Wood, *Black Majority: Negroes in Colonial South Carolina from 1670 through the Stono Rebellion* (W.W. Norton, 1996).

—ELIZABETH PURDY, PH.D.

Speeches on July 4 Commemorations

On July 4, 1778, patriot and historian David Ramsay (1749–1815) gave what is generally considered the first July 4 commemoration speech in American history in Charleston, South Carolina. In "The Advantages of American Independence," Ramsay asserted that American independence would be historically honored because it redeemed one-fourth of the world from tyranny and oppression.

As time passed, Americans paid little attention to celebrating the Declaration, in part because the Federalist Party was attempting to negotiate an alliance with Britain and wanted to tone down anti-British rhetoric. By the 19th century, however, celebrations were again being held around the country. On July 4, 1821, then Secretary of State John Quincy Adams, the son of John Adams and the sixth president of the United States, told an audience of July 4 celebrants that America's road to independence had prepared it for spreading the desire for independence around the world, but insisted that the country made no attempt to guarantee independence for others. In 1851, statesman and orator Daniel Webster delivered a stirring July 4 oration in Washington, D.C., when laying the cornerstone of a new addition to the Capitol Building. Webster informed his audience that the Declaration of Independence had been inspired by the "Genius of Liberty" that had allowed the American colonists to throw off tyranny and oppression and seal it with blood.

In a speech in Chicago, Illinois, on June 10, 1858, Abraham Lincoln stated that July 4 celebrations were held to remind Americans of what it meant to be free. Lincoln was responding to the Supreme Court decision *Dred Scott v. Sanford* (U.S. 393, 1857), in which the justices had declared that slaves were not citizens but property. Lincoln heartily disagreed with Justice Stephen Douglas, who claimed that the phrase "all men are created equal" in the DECLARATION OF INDEPENDENCE referred to the equal status of American colonists with English citizens. According to Lincoln, taking liberties with interpretations of the Declaration was dangerous and set the stage for future infringements of the Declaration's guarantee of basic rights.

Celebrating the 170th anniversary of the Declaration in 1946, John F. Kennedy reminded a Boston audience that the traditions of the Declaration had become an integral part of the American character. Kennedy asserted that the battle for political rights had not ended with the Revolutionary War. Quoting from the Declaration, Kennedy insisted that the battle would never be over as long as people the world over were denied those basic rights that the Declaration had claimed as self-evident: "That all men are

ABOVE *Frederick Douglass, ca. 1870. A former slave, Douglass was outspoken in his speeches, proclaiming that to the slave, all claims of liberty and equality were hollow.*

Frederick Douglass (1818–95)

ONE OF the most often quoted July 4 commemoration speeches was given by former slave Frederick Douglass at Rochester, New York, in 1852. Speaking at an antislavery rally, Douglass began "What to the American Slave Is Your Fourth of July?" by praising the Founding Fathers and the Declaration of Independence. Midway through his speech, Douglass admitted that a commemoration of independence had little to do with slaves who had always been considered property rather than people.

Answering his own question, Douglass assured his audience that to slaves July 4 was the day that "more than all other days in the year" reminded them that they were victims of "gross injustice and cruelty" and that to celebrate such a day was a sham. To the slave, Douglass declared, all claims of liberty and equality were hollow.

However, Douglass was not without hope that former slaves would be granted political rights because he strongly believed in the guarantee of eventual fulfillment promised by both the Declaration of Independence and the Bible. Douglass believed that if slavery were abolished, political rights would be granted, creating an environment in which all Americans would live in harmony. A century later, Dr. Martin Luther King, Jr., also frequently quoted the Declaration of Independence and invoked its promise of freedom and equality for all Americans.

created equal [and] that they are endowed by their Creator with certain unalienable rights."

Further Reading: Frederick Douglass, "What to the Slave Is the Fourth of July?" http://douglassarchives.org/doug_a10.htm (cited January 2006); John F. Kennedy. "Independence Day Oration," July 4, 1946, www.jfklibrary.org (cited January 2006); Abraham Lincoln, "Lincoln at Chicago, Illinois, June 10, 1858," in Robert Ginsberg, ed., *A Casebook on the Declaration of Independence* (Crowell, 1967); Keith D. Miller, "Frederick Douglass, Martin Luther King, Jr., and Malcolm X Interpret the Declaration of Independence," in Scott Douglas Gerber, ed., *The Declaration of Independence: Origins and Impact* (Congressional Quarterly Press, 2002); Edwin P. Whipple, ed., *The Great Speeches and Orations of Daniel Webster* (Beard Books, 2001).

—ELIZABETH PURDY, PH.D.

Stockton, Richard (1730–81)

A distinguished lawyer from New Jersey, Richard Stockton was one of the 56 signers of the DECLARATION OF INDEPENDENCE. Born into wealth and property, he saw his livelihood and health destroyed by the Revolutionary War. Stockton was the eldest son of John Stockton and inherited a revered and respectable name and considerable property. He received an excellent private education and graduated from the College of New Jersey with honors in 1748. He then read law with David Ogden of Newark, the head of the legal profession in the New Jersey colony.

Stockton was known for excellent reasoning and eloquent speaking, in addition to a sterling character. In 1774 he was named a justice of the Supreme Court of New Jersey. Two years later he was elected to the Continental Congress (see CONTINENTAL CONGRESS, FIRST AND SECOND) along with Jonathan Witherspoon to replace delegates who opposed independence. Stockton was no zealot for independence. His judicial temperament meant that he wished to hear all arguments, and he was reluctant to make bold moves, the consequences of which had not been fully considered. A member of the Royal Council in New Jersey since 1765, he had

In Praise of Washington

ANNE BOUDINOT Stockton penned the following poem in 1783. She sent it to George Washington:

> With all thy country's blessings on thy head,
> And all the glory that encircles man,
> Thy deathless fame to distant nations spread,
> And realms unblest by Freedom's genial plan;
> Addressed by statesmen, legislators, kings,
> Revered by thousands as you pass along,
> While every muse with ardour spreads her wings
> To our hero in immortal song;
> Say, can a woman's voice an audience gain;
> And stop a moment thy triumphal car?
> And wilt thou listen to a peaceful strain,
> Unskilled to paint the horrid wrack of war?
> For what is glory—what are martial deeds—
> Unpurified at Virtue's awful shrine?
> Full oft remorse a glorious day succeeds,
> The motive only stamps the deed divine.
> But thy last legacy, renowned chief,
> Hath decked thy brow with honours more sublime,
> Twined in thy wreath the Christian's firm belief,
> And nobly owned thy faith to future time.

long held that the colonies should be represented in Parliament.

Stockton was convinced by JOHN ADAMS, as were so many others during the summer of 1776, that the time for severance of all ties with the English Crown had come. Stockton not only came to agreement, but also addressed the Continental Congress, proposing that a new country needed to be declared.

On a trip to England, Scotland, and Ireland over two years in 1766 and 1767, Stockton was well received in high establishments of government and academia. He was presented at Court and conferred with William Pitt, the Earl of Chatham. But perhaps most important, in Edinburgh, he met the Reverend Doctor Jonathan Witherspoon, a distinguished theologian and educator, and convinced him to serve as president of the College of New Jersey. In 1768 Witherspoon assumed that post. Eight years later, he joined Stockton as a delegate to the Continental Congress, where he said of the move toward independence that the time "was not only ripe for the measure, but in danger of rotting for the want of it."

As did a number of the signers who had pledged "our lives, our fortunes and our sacred honor" to the new United States of America, Stockton would forfeit his life and fortune to the American cause. As the British army of General Sir William Howe overran New Jersey in 1776, Stockton hurried home from Congress and ensured the safe evacuation of his family from his colonial home, Morven. Stockton stayed in the area to secure certain affairs, and was dragged from his bed by LOYALISTS. Imprisoned as a common criminal, without a trial, he suffered much privation and mistreatment, first in Amboy and then in New York. Food and clothing were withheld.

Anne Boudinot Stockton, Richard's wife, let Congress know of the circumstances under which her husband was being held. Following a Congressional resolution, word was passed, via a flag of truce from General GEORGE WASHINGTON to General Howe, that Stockton's treatment must improve forthwith or there would be retaliation in kind against British prisoners. Stockton was eventually released, but returned home to ruin. His property had been plundered, with all stock stolen or driven away. His business papers and library had been burned. Now a pauper, he was also in ill health from his time in prison. He died at Morven in February, 1781.

Further Reading: John Benson Lossing, *The Declaration of Independence—With Short Biographies of Its Signers* (Applewood Books, 1996); "Stockton," www.colonialhall.com (cited March 2006).

—RAY BROWN

Syllogism

Syllogism is a form of deductive reasoning, consisting of a major premise, a minor premise, and a conclusion. On July 4, 1776, seven words uttered, and then written down for posterity, were of particular importance: "We hold these truths to be self-evident." Following this sentence, the authors of the DECLARATION OF INDEPENDENCE utilized the rhetorical device of syllogism to outline their reasoning.

That they used such a device on this momentous day, was telling. The first sentences of the Declaration stated its overall intention "to declare the causes which impel [the Americans] to the separation" from Britain. It is in the presentation of these causes that THOMAS JEFFERSON and his fellow drafters used syllogism: Only such a form of 18th-century logical rhetoric could yield, on paper, the conclusion that "these United Colonies are, and of Right ought to be, Free and Independent States."

The device of syllogism allowed the framers to absorb the turbulent happenings that had come to a crescendo on July 4, 1776, and to use them rhetorically. That is to say, they could set in ink a series of propositions that, when set against these previous experiences with British forces ("the course of human events") could yield to the necessity of separation. It is syllogism that allowed Jefferson to label these propositions as "SELF-EVIDENT TRUTHS," thereby garnering human experience with philosophical certitude.

The Declaration's conclusion was syllogistically supported by two premises: The major premise contained the term that was the predicate of the conclusion. This related to the fact that individuals had self-evident rights that governments were organized to protect. When governments did not protect these rights, people had the right to change their government. The minor premise contained the term that was the subject of the conclusion. This was the self-evident need for separation from Britain. Common to both is a middle term (the evidence, or "facts," of British corruption) that was excluded from the conclusion.

This understanding of syllogism in the Declaration should negate the contention that on this day in 1776, Jefferson could only respond to complicated and ever-changing events with disjointed prose and paragraphs. Rather, the structure allowed by syllogism brought about what was, according to Michael Zuckert, "tightly constructed, like a geometric proof."

That the "facts" were to be submitted on this day to a "candid world" suggests that their rhetorical basis would be amenable to fair-minded people, whose candor could judge American separation positively. Rhetorically at least, they could only but conclude that "the present King of Great Britain" has "in direct object the establishment of an absolute Tyranny over these States."

The Declaration's first paragraph thus proclaimed the just cause and effect that was to be proved, while the longer second paragraph utilized syllogism in order to demonstrate the general axioms of proof that the following list of short sentences would be judged against.

The "bill of particulars" thus listed 28 specific grievances. Yet the fact that the Declaration's drafters chose to make a rhetorical case for separation suggests that they did not on the very day of July 4, 1776, necessarily believe that, in practice, other nations would look favorably upon their actions.

Indeed, the Declaration's "decent respect to the opinions of mankind" related more to an appeal to the philosophy of John Locke. Here, Jefferson and his fellow authors were perhaps aware that as they declared their support for America against the more powerful Britain, there were those in the world who differed from Locke and assigned legitimacy solely to power and force, using the philosophy of Thomas Hobbes to their own end.

In this way, the authors of the Declaration wrote in a Lockean manner that they did not wish to give people "just occasion, to think that all government in the World is the product only of Force and Violence, and that men live together by no other Rules, but that of Beasts where the strongest carries it, and so lay a Foundation in perpetual Disorder and Mischief, Tumult, Sedition, and Rebellion." Importantly, the device of syllogism was a means by which a written stylistic device could reflect the same philosophical difference between Locke and Hobbes. It enabled words to be ordered and logical, based on clear principles and structures.

It was only with such syllogistic proofs, that the likes of Jefferson could draw a counterpoint to the political "disorder" of British "tyranny," and show what "We [the Americans] hold," even if other Hobbesian international powers did not.

Charges 1 through 12 outlined the abuses of the royal executive power in terms of the suspension of colonial laws such as habeas corpus, a lack of due respect for colonial legislatures and justice mechanisms, and the deployment of a standing army during an ostensible time of peace.

Charges 13 through 22 attacked and linked British royal corruption to British parliamentary corruption, with regard to the subjections of Americans to unconstitutional duties, such as their taxation without representation or consent, and the alteration of their colonial charters. GEORGE III's violent conduct and military cruelty was the subject of charges 23 through 27. The final charge stated that the colonists' "repeated Petitions" regarding their complaints had only been met with "repeated injury."

That the colonists' grievances against George III were "facts" allowed the syllogism to take full effect: They were unmediated demonstrations of empirical reality, rather than mere human interpretations of reality. The passive voice was deployed in the injunction to "let Facts be submitted."

Neither the Continental Congress (see CONTINENTAL CONGRESS, FIRST AND SECOND), nor any other human agent, had synthesised these "facts." Rather, they were submitted, passively from direct experience.

The points in the Declaration's middle section—its minor premise—could therefore be syllogistically related to the document's major premise, which stated that "self-evident" truths would be demonstrated.

Further Reading: Daniel Boorstin, *The Genius of American Politics* (University of Chicago Press, 1958); Bruce E. R. Thompson, *Introduction to the Syllogism and the Logic of Proportional Quantifiers* (Peter Lang Publishing, 1993).

—GIDEON MAILER

ABOVE TOP *A Revolutionary War era compass.* **ABOVE BOTTOM**, *a placard on the gravesite of Benjamin and Deborah Franklin in Philadephia, Pennsylvania.*

T

Taverns and Residences, 1776

In the late 18th century, taverns and inns played an important role in the social and political lives of American colonisits. Literacy rates were low in revolutionary America, and many individuals were unable to read the newspapers that were printed in most large cities. In taverns, someone was always ready to share available news and offer opinions, often reading aloud from newspapers or pamphlets. Many taverns had separate meeting rooms that were used by patriots during the Revolutionary War period.

At local taverns and inns, the colonists were able to share their dissatisfaction as resentment against Britain mounted. Because land was readily available in the American colonies, most tavern patrons were landowners with a definite interest in politics. As a result, taverns were often used for protests and other forms of political demonstrations.

In each major city, particular taverns served as gathering places for patriots who planned strategy and encouraged revolutionary fervor among other patrons. In Williamsburg, Virginia, for example, whenever Governor Dunmore dismissed the House of Burgesses because of its refusal to adhere to his wishes, the legislature adjourned to the Raleigh Tavern and continued their sessions.

Members of the Virginia legislature who regularly gathered at the Raleigh Tavern included GEORGE WASHINGTON, THOMAS JEFFERSON, George Wythe, and Peyton Randolph. In New York, local merchants met at the George Burns City Tavern, where they plotted strategy

THE CITY TAVERN, AT LEFT, *in Philadelphia witnessed more pivotal events in America's early history than any other building other than the State House. The great colonial men—and some notable women, including Martha Washington and Abigail Adams— passed through its doorway on a regular basis. In 1774, after a long ride, Paul Revere reined up at the tavern to inform John Adams and Thomas Jefferson that Boston Harbor had been closed.*

Ordinaries

INITIALLY, COLONIAL Americans referred to establishments that housed travelers as ordinaries. Over time, the term changed to *taverns* and, ultimately, to *inns* or *houses*. These taverns and inns were regularly used by both travelers and local residents. Tavern owners encouraged locals and visitors to use their premises as gathering places, knowing that politically savvy visitors were likely to stay in inns that hosted an intriguing assortment of locals with whom they could engage in lively political discussions.

The first ordinaries were often small log buildings, where visitors slept on the floors of bars and dining rooms. By the 1770s, however, large cities such as Philadelphia had a number of large, lavish taverns and inns. The City Tavern, for instance, was a two-story brick building with a bar and public rooms on the first floor and clubrooms on the second floor. Another Philadelphia tavern, the Indian King, was a converted mansion that contained 18 rooms and 14 fireplaces. It provided facilities for stabling up to 100 horses at a time. By law, proprietors were required to furnish travelers with beds, drinks, three meals a day, and stables for their horses.

TOP RIGHT *"An Extraordinary Gazette, or the Disappointed Politicians." The print depicts British politicians discussing the latest news from General Henry Clinton. On the wall in the background are maps of the English territories in America.*
BOTTOM RIGHT *The Man Full of Trouble Tavern, located at Second and Spruce Streets, is the only surviving tavern building from pre-Revolutionary Philadephia. Built in 1759, the tavern was licensed to dispense only beer and cider. The Man Full of Trouble was built on the banks of the Little Dock Creek, where shipwrights, dockhands, and cordwainers clustered. The creek was eventually filled in. In the colonial era, there was very little difference in the design of residential and commercial buildings.*

designed to block British efforts at denying political rights to the American colonies. In Georgia, the provincial Congress met regularly at Savannah's Tondee Tavern, even as the British controlled the colony.

In no colony were taverns more important to the revolutionary cause than in Massachusetts, where local political leaders rubbed elbows with locals of other social classes. John Adams, for instance, found that Boston's taverns provided an excellent means of recruiting local Whigs to the cause of patriotism and independence.

Heated discussions in local bars gained in intensity after the Boston Massacre and the battles of Lexington and Concord. Bostonian Patriots sometimes dropped by the British Coffee House on King Street, where British officials and LOYALISTS spent time, to unobtrusively learn whatever information they could.

A number of the SONS OF LIBERTY owned taverns, and one out of every five tavern owners in Boston was actively involved in the leadership of the revolutionary movement in the years leading up to the Declaration of Independence and the outbreak of war. John Marston openly distributed revolutionary literature at his Boston tavern.

PHILADELPHIA had its own taverns and inns, where some delegates to the Second Continental Congress (see CONTINENTAL CONGRESS, FIRST AND SECOND) resided and others gathered to relax and share a tankard of ale or a glass of rum. These informal meetings gave the delegates opportunities to chart progress toward achieving independence and to assess public opinion.

The most significant of these establishments was the City Tavern, which served as a meeting place for local political leaders and for the members of both the First and Second Continental Congress. When the Second Continental Congress met in Philadelphia in 1776, there were 120 taverns in the city. The oldest of these was the Man Full of Trouble Tavern at Second and Spruce streets.

RESIDENCES

In their own states, the signers of the DECLARATION OF INDEPENDENCE lived in homes that varied from simple to palatial. In the 21st century, those residences have come to be regarded as significant historical sites. Unfortunately, earlier generations did not share this regard, and many of these homes have not been preserved for posterity. By the 2000s, 21 residences of the signers had been destroyed by war, fire, neglect, vandalism, weathering, and urbanization. Although not destroyed, other residences have suffered from similar fates. The signers whose homes no longer stand include SAMUEL ADAMS of Massachusetts, Lyman Hall of Georgia, ROGER SHERMAN of Connecticut, and CAESAR RODNEY of Delaware.

The National Park Service has worked to preserve those residences that remain and to bring attention to surviving residences of those signers that have not been recognized as historic sites. In addition to Independence National Historical Park in Pennsylvania, the National Park system has accepted responsibility for the Adams Historical Site in Massachusetts, the Floyd House on Fire Island National Seashore in New York, and the Nelson House in Colonial Williamsburg, Virginia. Some surviving homes are owned by individuals and are still inhabited, while others are maintained by states, universities, businesses, or public and private organizations. Although some residences no longer stand, most states have created monuments to their own signers.

Philadelphia

WHEN MEMBERS of the Second Continental Congress convened in Philadelphia on May 10, 1775, they knew that the Pennsylvania summer would present problems as weeks passed. In addition to the rare breeze, the open windows of the State House provided entry for horseflies and other insects. At the end of each day, delegates were glad to retire to their respective residences and inns. Local taverns provided sumptuous breakfasts, lunches, and dinners for the delegates.

Some delegates, such as Thomas Jefferson, chose to rent rooms in private homes. Jefferson rented two rooms in a brick home located at Market and 7th Streets (see DECLARATION HOUSE (JACOB GRAFF HOUSE). Jefferson composed the Declaration of Independence in his second floor parlor, using a lap-top desk that he had invented.

The house later served as the residence of James Wilson, one of the Pennsylvanians who signed the Declaration of Independence. In 1976, the National Park Service began reconstruction of both the Graff House and the City Tavern. Delegates from Philadelphia, such as BENJAMIN FRANKLIN, remained at their own homes. Franklin resided at 318 Franklin Court, which was located south of Market Street between 3rd and 4th Streets.

Philadelphians welcomed the signers of the Declaration of Independence into their homes and taverns. The residence of Dr. William Shippen, a member of the Continental Congress, served as a gathering place for local and visiting dignitaries, including Francis Lightfoot, Arthur Lee, John Adams, John Witherspoon, BENJAMIN RUSH, and Robert Livingston.

RICHARD HENRY LEE, the man who introduced the Virginia Resolution that directly led to the writing of the Declaration of Independence, resided at the Shippen-Walter House while in Philadelphia, because Shippen was his brother-in-law. Other Philadelphia residents who opened their homes to visiting delegates included patriot Thomas Mifflin and John Dickinson, the author of "The Farmer's Letters," a widely distributed revolutionary-era pamphlet. Dickinson was known to enjoy hosting the lively gatherings of his congressional colleagues.

ABOVE *The back of the reconstructed City Tavern in Philadelphia. The original establishment hosted numerous Congressional delegates.*

Further Reading: Robert G. Ferris, *Signers of the Declaration: Historic Places Commemorating the Signing of the Declaration of Independence* (National Park Service, 1975); Sharon V. Salinger, *Taverns and Drinking in Early America* (Johns Hopkins University Press, 2002); Peter Thompson, *Rum Punch and Revolution: Taverngoing and Public Life in Eighteenth-Century Philadelphia* (University of Philadelphia Press, 1998).

—ELIZABETH PURDY, PH.D.

Travel, 1776

The people who came to North America chose to live by the water. It might be a harbor on the Atlantic, a river, or sometimes even a lake. Then, as now, water provided the cheapest means of moving any commodity. Water is a highway, a great common, and colonial America had few roads. Still water could not meet all the reaches of the 13 colonies. Moreover, water routes were subject to freezing in winter and storms year round, so roads to and from the waters and to other places had to be established.

Those who came to the New World came by ship, and the square-rigged sailing ship had the distinction of being the most dangerous and deadly means of travel ever invented. The North Atlantic is a capricious seaway and the coast just offshore the northeast United States is a region of swift and sometimes violent change: Hurricanes, nor'easters, cold fronts from the Saint Lawrence Valley, the Labrador current, and fog all combine to create a most inhospitable passage. It also became the birthplace of the best sailors and ships in the world.

The 13 colonies were agrarian, at a time when England was ushering in the Industrial Revolution. Outbound from the colonies to the West Indies, Britain, and Europe were wheat, corn, tobacco, rice, lumber, fish, horses, cattle, and indigo. In addition to the rapid growth and diversity of the population and the experience in representative government, the emergence of a prosperous agricultural and commercial economy in the colonies during the 18th century helped pave the way for the independence movement. This economic system was based on the production of wheat, cattle, corn, tobacco, and rice in America for export to the West Indies, Britain, and Europe.

The major port cities were Boston, Newport, New York, PHILADELPHIA, Baltimore, and Charleston. These shipping centers grew in size and developed associated commercial services, such as various insurance businesses and wholesale trade. There were also working waterfronts, with rope and sail manufacturing, ship chandleries, and shipbuilding.

The ports of the colonies built quite seaworthy ships, with the forests for wood close at hand, establishing shipbuilding industries that would eventually rank among the best in the entire world. These cities prospered. They influenced British imperial trade policies, and at times these cities profited by the trade policies and at other times were hurt by them. Boston even confronted the powerful East India Company, arguing whose ships would move certain products (see BOSTON IN THE REVOLUTION).

INLAND WATERS

The rivers and tributaries of North America were the first "roads." The Merrimac, Charles, Connecticut, Hudson, Raritan, Delaware, Susquehanna, Potomac, Shenandoah, James, Roanoke, and Savannah rivers and many others were the quickest and easiest means of movement to and from coastal regions. The rivers were also a primary source of power in an agrarian society. The mills were, of course, all by inland waterways. Many settlers owned small boats or canoes for their personal transportation. However, the supply and demand for trade created businesses specializing in transportation.

Moving crops, livestock, furs, fish, and supplies up and down rivers required something more than small craft. Barges and rafts became an ongoing business in a land of few long roads and few bridges. Rivers themselves could be difficult passages, and navagation was best left to an experienced pilot.

Ferries acted as bridges, and bateaux and rafts were the means of distant transport. The first ferry system was established in Massachusetts in 1631. Similarly, packet ships, sloops, and schooners were often built both to travel the inshore coastal waters and to proceed up rivers. They carried both goods and passengers. River traffic was important in all the colonies, but particularly so in the South, as there were fewer roads. It took five days to travel on the river from Augusta to Savannah, Georgia, a distance of 250 miles.

ROADS

By 1717 there was an established road system connecting all 13 colonies. Massachusetts, Connecticut, Pennsylvania, and Maryland all had serviceable highway systems. Boston had surface land connections to more than 70 inland and coastal towns. Boston and New York City were connected by the Boston Post Road, still sometimes called that in local towns, but now officially designated as U.S. Highway 1.

In 1776 the most traveled road in the colonies was the Great Wagon Road, which extended from Philadelphia to the hinterland of Georgia. There were also trails being blazed west, opening up the North American continent to pioneers and settlers.

Most country roads were subject to mud and dust and ruts. The first American highways avoided hills or mountains whenever possible. Most city roads were paved with bricks or cobblestones. Some of these last to this day, as in Alexandria, Virginia.

Road construction and maintenance were always challenges. Taxes, fines, and lotteries were used to fix potholes and widen streets. Some locales and colonies even had a draft of able-bodied males to perform compulsory maintenance each year. Bridges were never popular with town fathers, as they were expensive to build and repair. Fords were preferred, or even logs placed side by side through nearby wetlands. Poor roads were a source of consternation, argument, and political debate—and there were many poor roads.

In 1776 the Conestoga wagon had been in service for half a century. Able to carry six tons, this covered wagon was used by some 10,000 owners in Pennsylvania alone. It was a mode of travel that continued for more than a century and played a major part in the American westward expansion in the 19th century.

Stagecoaches were also well established by 1776, having been introduced almost two decades before. A system of stagecoach services connected all major cities. New York and Philadelphia, 100 miles apart, were a matter of 36 hours of travel. Horse-drawn transportation was available everywhere in the colonies in 1776.

Further Reading: James Deetz, *In Small Things Forgotten: An Archaeology of Early American Life* (Alfred A. Knopf, 1994); Helen Gilbert and Anna Johnston, eds., *Travel, Text, Empire: Colonial and Post Colonial Travel Modalities* (Peter Lang Publishing, 2002); Wendy Martin, ed., with Mary Rowlandson, *Colonial American Travel Narratives* (Penguin Group, 1994).

—RAY BROWN

AT LEFT *An example of the Durham boats commandeered by Colonel John Glover's Marblehead regiment prior to the attack on Trenton, New Jersey.* BELOW *A typical Revolutionary War–era one-horse wagon.*

Crossing the Delaware

GENERAL GEORGE WASHINGTON's crossing of the Delaware River in the surprise attack on Trenton, New Jersey, on December 26, 1776, was a tremendous feat of transportation. He had Colonel John Glover's Marblehead regiment of seafaring men commandeer all Durham boats within 30 miles north and south, and ordered all other boats nearby destroyed.

Durhams were large flat-bottomed boats with high gunwales. They could carry up to 17 tons downstream or two tons upstream. On Christmas 1776, they were handled by some of the best boatmen in North America. Washington was also wise to cross far enough north of Trenton, where set and drift caused by downriver current would not force a landing too far south where enemy patrols might see them.

The feat of furtively moving an army across a wintry river in night and storm would be no small accomplishment even in the 21st century. This endeavor was the hardest part of the battle for Trenton, and took four hours longer than planned. All the soldiers of the Continental Army crossed safely in the boats—including future presidents James Madison and James Monroe, future Supreme Court Justice John Marshall, and future Treasury Secretary ALEXANDER HAMILTON, Washington's aide.

U

Unanimity

THOMAS PAINE AT LEFT

Born in Thetford, England, on January 29, 1737, Thomas Paine emigrated to Philadelphia as a result of his friendship with Benjamin Franklin. Paine's writings, including **Common Sense** *and* **The Crisis,** *stirred the hearts of colonists and the Continental Army. He was staunchly antislavery, and one of the first to advocate a world peace organization as well as social security for the poor and elderly. Paine died on June 8, 1809, in New York City.*

After RICHARD HENRY LEE's Virginia Resolution was introduced in the Second Continental Congress (see CONTINENTAL CONGRESS, FIRST AND SECOND) on June 7, 1776, the more conservative and cautious members of Congress managed to delay a vote on independence until July 2, 1776. By that time, only South Carolina, Delaware, and Pennsylvania refused to vote for independence. Because the delegates from New York had not received specific instructions allowing them to vote for independence, the delegation continued to abstain whenever votes were taken on the issue. There was no set number of representatives to Congress from the various colonies, but each colony had only one vote. A colony's vote was determined by a majority vote of the state's delegation. Deadlocked votes were discarded.

The practice of allowing a majority of a state's delegates to determine the state's vote became extremely important once South Carolina and Pennsylvania agreed to vote for independence. South Carolina switched its votes after succeeding in forcing THOMAS JEFFERSON to remove his provision abolishing slavery from the DECLARATION OF INDEPENDENCE. Although Jefferson believed that it was gross hypocrisy to declare that all men are created equal while continuing to support the institution of slavery, he was aware that South Carolina could influence other southern states to withdraw support for independence. Jefferson reluctantly agreed to withdraw

Majority Vote

IF CONGRESS had been willing to settle for a majority vote, the Declaration would have passed immediately after the Virginia Resolution, declaring the right of the colonies to be free, as introduced on June 2, 1776. Doubt about the outcome of a vote for independence would have caused leading congressional patriots to wait until they were sure of essential support before pushing for a vote on independence. Despite the large base of support for the patriot cause, congressional leaders on both sides of the independence issue believed that unanimity was essential in achieving independence from such a powerful mother country as Great Britain.

Members of Congress well understood that they could all be hanged if they lost their bid for independence. Also, raising and supplying armies would have been made extremely difficult if some colonies had chosen to remain loyal to Great Britain. In the midst of the independence debate, a dispatch from George Washington, the commander in chief of the Continental Forces, informed Congress that British ships were already arriving in the waters around New York. This dispatch highlighted the dangers of a divided country. If New York refused to cast its lot with the other 12 states, the British would be presented with a strategically important base from which to organize its attacks on the remaining states.

At the time the Continental Congress was debating the issue of independence, public opinion in the colonies was sharply divided. One-third of all colonists either remained loyal to the mother country or were undecided on the issue of independence. This division in public opinion made it even more essential that the congressional vote for independence be unanimous. Congress felt that any hint of weakness or indecisiveness would doom its bid for independence and would be detrimental to future efforts to win over Britain's enemies to the American cause.

TOP LEFT AND RIGHT *The speaker's chair and the door hardware in Carpenters' Hall.* **MIDDLE LEFT AND RIGHT** *Table, chairs, and quill pens such as those used by the signers. Statue of Thomas Paine in Bordentown, New Jersey.* **BOTTOM** *A drawing of Independence Hall in 1776 by an unknown artist.*

the provision but insisted for the rest of his life that the God of the Declaration of Independence endowed unalienable rights on all people, including slaves and women. Although EDWARD RUTLEDGE, the most prominent of the South Carolina delegation, opposed independence as a matter of personal principle, he believed that unanimity of the colonists was essential to independence.

The makeup of Congress shifted to some extent when new delegate members arrived from both Delaware and Pennsylvania in the midst of the debate. Pennsylvania's hesitation in approving independence had been due in large part to the signficant influence of John Dickinson. Dickinson was afraid that Congress was acting precipitously in declaring independence.

Because Pennsylvania's split delegation would have prevented unanimity, and thus continue to stall the debates, two delegates agreed to absent themselves when critical votes were taken. The delegates' decision firmly united Pennsylvania with the larger portion of the colonies, and left only Delaware and New York unwilling to support independence.

Delaware's vote was split between Thomas McKean, who supported independence, and George Read, who did not. CAESAR RODNEY, the third member of the delegation, was a strong advocate for independence. However, Rodney had returned to Delaware to put down a loyalist uprising. McKean summoned an express rider and sent for Rodney, who suffered from cancer and asthma.

After riding some 80 miles in stormy weather, Rodney broke Delaware's deadlock, bringing the number of states voting for independence to 12, leaving New York as the sole colonial holdout. When these 12 states approved the Declaration of Independence on July 4, 1776, the New York delegation was still awaiting permission to vote for independence. The approval the other delegates were waiting for was finally received on July 15. Four days later, Congress passed a resolution requiring that an embossed copy be printed. This copy, which was signed by 56 men from the 13 states on August 2, 1776, became the official copy of the Declaration of Independence (see DECLARATION OF INDEPENDENCE, AUGUST 2 EMBOSSED).

Even after the embossed copy of the Declaration of Independence was signed on August 2, 1776, unanimous support for independence was not assured. Each of the 13 states was restructuring its own government, and state legislatures would play an integral role in conducting the Revolutionary War.

Even after the Articles of Confederation were approved in 1781, each of the 13 states held equal power. There was no federal executive or judicial offices or committees. With only limited power, Congress was unable to force the states to comply with its decisions.

As a result, no viable central government existed in the United States until 1787 when the U.S. Constitution was written and approved by a delegation chosen for that purpose. Consequently, the Revolutionary War was fought and independence won by continuous appeals to 13 sovereign states for soldiers, supplies, and monetary support. The support of state legislatures controlled by loyalists would have had the power to sabotage American independence.

Further Reading: Joseph J. Ellis, *Founding Brothers: The Revolutionary Generation* (Alfred A. Knopf, 2002); Lynn Montross, *Reluctant Rebels: The Story of the Continental Congress, 1774–89* (HarperCollins, 1990); Jack N. Rakove, *The Beginnings of National Politics: An Interpretive History of the Continental Congress* (Alfred A. Knopf, 1979).

—ELIZABETH PURDY, PH.D.

V

Virginia in the Revolution

In 1607, English immigrants arrived in Jamestown, Virginia, where they established the first English settlement in what would become the United States. Over a decade later, the *Mayflower* brought the Pilgrims to Massachusetts, establishing a pattern of migration of Europeans that would swell the population of the colonies to 2.5 million by 1776. Williamsburg, now restored to approximate its colonial state, became the capital of Virginia in 1699. It was there that the House of Burgesses convened in the Raleigh Tavern after the royal governor dismissed them during protests against GEORGE III's arbitrary taxes. Virginia became known as the "Mother of Presidents" because four of the first five presidents were Virginians: GEORGE WASHINGTON, THOMAS JEFFERSON, James Madison, and James Monroe. (Other Virginia presidents included William Henry Harrison, John Tyler, Zachary Taylor, and Woodrow Wilson.)

In the interval between the passage of the Stamp Act in 1765 and the signing of the Declaration of Independence in 1776, Virginians were in the vanguard of the independence movement. The House of Burgesses, established on July 30, 1619, was the first legislature founded in the American colonies. During the revolutionary period, members of this legislature included Washington, who became the commander in chief of the Continental Army; Jefferson, who wrote the DECLARATION OF INDEPENDENCE; and PATRICK HENRY, who is best known for his impassioned defense of liberty in which he declared "I know not

"FLIGHT OF LORD DUNMORE"
AT LEFT *Governor of the Virginia colony, Lord Dunmore, is shown fleeing to England after he could not regain control of the colony in July 1776.*

what course others may take but as for me, give me liberty or give me death."

INDEPENDENCE

After the passage of the Stamp Act, Washington proposed that the House of Burgesses adopt a non-importation law. The measure banned trade with Britain except for cloth and thread, which were essential to Virginia's economy. The legislature complied, taking its first steps toward rebellion. The *Virginia Gazette* played an active role in spreading revolutionary fervor. After learning of the nonimportation agreement, 400 merchants arrived in Williamsburg, where they made plans to coerce reluctant merchants into compliance.

In the fall of 1774, Virginia dispatched Peyton Randolph, RICHARD HENRY LEE, George Washington, Patrick Henry, Richard Bland, Benjamin Harrison (not the future president), and Edmund Pendleton to Philadelphia to serve in the First Continental Congress (see CONTINENTAL CONGRESS, FIRST AND SECOND).

By the time Virginia chose delegates to the Second Continental Congress, the revolutionary spirit had taken firm hold in the state. At the state convention on March 20, in an often-quoted speech, Henry informed his colleagues that war with Britain was inevitable and declared that death was preferable to a life of tyranny. The convention appointed the same contingent to represent Virginia in the Second Continental Congress, which convened in May 1775. In May 1776, Virginia passed what became known as the Virginia Resolution, and Lee introduced the measure in Congress on June 28. Virginia proposed that Congress declare the 13 British colonies in America "absolved from all allegiance to, or dependence upon, the Crown or Parliament of Great Britain." Virginia also declared its own independence from Britain and began establishing a state government.

By the time the Virginia Resolution was introduced in Congress, Jefferson had replaced Randolph, who had become ill. Jefferson was appointed to the DRAFTING COMMITTEE, which was charged with explaining the rationale for seeking independence. At the urgings of the committee, particularly those of JOHN ADAMS, Jefferson wrote the Declaration of Independence. After a number of changes and compromises, the Declaration was approved by majority vote on July 2.

However, Congress knew that UNANIMITY was essential and scheduled another vote on July 4. After much maneuvering, the Declaration was unanimously approved on that day. When members of Congress signed the official copy on August 2, 1776, Virginia's signers included Jefferson, George Wythe, Richard Henry Lee, Harrison, Thomas Nelson, Jr., Francis Lightfoot Lee, and CARTER BRAXTON.

WAR

From the beginning of the Revolutionary War until the end, Virginia's forces were involved in some of the most significant battles of the war. When Congress sent out a call for troops to form the Continental Army in the fall of 1776, Virginia supplied 15 of the 88 battalions that responded. Virginians fought with BENEDICT ARNOLD when he stormed Quebec in September 1775 and were with Washington at Valley Forge in 1777–81. Virginians were present when Americans were devastated by the fall of Charleston, South Carolina, on May 12, 1780, and at the heart-rending Battle of Camden on August 16 of that same year. Virginians were also there in large numbers when Lord Charles Cornwallis surrendered to Washington on September 19, 1781, in Yorktown.

The Virginia Constitution

WHEN VIRGINIA ratified the first state constitution on June 12, 1776, less than a month before the Declaration of Independence was approved by the Second Continental Congress, the liberal philosophy of Thomas Jefferson, Richard Henry Lee, and Edmund Randolph was evident in the Preamble. The Virginia Bill of Rights, which was founded to a large extent on the English Bill of Rights of 1689, in turn became a model for other guarantees of rights, including the Bill of Rights introduced in the first session of Congress in 1889 by Virginian James Madison and added to the U.S. Constitution.

Based on a Lockean foundation of government by contract, the Preamble to the Virginian constitution declared that all humans are born free with certain "inherent rights" that no government can take away. Those rights included the "enjoyment of life and liberty," the right to own property, and the right to be happy and safe. In order to protect these rights without infringing on the sovereign rights of the people, the Virginia Bill of Rights guaranteed the right to free and regular elections, trial by jury, freedom of the press, and the subordination of military to civilian law. The most controversial phrase of the Preamble was the guarantee of freedom of religion inserted by Edmund Randolph.

On October 17, 1777, British General JOHN BURGOYNE surrendered to Washington at Saratoga, New York. The following year, British General William Howe evacuated Philadelphia. The British then turned their attention to the south. Ironically, Benedict Arnold, the same hero who had led American forces to both victory and defeat through several years of war, led the British campaign to overrun Virginia from December 30 to March 26, 1781. Arnold had sold out his country for £20,000 and a commission in the British army.

The British occupied Portsmouth on May 9, 1779, without a fight. Recognizing that Williamsburg was also vulnerable, the capital was moved to Richmond. A force made up of militia and 2,000 recruits on their way to join the Continental Army was unable to prevent the British from occupying Williamsburg. By January 5, 1781, Arnold was on his way to Richmond, and the Virginia government was again forced to relocate— this time to Charlottesville. Arnold burned parts of Richmond, and then followed the government to Staunton, managing to capture a major store of supplies at Point of Fork. Tarleton's infamous dragoons swept through the area, looting and burning homes and warehouses. Seven state assemblymen were captured before they could escape from Charlottesville, but Governor Thomas Jefferson escaped. The British fell back to the James River and headed for the Carolinas as Franco-American forces arrived in Virginia.

On April 29, the Marquis de Lafayette (see LAFAYETTE, MARQUIS DE), along with General Anthony Wayne and his Pennsylvania troops, arrived in Virginia in time to prevent Arnold from destroying all of Richmond. General Cornwallis was in the Carolinas, where he was constantly threatened by General

Commander in Chief

ON JUNE 15, 1775, George Washington of Virginia was named commander in chief of the Continental Army. When he took command, Washington's military experience was poor in comparison to that of most British generals, consisting chiefly of having fought with distinction in the French and Indian Wars and in serving with the Virginia militia. However, Washington had an uncanny ability to know when to attack and when to retreat. Most of all, he knew how to learn from his mistakes. Such was the case when his entire army barely escaped capture at the Battle of Brooklyn Heights on August 26, 1776. By 1777, even though Washington had failed to free New York City from British occupation, he had earned the title of "Indispensable Man."

Washington's task as commander in chief was made extremely difficult because he was forced to work with untrained men who sometimes deserted to return to their families. He was undercut by loyalists and was often unable to purchase supplies even from patriots or neutrals, who had sold their supplies to the deep-pocketed British. After the Americans accomplished what had seemed impossible by winning the Battle of Saratoga, Washington received much-needed help from the French, who sent troops, fleets, money, and supplies. Even before this alliance, a number of foreigners had joined the American army. Most notable among these was the Marquis de Lafayette, who became Washington's protégé and whom he reportedly loved like a son.

Washington had won the respect of Americans when he went directly from the dark days of Valley Forge to a surprise attack on the British at the Battle of Trenton on December 25, 1776. It was entirely fitting that when the arrogant Lord Cornwallis was forced to surrender his entire army at Yorktown, Virginia, in 1981, Washington was present to reclaim his beloved state.

Nathanael Greene. Instead of confronting Cornwallis head-on, Greene led him around the southern countryside, staying just far enough away to avoid direct contact. Greene finally engaged Cornwallis at the Battle of Guilford Courthouse on March 15, 1781, pitting 4,400 men against Cornwallis's force of 1,900. When the battle seemed to be going against the Americans, Cornwallis demonstrated his ruthless dedication to winning by ordering his gunners to shoot into the crowd, felling both British and American soldiers.

Admiral Marquis de Grasse arrived in Virginia with a French fleet on August 30. By the time Washington arrived, the French fleet had taken control of the Chesapeake in the Battle of the Capes. Franco-American forces had also prevailed at the Battle of Eutaw Springs on September 8.

Before the month was over, Washington and the Comte de Rochambeau (see ROCHAMBEAU, COMTE DE) had encircled Cornwallis's forces. Cornwallis surrendered to Washington at Yorktown, Virginia, on October 19. For many, the surrender brought an end to the Revolutionary War. In reality, the fighting continued until the British were driven out of Georgia and the Carolinas. The Treaty of Paris on September 3, 1783, brought an official end to the hostilities and the British evacuated New York two months later.

Further Reading: James A. Crutchfield, *The Grand Adventure: A Year by Year History of Virginia* (Dietz Press, 2004); Alf J. Mapp Jr., *The Virginia Experiment: The Old Dominion's Role in the Making of America, 1607–1781* (Hamilton Press, 1987); E.M. Sanchez-Saavedra, *A Guide to the Virginia Military Organization in the American Revolution, 1774–87* (Virginia State Library, 1978); James Titus, *Old Dominion at War* (University of South Carolina Press, 1991); "Virginia Bill of Rights" www.constitution.org/bor/vir_bor.htm (cited January 2006).

—ELIZABETH PURDY, PH.D.

The Virginian Navy

PATRICK HENRY founded Virginia's navy, which was chiefly composed of half-decked, mastless gunboats intended to protect Virginia from the bands of Tories and Native Americans that roamed the area. Even though Virginia's loyalist population was relatively small compared to that in most colonies, it served as an irritant throughout the Revolutionary War. Privateers also presented a constant threat to the lives and property of Virginians. At times, the Virginian navy also ferried supplies to the Continental Army. In 1776, Virginia's new state constitution created a board of navy commissioners charged with overseeing the activities of the Virginian navy. The commission brought an end to the navy's trading in the West Indies and assigned those duties elsewhere.

The first boat in the Virginian navy was a small vessel assigned to patrol Virginia's waters after Patrick Henry saw two ships lurking in the Chesapeake Bay. Within two weeks, the navy had added nine more vessels to its fleet. Thomas Jefferson added additional boats, and the small Virginian flotilla joined Maryland's in patrolling the Chesapeake. When recruiting decreased, the navy raised pay to $10 a day, plus clothing and any bounties collected. However, at 78 crewmen rather than the 590 needed, the Virginian navy remained undermanned. During their first encounter with the powerful British fleet, a shot hit the mooring of the Tempest and placed it in a precarious position. The crews panicked. The result was disastrous, and the fleet was lost.

W

Washington, George (1732–99)

George Washington was a farmer and he kept farmer's hours, rising early to get a start on the day's business. This was the case on the morning of July 4, 1776. It was probably still dark when he arose in his headquaters in New York City.

His morning was filled with routine correspondence, much of it to the Continental Congress (see CONTINENTAL CONGRESS, FIRST AND SECOND) in PHILADELPHIA. He was upset by a shortfall in troops and supplies from New England. There was new intelligence from Canada to pass along. He was organizing a "Flying Camp," a mobile unit made up of 10,000 militia from Pennsylvania, Delaware, and Maryland.

Every day brought many small details for the busy commander in chief. The letters were handed off to a messenger who would take them on to Philadelphia, about 100 miles away. It took about four days to make the trip.

So Washington did not learn of the passage of the DECLARATION OF INDEPENDENCE until July 10, 1776. When he received the news, he immediately wrote the Congress with congratulations:

Sir: I am now to acknowledge the receipt of your two favors of the 4th and 6th instants, which came duly to hand, with their important inclosures. I perceive that Congress have been employed in deliberating on measures of the most interesting Nature. It is certain that it is not with us to determine in many

GENERAL WASHINGTON AT LEFT

In his early 40s when he was appointed commander in chief of the Continental Army, Washington inspired tremendous loyalty in his troops, and through the sheer force of his personality, kept the army together through eight hard years of combat. Painting by C.W. Peale, 1772.

instances what consequences will flow from our Counsels, but yet it behoves us to adopt such, as under the smiles of a Gracious and all kind Providence will be most likely to promote our happiness; I trust the late decisive part they have taken, is calculated for that end, and will secure us that freedom and those priviledges, which have been, and are refused us, contrary to the voice of Nature and the British Constitution.

Agreeable to the request of Congress I caused the Declaration to be proclaimed before all the Army under my immediate Command, and have the pleasure to inform them, that the measure seemed to have their most hearty assent; the Expressions and behaviour both of Officers and Men testifying their warmest approbation of it.

Washington did not start out to be a revolutionary. He had made his military career as an officer in the British Army in the 1750s. Even in this second season of the war, he was as highly regarded in Britain as he was in America. As a member of the Virginia planter class, his tastes and habits were thoroughly English, from the imported glass in the windows at Mount Vernon to his favorite sport of fox hunting.

But the levying of several new taxes and acts in the 1760s and early 1770s turned him toward political action. Not only did they cost him money; they violated his rights as an Englishman. "At a time when our lordly Masters in Great Britain will be satisfied with nothing less than the deprivation of American freedom, it seems highly necessary that something shou'd be done to avert the stroke and maintain the liberty which we have derived from our Ancestors; but the manner of doing it to answer the purpose effectually is the point in question," he wrote his friend George Mason in April 1769. "That no man shou'd scruple, or hesitate a moment to use arms in defence of so valuable a blessing, on which all the good and evil of life depends; is clearly my opinion; Yet Arms I wou'd beg leave to add, should be the last resource. ..."

He was appointed to the First Continental Congress in the summer of 1774. In the spring of 1775, British troops clashed with the Massachusetts militia in Lexington and Concord. When Washington joined the Second Continental Congress several weeks later, he wore his old officer's uniform to the sessions—a clear sign that he was ready and willing to take command of the fledgling Continental armies.

Washington was in his mid-40s when the war began. His reddish brown hair had begun to go gray. He needed glasses to read, and his search for a comfortable set of false teeth was never-ending. Yet he was in top physical form. Standing 6 foot, 2 inches tall and weighing over 200 pounds, he had the proud build of a lifelong outdoorsman. He was one of the best horsemen in the country, able to ride cross-country at top speed for hours at a time.

Many found his persona to be cold and formal, largely because he felt that was how he *should* act in public. Few saw the relaxed inner man—a man who, if the joke were funny enough, would actually roll on the floor laughing. A French officer during the war never forgot the sight of General Washington playing catch with some of his young staff outside his headquarters.

Washington's contribution to the Revolution was enormous and went far beyond his tactical skills. When he took his post in 1775, the army was little more than a ragtag collection of New England militia. He turned it into a truly "national" army, with

George Washington: An Overview

soldiers from all colonies joining in. He inspired tremendous loyalty in his troops, and through the sheer force of his personality, kept the army together through eight hard years of combat.

When he resigned his commission at the war's end in 1783, he planned to spend the rest of his life in quiet retirement at Mount Vernon. Instead, he served two terms as the country's first president. In 1798, when President JOHN ADAMS was faced with the prospect of war with France, he appointed Washington as Lieutenant General of the Army, as a message to the French that he meant to fight. Washington was never called to active service and died of acute laryngitis on December 14, 1799. His fellow Virginian "Lighthorse" Harry Lee eulogized him as "a citizen, first in war, then in peace, and first in the hearts of his countrymen."

Further Reading: Joseph J. Ellis, *His Excellency: George Washington* (Knopf, 2004); David Hackett Fischer, *Washington's Crossing* (Oxford University Press, 2004); David McCullough, *1776* (Simon and Schuster, 2005).

—HEATHER K. MICHON

Weather Report

M eeting in PHILADELPHIA in the summer of 1776, the Second Continental Congress (see CONTINENTAL CONGRESS, FIRST AND SECOND) was forced to cope with hot weather and uncomfortable conditions. The temperature tended to be hot and sticky, even early in the morning when congressional committees met to discuss business. On July 2, for example, the temperature was already 70 degrees Fahreheit when delegates made their way to committee meetings. The weather had cooled somewhat because of the thunderstorms that had raged through the area the night before. CAESAR RODNEY of Delaware had spent the night riding through the storms in order to get to Philadelphia to cast his vote for independence. Rodney's vote was particularly significant because it broke a tie between the other two delegates and allowed the colonies to cast their votes for independence with dissention.

By 9 A.M. on July 2, when the day's session began, the temperature had risen to 78 degrees Fahrenheit. THOMAS JEFFERSON took readings at least three times each day with the new thermometer for which he had paid £3, 15s. Jefferson was a keen observer of weather. In addition to maintaining a weather diary, he convinced several volunteers in his home state of Virginia to do likewise. The idea caught on, and by 1891, over 2,000 weather stations had been established across the United States.

On Thursday, July 4, the day that would come to be known as Independence Day, Jefferson left his suite of rooms for a committee meeting at 6 A.M. and noted that the current temperature of 68 degrees Fahrenheit was cooler than the readings of the last few mornings. He hoped that the heat of the sun would be somewhat mitigated by a southeasterly wind. By the time the delegates arrived at the Philadelphia State House at 9 A.M., the temperature had risen to 72.5 degrees. Later in the day, the room would become stiflingly hot. On most days during that hot summer, the meeting room had been almost unbearable because the windows were cracked only a small amount at the top to maintain the secrecy required for debating the issue of independence, which some defined as treason. Americans convicted of treason could be taken to England and hanged. Since the State House was near a livery stable, the smell from the animals was often overpow-

Summer of '75

THE WEATHER also played a major role in the Revolutionary War in the summer of 1775. Thunderstorms continued throughout the summer, and the hurricane season was particularly memorable. The worst of these was a hurricane that raged from September 2 to September 9, which came to be known as the "Hurricane of Independence." The hurricane caused damage along the coast from North Carolina to Nova Scotia in Canada. In Norfolk, Hampton, and York in Virginia, the hurricane created major havoc in the Chesapeake Bay area, and several supply ships were lost.

By the time the hurricane exhausted itself, 4,170 people in America and Canada had been killed. Corn and tobacco crops were completely destroyed, and mill-dams broke throughout the area devastated by the hurricane. The loss of crops made it even more difficult than normal for colonists to feed themselves while meeting the needs of the Continental Army.

ering. To add to the delegates' discomfort, horseflies flew in and out the window. The clothing and silk stockings worn by most delegates were no protection from the horseflies and often made the heat even more uncomfortable.

At 1 P.M., Jefferson registered the temperature at 76 degrees and noted that the sky was somewhat cloudy. To Jefferson, the day seemed to go on forever as Congress continued to delete what Jefferson saw as important sections from the DECLARATION OF INDEPENDENCE. During the day, the winds backed from north to southwest, and the barometer fell by 0.25 inches. The Declaration was finally approved by Congress in the afternoon, and the delegates moved on to other matters. By 9 P.M. when patriotic Philadelphians were celebrating the birth of the new nation, Jefferson's thermometer revealed that the temperature was 73.5 degrees. Celebrants were thankful for the cooler weather because, normally, Philadelphia's temperature would have been in the high 80s for most of the day and the night would have been hotter.

The weather continued to be of major importance in America in the months following the signing of the Declaration of Independence. When a fleet carrying Hessian soldiers (see HESSIANS) arrived at Staten Island, New York, on August 15, it had to wait out a storm that went on for four days before launching an attack. The vessels of the fleet were unable to move, with rudders and sails useless. Currents carried the ships in all directions. Many soldiers died of injuries, and diseases multiplied. Two weeks after the storm that terrified the Hessians because it was so much fiercer than the storms they experienced in Europe, another thunderstorm drenched Georgia and the Carolinas, and a record 4.10 inches of rain fell on Columbia, South Carolina.

The English population also suffered the effects of weather in 1776. It was hot in England during the summer of 1776. Records show that during a 14-day heat wave, temperatures registered above 30 degrees Celsius, or 86 degrees Fahrenheit. The hot summer followed a period of unusually severe cold in Britain and the rest of Europe, a winter in which frost had

blanketed the area for days on end. In Maidstone and Kent, temperatures had frequently dropped to minus 23.9 degrees Celsius, or minus 11 degrees Fahrenheit.

Further Reading: Edward G. Lengel, *General George Washington: A Military Life* (Random House, 2005); David Ludlum, "Independence Day Weather: 1776," *Weatherwise* (January–February 1998); David Ludlum, "The Weather of Independence," *Weatherwise* (November–December 1998); Weather History, "The Independence Hurricane of 1775," www.easternuswx.com (cited March 2006).

—ELIZABETH PURDY, PH.D.

Whigs, English

English political parties of at least a rudimentary nature were in existence in Great Britain as early as the 17th century. The conflicts between the Stuarts and Parliament were resolved in Parliament's favor during the Glorious Revolution. Because the Whigs stood for the interests of large landholders, businessmen, and dissenters and advocated parliamentary rule as well as religious and political tolerance, they became Britain's dominant party for decades after 1688–89. For the most part, the opposition Tories, supporters of a strong church and Crown, were political outsiders.

The Whigs were an English political faction whose name reportedly came from the Scottish *whiggamor*, meaning horse driver or horse thief. The Whigs were named by the Tories, who in turn named the Tories from the Irish for cattle rustler or outlaw. *Whiggamor* dated from the West Scottish insurgency of 1648, when it was used as a derogatory term for Scottish Presbyterians. Whigs were political heirs of the Roundheads of the English Civil War, who supported a strong Parliament in opposition to the Cavaliers, who were royalists and strong backers of the official church. The first modern usage of the term *Whig* was during the exclusion crisis of 1678–81.

Since 1215, when the Magna Carta established that no person was above the law, the English had sought to limit the power of the king. The resistance to the divine right of Stuart kings was in keeping with this position. In 1678, nonconforming and rebellious Protestants wanted to keep the Roman Catholic Duke of York, James II/VII, from the thrones of England, Ireland, and Scotland. The opposition culminated in the Glorious Revolution, in which Tories joined the Whigs in guaranteeing a Protestant succession as well as the supremacy of Parliament over the king.

After the resolution of the succession crisis, Whigs and Tories maintained their identities but lost their issues. Their differences were more in political mentality than in policy or social differences. Both parties were parliamentary coalitions that the Crown struggled to use without succumbing to. The government means of maintaining its autonomy was to buy individual members through patronage and influence. It also worked to keep sympathetic members of Parliament of either party elected. By late in the 18th century, the system was being described as government by corruption. The search for alternatives to the Crown-dominated system led to the creation of party government. The parties represented no electorate, lacked any manifesto, and had no significant social or organizational ties. National parties, really factions, provided cover for local aristocratic domination, with certain aristocratic families controlling several boroughs. Commonly factions secretly agreed not to run candidates in the boroughs of their opposition. The condition persisted until the reforms of 1832.

Political parties in the 17th century were factions or groups that came together over specific issues then disbanded when the issues faded. Tories were generally the landed gentry and the Church of England. Whigs were of the old nobility and the moneyed class, and were dissenters. There was a great deal of overlap between the two parties because they were not parties in the modern manner. Whigs tended to support merit over pedigree, so they could bring in a wider group than the Tories did. They were a minority prior to the Industrial Revolution because the landed aristocracy and church had superior numbers. The Whig interest in the constitutional monarchy, which had provoked the Glorious Revolution, faded as an issue after the accession of William III.

After 1688 William III used both Tories and Whigs in his governments, even though some Tories were of questionable loyalty, remaining backers of James II. On the other hand, Tories were more friendly to royal authority than were Whigs. William called the first cabinet based on a parliamentary majority in 1693.

Queen Anne was pro-Tory, but she also used both Whigs and Tories in her governments. During her reign, the Whigs became increasingly linked with aristocratic landowners and wealthy merchants. Being generally in the minority, the Whigs had to keep tight discipline and hope for the opposition to split. Whigs at this time supported religious toleration, war with France, the Scottish union, and the Hanoverian succession. Tories argued among themselves over these issues.

Prominent Tory moderates included the Duke of Marlborough and Lord Godolphin. These two leaders got involved in the increasingly unpopular War of the Spanish Succession, and as their Tory base became alienated they had to look to the Whig party for support. By 1708 the ministry of these two To-ries was virtually all Whig. Anne began having personal difficulties with the Duchess of Marlborough and she did not feel comfortable with such an overwhelmingly Whig ministry. In 1710 she replaced the Whig ministers with Tories, allowing the Whigs to move into opposition.

The Treaty of Utrecht of 1713 was strongly opposed by the Whigs, who blocked it in the House of Lords until Anne created a sufficient number of Tory peers to overcome the Whig majority. Anne's Tory ministers had connived to bring James II back after Anne died, and they lost power in disgrace. The Jacobite uprisings of 1715 and 1745 further tied the Tories to an absolute monarchy and to treason. With the Tories discredited, Whigs were England's dominant party between 1714 and 1760. The To-ries retained a significant presence in the House of Commons.

The Hanoverian succession began in 1714 when Elector George Louis of Hanover became King George I. George invited the Whigs to form a government. The first prime minister was named in 1721, and he had the duty of heading the cabinet when the king or queen was away. Because of these responsibilities, party leaders became more significant, and the party system became more valuable under a constitutional monarchy.

George I and George II generally had governments consisting of those representing the aristocratic interest; these governments were more or less Whig. With only few breaks, Robert Walpole and the Pelhams, and Henry and his elder brother, the Duke of Newcastle, ran the government between

Edmund Burke (1729–97)

EDMUND BURKE was born in Ireland of a Catholic mother and an Anglican father. He was educated at a Quaker school but grew up an Anglican to avoid the legal disabilities against Catholics enacted under William. He trained for the law but failed to finish. In the 1750s he began writing such works as *Vindication of Natural Society* (1756) and *Philosophical Inquiry into the Origin of Our Ideas of the Sublime and Beautiful* (1757).

Between 1761 and 1782 he served as private secretary to first Gerard Hamilton, then the Marquis of Rockingham. Burke remained in Rockingham's employ from 1765 until the Marquis's death in 1782. Rockingham arranged for Burke to enter Parliament from a pocket borough.

Burke once allegedly told his constituents that he did not care what they thought because he was not representing them anyway.

Burke was the most prominent writer of party philosophy. His 1770 *Thoughts on the Causes of the Present Discontent* contended that George III was indulging in favoritism by appointing ministers for personal reasons rather than letting the people, through Parliament, select their own. The work also defined a party as a body of men, joined by principle, who would serve as the constitutional link between king and Parliament. The party would give consistent and strong administration when in power and provide principled criticism when in opposition.

1721 and 1756. Their opponents also called themselves Whigs.

The second half of the 18th century was a time when faction prevailed. GEORGE III came to the throne in 1760, and initially there were no serious issues to generate party coalitions. George III wanted out from under the Whig thumb and he had aspirations to a stronger monarchy. His old tutor, Lord Bute, became prime minister, and the Whigs lost their royal support. Bute abandoned Newcastle. For a decade there was chaos and factionalism before the new system produced two opposition groups. The Rockingham Whigs claimed to be the Old Whigs of the Pelhams and the Whig magnates.

They had intellectuals such as Edmund Burke, and they developed a defense of faction as a virtue. The other group followed Lord Chatham, hero of the Seven Years' War. The Chathamites opposed both party and faction. Both groups were opposed by Lord North's government, comprised of many former Whigs–Pelhamites as well as former followers of George Grenville and the Duke of Bedford—as well as some of Lord Bute's Tory-leaning Kings' Men.

During the American Revolution, pro-war sentiment was widespread among country gentlemen, universities, Anglican clergy, Methodists and John Wesley, Adam Smith, and many merchants, traders, and the mass of the common people.

After 1774 the opposition in both houses of Parliament became increasingly powerful as defeats in America continued. Antiwar politicians included the Chathamites and the Rockingham Whigs. The Rockingham Whigs included Burke and Charles James Fox. The Rockingham Whigs did not reflect the king's or the majority of the people's view of the war. The Rockingham Whigs regarded Parliament

American Whiggery

WHIGGERY WAS widespread in prerevolutionary America. Its leading exponents included John Dickinson and Daniel Dulany of Maryland. Dickinson was a Quaker country squire with a good family name and a large estate. He married into a prominent and wealthy Pennsylvania merchant family; his father-in-law was the long time speaker of the Pennsylvania Assembly. Pennsylvania's merchants had close to a patriarchy. Dickinson moved to a Philadelphia mansion, Fairhill, noted for its luxurious interiors and unostentatious display of wealth.

as a revolutionary body and felt that the Americans were merely defending their rights as Englishmen. A major antiwar faction was the Independent Gentlemen. Opponents called North a Tory, but he labeled himself a Whig.

By 1778 the opposition was growing because Rockingham had correctly predicted the path the war would take. Both Burke and Fox spoke in Parliament in opposition to the war. North was the first prime minister to endure the brunt of popular opinion; opposition and criticism increased as the war deteriorated for the British. In 1776 many democratic publications appeared, with much influence on public opinion. Also, Ireland was reemerging as a problem. Then in 1778 the French joined the fight against Britain, making the Revolution into a global war for Britain. Domestic crises were also distractions for North. He asked George III for permission to resign several times, including in 1777 after the British defeat at Saratoga and again in 1778 after France entered the war. The king refused.

Still, North held the majority in the election of 1780. When Yorktown fell, so did North. He resigned in March 1782, and in succession Rockingham, Shelburne, and Portland attempted to govern in the 21 months until the beginning of ministerial stability with the ministry of William Pitt the Younger in December 1783. The period between 1783 and 1806 also saw the formation of Whig and Tory parties with distinct philosophical differences.

Once Pitt formed a government, opposition coalesced around Charles James Fox in 1784. The party at that time called for electoral, parliamentary, and social reforms, but it split over the French Revolution and the French Wars of the early 19th century. The partisans of Fox supported dissent, industrialism, and reform of society and parliament. They had the sympathetic ear of the Prince Regent, later George IV. Whigs took power in the 1830s and later in the 19th century became a conservative wing of the Liberal Party.

Cynics defined the Whigs as believers in the divine right of Whig families to govern, to have government maintenance, and to humiliate the ruler to demonstrate their own superiority. Lord Grenville embodied this form of Whiggery. Whiggery has long been associated with human liberty and liberalism because of its protest against divine right kingship. But it was not exactly liberal. It was the party of the rising class, the industrial interests against the aristocracy and the old-style merchant princes. Its underpinnings were economic. Its basic beliefs were in a limited constitutional monarchy, religious toleration, and an aggressive foreign policy.

Whig accomplishments were many. Whigs created the modern House of Commons and established ministerial government in its modern form. Whigs established the British constitutional principle of no taxation without representation. Whigs also established as first principle that the purpose of government is the protection of property. This principle led to the idea that government should use its power to expand the area of profitable enterprise and protect those who exploit, that is, imperialism.

Further Reading: Elija Gould, *The Persistence of Empire: British Political Culture in the Age of the American Revolution* (University of North Carolina Press, 2000); Conor Cruise O'Brien, *The Great Melody: A Thematic Biography of Edmund Burke* (University of Chicago Press, 1992); Lee Ward, *The Politics of Liberty in England and Revolutionary America* (Cambridge University Press, 2004).

—JOHN H. BARNHILL, PH.D.

Women in the Revolution

Traditional roles of women of the Revolutionary period were centered around the home. When husbands were at home, wives took care of the child rearing, cooking, cleaning, and production of household necessities like candles and soap. They served as nurses and midwives in times of need, and in times of war, served as very capable heads of household. Many times, women who were left at home by their soldier husbands tended not only the domestic chores, but also any crop production, as well as business duties from family-owned businesses that needed to be sustained in the absence of their husbands. Women were required to step in and fill these roles for their husbands.

WOMEN'S STATUS

Women did not have the right to vote, hold office, or possess land in their names. Only spinsters and widows were allowed to manage their own business affairs or hold property in their names, but that lasted only until they chose to marry or remarry. Once that relationship was made, all of the woman's business interests became subject to her husband's dispositions and all property automatically was awarded to the husband. Many women refused to give up the power and independence associated with the land they obtained or the businesses inherited after the deaths of their husbands. So some widows took over their husband's business affairs and continued as successful entrepreneurs for decades. Most widows, especially those who were left with children to raise, remarried quickly in order to have a man in the household who could care for the business and farming interests of the family. Conversely, men also sought to remarry quickly to provide a mother for their children. Hard lives, battle, and epidemics took their toll on the population, creating an environment where it was not unusual for a person to marry more than once in a lifetime.

Divorces were rare, and obtaining one would make a woman a social pariah. Women either put up with the unfortunate circumstances or ran away. At the time, husbands were legally allowed to beat their wives. When a wife did run away from a bad marriage, the husband would advertise for her in the same manner that he would advertise for a runaway slave.

The framers of the Constitution may have written *all men*, but only white males who owned property were protected under the provisions of the Constitution. Long before Elizabeth Cady Stanton and Carrie Nation made a name for themselves in support of the equal treatment of women, patriots like ABIGAIL ADAMS were standing in strong support of a government in which women were able to participate in an equal standing as their male counterparts. Many of Adams's now-famous letters to her husband expressed her adamant opinion that women were not inferior to men and that they should be protected in the new government. Not only did Adams push for protection; she wanted the liberties and rights extended to men regarding ownership of land, voting, and participation in political matters to also extend to women. By 1787 women in all states except New Jersey had lost the right to vote. Adams died more than 150 years before women would receive the right to vote in 1920.

WOMEN AND THE MILITARY

More than 20,000 women became army camp followers. British soldiers were notorious for their brutal treatment of women and children in towns that they occupied. Women who could not flee to neighboring townships to live with family members were forced to stay and risk brutalization at the hands of the enemy or brave the hardships of life in the shadow of the military. The women who followed units would launder the soldiers' clothing, mend their stockings, cook, and act as nurses for the wounded and dying. The women not only received a half food ration; they also received a minimal amount of monetary compensation for their efforts.

During the heat of battle many women who witnessed their husbands being wounded or killed took up their husbands' posts in order to help ensure the success of the battle. Though the inclusion of the women and children slowed down the movements of the military unit, their presence was necessary because of the services they provided for the soldiers.

One such example of this is Margaret Corbin. After seeing her husband shot, she took up his

AT LEFT *An engraving by J. C. Armytage of Molly Pitcher at the Battle of Monmouth. There is great debate as to whether Molly Pitcher actually existed or if her story is fictional. Nevertheless, the actions attributed to her during the Battle of Monmouth on the evening of April 26, 1777, exemplify the courage and spirit of patriotic colonial women.*

Molly Pitcher (1744–1832)(?)

MOLLY PITCHER or Mary Ludwig Hays are names attributed to one of the Revolutionary War's most endearing women. There is great debate as to who she really was, and if she existed at all. A woman called Molly was a camp follower who brought water to the American soldiers at the Battle of Monmouth, New Jersey, a particularly fierce encounter between the patriots and the British. Carrying the water, she got the nickname Pitcher. On the evening of April 26, 1777, she saw her husband wounded by a musket ball. Mary loaded and fired the cannon several times by herself at the advancing British army. She kept firing the cannon as a cannonball flew through her legs and tore a portion off the bottom of her skirt.

Because of the courage she exhibited and the actions she took against the invading British, she was awarded a soldier's pension in 1822 which totaled $40 per year. This pension was higher than a widow's pension. In 1876 she became recognized as a woman veteran of the Revolutionary War.

Legend states that after the battle, stories of the courageous actions of a camp-following wife made their way back to General Washington, who offered his gratitude. The story exemplifies the spirit of the patriotic woman.

Deborah Sampson (1760–1827)

IN OCTOBER 1778 Deborah Sampson created an elaborate disguise and volunteered to enlist in the Continental Army. She enlisted as Robert Shurtliffe and for three years served her country as a soldier under Captain Nathan Thayer. She was wounded twice. The first wound was a cut from a sword on the side of her head. She was able to keep her identity concealed throughout her treatment for this wound. Samson was not as lucky with her second wound.

After being shot in the shoulder and coming down with a brain fever, her identity was discovered by the attending physician. The doctor took her to his home where she received better care in a more private environment. Once well, the doctor met with her commanding officer and revealed what he had found. Historical reports confirm that she was presented with a discharge from the military and sent home.

She eventually married Benjamin Gannett, with whom she had three children. General Washington became president, and Robert Shurtliffe was invited by letter to come to Washington, D.C. Samson went to the capital and was awarded a soldier's pension and a tract of land in appreciation for serving her country as a soldier.

musket and his post. She suffered three gunshot wounds that permanently disabled her but did not take her life. She later petitioned Congress for a soldier's pension and received half of that amount, as well as a complete outfit of clothing. Upon appeal, she was awarded the full pension with the inclusion of her choice of whiskey or rum. Corbin was re-interred at the insistence of the Daughters of the Revolution and was the only Revolutionary War veteran to be buried at West Point.

Hundreds of women served as soldiers, caretakers, and even spies. Women were less likely to be detected by the British as spies and were able to gain more information than their male counterparts. Lydia Darragh, who lived in PHILADELPHIA, convinced a British officer who was attempting to commandeer her home that she needed to stay there with her children but told the officers that they were welcome to stay as well. The officer agreed and Darragh hid notes behind the buttons of her young son's coat that contained information overheard from the officers.

She would then send him to visit his older brother who was stationed at a fort nearby. She eventually overheard plans of a surprise attack, and while pretending to fill her flour sack at a neighboring town, Darragh was able to find a friendly soldier and pass along her information. She prevented a disastrous attack from happening that would have weakened the already struggling colonial army.

WOMEN IN BATTLE AND ESPIONAGE

Filled with pride and patriotism, women would often dress as men and take up arms against the enemy. Shortly after the conclusion of the battle at Lexington, a woman named Prudence Wright did more than impersonate a male soldier in order to serve her country. She enlisted an entire troop of women. The women gathered, dressed in the clothing of their husbands and male family members, and brought with them muskets and pitchforks. Armed with only these weapons, the women steeled themselves to defend their home, Pepperell, Massachusetts. The women ambushed a spy sent to the town by the British and gathered his intelligence, which was promptly delivered to the Americans.

Women as young as 15 years old are recorded as having braved potentially deadly journeys to ensure that the Americans had any new intelligence gained from the British. Dicey Langston crossed a river in which the waters reached her neck. Sixteen-year-old Langston was determined to reach her brother's camp and deliver recently gained information about the movements of British troops.

Another 16-year-old with nerves of steel rode over 40 miles to Danbury, Connecticut, in order to alert the militia of the impending arrival of the enemy. This occurred the same fateful night Paul Revere made his famous ride, though history glorifies his actions and barely remembers her journey—which was longer. By the time Revere was able to take his famous ride, Sybil Luddington had already begun her journey warning everyone she came in contact with that the British were on their way.

Emily Geiger was stopped by British Regulars who wanted to search her. A female was summoned to proceed with the search. As Geiger waited for the other woman to arrive, she swallowed the paper she was carrying that held the information she was supposed to deliver to the Americans. Geiger continued her journey and successfully delivered the information to the American army, reciting the message from memory.

African American Women

AFRICAN WOMEN imported to America for service had no rights. They were subject to the whims of their mistresses and masters. African slave women also were forced to work in the fields during harvest and planting seasons, as well as work in the house and assist with the rearing of the children. Slave women would return to their own shanties, constructed as rudimentarily as possible by their masters, to tend to their own children and husbands, constantly fearing separation at the hands of their owners.

African families had no legal rights, which also meant that they had no legal marriage bonds. Families united in any manner they could, which created a sense of belonging to a greater community as opposed to an individual family. African women were forced to survive only on what their masters provided for them. Yearly, an allotment of cloth was given to each person to make a new set of clothing, which had to be done on her own time, after a day of working in the master's house or fields. Food was scarce, and also provided by the master. African women were also subject to the physical and verbal abuse of their male supervisors. Many women were brutalized at the hands of their owners.

EDUCATION

Women only had limited access to a formal education. They learned only what they needed to establish a well-run household in their adult years. The remainder of their "education" consisted of years of assisting older women within the family. Wealthy citizens were able to afford private tutors to teach their children, but girls were rarely included. Reading was a favorite pastime of the colonists, and females were allowed to read any literature that they could acquire.

In the early 18th century most literature was imported from England and could be expensive. Many women were as avidly learned as their male counterparts and fueled their educational drives by reading anything they could get their hands on. Colleges and universities were for men only, and the presence of women was strictly forbidden.

Women served in various leadership and support roles during the Revolutionary War. Extended absences of husbands, perilous situations, and death forced women to take on additional responsibilities in order to survive.

Women were compelled by the need to care for themselves and families to push the bounds of the "traditional" wife and create their own norms. Though faced with the oppression forced on women by laws, societal bonds, and personal desires, some women were able to rise above their situations in favor of a greater cause: national independence.

Further Reading: Kathleen M. Brown, *Good Wives, Nasty Wenches, and Anxious Patriarchs: Gender, Race, and Power in Colonial Virginia* (University of North Carolina Press, 1996); Suzanne D. Lebsock, *The Free Women of Petersburg: Status and Culture in a Southern Town* (W.W. Norton, 1984); Cokie Roberts, *Founding Mothers: The Women Who Raised Our Nation* (HarperCollins, 2005).

—CARLISE E. WOMACK

INDEX